W9-BQU-993

ROOKIE —

WE HAD THE GREATEST
YEAR EVER & YOU ARE
THE GREATEST FRIEND
EVER, AND WE'LL BE
FRIENDS FOREVER, &
I CAN'T BELIEVE WE
CAN'T SPEND THE
ENTIRE SUMMER TOGETHER.
I CAN BARELY STAND IT.
I CAN'T WAIT UNTIL
NEXT YEAR.
S.W.A.K.
Damian Kulash

Rookie—
Congrats on a great year! I'll
never forget hanging out on the same
page as Jon and Paul and Hannibal—
so far. ALWAYS STAY YOURSELF!
B.J.N.

WHATS A ROOKIE?
I CAN'T BELIEVE THE
SCHOOL YEAR IS ALREADY
OVER! I'M SO SAD I
WON'T SEE YOU AT MY
LOCKER EVERY MORNING
ANYMORE. I KNOW WE
HAD OUR UPS & DOWNS
OVER THE YEARS, BUT I JUST
WANTED TO SAY HOW LUCKY
I AM TO HAVE YOU AS A
FRIEND. YOU ARE LIKE A
SISTER TO ME AND I'LL NEVER
FORGET THAT. WHEN TRACY
TRIED TO START ALL THAT
DRAMA AFTER KYLE AND I
BROKE UP, YOU STUCK BY ME
AND WE BECAME STRONGER
THAN EVER AND I WILL
ALWAYS ♥ U 4 THAT. I REMEMBER
WHEN LESLIE AND I GOT IN
THAT CAR WRECK IN THE SCHOOL
PARKING LOT, YOU WER THE FIRST
PERSON I TEXTED WHEN WE WERE
WAITING FOR THE TOW TRUCK. IT MEANT
SO MUCH TO ME TO KNOW THAT YOU WERE
THERE FOR ME THAT DAY. OH, AND REMEMBER
BETH'S PARTY WHEN HER PARENTS
WERE OUT OF TOWN? LOL!!!!!
WE HAVE SOME REALLY GREAT MEMORIES
AND I'LL ALWAYS REMEMBER THEM,
MOSTLY IN MS. STEPPERS SCIENCE CLASS!
HAHAHAHA!!!
IF WE BOTH GET INTO U OF PHOENIX IN
SEPTEMBER, I THINK I'LL D-I-E!!
YOU HAVE TO BE MY ROOMIE, GIRL!
GOOD LUCK WITH DAVID OVER
THE SUMMER, DON'T DO ANYTHING
I WOULDN'T DO! J/K!!
YOU GUYS MAKE SUCH
A CUTE COUPLE.
GO COUGARS!
LOVE YA!
— Tia

ROOKIE
YEARBOOK ONE

ROOKIE
YEARBOOK ONE
EDITED BY TAVI GEVINSON

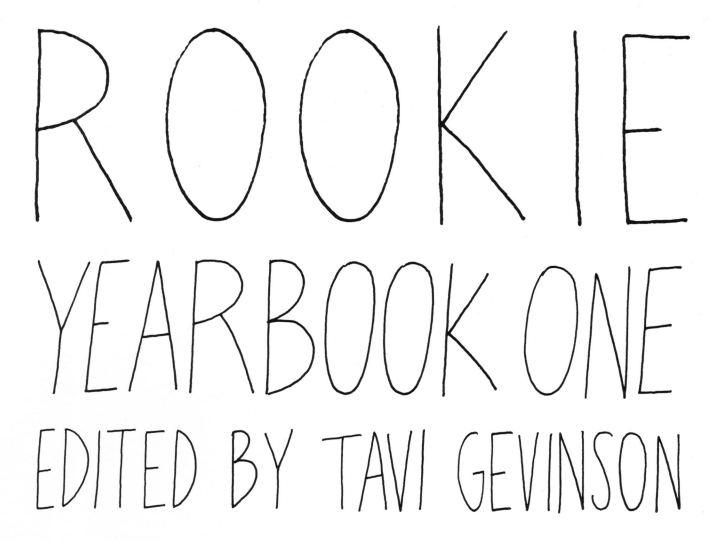

MILWAUKIE LEDDING LIBRARY
10660 SE 21ST AVENUE
MILWAUKIE OR 97222

razor
bill

RAZORBILL
AN IMPRINT OF PENGUIN GROUP (USA)

YA 305.23

Editor-in-Chief: Tavi Gevinson

Editorial Director: Anaheed Alani

Art Director: Tavi Gevinson

Lead Artist: Sonja Ahlers

Designer: Tracy Hurren

Managing Editor: Lauren Redding

Story Editors: Anaheed Alani & Phoebe Reilly

Production Manager: Tracy Hurren

Publisher: Chris Oliveros

Associate Publisher: Peggy Burns

♦ ◇ ♦

Cover Design: Sonja Ahlers
Cover art by:
Mike Bailey-Gates
Olivia Bee
Petra Collins
Minna Gilligan
Eleanor Hardwick
Beth Hoeckel
Cynthia Merhej
Lauren Poor
Erica Segovia
Leanna Wright

razor bill

A division of Penguin Young Readers Group • Published by the Penguin Group • Penguin Group (USA) LLC
345 Hudson Street • New York, New York 10014

USA / Canada / UK / Ireland / Australia / New Zealand / India / South Africa / China • Penguin.com
A Penguin Random House Company

Copyright © 2014 by Rookie, LLC. Writing and art © copyright 2014 by their respective authors and artists. All rights reserved.
Rookiemag.com

Penguin supports copyright. Copyright fuels creativity, encourages diverse voices, promotes free speech,
and creates a vibrant culture. Thank you for buying an authorized edition of this book and for complying with copyright laws
by not reproducing, scanning, or distributing any part of it in any form without permission.
You are supporting writers and allowing Penguin to continue to publish books for every reader.

ISBN: 9781595148261 • Printed in the United States of America • Originally Published by Drawn & Quarterly

1 3 5 7 9 10 8 6 4 2

CONTENTS

CONTRIBUTORS

Kelly Abeln
Lori Adelman
Sonja Ahlers
Ruby Aitken
Anaheed Alani
Lesley Arfin
Fred Armisen
Liz Armstrong
Olivia Bee
Ruby Book
Jack Black
Krista Burton
Lilli Carré
Pixie Casey
Naomi Christina
Hazel Cills
Suzy Coady
Petra Collins
Emily Condon
Joe Coscarelli
Bethany Cosentino

Emma Dajska
Katherine Denney
Pamela Des Barres
Zooey Deschanel
Sady Doyle
Leeann Duggan
Dum Dum Girls
Lena Dunham
Karen Elson
Anna Faris
Paul Feig
Shelby Fero
Anna Fitzpatrick
Kathleen Fraser
Tavi Gevinson
Laia Garcia
Minna Gilligan
María Inés Gul
Lexi Harder
Eleanor Hardwick
Beth Hoeckel

Winnie Holzman
Jessica Hopper
Amber Humphrey
Hannah Johnson
Miranda July
Lexie K.
Jamie Keiles
Meadham Kirchoff
Stephanie Kuehnert
Marlena Pope
Edward Meadham
Cynthia Merhej
Brooke Nechvatel
Patton Oswalt
Liz Phair
Lauren Poor
Rachael Prokop
Charlotte S.
JD Samson
Dan Savage
Erica Segovia

Leanne Shapton
Alia Shawkat
Arabelle Sicardi
Sarah Silverman
Kid Sister
Amy Rose Spiegel
Supercute!
Kevin Townley
Dylan Tupper Rupert
Spencer Tweedy
S.U.
Joss Whedon
Chrissie White
Autumn de Wilde
Jamia Wilson
Shannon Woodward
Leanna Wright
Suzy X.
Jenny Zhang

ACKNOWLEDGMENTS

Thank you to our amazing staff of editors, illustrators, photographers, and writers for their consistent honesty and sincerity. I don't think I could have dreamed up a team of people who so perfectly strike the balance between following their own voices and caring this much about their readers. Thank you, also, for the awesome group therapy.

Thank you to Sonja Ahlers for creating all the beautifully scripted titles and monthly opening spreads, perfectly embodying Rookie with her collage magic.

Thank you to all the very special artists who created new content especially for Yearbook: Kelly Abeln, Ruby Aitken, Sonja Ahlers, Lilli Carré, Suzy Coady, Kathleen Fraser, Minna Gilligan, Beth Hoeckel, María Inés Gul, Cynthia Merhej, Brooke Nechvatel, and Leanna Wright.

Thank you to Cynthia Merhej for creating the perfect handwritten Rookie logo and cover lettering.

Thank you to Geneviève Champagne of (Found)erie in Montreal of letting us raid her shelves for furs, fabrics, and general treasure.

Thank you to Edward Meadham for creating a beautiful crown for us all to wear and consistently letting us into his world.

Thank you to Suzy X. for creating a wonderful comic about her own teen years.

Thank you to the Dum Dum Girls and Supercute! for recording such rad theme songs and letting us use them for the extra special flexi-disc included here. Thank you to Leanne Shapton for letting us print an awesome excerpt from her high school sketchbook.

Thank you to Autumn de Wilde for letting us use her gorgeous photos of Shirley Kurata.

Thank you to Daniel Clowes for letting us use his wonderful painting of Enid Coleslaw.

Thank you to Chris Ware for making Rookie's introduction to Drawn & Quarterly.

Thank you to everyone at D+Q for invaluable assistance in putting this publication together: Peggy Burns, Jessica Campbell, Tom Devlin, Alyssa Favreau, Maddie Howard, Tracy Hurren, Amy Jo Tompkins, Chris Oliveros, Julia Pohl-Miranda, and Maddy Trower.

Thank you to Dad, Momma, Rivkah, and Miriam, for being the best people I know. Thank you to my other "family," which sounds like a cult but isn't. Thank you to Amelia, Ana, Anne, Autumn, Caroline, Claire, Dania, Ella, Emily, Franka, Gina, Grace, Heather, Lizzy, and Siobhan for being the best friends and Rookie readers I could ask for. Thank you to my grown-ass women friends and role models: Anaheed, Elizabeth, Kiwi, Laia, Sheba, and Susie. One day I will write a ladies' comedy about you all, and the critics will call it "raunchy."

Thank you to our readers for existing and helping us to exist.

WELCOME

One year ago, I started Rookie because I felt that there wasn't a magazine for teenage girls that respected its readers' intelligence. I started it online because it was the best way to spread the voices of our contributors far and wide, the best way for our readers to share their own, and the best place for our readers to connect with one another.

Despite how well this has worked out, our staff has a knack for creating work that is more timeless than articles online typically get to be, and more beautiful than photos and illustrations can look on a computer monitor. And so, we created *Yearbook* in an attempt to do justice to our very best pieces from the September 2011–May 2012 school year. This is the stuff that needed to be in pages adorned with doodles and glitter; that is revisited in times of angst and crisis, and that couldn't be just stared at on a screen for such an occasion. I mean, being able to actually HOLD art and writing that you love is kind of sort of really special.

There are acknowledgments on the previous spread, and I really, really have to use this inch of space to tell you how exaggerated those thank-you's ought to be. And thank you, also, for being here. It is still nuts to me that Rookie exists and people like it, but I will happily go along.

Isn't this weird, with no Cheeto-crumb-covered keyboard or Netflix streaming window between us? I'm really into it.

love,
tavi

SEPTEMBER 2011 BEGINNINGS

When I started thinking about the possibility of Rookie, it seemed like a good venue for pure aesthetic enjoyment and smart, fun writing. As my freshman year of high school progressed, I found myself needing something that could be more than that. I suppose that was a result of some experiences specific to me, and some more typical among females my age. But I don't want to even think about what makes someone "just your average teenage girl," or whether I fit that mold, or if that's who will read Rookie. It seems that entire industries are based on answering these very questions. *Who is the typical teenage girl? What does she want?* (And, a lot of the time, *How can we get her allowance?*)

I don't have the answers. Rookie is not your guide to Being a Teen. It is not a pamphlet on How to Be a Young Woman. (If it were, it would be published by American Girl and your aunt would've given it to you in the fifth grade.) It is, quite simply, a bunch of writing and art we like and believe in. While there's always danger in generalizing about a whole group of people, I do think some experiences are somewhat universal to being a teenager, specifically a female one. Rookie is a place to make the best of the beautiful pain and cringe-worthy awkwardness of being an adolescent girl. When it becomes harder to appreciate these things, we also have good plain fun and visual pleasure. When you're sick of having to be happy all the time, we have lots of eye-rolling rants, too.

Infinite big fat thank-you's to late-night superhero Anaheed Alani, life- and butt-saver Emily Condon, Cool Dad Ira Glass, fairy godmother Jane Pratt, my dad, our amazing site-building team, and all of our wonderful writers, photographers, illustrators, collagers, and thinkers. All of these rascals agreed to take part in this project before there was the slightest possibility of paying them in grown-up cash and not candy and mix CDs. THIS IS AMAZING. Do you know how much human beings like money?? We've got a special bunch here! They have dug deep into their hearts and souls and Netflix Instant queues to provide the wonderful content for Rookie, so please, please respect what they have to say. If something rubs you the wrong way, tell us, but be levelheaded and thoughtful. Internet fighting is not only redundant, it makes other people too shy to share what they want.

Every month on Rookie will be a differently themed issue, and our theme for September is Beginnings. Firsts and starts and back-to-school, etc. And, of course, the beginning of Rookie.

From here, you write your own handbook.

Love, ☆
☆Tavi

LET IT OUT

GOODBYE BAD TIMES

HELLO NEW UKULELE SUPERSTAR

Our guide to stomping out stress, exorcising your demons, and restoring your sanity after a terrible, horrible, no-good, very bad day…or week…or year.

Writing by Stephanie.
Illustration by Cynthia.

Let's talk about bad days. Everybody has them. Maybe yours was caused by a series of seemingly minor events, like you got out of bed and stubbed your toe on your way to the bathroom, and after your eyes stopped watering, you noticed the biggest zit ever on the tip of your nose and spent so long trying to pop/cover it that you were almost late for school, but as it turned out, it actually would've been good if you'd missed your first class because you had to take a test you totally forgot about. After that, your whole day fell apart and you wanted to cry or scream, but you felt stupid about it because your reasons seem so trivial. They aren't. If you feel bad, it's a bad day.

Or maybe you have a big reason to be upset. Maybe you've been fighting with your parents or your best friend or your boyfriend or girlfriend. Maybe you didn't make a team or land the role you wanted in a play or get a good grade on a test even though you worked your butt off. Maybe someone you care about got hurt, or worse. Maybe a few of those things happened at once. Maybe your bad-luck streak has been going on for a while now. A bad day became a bad week became a bad month, and you're starting to lose hope that it will ever get better.

During my junior year of high school, I could have been crowned the Queen of Bad Days. I did a lot of destructive things that I thought would make me feel better: smoking, drinking, getting high, and cutting myself. They never worked. Sometimes I felt better in the moment, but later I would feel worse.

However, there were other things that actually helped to relieve the stress, sorrow, or pure pissed-off-edness I was feeling, things that didn't come back to haunt me. I started to keep track of these things so I could use them again. Since bad days can happen for a bunch of different reasons and you can't predict what awful mood they are going to put you into, it's important to develop an arsenal to use against them. Here's a list of possibilities with plenty of options, so you can choose according to your personal interests and whatever's behind the icky mood you need to squash.

⧫ Crank up your favorite upbeat song and dance around your room to it. Bonus points if you sing into a hairbrush.

⧫ If that made you roll your eyes, this may be the better option for you today: crank up your favorite angry song and scream along with it. Head-banging helps a lot.

⧫ Make a playlist that suits your mood. If you're fighting with someone or coping with the end of a relationship, create the soundtrack to that relationship. Include the songs that make you miss them, the songs that make you angry at them, and the songs that remind you why you're fine without them.

⧫ Go to a concert. Even if it's a band you don't know well or have never heard of, they may surprise you.

⧫ Make your own music. Pick up your favorite instrument and start playing—loud or soft, bad or awesome, it doesn't matter. Or write lyrics and sing them.

◊ Journal. Write a rant or the saddest letter ever. Put all your feelings on the page knowing you can be as pissed or as whiny as you want because no one is going to see it but you. You can even burn the pages if it makes you feel better. Or you can save them to see how far you've come later.

⧫ Write really angsty poetry. Just, um, don't turn it in for an English assignment or you'll get sent to the guidance counselor. I know this from experience.

⧫ Write a story. Turn someone who wronged you into a zombie. Give yourself the most fabulous life you can imagine. Make your favorite celebrity fall in love with you. Live happily ever after in the city you've always wanted to move to.

⧫ Draw, paint, take photographs, get some clay and make something with it. Don't worry about if it's bad, just enjoy doing it.

⧫ Make a collage. This is one of the best things on earth, because you get to cut things up and piece them together.

⧫ Combine writing, drawing, photography, and collaging to make a zine. If it's something you're willing to share with others, photocopy and distribute it. Look up other zinesters online; see if they want to trade.

⧫ Do a tarot card reading or check your horoscope. There's no way to predict your future with total accuracy, but this can help you get into a more positive mindset about what lies ahead.

⧫ Cleaning your room can help, too. Or totally messing it up. Or rearranging all of your furniture and making plans to redecorate.

◊ You can also window shop or browse online for new clothes, shoes, books, music, etc. Make a wishlist and a savings plan. Or, if you have been saving, treat yourself to something you've wanted for a while.

⧫ If you're broke, find a piece of clothing you really loved but haven't worn lately for whatever reason (holes, too small, too big)

and turn it into something new. This is very satisfying in the same way as collaging, plus you get something new for free or next to nothing. Look up D.I.Y. clothing guides and get crafty!

◊ Give yourself a makeover. If you don't normally wear much makeup, go all out. Put on that funky lipstick shade you bought but never wear. Look up YouTube videos on eye makeup techniques and try them.

♦ If you wear makeup religiously, take it all off and go fresh-faced.

♦ Make your bathroom into an at-home spa. Get one of those clay facial masks; give yourself a mani/pedi.

♦ Dye your hair. Yeah, it's more extreme, and depending on the dye, more permanent than painting your nails, but sometimes we need extreme. Hell, chop off your hair or shave your head if you want. It grows back.

♦ Look at old pictures of yourself for inspiration or nostalgia, or to see how far you've come. Rereading old journals is good too.

♦ Purge your closet. Get rid of the things you don't need or want anymore.

♦ Donate your clothes to Goodwill or a similar organization. You can also donate food to a local food pantry, old toys and books to a shelter or children's charity. Give yourself and someone else a fresh start.

♦ Time is another great thing to donate. You can volunteer at a soup kitchen or an animal shelter, find a program where you read to people who can't, or help children or the elderly.

◊ Get politically active. Maybe what is upsetting you is part of a larger world issue, or maybe you just want to channel negative energy into something positive and create change. Call a local politician to speak out on an issue that you care about, plan a march or demonstration, start a petition, or make a website for an organization whose work you support.

♦ Get physically active. It's scientifically proven to make you feel better. Go for a walk or a run. Have you always wanted to try yoga or Pilates or martial arts or boxing? A lot of places offer free introductory classes, so check around. Bust out your skateboard and visit the skate park. Round up some friends for a kickball, softball, or basketball game.

♦ Go to your neighborhood playground and swing, go down the slide, and use the monkey bars.

♦ Play with a younger sibling, cousin, or neighbor. They'd be happy to go to the park with you. Or you can break out an old favorite board game or video game and teach them to play.

♦ Pets make fabulous playmates, too. Take your dog to the park, find your cat's favorite toy, or just sit and pet or brush them.

♦ Reread a favorite book or watch your favorite movie or TV show for the millionth time. Indulge in trashy magazines, bad TV, or a movie that's so incredibly stupid but makes you laugh your butt off.

♦ Nothing goes better with a lazy day than junk food, so indulge in that, too. Cooking or baking for yourself is great, because you get so focused on the recipe and the mouth-watering smells that you can't think about anything else. And there's a tasty reward at the end.

♦ Invite a friend over to enjoy your lazy day with you. Call that friend you know you can just sit and veg with, the one who won't make you talk unless you want to.

♦ Or call the really fun friend who will do the makeovers, play the games, make the collages, tell a bunch of funny stories, and bake the brownies, and have a slumber party or an all-day extravaganza of silliness with them.

♦ Or call the listener, the one who will let you vent and cry and yell if you need to. The friend who will say the right things

whether it's exactly what you want to hear or the tough, honest advice that you don't want to take, but know you need to think about.

♦ I'm gonna get serious for a moment. Sometimes you really need to talk. You may not want to, but in the long run it might be the only way to get through a difficult situation. So find a guidance counselor or a therapist or someone else you really trust and reach out. There's absolutely no shame in that.

♦ There is also no shame in having a serious cry. Wail at the top of your lungs. Sob until there are no more tears and you don't want to cry anymore.

◊ Break stuff. Sometimes you just need to, but try to do it carefully. Don't break anything that you're going to regret wrecking later or that's going to cause trouble at home. But you can buy some cheap glassware at the thrift store and smash it in the basement or on the concrete in the backyard. Just make sure to clean it up so your little sister or your dog doesn't get hurt.

♦ Take a long shower or a bubble bath.

♦ Burn some incense or a fragrant candle and meditate or daydream.

♦ Masturbate. It gives you a nice endorphin rush that can combat stress, tension, and, in some cases, even headaches and PMS symptoms. Plus it can help with the next item on this list.

♦ To quote a Hole song, "Just relax, just relax, just go to sleep." Sometimes you're so emotionally drained that you just have to. And sometimes a nap is all you need. You'll wake up feeling refreshed and reinvigorated, maybe even inspired by a good dream. And if you don't, that's OK. Skim this list again and try something else from it that sounds like it fits your mood, or do something that this list helped you think of. Rinse and repeat. Do it until you feel better, and come back to this whenever you need to. ♦

GREAT EXPECTATIONS

"If school days are the happiest days of your life, I'm hanging myself with my skip-rope tonight."
—Jackie O at 16, in a 1945 note to her boyfriend
Writing by Sady. Illustration by Brooke and Suzy.

In 1995, there was nothing I wanted more than to finally become a teenager. That was the year: the year I crossed over from being just an ordinary, awkward 12-year-old and entered the mystical world of teendom.

Everything in my life told me that becoming a teenager was the solution to all my problems. To be a teen was to be beautiful, popular, stylish, and free.

I would bond with an unlikely group of misfits, who would become my friends for life! I would fall in love with Judd Nelson in detention! Should I fail to be pretty enough to entice Judd right away, I would get a makeover from kindly popular girls and/or new BFFs! Also, I would go to school dances; at these school dances, it would become immediately apparent that, when I took my glasses off, I was just so *pretty!*

Imagine my surprise when I turned into just a regular teenager.

Look: I am going to break this to you now. Your teen years are a very valuable commodity to some very wealthy adults. They have learned that packaging and promoting the experience of "teen" is a great way to get you to buy things. Movie tickets, music, clothes: you name it. The unfortunate side effect of this is that you can wind up, as I did, expecting your teen years to resemble a scripted drama by a 45-year-old male screenwriter. Or, worse yet, expecting *yourself* to resemble one of the very pretty 23-year-olds who are routinely called upon to play "awkward" high school students. And when you expect this, you are setting yourself up for some fairly hideous disappointments.

Hideous disappointments like mine! Which I will now tell you about. Because, you know what? I learned something from every single one.

EXPECTATION: I will find my clique and settle into a life of acceptance, friendship, and wacky adventures!

REALITY: Dumped by all of my friends, publicly, in a cafeteria. Twice.

I was just not very good at clique-finding. First, I tried to hang out with the popular girls—the ones who knew about fashion, wore makeup, and were a hit with dudes. I liked fashion magazines! I knew a bit about makeup! I *wanted* to be a hit with dudes. Unfortunately, the things I liked other than fashion magazines and makeup were talking about what I saw last night on the news, and feminism, and how gay people ought to be able to get married. This was not a turn-on. One day, when I went to our usual cafeteria table, the girls all just turned their backs on me in unison, and that was that.

So next, I went to the alterna-teens. The ones who played guitar and talked about how they wanted to move to Seattle. I liked music! I could do this! Unfortunately, I was still talking about feminism, and this time around I was trying to get them all to listen to Hole (them: "Oh, yeah, she's Kurt Cobain's girlfriend") and Tori Amos ("Oh, yeah, wasn't she maybe Trent Reznor's girlfriend?") and PJ Harvey, who was not anybody's girlfriend that they knew of, and therefore was not worth lis-

tening to. This time, the dumping was even more theatrical: I sat down at the cafeteria table, and they all got up and walked to the next table.

LESSONS: Surprise: I am now an adult. I still like fashion magazines; in fact, I get to write for a website that talks about fashion a fair bit. And how did I get to write for it? I started a website, Tiger Beatdown, where I talked about what I had seen recently on the news, and feminism, and how gay people ought to be able to get married, and also sometimes PJ Harvey.

Having friends is great; you should definitely make friends! I made some real ones, eventually. But having a "clique" is awful for you. Cliques teach you to fit in. The only way to know your value is to know what makes you different. If everyone agrees with you all the time, odds are that you don't have anything interesting to say. When people reject you for not fitting in, take note: they're pointing out what makes you unique. And that's going to come in handy later.

EXPECTATION: My true beauty will be revealed, through the magic of makeovers!

REALITY: Got called "young man," on a regular basis, for an entire year.

As a teen, I adopted Winona Ryder as a role model. My goal was to transform myself from an ordinary-looking, skinny brunette into an edgy brunette "waif" of the sort who might possibly date Johnny Depp. Thus, I got all my hair chopped off,

adopting what the magazines were calling a "pixie cut," put on my dad's flannel shirts, and went to town.

I just sort of forgot that when someone wears androgynous clothes, has short hair, is completely flat-chested, and is of an age where many boys don't have facial hair or deep voices, there are several different ways you can read that look. And what people read on me was "Hey, a dude!"

Teachers did it. School bus drivers did it. Sales clerks did it. But my fellow students, for some reason, never did it. They just waited for me to have to clarify that I was a girl so that they could laugh and laugh at this latest hilarious misunderstanding.

LESSONS: Well, we should deal with the serious lessons first. There are plenty of people who get mis-gendered, or bullied for not conforming to stereotypes about their gender, and most of those people have it way worse than I did. Transgender people, in particular, often have to go through their entire adolescence in bodies and gender roles that just don't line up with their inner selves, and it can take a lot of work and a lot of time to get their inner and outer selves to match. Gay, lesbian, and bisexual teens are often bullied mercilessly. I had none of those problems; all I had to do was grow my hair out and start wearing skirts. I had it easy. But in my year as a "young man," I did learn a lot about how screwed-up stereotypes and gender expectations are, and I'm grateful for that.

Also, haircuts, much like assault rifles, should probably require a 48-hour waiting period. I'm serious. Those things can ruin your life.

EXPECTATION: With my popularity and beauty duly attained, I shall now find that most important of all things: my very first high school boyfriend!

REALITY: You know what? College is a very exciting time in a young woman's life. It's totally fine to get your first real kiss in college. No, really. It is.

LESSONS: Oh, all right. I'm still bitter about this one. I'm told this bitterness can be assuaged by watching a little show called *Teen Mom*, but I'm having none of it.

But, hey. You know how they tell you that dating isn't the most important thing in the world? That's something you get to figure out firsthand when you go through pretty much the entirety of your teen years dateless. Life goes on. Your friends still like you. In fact, they like you more than usual, because you're not one of those girls who go AWOL every time they start dating someone.

And, while actually falling in love is great, *wanting* to fall in love is usually just another way of wanting validation. People often want boyfriends or girlfriends because they want to know if they deserve them. But who deserves the power to decide whether you deserve love? Whose judgment is really that great? OK. This is the person you want to date, correct? Are you, by any chance, basing your assessment of this person's judgment on the fact that he or she has really, really shiny hair? Does this person, by any chance, still have bed sheets with Pokémon on them? DOES THIS PERSON STILL LIVE WITH HIS OR HER PARENTS AND RELY ON THEM FOR FOOD AND SHELTER??? Great. Let's acknowledge that this person might not *quite* be ready to tell you whether you *deserve* to live just yet, and move on.

EXPECTATION: If all else fails, I can at least pull it together for the prom. It is the most magical and romantic night of a young girl's life! I deserve at least one of those!

REALITY: Here is how I spent my prom: crying in the back of a station wagon.

At first, everything looked good. I got the dress, the hair, the makeover—and it actually worked. I looked great. I went with a guy friend I was not even remotely attracted to, but at least I had a date. My best friend was there, with her boyfriend; I had people to hang out with. But then I was at prom, and I didn't have a real date, and everybody else was smooching, and nobody complimented my dress, and the expensive necklace I'd bought for the occasion turned out to be flimsy and it ripped right off on a piece of the decoration, and my best friend wandered off to have intensive smooch times with her boyfriend, and I went back to my fake date's station wagon and cried about it. And then he sort of cried, too, because he wasn't aware that the date was fake. And then, we had the awkwardness. Oh, the awkwardness.

LESSONS: This, too, shall pass. After I cried, my best friend came back, witnessed awkwardness, and declared it was time for both of us to leave. We got in her car and rode around in the dark, singing along to the radio. It wasn't magical, it wasn't romantic; it was just the two of us, doing what we normally did, in more-expensive dresses. But when I remember all of this, it's her I remember. More than anything else about my high school years I remember the several thousand times we rode around town in her car, going to no particular destination, circling around on the highway and singing. It wasn't cinematic and it wasn't glamorous, and the two of us were the nerdiest nerds who ever nerded, and we were treated as such. But that didn't stop us from having fun. That's the other lesson: there is goodness in all of this too. Beneath the hideous disappointments, behind all the shattered hype, there's always some kind of goodness. It just never looks like what you expect. ◆

HIGHER LEARNING

Remembrances of the first year of high school, and advice for getting through your own, from some of our favorite grown-ups.
Illustrations by Brooke and Sonja.

JOSS WHEDON

I went to the same school, with the same people, for 10 years. I knew everyone—including the teachers, as my mother taught history there. In the middle of 10th grade my mother took a sabbatical abroad and I found myself going from Riverdale Country School in the Bronx to Winchester College, a 600-year-old all-male boarding school in southern England. I had never traveled alone. I had barely left the house. Also, I was quite small.

Winchester is timelessly beautiful, famously academic, and a bastion of blithe cruelty. Everyone else was used to this; I was the only new kid. Older boys relentlessly bullied the younger, and teachers (called "dons") bullied everyone, often physically. All the students, even boys younger than I, knew one another and came from the same social strata. The school had its own language—

literally; there was a book of "notions" to be memorized and tested. And on top of it all, I was of course that most dread creation, an American. It was clear to me from the start that I must take an active role in my survival.

Rule One: DON'T BE LIKE THEM. I knew I was going to be mocked as an outsider and a weirdo, so I established my weird cred before anyone had time to get their mock on. Our study area was a great room ringed by tiny wooden cubicles (called "toys," in both the plural and the singular—Know Your Notions!), about 50 to a room. On the first day of term I posted a notice outside my toys that was pure nonsense, a portentous abstraction that conveyed the simple message that ridiculing me would not only be weak and redundant, but might actually please me in some unseemly way. As boy after boy read the notice and either laughed or puzzled, I could feel a small patch of safe turf firm up under my feet.

Rule Two: BE LIKE THEM. My next defensive aid appeared quite unexpectedly, as we were all bunking down (12 to an ice-cold room) for the night. All the boys started doing a bit from an episode of Monty Python (which was a cool thing to do back then—no, you're mistaken; it was). When there was a lull, I unthinkingly chimed in with the next line. I was answered with unfiltered silence, and then one of the older boys called out from the corner, "OK. He's in." He literally said that. Like a cheesy movie: "He's in." And I, in whatever limited capacity I have to be, was. Speaking their language startled them as much as making up my own had.

Rule the Most: F@#K 'EM. We all want to be accepted. If possible, liked. Loved. But nobody ever got to be popular by desperately wanting to be. (Well, maybe Madonna.) Whether you crave attention or anonymity, you'll be thwarted if you

focus on those goals. I was actually gunning for a bit of both, but I only succeeded, in the end, because I knew I had the right to be myself. The judgments of others, however painful, would always be external. I was fiercely calculating about establishing myself as someone not to be trodden on (I'd had plenty of that from my brothers, thank you), but it really only worked because I knew, as much as a tiny-15-year old can, who I was. I was a short, annoying, existential, girl-repelling mess—but I KNEW that. I honored that. I defended that. And as intimidated as I super-incredibly was in those alien environs, I never lost that.

Rule Where You Realize I'm Super-Old and Skip to the Next Article: LEARN. High school is, among other things, *school*. If you have teachers worth a damn, stop worrying about where you fit in and work for them. Knowledge will serve you long after you've forgotten the names of everyone you feared or admired. And will prove subtly invaluable the next time you find yourself in a new situation, trying to fit in. You know the old saying: Knowledge is power.

And it's always, always about power. (Should this have been a Rule?) Everyone has it. Not everyone knows how to express it. And, institutionally and hormonally, high school is an easy place to forget you have it, particularly since so many people are focused on establishing or abusing it. But the power people take from others is nothing next to the power that comes with simple self-acceptance, with being comfortable in your (changing) skin. It's not just Survival of the Fit-ins. There's room for something new.

Joss Whedon is the creator of Buffy the Vampire Slayer, Angel, Firefly, *and* Dollhouse, *and writer and director of* The Avengers.

ZOOEY DESCHANEL

If only high school were as simple as a teen movie. I would have loved to have been as single-minded as your typical teen heroine (*must get in with the popular crowd, must get floppy-haired dude to take me to prom, etc.*), but as a teenager I had a lot on my mind. For instance, *infinity*. How was I supposed to think about prom when I spent so much time thinking about the concept of infinity? Prom was OK, but infinity was interesting and terrifying. This made it a lot harder to think about the dudes with floppy hair.

I often liken my high school experience to the opening scene in *Stardust Memories*, where Woody Allen is sitting on an unmoving train with a lot of really miserable-looking people, when out the window he sees an identical train, only on this train, as I remember it, everyone is happy and attractive, and there is a young Sharon Stone wearing a feather boa, and there are men in sailor suits popping bottles of pink champagne. He can no longer accept his sad train existence now that he has seen the happy train, and he tries in vain to escape. The difference between Woody Allen and me was, I kind of liked my sad train. I saw that there was another version of high school that was being peddled by the media, but I could never connect with it.

Of course, I went to an artsy sort of school, so things were a little bit different. It wasn't unusual to find a young gentleman wrapped in a piece of duvetyne theater curtain fashioned with safety pins into a makeshift toga. And no big deal guys, but we had Guys Wear a Dress to School Day. But even surrounded by all these unicorns, I felt like the unicorniest. I just did not fit in.

One day my history teacher asked our class, "Do you guys think about infinity?" Most of my classmates gave him the *you're totally lame* blank stare, but my mind started racing. *How does he know?!* I wondered. He said, "I used to think about infinity, and then I stopped." He chuckled to himself. For me, this moment mapped a strange intersection of emotions: whereas I now knew I wasn't alone, the people I wanted to connect with, my peers, seemed even farther away. I guess it was then that I realized I wasn't required to LOVE high school, like the movies demanded; I didn't have to want to go to prom and homecoming or be the center of the social world—I just had to make high school a place where I could get better at the things I wanted to do. And that's exactly what I did.

Zooey Deschanel is an actor on screens small and big, half of the indie folk band She & Him, and co-founder of HelloGiggles, a comedy website for women.

DAN SAVAGE

The first morning I walked through the doors of Quigley Preparatory Seminary North—a school for boys who were thinking about becoming Catholic priests—wasn't just my first day of ninth grade, it was my first day in a school where I didn't have any of my siblings to fall back on or to smooth the way for me. I was on my own, and I wanted things to be different. I didn't want to be the geeky kid anymore, or the sissy, and I didn't want to get picked on or bullied. But things couldn't change if I didn't change. So I made up my mind to be tough, one of the cool kids, fearless.

So there I was, on my first day, sitting in the library during study hall. When the librarian—one of the ancient priests who'd been parked at Quigley—stepped out, this kid started walking around, picking out freshmen and punching them as hard as he could. The freshmen in the room were terrified—they looked nervous, they looked away, they looked at the door, praying for the ancient librarian to come back—so I figured that he might not think I was a freshman, and not punch me, if I didn't look away. So I stared right at him.

"What are you looking at?" he asked.

I still didn't look away. I held his gaze. And then I said, my voice dripping with subtle contempt, "*Nothing.*"

I was calling him a nothing and I sorta thought the insult would fly over his head—his meaty head—and that everyone else in the room would get it, and admire me for it, but he wouldn't realize that I'd insulted him. After a pause that filled me with false hope, the bully strode over and beat as much of the crap out of me as he could before the door opened and the librarian walked back in. He beat me up again later that day in the hall, and again in the cafeteria, and again after school.

It didn't take me long to realize that I had picked the wrong high school. It wasn't just that I had attracted the attention of the school's meanest and most accomplished bully on my first day. No, I hated *everything* about Quigley. I didn't like my classes, or the priests, or how fake everyone was. This kid, my bully, and all these other bullies—my bully was the biggest but not the only bully—they all wanted to be *priests*?

And then there was my Latin teacher, also a bully, and my gym teacher, who was an actual ex-Marine and a bully.

Quigley—the high school I had picked—was hell.

RING BINDER

STUDENTS PROTEST!!

And here's how I got through ninth grade in hell: when I realized that I was going to be an outsider at Quigley, I embraced lonerhood. Quigley was near downtown Chicago, and I skipped classes when I could. I went to museums, I snuck into theaters. I didn't do any extracurricular activities, opting to spend my time exploring a city full of adults instead of a high school full of assholes. I did as little of my class work as I could get away with. And every day, when I walked through those doors, I told myself that I wasn't going to be at Quigley forever.

My parents insisted that I return to Quigley for sophomore year. But I quickly realized—sometime around the pope's visit to Chicago (he dropped by Quigley)—that I just couldn't take it anymore. And that's when I did something…um…well, that's when I did something that no high school student in America could get away with doing today. No kid should do today what I did 30 years ago, not in our post-Columbine (google it), zero-tolerance world.

I brought a brick of firecrackers to school. I placed them in my locker, lit the fuse, and walked out the front doors, listening to the explosions echo down the halls behind me. I was expelled. (But that was then. Try something like this today and you'll get arrested.) I wound up at St. Gregory the Great, the school two of my siblings chose, for the rest of my sophomore year, because I had nowhere else to go. (No other school would take me.) It was a teacher at Greg's who told me about a school where I might be happier: Metro High, an alternative public school in downtown Chicago, near the same museums and movie theaters and restaurants where I hid out in ninth grade.

Metro encouraged its students to explore the city—you could actually get class credit for going to museums—and I spent my last two years there. I did my schoolwork, I made friends, I didn't cut classes, and I never felt a need to bring explosives to school.

I got terrible grades at Quigley—and for a while they refused to release my transcripts that proved it—and my grades at Greg's were a bit better, but not that much. At Metro, though, I was an academic superstar: straight A's, glowing reports from teachers, counselors pushing me to go on to college. I don't know who was more shocked, me or my parents.

Which just goes to show…

Sometimes the problem isn't *who* you are, despite what you're being told by everyone around you, but *where* you are. And sometimes the solution can be as simple as finding a new place, a better place, the kind of place where a kid like you can thrive.

Your place is out there. Go find it.

Dan Savage is the author of the syndicated sex-advice column "Savage Love," star of Savage U *on MTV, and founder of the It Gets Better project.*

JD SAMSON

I decided to include my lyrics to the song "Keep on Livin'" by Le Tigre. I wrote these words in 2001 while trying to give advice to kids coming out of the closet, and it's the same advice I would give today. I came out when I was 15, and high school felt nearly impossible to trudge through. But once I emerged from the bubble of my town, I realized that there was a lot more for me out there.

Look up to the sky sky sky
Take back your own tonight
You'll find more than you see
It's time now now get ready
So you can taste that sweet sweet cake and
Feel the warm water in a lake
What about the nice cool breeze and
Hear the buzzing of the bumblebees
Live past those neighborhood lives and
Go past that yard outside and
Push thru their greatest fears and
Live past your memories' tears cuz
You don't need to scratch inside just please
Hold on to your pride
So don't let them bring you down and
Don't let them fuck you around cuz
Those are your arms that is your heart and
No no they can't tear you apart cuz
This is your time this is your life and
This is your time this is your life.

JD Samson is a music player/maker with Men and Le Tigre.

WINNIE HOLZMAN

Recently I ran into someone I hadn't seen since high school. Back then, I admired Bonnie—she seemed to know how to dress for and handle every situation. There was a group of guys we both hung out with, and she also seemed to know better than I how to handle them. But we weren't really friends.

Suddenly we bump into each other, out of nowhere, at a concert, lo these many decades later, and I'm thrilled—it's like spotting a celebrity! And it gets fascinating right away. We're explaining to a third person how we knew a lot of the same people, but hadn't been actual *friends*, when Bonnie says, "Oh, I could never talk to Winnie; she was way too cool for me."

Stunned, I splutter, "WHAT?! What are you TALKING about?! I was NEVER cool. YOU were the cool one. I would have given ANYTHING to have been as cool as you!"

She looks at me like I'm out of my mind. Facts that we've both taken for granted for over 30 years vaporize before our eyes. Bonnie mentions a guy we both knew: "He was so in love with you."

OK—*whaaat?!* Why is this quasi-stranger lying to me? My most fervent wish during those four terrifying years was that someone would somehow see past my uncoolness and fall in love with me. A huge part of my identity was (and still is) based on the firm belief that *that never happened*. In Bonnie's parallel universe, however, it did. How can that be?

In high school, we become pretty convinced that we know what reality is: We know who looks down on us, who is above us, exactly who our friends and our enemies are. We know what's true, and what isn't, and there's no room for doubt. Sadly, this condition will likely continue throughout the rest of our lives, unless we actively work to combat it.

How do we combat it? By allowing ourselves to realize how very little we know about all the people we're so certain about. And that what seems like unshakeable reality (he thinks I'm a fool, she hates me, they're better than me, I'm better than them, *I know what they're thinking*) is basically just a story we learned to tell ourselves. Until we know it by heart.

A few years ago I heard a rabbi explain that there's a specific Jewish prayer meant to be recited when you find yourself in a crowd. I never learned the exact wording of this prayer—but the idea is basically this: Remember, everyone bears a hidden pain. Everyone. It may not show; it may be something you'd never guess in a million years. But every person has a secret burden.

When I remember the truth of that prayer, I feel less alone. When I write, the idea behind that prayer is my guiding principle. I want my characters to seem alive—so no matter what they appear to be on the surface, when the audience first meets them, I know there's got to be more to them. Something hidden—maybe even from themselves.

I almost wish someone had talked to me about all this when I was in high school. But if they had, would I have believed them? I was so sure of everything I was so sure of.

By the way, Bonnie and I are friends now. For real.

Winnie Holzman is the creator of the TV show My So-Called Life *and a writer (with Stephen Schwartz) of the musical* Wicked.

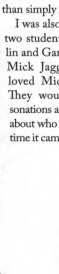

JACK BLACK

I was running with a pretty rough crowd in 1984. It was a gang of kids from the tough part of the neighborhood. We'd listen to heavy metal and watch *The Exorcist*. We'd wear jeans and flannel shirts. We'd BMX and skateboard around town.

Things got pretty hairy. I wanted desperately to belong to something cool, and fitting in with these guys was everything to me. I stole some money from my mom. I got caught and confessed all my badassery to my parents. I felt like I needed a fresh start, and my folks agreed. They decided to send me to a school for troubled youths. It was called Poseidon.

It was a very small school in West L.A. that featured a student psychologist named Roger. In addition to being a kick-ass therapist, he was also a big bodybuilder who could defend himself and break up fights in the yard if necessary.

I was not required to have sessions with Roger. But I saw the other kids going into his office, and I was curious. I wanted to tell him my story and see if I needed counseling. So I signed up for a session and went into his office the next day. I spilled my guts about stealing from my mother and cried my eyes out. It was an intense catharsis. All the guilt and stress I'd been holding on to for years just melted away.

I continued seeing Roger, but never had that kind of mind-blowing release again.

The rest of my ninth grade was mainly focused on animation drawings and improv classes with my incredible theater teacher Deb. Deb was inspiring. She encouraged me to get involved in all aspects of theater. She insisted that writing and directing were far more interesting endeavors than simply acting.

I was also obsessed with two students named Collin and Gary. Collin loved Mick Jagger and Gary loved Michael Jackson. They would do impersonations all day and argue about who was better. One time it came to blows, and

I tried to jump in to defend Collin, who was getting his ass kicked. I punched Gary in the side of the head, and he just stopped and looked at me with confusion in his eyes. I had never done anything like that before. Or since.

I started reading *Siddhartha* by Hermann Hesse. I drank it up like a delicious nectar. It is the story of the young Buddha's journey. Reading that book marked the beginning of a spiritual journey that lasted for years.

But that is another story.

Good luck in high school. Being a person is hard.

Jack Black is an actor, comedian, and musician.

ALIA SHAWKAT

Try your hardest to say what you think. Most of the time, you'll get egg on your face—not literally—but there are a lot of fresh egos buzzing around with no direction at this stage in life, and high school kids who fit in and morph into one another are usually very dull. So speak your mind, and state your funny observations, even if there's only one other person who understands them. High school can feel disconnected and painful, but such places are perfect for sharpening your opinions and your confidence.

The best thing to do—because, let's face it, you have to be there—is to soak in the torture and try to remember everything. I suggest writing every day about your experiences, your friends, your enemies, your crushes. Because one day soon, you'll see the absurdity of what you thought was important, and that perspective will teach you something.

God knows there are many films made about these precious four years of life, so you never know—living through it might be good research for the growing artist inside you. And don't lose hope. In my experience, the worse high school is, the better your adult life seems to be. (Not that it can't occasionally be fun.)

Be nice to the weird kid in class, who doesn't shower or talk. They need your help, and they're usually much more interesting than you think.

*Alia Shawkat is an actor (*Arrested Development, The Runaways, Whip It, *etc.).*

BIG

LESLEY ARFIN

Dear Kid in High School,

Not that you really give a shit what I have to say, cuz kids in high school love not giving a shit, but I also know that you actually give a huge steaming pile of shit, so shut up your face and listen.

You're allowed to care about stuff. That's the first thing. Even if you think it's stupid or weird, like polka music or "being obsessed with mimes." One day you will look back not at all the things that made you cool enough to fit in, but at the things that didn't. And you will love them.

The second thing is write everything down. Even if you don't like writing, just write about every obsession, story, hatred, happiness—whatever. And save it. All of it. I say this because when you're an adult, you will get drunk with your friends one night and read your diary out loud to them.

It will be the funniest night of your life.

When teachers say, "This is the best time of your life," they are wrong. They are only saying that because they're teachers and they have to look at your weird faces every day. There is no "best time of your life," but rather perfect moments, like when someone's gum falls out of their mouth while they're telling a story, or when a jerk is walking toward you and accidentally gets hit in the head with a soccer ball. Make sure to store these moments in a safe place in your brain. They will be useful to you in the future, I promise.

But also, quit bitching about being in high school. At least your mom still makes you dinner at night, and that rules.

I'm not gonna say don't do drugs because that's ridiculous, just don't take anything that is known as an "epidemic" (crystal meth, OxyContin). When they tell you in health that they're addictive, they're not "just trying to scare you into

being a normie," and it's not all "government propaganda."

Stick with pot, acid, and booze and you will have way better memories. When you do acid or shrooms and you think you might be having a bad trip, get a piece of candy and hold your friend's hand and it will go away. Try not talking for a while, too. If it's still bad, well, whatever, it will be over in 14 hours.

If you want to stay out all night, say you're sleeping at a friend's house. If you come home super early and your mom says, "Why are you home so early?" you say, "I got homesick and I missed you." She will then make you eggs and you can watch TV.

If you don't want to change for gym, a good trick is putting sweatpants on over your jeans. If you don't want to go swimming, say you have your period. If you want to go home early or get out of a class, give the nurse a general "my stomach hurts." If she asks you, "How does it hurt?" you say, "It's just pain." There's no cure for that.

You might feel at times that you are ugly and disgusting and unlovable. Some of you might feel as though you are beautiful and hot and cool and awesome. Know this: When you're in your 20s you go through, like, a time machine of opposite days. What I mean is, everyone who thinks they are hot shit in high school eventually turns into cold diarrhea by their 30s. And all you ugly nerds will eventually start to sparkle like geodes. If you don't believe me you can ask Facebook.

Hmm, what else what else? Some things I regret: not learning an instrument (I gave up playing the sax, wish I hadn't), not learning a foreign language (got kicked out of Spanish), not taking more acid (was afraid of bad trips but regret now due to lack of funny stories).

I don't know what else. You guys are gonna do whatever you're gonna do, fuck that up, do it again, and so it goes.

You all probably know just what you're doing anyway and don't need any advice at all, isn't that right, you little smartass?

I'll be watching you. I am the eyes and ears of this institution.

Lesley Arfin is a writer for Rookie and Girls.

KID SISTER

My only advice on surviving high school is this: Superfine Sharpies CAN be used as makeup and RANCH. CAN. GO. ON. ANYTHING.

Kid Sister is a rapstress, actress, and professional snackstress.

FRED ARMISEN

To me, ninth grade was very much about defining my personal tastes. I started to think of my favorite bands as part of my identity. That only got more intense as I got further into high school. I bought so many band pins. They meant so much to me. THIS is who I listen to! THIS is their official logo.

I remember also seeing my teachers more as people, as opposed to just classroom disciplinarians. It seemed like many of them were trying their best to connect with us. They got nicer all of a sudden. Maybe eighth graders were more rowdy or something.

Seventh and eighth grade I did not enjoy. I picture bigger kids in jean jackets throwing M80s everywhere. Parking lots, suburban street corners, everywhere. Those are the worst kind of fireworks. You don't see anything. It's just that loud, stupid boom. Today, when I hear super-loud motorcycles go past me, I get that same feeling.

Ninth grade was also around the time when me and my friends started becoming more of a tight group. We developed our own sense of humor, like in our own language, and our own sound effects for everything.

We did some pointless, stupid stuff too. One time along Central Avenue, I was with my best friend, Kenny Young. We saw these huge shipping pallets in an alley. Those wooden ones. We decided for some reason that they would make a good drum riser.

Why we thought we needed a drum riser in that moment I'll never know. So we took one each and just dragged them down the street. These big heavy pallets. Why? Even as an adult those things are heavy to me.

In my opinion fear starts melting away a little in ninth grade. It's a good time for choosing friends and appreciating teachers. And for wearing band pins.

Fred Armisen is an SNL cast member and the co-star and co-creator (with Carrie Brownstein) of Portlandia.

ANNA FARIS
LAY LOW.

Anna Faris is an actor (Lost in Translation, *all the* Scary Movies, *etc.).*

SHANNON WOODWARD
I'll be straight with you. No matter what anyone tells you, your trek through the explosive adolescent social experiment that is high school will be inspirational, iconic, tragic, stressful, giddy, odiferous, awkward, hysterical, painstaking, romantic, and, in hindsight, an all-around blur. But, most important: it will be completely, uniquely yours. So, seeing as I don't know you (to be fair you haven't introduced yourself), here are a few entirely random personally gleaned nuggets of wisdom. Hopefully, at least one of them will be credited with saving your life.

Wave your freak flag. I know. It feels counterintuitive. Teenagers are generally wary of standing out, and aren't going to take well to your refusal to go with the flow. But if you can get down with your bad self this early in the game and not look back, it will be the real-life equivalent of scoring Boardwalk on your first roll (yes, I'm talkin' *you*-themed Monopoly here).

Avoid "freak dancing" at all costs. During such an important and developmental stage in your life, it is hard to fathom the long-term repercussions of some decisions. Some reckless behaviors leave eternal stains on the permanent record that is your soul. Absolutely do NOT freak dance at homecoming. Or prom. Or the Sadie Hawkins Dance. Or sporadically in the hallway. The memory flash of your knees Tootsie-Rolling with some smelly teenage boy repetitively knocking into your back with his pelvis is one that will haunt you into retirement. Just don't do it. It's not worth it. (Neither is the school cafeteria's taco salad. Trust me.)

Learn stuff. I know you're angry. That's OK. Whether your parents are the actual worst (my condolences) or you merely can't bear their presence unless they materialize for the sole purpose of providing you with food and/or money: I assure you that the best and only revenge you can wreak on your parents is your own success. So, hit the books. It is the only thing we high school survivors uniformly do NOT regret.

Avoid an aerial attack! Even in cases of absolute emergency, avoid standing in an open courtyard where birds are likely to congregate. Living down a fly-by bird pooping is hard to do. I hardly survived to tell the tale.

Go get 'em, tiger. We'll be rooting for you here in adult-world.

Shannon Woodward is an actor and a consumer of vast quantities of food.

PATTON OSWALT
First off, everyone else giving you advice in this article is more wise, articulate, and helpful than me. Read what they've written and take it to heart. Follow their advice—they've all gone through versions of the same things you're about to go through. They're not trying to scold you or judge you or make you feel stupid. They want to save you time and heartache.

So here's what I'm saying—go ahead and screw things up. You're young—you're *supposed* to do that for a while. Rebel. Write bad poetry. Listen to bad music and roll your eyes at the adults. Be concerned with things that don't matter. Because when you get to be my age—23 years old and not 42 *no matter what my stupid Wikipedia page says*—you'll realize how valuable all of your mistakes were in making you the person you'll end up being. The mere fact that you're *reading*, right now, puts you so far ahead and above the bulk of the population that I'm really not too worried about how any of you are going to turn out. If you're reading and curious, you'll be fine. Trust me. ♦

Patton Oswalt is a comedian who also writes and sometimes acts but mostly is a comedian.

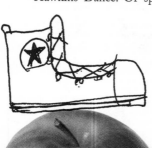

SCHOOL SPIRIT

Admit it—you're excited for school to start. If not, at least you have knee socks and plaid skirts to look forward to.
Shoot styled and photographed by Petra. Thanks to Anna, Aleks, Raevv'n, and Aurora for modeling.

FIRST KISS

Ten years after the fact, Jenny interviews the first boy she ever smooched.
Interview by Jenny. Photos by Petra.

When I was 15, I went around school in my mom's old dresses and a pair of platform PVC combat boots that I had begged my parents to order for me from the Delia's catalog. I wrote poetry about dying in the suburbs and was convinced there had never existed a teenager more misunderstood than me.

It was hardly a surprise when I became infatuated with my friend Chris's older brother, Pete. He was two grades ahead of me, wore T-shirts that said "Fuck White Supremacy," made me a mixtape titled "Punk Rock 101," had friends who made zines about feminism and went to shows in the city, got me into Billy Bragg and Bikini Kill, quoted from *The Dharma Bums* before I had cracked open *On the Road*, had an encyclopedic knowledge of radical progressive movements when I was still trying to articulate why I was pro-choice, argued beautifully against the sanctions in Iraq, wrote impenetrable poetry that referenced *Moby Dick*, and sometimes gazed at me in a way that I described in my diary as "so intense I could DIE!!!!!"

The next year, Pete went away to college in the Bronx, and I started my junior year of high school even more crotchety and disenchanted than I was the year before. I started writing him long, painfully loving emails and assaulting him with my irresistible wit over late-night sessions of AOL Instant Messenger. Looking back over these emails, I'm pretty pleased to find that while there was a good amount of LOVE ME LOVE ME LOVE ME, I also wrote about stuff that really mattered to me. Like how starved I was for any kind of artistic/intellectual/creative action. How badly I wanted to be part of a community of people who inspired and challenged me. Or how in high school, it seemed like your only choices were to be either someone who was obsessed with getting perfect grades, or someone who didn't give a shit. Where were the people who just wanted to learn new things and be exposed to everything there was? I wrote to him about my family and how they didn't want me to write. I wrote about how badly I wanted to be a writer and how scared I was of finding out that I sucked big time.

At 16, while I believed I was interesting and funny, it seemed crazy that anyone else would. So when Pete came back to Long Island for the holidays and asked me if I wanted to meet him in front of the elementary school, I was shocked. I remember shakily waiting for my parents to go to sleep before sneaking out the back door, cutting through the woods behind my house, and running across the elementary school playground toward his car. *Is it possible?* I wondered as I sprinted across the grassy field. *Can Pete possibly like me?*

He was the first boy I ever like-liked and that night he became the first I ever kiss-kissed. Pete goes by Peter now. He's a Ph.D. candidate in history, and I'm still writing poems about the boys I've loved and love. I caught up with him on the phone to ask him what he remembered about our first kiss. Ten years later, and he's still every bit the dreamboat he was in high school.

JENNY Are you ready to do this?

PETER I am.

Can you tell me what you think you were like in high school?

Misunderstood is the word we all used, I think, looking back on it with some self-deprecation. Adolescence is an awkward time for anyone.

Do you remember the first time you noticed me?

You were hanging out with Malgorzata. That was the first time I took notice of you physically. And because you were friends with Malgorzata, I thought you were probably a little different, and that made me interested. I learned at some point that you were this literary genius who was the star of your class. So I was drawn to your tortured genius, of course.

I don't know about that…

Especially since I imagined myself as a quiet, tortured genius.

Do you think I chased after you or do you think you chased after me or do you think there was mutual chasing happening?

I think we did like a Jordan Catalano–Angela Chase thing. We noticed each other.

Do you remember anything about the first time we kissed? Where were we and what were we doing? I'm thinking it was at Prybil Beach.

Were we in the car when it happened or were we on the beach?

I vaguely remember leaning against the hood of your car. But maybe I'm just openly fantasizing.

That was probably it…I remember you were very cutely shy about the kiss. You were a sweet kisser. You were…I don't know how to describe it. You were…

Gentle?

You were soft. You weren't jumping on top of me or anything. It was more awkward than that.

I don't know if you know this, but earlier that same day, I had pecked another boy on the lips. It was this kid who had a crush on me in high school. We went to Morgan Park and very awkwardly embraced and he very awkwardly asked me to be his girlfriend and I just said yes because I was super passive back then. And then I came home and started chatting with you on AOL Instant Messenger or something, and you asked me if I wanted to go for a ride in your car, and I immediately messaged the boy I had embraced in the park earlier and was like, "Um, I'm calling this whole thing off. I just want to be friends," and then dashed off to meet you. I think that was the same night we ended up kissing on the beach. I don't know if I ever told you that.

What a heartbreaker you were. Having your first kiss and leaving a trail of broken hearts behind you.

Yeah, so calculating, already. How many times do you think we've kissed each other?

I don't know…we did a lot of kissing.

Just throw out a number.

Maybe a hundred times? How do we distinguish between one night and one kiss? I don't know how we break that up mathematically. A lot of times.

What do you do now? Do you think you are the person you thought you would be in high school?

Yeah, I think I turned out the way I expected. I have my self-criticism, of course. But I'm finishing a Ph.D., and hoping to use it to write. The road has been very unexpected and circuitous, and not without some regrets, but I think I'm generally about where I expected to end up.

Is there a part of you that's still the punk heartthrob I thought you were in high school?

Oh, man. You know, I hope so. I've largely abandoned the music, beyond nostalgia—apologies to Kathleen Hanna—and I dress more bourgeois and suburban than I could have admired back then, but in social and political thought I'd like to think I've kept the rebelliousness against conformity and conservatism that first attracted me to that scene. The anti-conformists can also be just as herd-like and fashion-obsessed as the crowd…but I still light up like a kid on Christmas morning whenever I hear a Dead Kennedys song…

What kind of lady do you think I've become since high school?

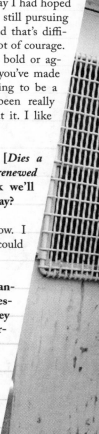

You turned out the way I had hoped you'd turn out. You're still pursuing dreams, like I am, and that's difficult to do. It takes a lot of courage. Neither of us is very bold or aggressive, but I think you've made a bold choice by trying to be a writer. And you've been really successful and kept at it. I like who you've become.

That's really sweet. [*Dies a little bit inside with renewed love.*] Do you think we'll ever kiss again someday?

[*Laughs*] I don't know. I don't know. Anything could happen…

All right. Thanks for answering all of my questions even though they were kind of embarrassing.

You're very welcome. ♦

FIRST LOVE

1. Is This Love? ♥ Clap Your Hands Say Yeah
2. A Teenager in Love ♥ the Pains of Being Pure At Heart
3. Super Crush ♥ Tiger Trap
4. Don't Laugh (I Love You) ♥ WEEN
5. Lover ♥ Devendra Banhart
6. Abducted ♥ Cults
7. Why Do Lovers Break Each Other's Hearts? ♥ Bob B. Soxx and the Blue Jeans
8. Breakin' up ♥ Violent Femmes
9. Gimmie Gimmie Gimmie Back Your Love ♥ Hunx and his Punx
10. Don't Throw Your Love Away ♥ Fabienne Delsol

BECAUSE YOU CAN

Our monthly column where Leeann gives you easy ideas for having more fun with your clothing.
Writing by Leeann. Illustrations by Kelly. Playlist by Hazel. Photos by Olivia Bee.

◆ Borrow your dad's gigantic wooly sweater and wear it over the shortest kilt you can find. Try to get it so the hem only just peeks out from under the sweater.

◆ Thrift an old lunchbox to carry your pencils and other school junk around in.

◆ Style your hair into a nice, big '60s ponytail and stick your favorite badges in the poufy part.

◆ Wear knee socks with everything! You can cut them from an old pair of tights, or get the slouchy old-lady kind from the drugstore for 99 cents—they look great with a cute skirt and flats. Black knee socks and a leather jacket bring your favorite summer dress into fall; white socks give a little plaid jumper a schoolgirl vibe.

◆ Tie an old belt around your schoolbooks like kids used to in the dark ages before book bags. Your brother's old brown belt will look very classic '50s Ivy League; bonus points if you can find one of the crazy neon rubber ones they made in the '60s.

◆ Speaking of book bags, never buy one from a regular store. Army/Navy surplus stores have a million awesome bags that are sturdy and dirt cheap.

◆ Plaid might as well be the official pattern of fall. Go all in and wear two or three different plaids that clash delightfully.

◆ Have some school spirit for once and get a varsity jacket in your school's colors. If you don't play a sport, they can almost always be found in the men's section of the thrift store for super cheap. They look great when they fit nice and loose, worn with a pair of skinny jeans, and your hair hanging in your face just so people know you haven't totally gone Spirit Week.

◆ Even if you don't have to wear a school uniform, you can put together amazing outfits at a uniform supply store (for incredibly cheap). Try wearing a knife-pleat miniskirt with a little shrunken polo, or a Peter Pan–collar blouse with an A-line jumper. You can carry a plaid pencil case as a clutch!

◆ If you have a little brother, definitely raid his closet for the blazer he wore to your aunt's wedding when he was 11. It'll look perfectly shrunken and cute on you. Put your favorite pins all over the lapel and wear it with a big scarf, a shirt buttoned all the way to the top, and close-fitting khakis or jodhpurs.

◆ Saddle shoes are the cutest and most classic shoe you can wear with any sort of schoolgirlish look. The school uniform store should be able to help you out here, or you can do what I once did in a pinch and take a black Sharpie to a pair of basic white canvas sneaks.

◆ If you're the arty-crafty type, swap out your regular shoelaces for a piece of yarn. It looks extra cute when the yarn starts to fray and get all fuzzy. You can also tie a same-colored piece of yarn around your ponytail, but only if you want to be the most adorable girl in school. ◆

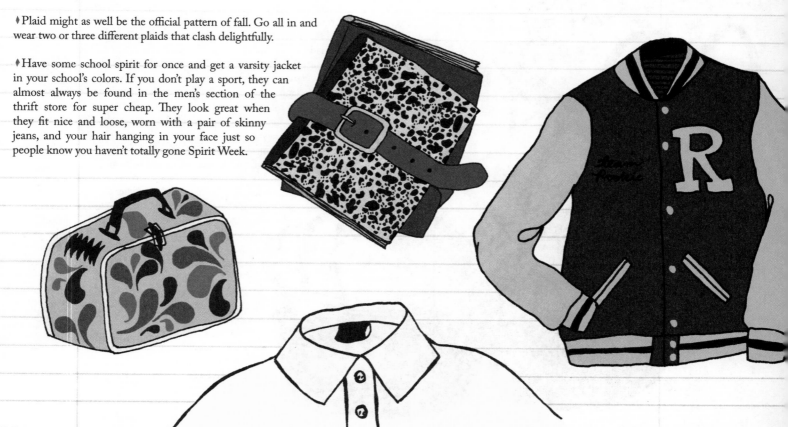

A SUPER-CLASSY GENTLEMAN'S GUIDE TO BEING
A CLASSY FELLOW

The subtle art of seduction.
Writing by Paul Feig. Illustrations by Cynthia.

It happened in my seventh-grade science classroom. A weird place to have your first kiss, although I have to admit that it was only a kiss on the cheek. But for a kid who pined hopelessly after every pretty girl in my junior high, getting a kiss on the cheek from any female outside of my family's gene pool was an event worth celebrating. The problem was, as with most things in my life, I turned something that should have been a sweet memory into yet another self-generated humiliation.

No, this isn't a boner story, although I believe a boner was involved. This, my friends, is a story of sheer misguided nerdiness.

Kim McKenzie was an extremely pretty girl who hung out with a group of other extremely pretty girls in our school. They were the ones who would show up wearing very similar rabbit-fur coats and tight bell-bottomed jeans that fit perfectly over their platform shoes so that they almost appeared to be levitating as they walked down the hallways. Kim was the friendliest-looking of the bunch, since the other girls had kind of a hard prettiness that said they would not only laugh in your face if you asked one of them out but also kick the crap out of you as they laughed in your face. But Kim seemed different. She was shorter than the other girls and had big eyes and a permanent smile that made her seem like "the nice one." I had spent the last several years staring at her from various hidden vantage points in classrooms and hallways and had often fantasized about asking her to a school dance or to see a movie at the mall. But, of course, I never did anything more than fantasize, because the chance of my working up the courage to ask out a girl that pretty was about as likely as my standing up on a cafeteria table in the middle of lunch hour naked and doing an interpretive dance.

But the first day of seventh grade, the Fates dealt me an amazing hand. As I sat down at my assigned desk in science class, which was a lab table that sat two students, a fringed suede purse dropped onto the chair next to me. I looked up to see that Kim had been assigned as my desk partner. We would be sitting next to each other every day for the entire year in the hour before lunch, close enough for our elbows to occasionally touch. I looked at her and she smiled back and said, "Hey, Paul." She knew my name!

It turned out that she actually *was* really nice. She immediately struck up a conversation with me and was so friendly that I lost a lot of my awkwardness and was able to joke around with her in a way that almost made me seem entertaining to someone who looked like her. I was in shock. Kim McKenzie was going to be sitting next to me every day for the next year. That had to mean she'd end up being my girlfriend, right? I thought as we sat taking notes about electrons. How couldn't it?

A few weeks went by, and things were looking good. I was able to regularly make Kim laugh, usually at the expense of our disheveled teacher, Mr. Durkowitz, who had apparently never heard that nose hairs can be trimmed. I also got pretty good at coming up with witty comments making fun of the pictures of old scientists in our textbook. Also, whenever possible, I'd try to ask her about herself and her likes and dislikes, since my father had given me a book a couple of years earlier entitled *How to Win Friends and Influence People* that said the key to getting people to like you was to ask them personal questions, as opposed to yammering on and on about yourself.

One day, before class started, we got to talking about music and what our favorite new songs were. Embarrassingly, I blurted out that the one I liked was "The Streak" by Ray Stevens, which was a really stupid song about the fad of that year, which was taking off all your clothes except for your shoes and then running through a public place. But fortunately for me, she said she thought it was a funny song and what was a potential relationship-ending admission by me turned out to be another small bit of bonding between the two of us. Then Kim said in a dreamy voice, "You know what song I absolutely love? 'I Honestly Love You.' It's *soooo* romantic."

For those of you who don't know that song (and I'm assuming that's most of you since I'm guessing I'm a lot older than the readers of Rookie), Olivia Newton-John had recorded a very syrupy song back then called "I Honestly Love You" that had become a big number-one hit in 1974. And it really *was* romantic. I had heard it many times on the radio and had had visions of slow dancing with Kim to it at the upcoming school dance. And so to have Kim tell me to my face that she loved that song almost seemed as if she was telling me that she honestly loved *me*.

She then said, "I really want to buy that record. I'd play it to death in my bedroom."

I had my mom drive me to the mall the minute I got home. I ran to the record store and bought a copy of "I Honestly Love You," inspecting several copies closely. I did this because back in 1974 all records were made of vinyl and if you accidentally bought a copy that was scratched or warped, you'd look like a total loser giving it to someone as a present because it would sound terrible when they played it and they'd think you were an idiot for not having checked it out before you bought it. I then went to the Hallmark store and bought some gift-wrapping paper. I wrapped the record to make it look like a present and even put a bow on it, since I was really hoping to blow her away with this incredibly romantic gesture of mine.

I barely slept that night as I tried to imagine how she would react. Would she scream with joy and throw her arms around me and kiss me? Would she just say thanks and put it in her bag because she was a pretty girl and pretty girls probably have guys giving them presents all the time? Or would she think I was a total weirdo and ask Mr. Durkowitz if she could change seats because she was sitting next to an insane stalker? I had no idea, but was definitely hoping for the first outcome.

I was so nervous when I got to science class that I considered not giving it to her after all. I was definitely running the risk of embarrassing myself not only in front of her but in front of my entire class, since if things went wrong it was going to be a very public failure. Fortunately, the Fates dealt me yet another good hand. As I walked in the classroom, Kim was already there at our desk, looking through her purse for something. Only a couple of other students had arrived, and so if I acted now and she screamed and ran out of the room in terror, there would be very few witnesses and I could always blame it on accidentally stepping on her foot or something.

I nervously approached the desk and said as nonchalantly as I could, "Hey, Kim, I got you something." She looked up at me, surprised. I held out the wrapped record. Her eyes went wide as she looked at it, and I waited to see if I had overstepped my bounds. But she gave a little laugh and said, "Oh my god, what did you do?"

She took the present from me, and I sat down next to her. "Pretty wrapping," she said as she carefully began to open it. I suddenly loved her even more, seeing she was someone who hated tearing wrapping paper as much as me. I always felt bad for wrapping paper because it does such a great job looking nice and making people happy when they see it and then two seconds later they tear it to shreds like it was just some ugly old newspaper. But then again, I was also a kid who couldn't throw out a Cap'n

Crunch box because it had a picture of the Cap'n smiling on the front of it and I felt like I was killing him if I sent him to the garbage dump. I think this is called *personification of inanimate objects* and it's probably what leads you to become a hoarder and look insane on national TV. But I digress.

Kim pulled the record out of the wrapping and read the label.

"Oh my god!" she gasped. "I can't believe it! Thank you!"

And with that, she threw her arms around me and kissed me on the cheek.

I almost fainted. It was very rare in my life at that point (and up to this day, sadly) that things went the way I hoped they would go. But this had worked. So well, in fact, that I was immediately kicking myself I hadn't waited until more people were in the classroom. A girl like Kim McKenzie kissing a guy like me in public would have given me some much-needed romantic cred in a place that knew me as a nerdy kid whose only skill seemed to be the ability to quote Bugs Bunny cartoons by heart. But it didn't matter, because I had accomplished exactly what I wanted. I had made Kim McKenzie like me.

At home that night, all I could do was relive the kiss. I played the moment over and over in my mind. I played it in slow motion. I could still feel her lips on my cheek. I could still feel her arms hugging me. I could still hear her saying, "Thank you!" I could still see her smiling at me during class and hear her saying, "Thanks again, that was really nice of you" as she headed out of the room when class ended and I delayed at my desk to let my boner subside. But it was the kiss that I couldn't stop thinking about. And I wanted more than anything for it to happen again.

And that was the moment that I made a very bad mistake.

I decided to write her a thank-you note, thanking her for the kiss.

It seemed like such a good idea at the time. What could be a more romantic follow-up to giving her a present she really wanted than the handwritten gift of my gratitude? And how else could I get her to kiss me again if she didn't know how much her small gesture meant to me? It was the perfect plan, I told myself.

I sat down and started to write the note. All I remember verbatim is the opening line, which was: "Dear Kim, I just wanted to write you this letter to say, thanks for the kiss."

I honestly don't remember the rest. I've torn it out of my memory. But I do know that it was a long sappy letter that drove home repeatedly how grateful I was that she had kissed me and that talked about

how girls didn't usually like me "that way." I went into great flowery detail about how I felt when she kissed me, referencing things like my heart feeling "light" and how I spent the rest of the day "walking on air." As I wrote, I played the Olivia Newton-John song over and over in my head and had visions of Kim in her bedroom playing the record repeatedly as she danced around with her eyes closed and imagined I was there holding her close, dancing along with her. I went over the letter many times and was convinced that it said all the things I knew I couldn't say to her in person. And I couldn't imagine that she wouldn't be completely swept off her feet once she read it.

I went to bed that night certain I would be kissed again the very next day.

My heart was pounding as I got to class. Kim wasn't there yet. Should I put the letter on the desk now, I wondered, so that when she arrived she'd be intrigued by this mysterious envelope with her name on it? Or should I hand it to her after suavely saying, "Kim…I've got something else for you"? Minutes ticked by and still no Kim. Just as Mr. Durkowitz walked in, Kim rushed through the door and sat down next to me. I gave her a friendly hello nod and she nodded back, looking a bit preoccupied. Then Mr. Durkowitz went into his lecture, and I spent the entire hour obsessing about the best way to give Kim the letter. I even considered handing it to her during class so that she could read it as Mr. Durkowitz droned on, but then the vision of him seeing her not paying attention and taking the letter and reading it to the entire class made me realize that wasn't a viable option.

When class was over, Kim got up pretty quickly. She looked like she was in a hurry to get somewhere, and so I awkwardly said, "Hey, um, you going to lunch?" She said she was and that she had to run to her locker before she met her friends and it was clear that I had to hand over the letter right then and there. And so I did.

"I have something for you," I said, holding out the letter.

"Something else? Wow." But she didn't say it the way you would if you were im-

pressed and touched that a person had now given you a present two days in a row. Her tone was more of the "Why are you giving me things all of a sudden? Are you some kind of psycho?" variety. She took the letter and thanked me and then rushed out of the classroom. And I immediately started to feel like I had made a huge mistake.

My stomach was in knots that night, and every time I reread the letter in my mind, what had seemed so romantic and poetic the night before now sounded desperate and pathetic, as well as catastrophically cringe-inducing. And when I saw her the next day in class, she didn't mention the letter and was decidedly colder to me. I was completely self-conscious and so pretended to read my textbook once I saw that there was no positive feedback coming as a result of my thank-you note and definitely not another kiss in my future.

Over the course of the next week things only got more awkward. I was too embarrassed to say anything, and it was clear to me that Kim didn't want to do or say anything that she thought would lead me to believe she had any feelings for me. Which meant she didn't want to say *anything* to me because in her mind, if I was a guy who could turn an innocent kiss of appreciation into a declaration of love from her, then I was like one of those people you don't even want to say hi to for fear they'll start talking to you and never shut up.

A few weeks later, when Mr. Durkowitz said we could pick our own lab partners to work on projects for the science fair, Kim picked one of the popular guys on the other side of the room and I picked someone else. She moved over to the guy's desk for the rest of the year and my new partner moved to mine, and Kim and I never really spoke again.

And to this day, whenever I hear the song "I Honestly Love You" on an oldies station, all I can think is one thing: "God, I hope Kim McKenzie doesn't still have that stupid thank-you letter." ◊

Paul Feig is a writer of books, a director of movies (most recently, Bridesmaids*), and the creator of* Freaks and Geeks.

AUBREY PLAZA: PHANTOM RAIDER

Our favorite stare master discusses her cheery alter ego, lab safety, and Justin Bieber's subconscious penchant for vaginas.
Interview by Tavi. Illustration by Brooke and Sonja.

If there are two things I find refreshing, they are milk with ice in it, and Aubrey Plaza. One of these items is especially refreshing because she brings us, on *Parks and Recreation*, April Ludgate, a good, dry, eye-rolling girl character the likes of which TV hasn't seen in too long a time.

Also refreshing is the way she began her comedy career: by making web videos with a couple of friends out of suburban boredom.

This refreshing being then put up with older comedians grumbling about her success after Judd Apatow started getting her standup shows, and I think it's *refreshing* that she just focused on how awesome she is and left other people to deal with it instead of apologizing.

When we started talking I was nervous because I'd forgotten my questions and couldn't improvise many good ones. But her inherent coolness refreshed my black heart, and by the end of our con-

versation, the inside of my chest cavity felt like a photograph on a water bottle label of flowers made out of Winterfresh gum blooming in May against the springs of Iceland.

Basically, she's refreshing because she does a lot of cool stuff because she wants to, and we less interesting people get to benefit by having our culture livened up a bit, despite her deadpan delivery.

And now I bring you: my interview with a glass of milk.

Just kidding. It's Aubrey Plaza.

TAVI I wrote questions for you in my chemistry class, but now I can only find my chemistry homework.

AUBREY What chemistry class are you in?

The...bad one? I don't know. It's been a long day and my brain is farting, so I

might just have to ask you about lab safety instead of thinking of real questions.

That's really weird, because I was a safety lab officer in chemistry class. I was really bad at science, and I just tried to talk my way through all those classes, so I asked my chem teacher if I could do extra credit because I was failing my tests and stuff, and she told me if I was safety lab officer I would get extra credit. I made T-shirts with my friend that said "Safety Lab Officer" on them, and then we would walk around and, like, tell other people how to handle their beakers. And somehow I passed that class.

That's a very hefty responsibility.

I kept the T-shirt, too. I have it somewhere in a drawer. I sleep in that T-shirt whenever I'm sad.

If you could go back in time and be in any teen movie or TV show, which would it be?

I would be Janeane Garofalo in *Reality Bites*. Because she's amazing—she was my hero, she's so funny in that movie. Or I would have to be Winona Ryder. I love Winona Ryder too. I would be either one of them. I would also totally be…oh, what's her name? In *Roseanne*?

Darlene?

Darlene! I would totally be Darlene. She was awesome and I love that show so much.

All good roles. Have you ever gotten to meet Janeane Garofalo?

I did actually get to meet her. I did a standup show with her two years ago and it totally blew my mind, because she was actually the first person I ever saw do standup. In high school I drove up to Allentown, Pennsylvania, and saw her standup and I was so psyched about it and then I got to do a show with her and it was awesome. She was really cool. It was really magical. I don't really get star-struck that often, but she was someone who I was really nervous to be around.

What other comedians did you look up to?

Well, Adam Sandler was a big one for me, too. When I was growing up I watched *Billy Madison* like once a day, probably. And I loved him and then I got to meet him, and that was pretty crazy.

Meet him? Weren't you guys in a movie [Funny People, 2009] together?!

Yes! [*Laughs*]

When someone really cool guest-stars on *Parks and Rec*, is it easier to be relaxed about it at this point? Because I think I would forever have a continuous anxiety attack.

It's weird, I don't have the anxiety attack when I meet people in the makeup

trailer, but then when I go and do a scene with them…like, Parker Posey was on our show last season, and I totally loved her growing up, too. I was obsessed with her. And when I met her in person I didn't really freak out, but then when we were shooting the scene and she was in it and the cameras were rolling and we had lines with each other, I couldn't even believe it. I was just like, *I can't believe I'm in a scene with her.*

That seems pretty surreal. Are you guys done shooting the fourth season now?

No, we're just in the beginning. I think next week we're on episode five, so we've only done four. We've already had some guest stars that have been really fun, like Patricia Clarkson was on two weeks ago. And we made out. Which was weird.

That is very weird and will be awesome. Wait, isn't Patricia Clarkson going to play Tammy 1 or 2 or whichever one it is? [*The Tammys are Ron's ex-wives.*]

Tammy 3. No—Tammy 2. No! Tammy 1! What am I talking about. Sorry…wait…

Now everyone will be mad at you.

I know! Shit. OK, so Tammy 1 is Patricia Clarkson, Tammy 2 is Megan Mullally, and then Tammy 0 is on the show, too—Ron's mom.

Oh! That exists?!

That exists. And that's something that no one knows. And they will be shocked to find out that there's a Tammy 0, and Tammy 0 is [played by] Paula Pell, who is an actress-slash-writer on *SNL* and *30 Rock* and she is amazing. She's so funny.

Now someone has to start a band called The Tammys.

Fine, I'll do it.

Good. What'll you play?

I'll play piano and you can play the drums. Or we can have an a cappella group called the Tammys.

Not to brag or anything, but I'm, you know, in a very serious and popular a cappella group at school, so that should be, like, no problem.

Seriously? I always wanted to do that, but we didn't have one.

I think in high school there are some nerdy things that you love but are a little ashamed of, and I'm glad I did this one.

I support you. That was my whole high school experience, doing nerdy things that I loved.

Like lab safety officer.

Exactly.

Were there any others?

Oh, so many things. We didn't have a mascot, so I created a mascot for the school and made my own costume and I kept it in the trunk of my car, and I would drive around to all the games and show up as this character I created called the Phantom Raider, and I had, like, this mask on and a cape and stuff, and I would run around and get everyone pumped up and then I would get back in my car and drive away. And everyone knew it was me but I pretended I was this mystery.

Exactly like Hannah Montana.

That's right. Me and Miley Cyrus have so much in common. It's crazy.

Was this agreed on with the school? Now I'm so curious about it.

No, it wasn't. I actually got in trouble. I climbed up the scaffolding in the gymnasium and I pretended like I was gonna fly off of it, and the nuns yelled at me. But then when I graduated, the school recognized the mascot. They've made it something now called the Spirit Officer, or something? And they pass the costume down to whoever is elected for that position. So now it's like a legitimate tradition, and my sister was that person.

That's a nice legacy. Did you say a nun yelled at you?

Yeah, we had nuns. I went to a really strict all-girls private Catholic school.

That's so intense! I'd want to do that for the aesthetic pleasure and then I would leave.

I feel the same way about public school. I'm still so jealous of people who went to the all-American high school. I was in an all-girls school my whole life up until college.

Do you think that you would ever play a bubbly character?

Yeah. Actually, I just shot a movie called *The Hand Job*, where I play a character like I've never played before. She is not sarcastic or depressed or ironic in any way. She's the valedictorian of her class and she's really focused and determined and Type-A, like a cheerleader almost. It's really different from anything I've done, and it was really, really fun for me to kind of get out of the April zone.

Do you ever go home after work and really feel like you hate everything? Like you're so into the psychology of April?

No, I pick up the April suitcase when I go to work in the morning and I leave it at work when I come home. That was a bad analogy.

That makes sense. That's good vibes I think.

Yeah. And also, April's kind of evolved, you know? She doesn't really hate everyone, she just has kind of an attitude problem—but secretly she really loves everyone.

That's why the wedding episode is so heartwarming, and all of the subtly paternal Ron stuff...ah! OK, anyway. What is *The Hand Job* about?

The Hand Job is about a recent high school graduate who has spent all her time achieving academic awards and focusing on her homework, and she graduates and kind of realizes that she hasn't really had any fun, and she hasn't really done anything with guys. She's warned by her older, kind of slutty sister, who's played by Rachel Bilson, that she must learn how to do stuff with guys before college or she'll be the laughingstock of Georgetown. So she takes this very seriously and decides to treat sex as like a homework assignment, like a summer work assignment. She basically makes a list of all these things that she wants to figure out how to do with guys, and then she takes it so seriously that she kind of becomes promiscuous without even realizing it, and it causes some tension with her friends. And it's set in 1993, so it's like a period piece, and there's some really amazing awful skorts and clothes happening. It's kind of like a female *Superbad*. Bill Hader's in it, Andy Samberg's in it. There's a lot of really awesome people in it. Alia Shawkat is playing my best friend. She's one of my really good friends in real life. It was fun to shoot a movie with her, because we got to just play.

1993 and graduation and promiscuity. It sounds kind of like you are playing Janeane Garofalo in *Reality Bites*.

Yeah, definitely. Kind of.

I can't believe there's a movie that takes place "in the past" but it's 1993. I like it.

I know, that's what everyone keeps saying, 'cause I keep calling it a period piece, which sounds funny, but it really is. There's some pretty amazing art direction in the movie.

There's this more recent Janeane Garofalo bit about how on *Ghost Hunters* and stuff, the ghosts are never from, like, the '90s or the '80s. But...yeah. I don't really

know where I was going with that. Except the other night, my friend and I did the Ouija board in my room and we actually got a ghost from the '80s.

A guy or a girl?

A girl.

Really? Like someone that you knew?

No, sadly not.

I just did a Funny or Die video with my friend Allan [McLeod] called "Ghost Walkers." It's a parody of a ghost-hunting show, and I play this weird witch girl and it's really witchy and ghosty. You'd probably like it.

I probably would. Is there anything else you'd like people reading this to look up right now? Just something you wish more people knew about?

I just saw something yesterday that was really funny. It's this guy who works in one of those stock-photo companies and he pulled a prank on his co-worker where he Photoshopped Justin Bieber's face into all of the stock photos. And you think it's gonna be just, like, covering other faces, but he does it in a really weird way where if it's a stock photo of a can of beans, Bieber's face is one of the little beans. It's really creepy, but it's one of the funniest things I've seen in a while.

I'll use my internet skills and find it. [I found it. It's at www.helpmesellmore booksthanjustinbieber.com/head.]

Rashida Jones just gave me Justin Bieber's...perfume, or whatever. The bottle kind of looks like a vagina. I think it's supposed to be like a flower, like a rose. The petals are, like, rubber petals. It's really weird and vaginal.

Does it smell all right?

It smells awful. Sorry, Bieber—I love you, but it smells really bad. ♦

FIRST ENCOUNTERS WITH THE MALE GAZE

Here's what the big deal is.
By Tavi

Everyone has a very personal relationship with their body. You live with this thing every day. You grew up with it. It has birthmarks and bruises and acne and battle scars, and holds lots of memories. And perhaps lately you've started noticing different things about yourself in the mirror every now and then. It's not a good or bad thing, it's just what happens. But still, it's weird, because it is change, and it does just *happen*, and without your permission. Which is why it feels so weird when other people start taking notice, also without your permission.

I'm talking about catcalls, and whistles, and comments from passing cars, and hallway touching, and rumors at school, and on Facebook, and Formspring, and another social-networking site that starts with an F. (I just typed in Farts.com BECAUSE THAT IS HOW MY BRAIN WORKS and got distracted from writing this for a really long time.) Sometimes this attention is positive, sometimes it's negative, and sometimes it's positive in a way that sounds like a compliment but is just an FYI to you from the deliverer that they apparently have the right to offer their two cents on the state of your body.

Last year, a big, obnoxious, piercing catcall rang through the halls of my high school. A junior guy made a list in which he ranked 50 junior girls and commented on their bodies and alleged sex lives. I say "catcall" because it was not positive attention, though it disguised itself as such, and under pet names like "the amazing bisexual" was this presumptuous entitlement. As if anyone should give a shit that this guy gave their breasts a 7 out of 10.

He posted the list to Facebook and left folders of printed copies all over the school. A mob of students cheered him on as he stood on the main staircase in our lobby, threw out copies of the list to the student body, and yelled, "Women are the future—unless we stop them now!" He didn't know how shitty what he did was, but he wasn't innocent. He intended to make girls feel bad by targeting the insecurities and criticisms that come up for us regularly. Too slutty, too prudish, too fat, too skinny. (Thank god, too, cause I was really worried for a while there that our world would soon be destroyed by all these damn women taking over, stomping around in their girly high heels and ruining everything!)

We have a little over 3,000 students at my school, so rumors never make it very far, but man, people were looking for any gossip about this scandal that they could find. That one guy may have written the list, but it took lots of people to pass it around. When it came up in conversation, even months later, after it was in the newspaper, and Jay Leno made a joke about it on his late-night show, there was always one person saying, "I don't see the big deal. If I'd been on that list, I'd be able to get over it pretty easily." And that person was always a guy.

I want these guys to know that they're able to be so cavalier because they don't hear unsolicited opinions on their bodies and alleged sex lives *all the time*. Because the changes they noticed in the mirror a year or two ago were not interpreted as permission by strangers to offer an opinion on their bodies. Because they don't put up with the kind of language the list used on the regular, and didn't have to see it manifested as some kind of official document or rulebook, shared and spread and broadcast for students and teachers and parents to see. I want these guys to know that of course it would be easy for you to get over, because your transition into puberty didn't include the same kinds of ridiculous beauty expectations, and then unsolicited evaluations of how well you measured up.

I want these guys to know that it's not their fault that they can't have empathy, but that it's ignorant to assume that their empathy is the only thing that could validate what we girls were feeling. I want them to know that it's not their fault that they don't know the feeling of your safety being threatened when a guy on the subway keeps edging closer to you, but that they look like jerks when they pretend it's no big deal.

I want the guys who regularly perpetuate the same bullshit that the list was made of to know that, congratulations on your high self-esteem, but you are mistaken if you think anyone is interested in your opinion of their body parts. I want them to know that I don't have to smile, or react at all, to their backhanded compliments. I want them to know that I don't exist for them to look at, I don't get dressed for them, and however I have put myself together on this day—it is not for you.

Most of all, I want to be able to walk around my neighborhood and school without its being assumed that I am looking for feedback on my figure. You know, it really shouldn't be so complicated.

I don't know that these wishes of mine will be granted. I'm grateful for organizations like SlutWalk and Hollaback because they respond to these guys in a way that is hard to do in the moment. A few things that work are: "No, I won't smile, I just found out my entire family was killed in a freak accident," or "You don't own this street and no one asked your opinion on my ass." But I shouldn't have to have a strategy for preserving my personal space.

The guy who made the list no longer goes to our school. He still comes up in conversation now and then, and there's always someone who shrugs when it's brought up, wondering what the big deal was. Recently a guy at our lunch table defended him. Part of me wanted to argue, but I was already tired of the frustration I knew I would soon feel. So were the rest of the girls at our table. We just rolled our eyes and took it in. We'd had plenty of practice. ◆

HANDS OFF

My first feminist action.
Writing by Miranda July. Illustrations by Cynthia.

YOU SAY : KEEP YOUR HANDS OFF MY CAR

WE SAY : KEEP YOUR HANDS OFF OUR BODIES

SINCERELY,
THE WOMEN OF THIS SCHOOL

This story begins when Xavier Reed* made an announcement in assembly. My high school was private, a prep school. Most announcements at assembly were about a bake sale or a basketball game, but Xavier Reed took the microphone and said, with complete seriousness, "Someone spilled their Coke on my BMW. If this happens again I'm going to be forced to sue for damages. Keep your hands off my car."

To understand how angry this made me, you have to know a little bit about Xavier Reed. He was a rich asshole. He made fun of people in mean ways. And he had a history of touching girls at parties when they were drunk or passed out. This was widespread knowledge; older girls told younger girls: watch out for Xavier Reed. He wasn't a stud, he wasn't well liked. His power came from being a brute in an Izod shirt. Thinking about it now I imagine he had his share of suffering, but to understand this story it's important that you feel no sympathy for him.

After assembly I had a free period. Still furious about Xavier's announcement, I sat and read a book I'd checked out of the school library called *Lipstick Traces*. Do you know this book? It's by the music critic Greil Marcus and it's about revolts and rebellions throughout history. It has a picture of Johnny Rotten on the cover. What exactly did I read? I don't know, maybe I just stared at the flier for a 1978 Slits show on page 40. Or maybe I read the lyrics to the Wire song on page 73: "I am the fly in the ointment."

Using a black marker, I made a poster. I went into the library and Xeroxed it, and then, while everyone was in class, I taped it up all over the school. Then I sat and waited. The bell rang; all the kids burst out of their classrooms and toward their lockers.

Then they saw the posters. I held my breath and watched them read>>>>>>>>>

I didn't have a plan beyond this moment. I wasn't sure anyone would even get it—who and what I was talking about. But they did. Everyone was whispering and soon there was shouting. Boys were forming factions, taking sides, and some girls were crying. I watched in shock, not sure whom to stand next to or where to look. I had assumed that nothing I said or did could ever have an impact on reality.

Somehow everyone knew it was me. Xavier's friends let me know I would be killed after school. A sophomore girl told me, in strict confidence, that Xavier had molested her. A girl from my class, a senior, made me promise never to tell anyone that she had had sex with one of our teachers. Everything was so much worse than I had known, it was actually terrifying. I waited for some authority to step in—and they did. I was sent home from school. They said it was for my safety, to protect me from Xavier's friends. Xavier himself had assured me I would be sued for slander.

When I got back to school everything was smoothed over. The faculty had decided it was best to ignore the outburst. I felt sick. What about all those girls who had told me their secrets with such shame? I couldn't bear it.

At lunchtime I walked into the headmaster's office. I put my hand on his telephone (I had a flair for the theatrical) and said, "If you don't do something, I'll call all the newspapers and tell them that you have, at very least, a sexual harassment situation here and you aren't doing anything about it."

This worked in part because of timing. Sexual harassment was a big new topic in 1992; just a few weeks before there had been an article about it at the local public high school, which is how I'd gotten the idea for my dramatic blackmail.

That Friday we had an extended assembly. Instead of the usual announcements, a group of energetic college students came and taught us about sex. They taught us that no meant no, and what was appropriate behavior for a date. They showed us sexist images from magazines and called them sexist. Some of them were openly gay, and that blew our minds. It was a start.

Right after this I graduated and became a riot grrrl, to the tune of: We want revolution, girlstyle, *NOOOWW!* ♦

* *This name has, for obvious reasons, been changed.*

Miranda July is a writer, filmmaker, and artist.

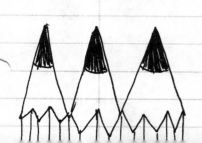

YOUNGER THAN YESTERDAY

The kind of day when you don't wanna get called inside for dinner.

By Erica

Thank you to Ariel, Beth, Eira, Hannah, and Zaira for modeling.

OCTOBER 2011:

We had a good first month, and we're ready to make this one even better. October's theme is Secrets, and we'll be talking about things people normally don't talk about, like depression and masturbation, along with candy, which people never shut up about, and for good reason. Candy is good. Loooove candy. Candy.

Even more interesting than secrets themselves are the people whom they belong to. October's spookiness is a perfect reason (not that it should ever need a reason, duh) to embrace more-mysterious heroines like Wednesday Addams, Margot Tenenbaum, Allison Reynolds of *The Breakfast Club*, and even Jane Eyre, who might be the godmother of teen witches.

When I use this term, I don't mean actual Wiccans, but rather the cultural clan of girls who have a kind of strange, dark magic about them that you can't quite place, and which they definitely won't help you figure out. *Lula*, one of my favorite magazines, worded it best when they did their angsty-girls issue: "They know that life, most of the time, really kind of sucks, and we shouldn't kid ourselves otherwise." Not to be a total downer or anything, but sometimes it's not that fun to pretend to be all happy, and the girl in the back of the class is always the most intriguing and endearing. Let me put it this way: my spellcheck just changed *angsty* to *gangster*. That should tell you enough.

I'm not quite cool enough to be that girl—I care about grades a little too much to be such a badass, and have trouble keeping my love for things like stickers bottled up—but I will always be her #1 mascot. Along with the mysteries and secrets in this issue, we'll celebrate angst and moodiness. It'll be like Rookie is on its period the ENTIRE MONTH! SO FUN! But an aesthetically pleasing period, and one that is not actually moody all the time, contrary to menstruation's bad rap in bro movies. We have CANDY, remember?

Thank you for being here.

LOVE,
TAVI

YES   NO

ABCDEFGH
NOPQRSTUV
123456

CLASS OF 2012

Exercise your right to roll your eyes this picture day.
By Petra and Tavi

Thanks to Anna, Arabelle, Billy, Molly, Nicki, and Rachel for modeling; Rivkah for assisting; Jonathan Young for Dior Beauty for doing all the makeup; Charles Olson for doing almost everyone's hair; and Continental Studios, School Photographers in Queens for letting us use their studio. All photos styled by Tavi. All makeup by Christian Dior.

MOST LIKELY TO SUCCEED

BEST SMILE

BIGGEST FLIRT

CLASS CLOWN

TEACHER'S PET

DRAMA QUEEN

HOW TO BITCHFACE

Channel your inner Martha Stewart with this crafty D.I.Y.
Writing by Tavi. Playlist by Stephanie.

If you are the kind of person to encounter human beings in your life, you probably will find yourself needing a bitchface eventually. A bitchface is a beauty essential for any true lady—the kind of accessory that says, "You are a fucking idiot, why am I still talking to you." Here, I show you multiple faces for reacting to varying levels of stupidity, including handy step-by-step how-tos.

UNAMUSED   REPULSED

This is your very basic bitchface. Your canvas, if you will. For the art of bitchfacing, and your many bitchface experiences to come, in your long, long lives ahead of you. Sigh, thinking about the children of our world makes me emotional!

STEP ONE: Look as much like you don't care as possible. Remember, the opposite of love isn't hate, it's indifference! So keep a straight face, and don't flinch. (It always helps me to pretend I am a corpse.) If you're one of those god-awful people who look all cheerful all the time, whose faces just naturally fall into a smile of any kind, you might have to use a little extra muscle to keep it looking like an emoticon.

STEP TWO: Hold this look until a little bit after the person stops talking. The extra time will make them nervous—they won't know if you can't tell the difference between the sound of the wind blowing and their voice, or if they've bored you so much that you've fallen asleep with your eyes open, or if you just don't even know how to respond because they are such a flaming imbecile. All of these are positive things. Keep staring. Stay strong. You go, girl.

This one requires a little more effort than the typical bitchface, and shows the beholder that their stupidity was bad enough to cause you to actually contort your face. Use sparingly. Few people are worth your muscle movement. And you can quote me on that the next time you want to get out of gym.

STEP ONE: Smize.

STEP TWO: Furrow your brow suspiciously.

STEP THREE: Open your mouth ever so slightly, like you're about to eat a mini cheeseburger. (NOT a mini plain burger. Then your mouth will be too small. This hypothetical cheese slice may be mini, but it makes a huge difference.) Crinkle your nose a little so the shape of your mouth is one of utter disgust. This may require a little nostril-flare action.

STEP FOUR: Here's the real zinger! When you add the brow furrowing to the smize, your eyes get a bit too small for all of your

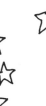

repulsion to show through. Open them up a leeeeetle more to give the onlooker a flash of ICE. And they'll be like, "What is this, a 2002 animated comedy about talking animals starring Ray Romano?!"

And you'll be like:

And then they will never bother you ever again.

"IS ANYONE ELSE HEARING THIS?"

This one is good for when you're with a group of people. Just crinkle up your face a bit—the sweet spots are the brow and the mouth—and look at the people around you. The person talking will feel like everyone has ganged up on them, just from the power of your eyes. This also works when you're not with other people, because they will see that you are so bored that you are utilizing your peripheral vision to look for somewhere to escape to.

"REALLY?"

This one requires a bit of sass, if you're game. Start with your *Unamused* look from earlier.

STEP ONE: Raise your eyebrows. Furrow them EVER SO SLIGHTLY in the middle to take your look from "surprised" to "in disbelief and a little skeptical."

STEP TWO: Push your face back, like the first half of that head-bob motion douchebags do when they're listening to dubstep on their iPods while walking to class. This will show that you are taken aback. By the talking person's stupidity.

HANDS

FACE ONE: Cup your hands around your nose and flatten them together. This will look like you are refraining yourself from telling this person the sad, bitter truth about how pathetic they are.

48

Closed eyes will give the effect of increased frustration. Don't worry too much if it looks like you're praying. The dumbass will probably think you are praying for someone to save you from this terrible conversation, or for them to shut up, both of which you probably are.

FACE TWO: For added effect, breathe loudly and deeply. Dip your head down and stare up from under the very tops of your eyelids. I can't explain why this works so well. It just does. Don't question it. Just *live* it.

FACE THREE: Massage your temples with the tips of your fingers. It will look like you have a headache from the other person's voice/ideas/existence. Widening your eyeballs and clenching your jaw add a special quality, too.

ACCESSORIES

A DRINK: You can make slurping noises to show how bored you are. I recommend milk, because a person who is not a baby drinking straight milk is mysterious and therefore disturbing and therefore intimidating.

YOUR TONGUE/JAW: If you shift your bottom jaw to the side a bit and move your tongue around inside, you will look extra impatient.

A GUN: Will just add to your general intimidatingness. But I don't condone violence.

And there you have it! Next time someone is wasting your life with their voice, any look from this rainbow of options ranging from passive-aggressive to aggressive-aggressive will help ward them off. Some might call you insensitive or rude, but to those haters, just shoot any other one of these looks right back at them. If you are continually criticized, just keep bitchfacing. Forever. And ever. (And don't sue Rookie when you eventually need surgery to be able to smile. For the day you want to smile, you'll have become one of *them*.) ♦

EVERY DAY IS HALLOWEEN

1. DISINTEGRATION † THE CURE
2. BELA LUGOSI'S DEAD † BAUHAUS
3. TRANSMISSION † JOY DIVISION
4. HALLOWEEN † SIOUXSIE AND THE BANSHEES
5. LUCRETIA, MY REFLECTION † THE SISTERS OF MERCY
6. SPIRITUAL CRAMP † CHRISTIAN DEATH
7. LOUISE † CLAN OF XYMOX
8. WALLFLOWER † SWITCHBLADE SYMPHONY
9. NOXIOUS (THE DEMON'S GAME) † CORPUS DELICTI
10. PREACHER MAN † FIELDS THE OF NEPHILIM
11. CRY. LITTLE SISTER † GERARD McMANN
12. TESTURE † SKINNY PUPPY
13. SPARKS † FAITH AND THE MUSE
14. THIS IS HALLOWEEN † THE CITIZENS OF HALLOWEEN TOWN

NEVER BEEN Kissed

The joys of living single.

Writing by Rachael. Illustration by Sonja.

A confession: I'm a 23-year-old virgin. Not just a sex virgin, but a kiss virgin. A kiss virgin who has never been on anything remotely resembling a date.

A bigger confession: I don't care.

If you took your cues from pop culture, you'd think the sole purpose of high school was hooking up. If you're not dating the coolest, hottest boy in school, you're a loser, and if you're not dating (or trying to date) anyone, you're not just a loser. You don't exist. But I do exist. I have hobbies and a social life. I was on the homecoming court and I went to prom. And I did it all without a boy or girl at my side. I'll admit, the homecoming-court dance was a bit awkward (I had to borrow a friend's date because apparently singletons can't slow dance), but

I'm told that I inspired at least one freshman to excitedly tell her mom, "There's a *nerd* on the court!" so I call it a success.

A lot of people want to know why. *Why* have I gone 23 years without so much as a first kiss? In fact, that's what Rookie's editors asked me when they suggested I write this article. Why did I choose to refrain from dating and making out and all that awesome stuff?

My answer was, "I don't know. Why are you asking?" Because I never made the choice to be single. I didn't wake up on the first day of high school and say, "I want to make it to the age of 23 without dating anyone!" The only choice I made was that I wasn't going to rush into a relationship just for the sake of being in a relationship. If the right person comes along, yeah, maybe I'll make a move, but so far I haven't met that person. Is that so weird?

What might seem weird to you is that I don't really get crushes. I never notice when someone is trying to flirt with me until someone else points it out. So maybe I am missing something, some social skill that other girls have. But I have a sense of romance, and just like most girls, I long to meet that special someone. Every time

I finish a book with a particularly good romantic plot, I get a little depressed and ask myself why I don't have a dashing suitor in my life. Then I remember that I was reading a YA paranormal romance and in real life there are no supernaturally gorgeous vampires who will choose a lifetime of love over my delicious, delicious blood. In real life there are fights and awkwardness and very few chances for my lover to dramatically throw me out of the way of oncoming bullets. And sure, there are plenty of good things about relationships, but I don't lie awake at night fretting over everything I'm missing out on. It's just not important to me.

I'm not saying that it's wrong to make dating a high priority in your life—if you're having fun, great! But if you're not happy in your relationship, or you just have no interest in dating right now, it's OK to be single. Really, it is. I made it through high school *and* college without dating and I'm not a crazy cat lady yet.

Singleness is not a lifestyle choice that's celebrated very often, but it can be a great thing. I had the freedom to move eight hours away from home this year, and I didn't have to worry about uprooting anyone else's life in the process. I dealt with way less drama in high school than most girls. And I have all the free time in the world.

Someday I expect I'll settle down with Mr. or Ms. Right (or have an accidental fling with Mr./Ms. Wrong), and I'll experience all the joys (and the drama) that most of you were experts at by 10th grade. But for now, I'm enjoying the single life.

So, fellow singletons, don't apologize for not living a storybook life. Whether or not you ever choose to pair up is your business, and no one else's. Because, as cheesy as it sounds, you don't need anyone else to make you happy. And a little alone time never hurt anyone. ♦

Do it Yourself

What we talk about when we talk about masturbation.

Writing by Jamie. Illustration by Emma D.

Among my friends that are girls, secrets about masturbating make up the largest category of things that I am ill-advisedly made privy to. As soon as things get a little drunk-after-prom or giggly-at-a-sleepover, everyone gets all, "I totally masturbate…isn't that CRAZY?!"

Having heard this at least 15 times by now, I have a less-than-difficult time accepting each new piece of OMG-so-crazy information. What still manages to blow my mind, though, is the fact that people have chosen to tell their secrets to *me*. Not only am I the worst secret keeper—whispering in my ear is basically the same as sending a mass text to everyone you know—I also was never exactly on the cutting edge of masturbation myself. While most of my guy friends made it very clear that they had been wanking since the waning days of elementary school, I didn't even know that female masturbation was a thing until my best friend came clean to me in the fall of freshman year.

"What do you mean you've never masturbated?" she asked. "I thought everyone did."

At that point in my life, the only thing more frightening than touching my own vagina was the possibility of being marked as a "late bloomer," so I decided to take my lady parts out for a spin. Here are a bunch of questions that I wish someone had answered for me before I started masturbating, as well as relevant anecdotes I gathered from strangers and friends:

1. IS MASTURBATING WRONG?

Some things are wrong: stealing from Claire's, murder, bullying, control-top pantyhose. Notice what isn't on this list? Masturbation. Masturbation is a healthy, natural, NORMAL activity. If you try it out, you won't go blind or grow hair on your palms. Your god of choice will not smite you. Your parents never need to know. The first few times you try it, though, you might feel guilty. This isn't weird. Lots of people (mostly female-identified people) feel bad about masturbation at first, because NOBODY EVER TALKS ABOUT IT. The more that it becomes part of your normal routine, though, the more you'll realize that it's just part of being a human, like breathing or farting or scratching your leg when it itches.

Relevant personal anecdotes from real live people:

"My parents never really talked about [masturbation], but I think I knew that generally it was something they probably didn't approve of. To this day I don't really know their opinions on it, but it's OK, because I generally know my own." —Abbi, 19

"I remember I used to feel awkward, even guilty, about masturbation. I felt like a freak, because I thought no one else did it. All [of my friends] said that masturbation was for weird, nymphomaniac girls because only boys did that. That kept me thinking I was weird and a nymphomaniac for years." —Laura, 18

2. AM I THE FIRST/LAST PERSON IN THE WORLD TO TRY THIS?

I asked a bunch of girls and women I know about their first masturbation experiences, and almost everyone prefaced her answer by saying she was either a "late bloomer" or an "early bloomer." Hilariously (or perhaps sadly), they said this no matter what age they started. Women who masturbated for the first time at the age of 12, and women who tried it for the first time at 20, both called themselves early bloomers. Other women who started at the exact same ages called themselves late bloomers. I guess this is what happens with something that nobody talks about—everyone thinks they're weird. But I have some news for you: no matter what age you start masturbating, or if you never start masturbating, in this regard, at least, you aren't special. You are neither the first nor the last person to try it out. Whatever age you decide to start masturbating, if you do, is "normal."

Relevant personal anecdote from a real live person:

"*I can't even remember the first time I masturbated. I constantly humped just about everything when I was little—pillows, stuffed animals, etc. I never attached any sexual feelings or concepts to it until about middle school, which was the same time I first fingered myself. I never considered humping or clitoral stimulation to be sexual until about that age.*"
—Danielle,* 19

3. WHY SHOULD I MASTURBATE?

The most obvious reason you should try masturbating is because you want to. I tried it because I wanted to be as cool as my friends (OH NO VICTIM OF PEER PRESSURE), but I'm glad I did, because masturbating is fun! And it can contribute lots of great things to your life.

Relevant personal anecdotes from real live people:

"*Masturbating has improved my general self-confidence. I am a sexy woman who can meet her own needs!*" —Danielle

"*Masturbating definitely helped my stress levels and self-confidence.*" —Zoë, 24

"*When I can't sleep or am stressed out I masturbate a lot, so I think it helps with sleep and stress.*" —Holly, 21

4. SO HOW DO I ACTUALLY DO IT?

This is probably the only question that I can't really answer for you. What feels good is a matter of personal opinion. Just like people have different tastes when it comes to food, they have different tastes when it comes to things related to sex. The best advice I can give you is to try a bunch of different techniques and then decide what you like and what you don't.

There are lots of different ways to masturbate. A good way to start is by using your hands, since that doesn't cost any money and you hopefully are already familiar with how to operate them. What you specifically do with your hands is up to you:

♦ You can stick varying numbers of fingers inside of your actual vagina (this is the part of the body that goes inside of you, like where you would put a tampon or get fingered). Not all women can orgasm from vaginal stimulation, but that doesn't mean that vaginal masturbation won't feel good for you.

♦ You can also try touching your clitoris. Your clitoris, or "clit," is located near the front of your genitalia, in front of your urethra (the place you pee from). Use your hands to massage your clitoris. Vary speeds and amounts of pressure that you use in order to determine what you like. You can try spitting on your fingers first; some wetness can feel good.

♦ In the same way that you can finger your vagina, you can also finger your anus (yes, that anus). If you plan on trying this, go slowly and use a lubricant (like spit) to make sure you're comfortable, as the skin in your anus is thinner and more likely to tear than the skin in your vagina. You might like masturbating your anus, as it's a good way to indirectly stimulate your clitoris.

Lots of people find masturbating more than one of these parts of the body at once to be pleasurable. If you are switching between anal and vaginal stimulation, be sure to wash your hands in between. Going straight from your anus to your vagina without washing can cause a nasty infection.

If masturbating with your hands is not for you, you might want to purchase a sex toy like a vibrator. Someone in a friendly, feminist sex shop (like Good Vibrations, Smitten Kitten, or Early 2 Bed) will be able to help you figure out the type of toy that is right for you. In most areas you need to be 18 in order to shop in a store for this sort of thing, but let it be noted that sex toys can be ordered online (just sayin'). You also might be living under the same roof as a free sex toy RIGHT NOW, and not even know it: lots of people I consulted sang the praises of "that shower sprayer thing on the end of a hose." If you have one of these in your bathroom, that might be something worth checking out. Spray it on top of your clit, not into your vagina. Start at a low setting.

Relevant personal anecdotes from real live people:

"*Back in the day, I mostly masturbated by lying in bed, face down, with a pillow between my legs, and humping the hell out of it. Eventually, in high school, some friends gave me a vibrator that was meant to be inserted, and I experimented with that quite a bit, including some anal play.*" —Ellen,* 33

"*I mostly use a vibrator, but sometimes I'm feeling nostalgic and I'll go back to my hands. I always use my middle finger. It's weird, but any other finger doesn't feel as good. And two fingers never really worked for me. One was always falling off the clit and not being a part of the action.*" —Amanda, 26

"*I like to use my hands. Sometimes I think about buying some sex toys, but I really can't afford them. I prefer clitoral stimulation, which I sometimes alternate with vaginal stimulation.*" —Laura

"I have never used a sex toy in my life. I always masturbate lying down, on my stomach, using my hand/pillow/something."—Katie, 26

"I don't know if I've really had an orgasm… it's just a success if I get a warm and heightened pleasure." —Abbi

5. DO I HAVE TO "COME"? HOW DO I KNOW IF I'VE HAD AN ORGASM?

You don't *have* to do anything when you masturbate. The success or failure of masturbating has nothing to do with whether or not you orgasm, and everything to do with your enjoying yourself and feeling good.

Orgasms come in different sizes. It is possible for you to have no orgasm, a small orgasm, a large one, or one of any size in between. All of these still qualify as successful masturbation outcomes, if you had fun, killed some stress, or alleviated your boredom. Here are some things that might happen to your body when you orgasm:

♦ The inside of your vagina might lubricate itself a lot at once ("get wet").

♦ You could feel a rush as blood flows quickly from other parts of your body to your genitals.

♦ Your breathing might get fast; your heart rate could increase.

♦ Your vagina (and maybe even some other parts of your body) might contract rapidly in a series of pleasurable waves.

Relevant personal anecdotes from real live people:

"I reach orgasm only about half the times that I masturbate. It's a success if I have fun, and I always do." —Danielle

"Truthfully, I have never orgasmed when I masturbate. I'm still in pursuit." —Sophie, 17

"With masturbation, I come once and am done. I've tried going for another orgasm, but I just lose interest." —Ellen

"I almost always orgasm, usually once, but sometimes twice. I guess I do consider it more of a 'success' when I do, but at the same time I don't think it's a failure if I don't orgasm." —Michelle, 18

6. SHOULD I WATCH PORN? IS THAT GROSS?

There is nothing weird or gross about watching porn, just as there isn't anything weird or gross about not watching it. Lots of people enjoy watching porn because it helps them get turned on or into a sexier mindset. Porn isn't the only way to do this, though.

Relevant personal anecdotes from real live people:

"I fantasize about having sex with different men or women. [I think about] the sex and how it would feel." —Danielle

"I watch a lot of porn. Like, a lot. I used to think it was kind of a dirty thing that I couldn't talk to a lot of people about. I felt a lot better about masturbating and watching porn, though, after I started talking to my friends about it." —Erinn, 19

"[I used to have a] TV with HBO and Showtime in my room—MAJOR PORN TIME USA!" —Katie

"I watch porn sometimes, but honestly, I read fan fiction or erotica at least as often. I'm so in love with my smartphone, [because] now I can read online things, AND be in bed lying down." —Kelly,* 29

7. IF I DON'T LIKE MASTURBATING, IS SOMETHING WRONG WITH ME?

No! The important thing is to know that there is nothing wrong with giving it a shot. If you try it and you don't like it, that's fine! Plenty of healthy and happy people go through periods of their life, and even their entire lives, without masturbating. You should do what makes you feel good, and if that does not include masturbating, then don't masturbate!

Relevant personal anecdote from a real live person:

"Sometimes I'll masturbate multiple times a day, sometimes I'll stop for weeks. It changes!" —Claire,* 17

8. IS THERE A WAY I CAN REFER TO FEMALE MASTURBATION WITHOUT SOUNDING LIKE A HEALTH-CLASS TEACHER?

There are tons of ways to refer to female masturbation without sounding clinical. I used a bunch in this article. Here are a few more suggested by some of the people I talked to:

"I always just call it rubbing one out." —Zoë

"I like having a wank, even though I know that [usually] refers to male masturbation." —Amie, 26

"My favorite word for female masturbation is the verb to frig, which I believe I first ran into in the works of the Earl of Rochester. I think it's a 16th- or 17th-century term." —Ellen

"I'm a fan of jilling off." —Sophie

"I usually just think of it as getting off, because jilling sounds to me like that last step in making Jell-O, where you let it chill in the fridge." —Michelle

♦ ◊ ♦

No matter what you call it, how you do it, or what you think of the result, getting to know the likes, dislikes, mechanics, and nuances of your body is a good and valuable way to become more comfortable with yourself. So go south, young lady, and grow savvy in the things that make you feel good! ♦

* These women asked me to change their names for this article, and I obliged.

THERE IS A LIGHT THAT NEVER GOES OUT

What The Rocky Horror Picture Show *meant to me (a lot).*
Writing by Kevin Townley. Illustrations by Leanna.

The year I turned 13 (exactly 20 years ago this month!), two very special men came into my life. While they both had long, flowing hair, androgynous costumes, a yearning for togetherness, and a flair for controversy, they couldn't have been more different. One of them was Dr. Frank-N-Furter, the Transylvanian transvestite from *The Rocky Horror Picture Show*. The other was Our Lord and Savior, Jesus Christ.

Let me explain how these two fellows wound up in my life. It was 1991 and my parents had been divorced for about seven years. I lived with my dad, but my mom would sometimes come over to our house and they would treat each other with the kind of stilted cordiality you usually reserve for people you run into at the airport—

you *know* you know them from somewhere, but you don't want to ask their name because it might offend them and you also vaguely remember that this person may have a tendency toward violence.

I've always been the perfect example of the introvert/extrovert personality-type dilemma. When I was young I was painfully shy, to the point that I think my dad was a little concerned. He went out of his way to enroll me in extracurricular activities: karate class, art class…he even forced me to be a mime ("PLEEEEEEEEEEEEASE DON'T MAKE ME BE A MIIIIME!" I'd sob on the car ride to mime class). I didn't want people to see me or know who I was. On the other hand, I loved making my friends pretend to be the band Blondie and force perfor-

mances on the mailman in the lobby of our apartment building, so go figure.

To further his campaign to bring me out of my shell, my dad also encouraged me to audition for my junior high's production of *The Phantom of the Opera*. I secretly yearned to be onstage, but I was petrified to let anyone know. My father helped me prepare, though, and I got a small part. I was over the moon! I had heard that junior high was a treasure trove of freaks and geeks, but didn't know where to find them. Turns out they were all lurking in the theater department (duh). That's how I first heard about *The Rocky Horror Picture Show*.

For those of you who don't know what *Rocky Horror* is (where have you been since 1975 aside from mostly not born?), I will try my best to explain it, though it is difficult because on one hand it is a silly piece of nonsensical fluff, and on the other it is a way of life.

While it was a huge hit onstage in London in the early '70s, *Rocky Horror* didn't do so hot in the movie theaters upon its release in 1975. It did, however, manage to generate a crazy midnight-movie cult following a year later, which continues to thrive around the world as we speak.

At the midnight showings, a live cast of performers act out the entire movie while it plays onscreen behind them. Almost everyone in the audience dresses up too, sings along, shouts audience-participation dialogue, and throws props at the screen. It is a giant slice of glittery mayhem and should be experienced by all before it is too late (death). (No, the *Glee* tribute ep doesn't count.)

The plot, in a nutshell: Newly engaged squares Brad and Janet are so jazzed about their upcoming wedding that they decide to rush to the home of their friend, Dr. Everett Scott, to share the news. Unfortunately, their car gets a flat, so they walk over to a nearby castle hoping to use the phone, only to find there is an intergalactic science convention going on, hosted by some singing, dancing aliens! The aliens' leader, Dr. Frank-N-Furter (played by the supernova of talent that is Tim Curry), informs everyone that he likes to wear ladies' undergarments and has just created a muscle-bound stud in his lab. Then there's some murder and Mickey Mouse hats and cannibalism and everyone gets turned into a statue and winds up really horny and runs amok in fishnets and sings in a swimming pool and the castle blasts off into outer space, the end.

My best friends, fellow theater geeks Tiffany and Lisa, had snuck out one Friday night and gone to a midnight showing at the Fox Theatre on the Hill in our hometown of Boulder, Colorado. They returned with scandalous tales of feather boas, squirt guns, flying toast, loud rock music, and men in ladies' underthings. It sounded terrifying, forbidden, and deeply, profoundly awesome.

A few nights later, my dad took my brother and me to his girlfriend's house for dinner. Her name was Janice, which was hilarious because she had the same dippy, easygoing demeanor as the Muppet with whom she shared a name.

"Have you ever heard of something called *The Rocky Horror Picture Show?*" I asked over dessert.

"TOUCH-A-TOUCH-A TOUCH MEEEE, I WANNA FEEL DIIIRTY!!!!" Janice bleated, to everyone's dismay. "Come ON!" she hollered at her ungrateful audience.

She left the dining room and came back with a CD. She handed it to me: it was the *Rocky Horror* soundtrack. "Try that on for size," she said.

At that time I don't think I even *had* a CD player (remember, this was sometime between when the unicorns vanished and when the internet was born), so I couldn't try it on for size until I was able to get to Tiffany's house. Tiffany made a cassette-tape copy for me and I played it all night long and all over the weekend. I had no idea what the hell the plot of the story was, but I later learned that wasn't really a concern.

One day after play practice, Lisa and Tiffany asked me if I thought my dad would let me go to the midnight showing of *Rocky Horror* with them. I broke out into a cold sweat. I was *dying* to see it, but I was also secretly terrified. I'd never gone out without a parent before, not to mention I'd heard that newcomers to the movie had to be "devirginized" onstage! What did that even mean?!

That evening at home I asked my dad, "Ummm, I was wondering if it would maybe be OK if I went out with Lisa and Tiffany and some of their friends to see *Rocky Horror* on the Hill Friday night?"

"Taking two ladies out on the town, eh?" my dad said, waggling his eyebrows at me. I had planned a few good arguments on my behalf in case he said no, but to my surprise he immediately said yes!

I called Lisa with the good news.

"Rad," she said. "What are you going to wear?"

"What do you think I should wear?"

"I don't know. What do you want to be devirginized in? I don't suppose you have fishnets and a garter belt?"

"Oh dang it, they're at the cleaners. I'm 13 for chrissakes, of course I don't have fishnets!"

"All right, just go as a Transylvanian, that's a safe bet. Black pants and jacket, white shirt, and a party hat."

I hung up the phone, but I couldn't shake the image of myself laid out in a white gown on a stage in front of an audience chanting: *VIRGIN! VIRGIN! VIRGIN! VIRGIN!*

At the time, I didn't really understand what that word meant. I'd heard it sung about in carols and talked about in church, so I knew it couldn't have anything to do with sex, which had no business being in Christmas! In fact, when it came to sex in general, I was absolutely clueless. I'm not really sure why—my father was a hip single dad who fancied himself very progressive and very permissive. Maybe that was part of the problem: he thought he was so ahead of the curve that he just assumed I knew everything already.

In the past, when I'd asked if I could stay over at Lisa's house, my dad would say, "OK, but make sure you wear a condom!" and laugh at me and wink, which made me blush nearly to the point of bleeding to death. I barely knew what a condom was. At this point I don't think I'd yet been cleared of the misconception that "oral sex" meant chatting about it (if you haven't been cleared of that misconception yet, don't be embarrassed—but just for the record, oral sex hopefully doesn't involve much talking, if any at all).

Looking back, I think there were a few contributing factors to my absolutely staggering sexual mystification. First of all, I was a late bloomer. I understood what sex was, technically, but I didn't know what anyone expected *me* to do about it. The surges of hormonal energy I felt never seemed to be directed at a particular object.

Also, whenever sex was mentioned in school it was always referred to in some man-lady context. Maybe I would have felt more interested in it if I knew other configurations were possible. I wasn't in denial about being gay; I just didn't get that it was an option.

Don't think I didn't hear it though, the tittering and murmuring behind my back and to my face: "Is he gay?" "Do you think he's going to grow up gay?" "Are you gay?" Or, from the sophisticated adults who prided themselves on being terribly open and accepting: "You're gay, right? Don't be embarrassed, it's fabulous!"

If I was too young to know what a virgin was, I was also definitely too young to know what *gay* meant. Besides, nothing deflates the fun of self-discovery like a bunch of loudmouths with the advantage of not being you telling you just who and what you are. By the time I realized that I was attracted to men, I was ready to stay in the closet for another six months like a big gay groundhog, not because I was ashamed or in denial, but because I was a teenager and was fully committed to being the opposite of whatever anyone said I was, so there!

The Friday we planned on going to the movie Tiffany handed me a note between two classes. At the top of some fringed paper ripped out of her spiral notebook, she had written, in big purple block letters: "ROCKY HORROR KIT." She then wrote out the list of props I'd need to bring to the theater for the audience participation part.

I started getting ready around 9:30 PM. I was wearing my Transylvanian party attire and spiking my hair with some glittery hairspray left over from Halloween. I thought some of the glitter might look nice on my eyes, and proceeded to mace my own self like an idiot. I had my face under the faucet until the doorbell rang at 11.

Tiffany and Lisa came in to meet my dad. He told us all to "have fun and be safe." That's when I realized that I was scared. I'd never been out so late before, nor been given so much freedom, and now I didn't know quite what to do with it. I wasn't so sure I wanted to know what went on in the streets after midnight. I am probably the only person whom the D.A.R.E. program actually worked on.

I will never forget my first night sitting in that giant old movie theater. It had a balcony and seated about 500 people, though there were probably only 40 of us in the audience. Lisa, dressed as Columbia, looked stunning with her bobbed hair and sparkling clothes. Tiffany's big, curly hair was teased into a nervous breakdown and

topped with a tiny doily (she was Magenta). People were milling about in the aisles, laughing loudly, hugging one another, and passing Ziploc baggies full of toast and rice around. Some of the boys were dressed in tighty whities and robes like the character Brad, some wore tiny gold underpants like Rocky Horror, and the really brave ones dressed in full lingerie like Frank-N-Furter. There were other girls dressed as Columbia with their tap shoes and gold sequined top hats, Magentas in maid costumes, and some Janets in white bras and slips.

Most everyone seemed to be in high school or college; I was definitely the youngest person there. Everyone was really friendly to me.

"Is this your first time here?" one Magenta asked.

"Yes," I said, blushing.

"*Oooh! A vir-gin!*" she squealed. "Hey, Joey, I got a *virgin* over here!"

"*VIRGIN! VIRGIN! VIRGIN! VIRGIN!*" the crown chanted. It was all happening just as I'd imagined, except I wasn't wearing a white gown. Magenta took my hand and brought me up onstage along with six or eight other people. The rest is kind of a blur. I remember a heavyset man with a tiny megaphone shouting at us, "On your knees, virgins!" I got on my knees, and then a girl in a nurse's uniform came around with a jar of maraschino cherries. She went down the line placing a single cherry between everyone's teeth.

"Do not eat the cherries, you greedy little piglets!" the man with the megaphone said. "You are our sacrificial virgins, and we are going to pop all of your cherries! MUAHA-HAHAHA!"

A cute guy, probably a freshman at the University of Colorado, with long brown hair, wearing just a vest and shorts, came up to me. He knelt down to face me and could probably see the animal panic in my eyes. "Don't worry," he said. "I won't bite you." He leaned in, caught the cherry out of my teeth with his, our lips barely grazing, and ate it. I had never been so close to another human being before in my whole life, and I would never even know who he was. "Nice lips," he said. My heart

felt like it was going to blast out of my chest and take off into orbit.

I was ushered back to my seat, no longer a virgin. The lights went down, the curtain rose on the screen and the famous 20th Century Fox logo appeared to its jangly piano accompaniment. Then everything went black, and in that dark void a red slash appeared. As it came closer and closer it became clear that the slash was a pair of lips, and Richard O'Brien, the writer of the movie, began to sing the song "Science Fiction/Double Feature," and I don't think I'd ever seen anything so beautiful.

The rest of the night was fun, but I remember kind of wishing people would stop shouting the audience-participation lines. I wanted to hear the movie on its own. The colors, the music, the actors—they were all gorgeous and strange and seemed like friends that I didn't want everyone laughing at.

And that, as they say, was that. My first real teen obsession (after Marilyn Monroe—that's another story) was born. My dad, thrilled that I was starting to come into myself more, encouraged my new mania. He sent away for a lot of cool memorabilia and I had a Very *Rocky Horror* Christmas.

Not long after this, Tiffany, Lisa, and I got the idea to reshoot the entire movie ourselves, scene by scene. I was put in charge of costumes, so I started calling local lingerie stores to get price quotes on teddies, feather boas, and garter belts. I was a little nervous to call about something so adult, so I started the phone calls by saying, "Hello. I am a filmmaker making a film, and I would like to know what you charge for satin corsets." What kind of film they thought I was making I can only guess; I just didn't want the decent, hardworking salespeople at Frederick's of Hollywood to think I was some creepster. This didn't end up being an issue, as most of the people I spoke to on the phone called me "ma'am."

I was so excited about this new project I even told my mom. She was lying in bed with my little brother, Sean, one morning and I came in like a jumping bean, telling her about our costumes.

"Wait, you're going to be wearing *what?*" she asked.

RICE.
THROW IT DURING THE WEDDING SCENE

SQUIRT GUN.
+ NEWSPAPER
TO SHOOT DURING THE RAINSTORM SCENE
NEWSPAPER TO COVER YR HEAD

LIGHTER.
HOLD UP DURING THE LYRIC "THERE'S A LIGHT OVER @ FRANKENSTEIN PLACE."

NOISE MAKERS.
BLOW @ THE END OF FRANK'S SCIENCE SPEECH

CONFETTI.
THROW WHEN FRANK AND ROCKY WALK INTO THE BEDROOM

TOILET PAPER.
THROW IT WHEN THEY SAY "GREAT SCOTT"

TOAST. THROW IT WHEN FRANK SAYS "I'D LIKE TO PROPOSE A TOAST"

PLAYING CARDS. THROW THEM WHEN FRANK SINGS "CARDS FOR SORROW CARDS FOR PAIN"

"A polyurethane vest, some stockings, and a low-heeled boot. Oh! And a ray gun."

She looked at me blankly. "Yeah. I'm not so sure this *movie* is such a good idea," she said.

I bet you thought I'd forgotten about Jesus, didn't you?! Well, this was right around the time when he gate-crashed the party. My mom met a charismatic bible-beater at a local watering hole called the Outback Saloon. The most religious thing my mother had ever done to date was to drop Sean and me off once a month at Sunday School so she could have coffee and doughnuts with her friends who liked to go to a club called "A Course in Miracles." But this was different. Ever since she had met Stan—Stan the Bible Man, as Sean and I called him—at the Outback, my mom had gone from zero to zealot in 60 seconds.

The first time my mom brought Stan over to my dad's to meet us she said, "Can we show Stan your room?" My teenage bedroom was epic, and I enjoyed showing it off to people. Every inch of wall and ceiling space was covered in Christmas lights and posters, and all of the posters were covered in Saran Wrap for protection. There were movie posters, Marilyn Monroe posters, and *Rocky Horror* posters.

"Sure," I said, eyeing him suspiciously. Stan was very tall with big teeth, a beard, an all-denim outfit, ringlets so tight it looked like he had pin-curled his hair, and a crucifix around his neck.

He looked around my room with its pink Christmasy glow. "Marilyn Monroe," he said. "She's hot." I supposed that was true, though *glamorous* was the word that first came to my mind.

As he was about to leave, I could feel his gaze get snagged like skin on a protruding nail. He was looking at a fold-out poster of Frank-N-Furter I'd gotten in a fanzine.

"*He*—" Stan choked out. "He should be burned."

My mother and I laughed nervously. "Yeah, Kevin," she said. "You really don't need to have that *thing* on your wall." *Traitor.*

"He reminds me of the band Queen," Stan continued. "I used to love them. Then I realized what kind of *queen* they were talking about. Now I only listen to Rush."

They left, and I was shaking with rage and shame. Was Frank-N-Furter a queen? Was Tim Curry? Was I? What the hell *was* a queen aside from an antiquated figurehead of a monarchy? And, more important, what was this band Queen and how could I get all of their albums immediately?

I turned off all the lights in my room except for a strand of red Christmas lights. I put on "Science Fiction/Double Feature," stood in my window looking out at the snowy parking lot outside my apartment building, and put one of the tiny red bulbs between my lips. In the darkness all I could see was my mouth, reflected back to me in the windowpane, electric red, as I lip-synched to Richard O'Brien's voice.

I was radioactive with yearning, but I didn't know what I was yearning for. It frightened me, because people can be defined by the things that they desire and even trapped by them. And yet maybe this yearning I felt wasn't for anything a person could actually hold on to—maybe it was just the desire to belong to the world.

When I was 13, I knew some of the hard (*tee-hee*) facts about sex, but I had no idea what the sex-ed stuff had to do with all of the symphonic, loud, technicolor hormonal energy and emotion I was feeling 24 hours a day. How could you even begin to depict that? Oh! I know! Get a bunch of fabulous, beautiful people, dress them up in hilarious, sexy, feathery costumes, paint their faces the colors of the rainbow, and have them sing and dance to a bitchin' rock score. And then blast them off into space.

I took the lightbulb from my lips and drew my curtains closed. I sat on the end of my bed and looked at the *Rocky Horror* CD insert with the pictures of its bizarre cast of characters: Magenta, Columbia, Riff Raff, Frank-N-Furter.

If there was a place in this crazy world for a man named Meat Loaf, then maybe, just maybe, there was a place for me, too. ♦

Kevin Townley is a New York-based writer and performer who still basically does all of the same silly stuff he did as a teenager, only on a slightly larger scale.

DON'T THROW STUFF AT THE ACTORS ON STAGE. THEY GET PISSED.
— Tiffany xox

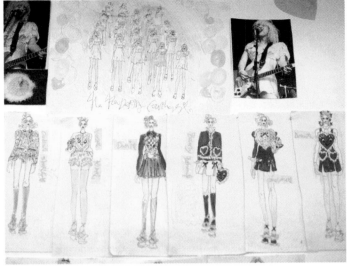

PRETTY ON THE OUTSIDE

Last month, Edward Meadham and Benjamin Kirchhoff were nice enough to let Eleanor come backstage at Meadham Kirchhoff's Spring/Summer 2012 show in London. Here are Eleanor's photos from that day.

By Eleanor

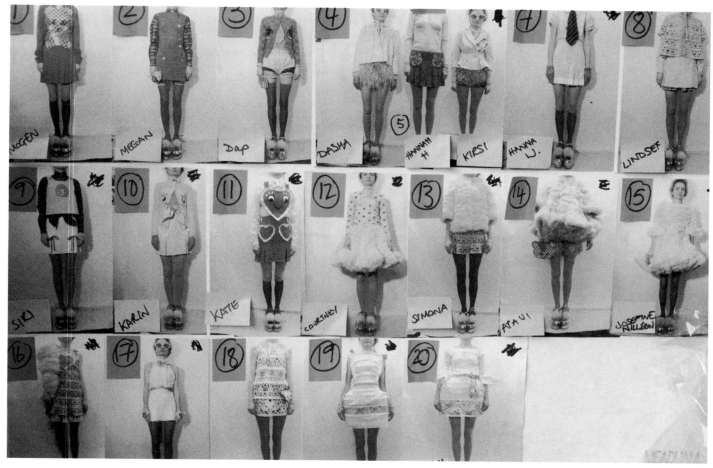

Season of the Witch

Why teenage girls are so dang scary.
By Sady. Illustration by Sonja.

When it comes time to write the history of Westerville, Ohio—a project that will be only slightly impeded by the fact that the historians will keep having to be replaced every few weeks, as they slip into boredom-induced comas—no one will include the following story. It is too strange, too eerie—to be frank, just too unbelievable. And indeed, many of the girls who experienced the strange phenomenon I am about to describe will deny it. Perhaps they've forgotten. Then again, perhaps they are only trying to forget. After all, they are respectable women now. The dark and eldritch forces they once encountered have no place in their lives today.

But it did happen. I know it. I was there. And so I alone shall recount to you this terrifying paranormal tale: for several months, the entire youth culture of Westerville, Ohio, was based on *The Craft*.

Yes, I'm talking about that one movie, with Fairuza Balk. *The Craft* was about four teenage girls—representing the elements of water, earth, air, and fire—who formed a "coven" to worship "Manon" and/or make some freaky stuff happen with their minds. They became prettier, caused the downfall of mean girls, made cute boys fall in love with them—you know, the usual witch stuff. As it turns out, *The Craft* was a horror movie, and the girls' spells ended in death, attempted rape, and psychiatric hospitalization. But nobody focused on that part. We, the teen girls of Westerville, Ohio, had just learned that banding together in groups could potentially give us freaky mind powers. And we wanted in.

We wore more eyeliner; we checked out our friends' astrological signs to see who could embody which element; we passed around a Wiccan spell book someone had shoplifted from Barnes & Noble; as one, we entered into one of the goofiest, most Yankee Candle–centric epochs of our young lives.

I've since learned that this bout of film-inspired teen witchery has struck other towns, and other women. Which, really, is not at all surprising. Much of the world's paranormal history has to do with adults being terrified of teenage girls.

Before there was *The Craft*, there were the Salem witch trials, which started because the young girls of the town were engaging in unearthly, demonic behavior—such as "screaming" and "throwing things." You know. The sort of thing you'd *never* do as a 12-year-old, especially not if you were stuck in a freezing cold Puritan settlement where the funnest activity was churning butter. Their parents took a quick look, were like, "Clearly, Satan has done this," and promptly went about slaughtering half the town. In the 20th century, Anneliese Michel—an epileptic, mentally ill girl who started to have seizures and hear voices at 16—died of starvation and dehydration because her parents chose to hire exorcists instead of getting her to a hospital. They were convicted of manslaughter, but her grave is still visited by people who believe she was possessed, and, thanks to two or three pseudo-biopics, Anneliese's story has become a central part of the disturbing pop-culture tradition of movies about young girls or teens who are possessed by Satan. Oh, and by the way: do you have a poltergeist? Check again! Many people who believe in ghosts believe that the presence of a teenage girl in the house attracts malevolent spirits, who feed off of their burgeoning sexiness and intense, girly emotions.

All of this is typical girl-fear. Once you realize that *The Exorcist* is, essentially, the story of a 12-year-old who starts cussing, masturbating, and disobeying her mother—in other words, going through puberty—it becomes apparent to the feminist-minded viewer why two adult men are called in to slap her around for much of the third act. People are convinced that something spooky is going on with girls; that, once they reach a certain age, they lose their adorable innocence and start tapping into something powerful and forbidden. Little girls are sugar and spice, but women are just plain scary. And the moment a girl becomes a woman is the moment you fear her most.

Which explains why the culture keeps telling this story. But it doesn't explain why girls are drawn to it, or why we would be compelled to play it out, even in its goofiest and Fairuza-Balk-iest incarnations. Why is the Ouija board inevitably brought to the sleepover, in spite of the fact that every single session brings on pants-peeing levels of terror? Why did at least one girl in 1999 claim that she had been converted to a whole new religion by watching *Charmed* and *Sabrina the Teenage Witch*? (Melissa Joan Hart has played many roles, but I'm of the opinion that "spiritual counselor" should not be among them.) Why can I, to this day, read your tarot cards and explain in some detail the importance of your sun sign as compared to your ascendant?

Well, note the differences between these stories. When one girl gets possessed by Satan, she is smacked and yelled at by the grown-ups until the evil leaves her. But in the stories about witches that made girls actually want to do magic—*The Craft*, *Charmed*, *Buffy*—the power comes, in some essential way, from being together. And together is what we were, or what we tried to be, in the time we thought we were magic.

There were a lot of things that my friends and I were scared of, during our *Craft* mania. We were scared of our bodies. We were scared of the attention that our bodies were receiving. We were scared of dating, and of sex. But we were also scared that we'd never date, or that we'd never have sex. We were scared of college; we

were scared that we might not get into college. We were scared of driving, and scared of not getting the license. We were scared that we might grow up to be our parents. We were scared that we didn't know what to do with our lives. We were scared of tests, auditions, try-outs, games, and recitals. We were scared of increased responsibility, and scared of our own powerlessness. We were scared of our classmates. And every day, we kept on turning into someone else—turning into our new selves, our grown-up selves—and we had no idea what the outcome would be, or if we'd like it. So, more than anything, we were scared of ourselves. But here's one thing that definitely didn't scare us: the idea that, if we supported one another and stuck together, we could somehow control all of this *just by wishing*.

And we didn't think we could do it without one another. That's the best part. There is something strong, maybe even magical, about teenage girls getting together and making very specific lists of what they want from life. Sooner or later, that stops taking the form of "I cast this spell of love, so that Travis Johnson will like me back" (or its inevitable follow-up, "I cast this spell of herpes upon Travis Johnson") and starts taking the form of real, practical strength. My friends and I honestly believed that if we stuck by each other and searched for power within ourselves, we would find it. And we weren't wrong.

There is something scary about being a teenage girl. There's something frightening about any state of life that involves so many mysteries, and so many drastic changes. But the thing that many people find scariest—the idea that there's a force in teenage girls that doesn't follow the rules and can't be controlled, that these girls might be going off together and forging something new, something unknown and surprisingly powerful—isn't scary at all. It's deeply awesome. And, unlike the deathly curses uttered by Ouija boards, it's real. ♦

Spell Bound

A set of witchy photos.

By Petra

All clothes and props, Petra's own.
Thanks to Allison, Anna, Aurora,
Jacqueline, and Raevv'n
for modeling.

Ghost Rider

Keeping a secret doesn't make it go away.
It just makes it grow and grow until it swallows you whole.

Writing by Pixie. Illustration by Sonja.

In high school, my best friend with (limited) benefits had a '94 Honda Civic that he used to *2 Fast 2 Furious* with on the weekends, racing up and down the turnpike in between parking-lot cigarettes behind a combination Pizza Hut and Taco Bell. When he wasn't living life and tasting death or what have you, he was driving me around the back roads so that I could get ice cream, listen to the radio, and try to stop crying.

It was senior year, and I'd spent most of it having panic attacks at his house, sitting on a waterbed and trying to remember to move the oxygen through my body. These attacks came at strange times, set off by a commercial, a song, by nothing at all. One minute I'd be OK, and the next I'd feel like I wanted to tear off my skin and separate myself from my bones. I'd get dizzy, then frightened, then angry, and then I'd cry for about an hour.

"I'm okay, I'm just REALLY TIRed"

"I think I'm going crazy," I'd say. "I think I already am crazy."

"You're not crazy," he'd say. "Come on, let's go for a ride."

People like to warn you about cars when you're a teenager, because they don't want you to die in one. You are constantly given instructions on how not to kill yourself or anyone else while driving. You're not always given instructions on how not to kill yourself while outside of a moving vehicle, aside from, well, *don't*.

The year I got my license was the same year I started feeling tired all the time. It was a tired beyond tired, the kind of exhaustion that makes your entire body ache. I assumed it was the standard summer-to-fall adjustment process: I'd started three-hour swim practices; I was waking up early after a summer of sleeping in; I was staying up late to finish my homework. But as the months wore on and my body adjusted to the changes, the exhaustion seemed to linger elsewhere—in my heart, in my head. I just felt *off*, as if someone had come along and dimmed the lights a bit. I started to drag, to sense something dark floating around the tiny file cabinets that I'd always imagined lined the inside of my brain. But whenever anyone else seemed to notice the dark thing—a parent, a friend, whoever—I'd always give them the same explanation: "I'm fine. I'm just really tired." Deep down I knew it was more than that, but

part of me believed that if I covered it up well enough, it would eventually go away.

It didn't.

Mental illness is a relentless ghost; no matter how many times I try to exorcise it, it finds a way to make a comeback. I had struggled with OCD in middle school—everything had to be done 11 times, or else—but by some cognitive-behavioral miracle I'd managed to shed my rituals after a year or so of mental torture. I never asked for help. I hid my rituals from everyone, with the exception of my seventh-grade science partner, who must have been born with the best heart in the world, as he never said a word to me or anybody else about the repeated prayers I'd do during our lab time together. I'd spend hours at night reciting special sayings over and over until I got them right, for fear that if I didn't, terrible things would happen. After about a year of tapping my foot and biting my lip and writing and rewriting my homework 10 times, I finally realized that terrible things happened anyway: my dog died, my perfect grades slipped, my softball team went 0–16, and I was miserable all the time. I forced myself to stop counting. I thought I finally had my brain under control.

But the ghost returned. It always does. It is a constant presence in my life. Sometimes it shows up as anxiety, sometimes it shows up as depression. In high school, it showed up as both. It was brutal and relentless and never lifted and I swore I could fix it by myself, which I couldn't.

I started hiding my depression right away in order to protect my parents. It sounds like a ridiculous idea now, 15 years later, but at the time I thought I could spare them a lot of pain by dealing with mine on my own. I didn't want them to worry, or to be disappointed in me. I thought if I admitted that I needed help that it meant that I was too weak or too dumb—or worse, too "crazy"—to fix things on my own. I started trying to rationalize the dark thoughts I was having, the behaviors I was engaging in. *Everybody gets sad*, I thought, though I imagined that not everyone compulsively scratched their arms or fantasized about flinging themselves out of a third-story window.

I tried so hard to beat it, to keep it controlled, to keep it away from everyone else. I put it all in notebooks so that I wouldn't be tempted to actually talk about it out loud. I kept all of my scratches well hidden, and blared music in my room when I needed to cry. I pulled A's in school and smiled when necessary and made sure to wash my face before coming to dinner, so that nobody would know I'd been crying. I faked it so real I was beyond fake, if you will. It was horrible.

Sometimes I have dreams where I'm forced to sit in a movie theater and watch something awful onscreen. I try to close my eyes, but then I realize that I'm dreaming and my eyes are already closed, and there's nothing I can do. I try to scream, but no sound comes out. I can try to look away but the terrible thing just keeps playing, and I sit there, unable to stop it, until everything goes black and I finally wake up.

That's the best way I can describe what it feels like to deal with clinical depression on your own.

During my senior year of high school I drove around my hometown so often that I began to build an affinity for stupid things. I grew attached to the lights at the municipal airport, the seasonal flags everyone hung from their porches, the ugly green electrical boxes that lined the streets. Whenever I was moving, I felt better, as if the world couldn't catch up to me while I had four wheels beneath my feet.

My best friend and I would drive for hours, him with a cigarette hanging out of his mouth and me with my left hand glued to the radio. We always seemed to end up at Dairy Queen, eating Peanut Buster Parfaits and talking about where we'd be in two years, two months, two hours, two minutes. We decided we'd still be friends. Maybe we'd have sex, or something, since everyone thought we were doing it anyway. Maybe we'd have sex and I'd get pregnant and my parents would kill him and then he'd be a badass ghost. Maybe we'd just build a boat and float away somewhere. Maybe we should get another Peanut Buster Parfait.

"Do you think I'll always be this fucked up?" I asked him.

"You're not fucked up," he said. Then he laughed. "Well, I mean, you're fucked up, but it doesn't have to be, like, forever."

Only your best friend can tell you you're fucked up and mean it in the nicest possible way. You are a mess, but you know, that's OK, because I still love you.

"I think you just need, like, help," he said. To know that you need help is one thing. To hear someone say it out loud is another. I realized that I needed someone to give me permission to stop hiding, to admit that I couldn't do it on my own. I started to cry again, tears of sadness and acceptance and a tiny bit of relief, and he started the car and began to drive.

Here is something to remember about the people who love you: they love you.

It took me a few more months to admit that I needed help. By that time, I'd stopped eating Peanut Buster Parfaits. Unfortunately, I'd stopped eating everything else, as well. I was about a month into my first semester of college when I came home and was promptly taken to a hospital by my parents, who barely recognized me. I was diagnosed with a variety of things, officially, and I finally started getting the help I needed. I apologized over and over again to my parents, for letting them down, for "being so dumb," for things I can't even remember now. My parents, in turn, kept apologizing to me. They blamed themselves for missing the signs, for not recognizing how bad it really was. But I was an Oscar-worthy actress: I hid everything so well that I was often in denial of how bad it was myself, until it knocked my heart rate down to 43 bpm and almost killed me.

In the end we realized that nobody is to blame for mental illness. It is not something that people choose to have. Anyone who tells you otherwise is a creep and a liar, and you can tell them I said so.

What I've learned over the years is that the people who care for you will not be disappointed in you for having to deal with things beyond your control. They will not think you are "crazy." They will not think you are weak or stupid for not being able to pull yourself out of it. If you stick out your hand, they will take it. They won't be able to make all of it go away, either, but they can help you find the path and the professionals that will lead you to brighter places. They will support you. They will listen to you. They will never stop loving you. You don't have to suffer, and you don't have to be alone. You're not the only one, even though it totally feels that way sometimes. I can't tell you how things will work out, or how long it will take, but I can tell you, from personal experience, that there are lights even at the end of the deepest, darkest tunnels.

I still struggle sometimes; the ghost won't ever leave me entirely. But I no longer hide what I'm going through, and I am very fortunate to have a team of professional people and a few medications helping me along the way. I've learned how to deal with anxiety without trying to cut or starve it away. I've learned how to ask for help whenever I need it. I've learned how to help myself without spiraling into a black hole. Keeping it a secret doesn't make it go away. It just makes it grow and grow until it swallows you whole.

My old best friend and I haven't spoken in years; I don't know where he is or what he's doing. We drifted apart during college, separated by state lines and significant others, and now we are slowly fading memories of each other. He is always 17 when I see him. He smells like cigarettes and ice cream. The last time we talked, we were both in a good place. We both had new and totally different plans for two years, two months, two hours, two minutes into the future.

Whenever I drive back to my hometown and see the lights at the municipal airport, I blow a wish in their direction, and hope that he is as happy as I am. ◊

Everybody Farts

Terrifying secrets of the human body!
Writing by Sady. Illustration by Cynthia.

Here's a story for you: Not so very long ago, I was a teenager, and read magazines. I know! It was exciting for me, too! But the thing is, these magazines were often not so great for my self-esteem. Because here is what I remember about those magazines: 9,000 articles by girls about why their bodies were disgusting.

Sometimes there was a whole section: readers would contribute "stories" along the lines of "One time I dropped a tampon in front of a boy and was *soooo* embarrassed," or "One time a boy found out that my bra was padded and I was *soooo* embarrassed," or "This one time, I found out that I have a body, and I'm not just a cloud of pure consciousness, and that means that I have to eat and sleep and stuff. I was *soooooooooo* embarrassed!"

My theory at the time was that if these apparently normal girls were embarrassed by their bodies, I clearly needed to be super embarrassed. Their bodies were in magazines, after all; mine was just the ever-evolving deal I had to confront in the shower. In this attitude, I was just like every other girl I knew. The fact that (a) I thought my body was the worst, and (b) I spent a lot of time reading magazines about how to make my body less hideous and which terrible things might happen if I didn't… Well. I never really connected the dots.

But here's the good news: I grew up. And I found out that my theory was BS. It's true: bodies are goofy, and never do exactly what you'd like. But the idea that you have to be embarrassed about your own bodily functions? That idea exists solely to make you less confident, so that no one has to encounter you at your full, natural level of awesomeness. Also, it exists

because for some reason people think certain facts about the human body are unspeakable. Even though you are going to find out most of those things sooner or later. Preferably sooner! Because I will now share with you several TERRIFYING SECRETS of the HUMAN BODY, such as:

YOUR PERIOD IS GOING TO COME WHENEVER IT WANTS.

When I was young, I could not wait to get my first period. My older cousins were always talking about theirs, and trading war stories, and I envied them intensely. So, when my period hadn't shown up by my 13th birthday, I did what anyone would do: I lied. For several months, I faked my own period.

I faked it so well, in fact, that I forgot I might actually get one. Imagine my surprise, then, when it showed up. One fine summer evening, after I'd been jumping around on a trampoline and flirting with a boy, someone pointed out to me that I had, indeed, finally gotten my period. I had Become a Woman after all, without even knowing.

Unfortunately, everyone else did know. Because I Became a Woman in skin-tight white cotton leggings. That I had borrowed. From my cousin. In front of whom, a week earlier, I had faked my period.

If you have a functioning uterus, eat well, and are reasonably healthy, you are going to get your first period eventually. But that doesn't make you a woman. It doesn't make you anything but a risky candidate for borrowing tight white pants. So you don't need to obsess. Also, the first few times it does show up, it's going to be messy. You have to learn to expect it, and deal with it in the way that works best for you. But as long as you have a period, there will be spills, overflows, and stains; none of this is a reason to be humiliated, or even especially surprised. Some jerks might laugh, but guess what? Jerks laugh about things. That is what makes them jerks. They do this so that they can convince the world that the things that happen to everyone have never happened to them, which keeps them from getting any sympathy when bad stuff happens. So just imagine them writhing in their lonely

insecurity every time something unfortunate happens to them, planning how they are going to make *so much fun of everyone else it's ever happened to*. What powerful, fulfilling lives these people lead! Oh, and by the way:

DUDES ALREADY KNOW WHAT TAMPONS ARE.

It's true! Even the most clueless dudes have sources of uterus-related knowledge, such as their sisters, their moms, or health class. Or television, where there are always pretty ladies between the daytime programs talking about how they just love to wear sexy outfits to the club, except "sometimes," when they feel "not so confident," but now, thanks to WINGS and RESERVOIRS, they can basically go to the club naked. No matter how oblivious this guy is, he's probably figured out that they're not talking about the Hoover Dam.

So, if a guy has female relatives, a health class, or sick days, he knows that uteruses shed their linings, and that various devices such as pads and tampons are used to catch the wave. Unfortunately, he—like you—has also received the message that these things are icky and forbidden, and that he must freak out every time he sees or hears about them. Because if he didn't, he'd be suggesting that he's comfortable with his own body, and the bodies of various others. And that's not going to help him, right? Too many dudes think they're supposed to go through life horrified by their own and other people's crotches.

Don't help to maintain this silliness. If you get embarrassed every time you drop a pad or tampon—and it will happen—or every time a dude looks through your bag for a pen and finds one of these items instead, he gets to pretend that he is ignorant and that you are yucky for one more day. And that's a day none of us can afford. Sooner or later, he's going to be 53, and in Congress, and saying that he just doesn't understand why people NEED birth control, all because no one had the decency to sit him down and tell him to stop pretending he doesn't know about vaginas.

Now that we've covered the downstairs furniture, it might be time to mention that:

YOUR BREASTS ARE NORMAL.

I was a skinny kid. I took a lot of dance classes, rode my bike everywhere, and did a lot of swimming; I also went from being the shortest girl in my class to one of the most medium-size, almost overnight. So, I was bony. I was fine with this; "skinny," after all, was what the world taught me girls should be. But one aspect of my body made me deeply insecure. I could not figure out why I, a person with no visible body fat, did not have big breasts. The skinny girls in magazines did! The girls on TV did! The girls in the *Sports Illustrated* Swimsuit Edition *definitely* did—that was the whole point of that issue. Why not me? WHY WAS I SO UGLY?

To be honest, if you have breasts, the odds are high that your breasts are normal. But the odds are also high that you haven't seen a normal, unretouched human breast since you were nursing from one. So, when you grow some, they'll look unfamiliar. Here, therefore, is a short questionnaire to help you determine whether you have normal breasts.

Are you a skinny person with small breasts? Congratulations, you have normal breasts. Do you have bigger breasts than most of your classmates? Maybe they're behind you hormonewise, maybe you have more body fat to work with, maybe it's genetics: in any case, you have normal breasts! Large nipples, small nipples, light nipples, dark nipples, bumpy nipples, smooth nipples, inverted nipples, hair around nipples: all of these are regular features on normal breasts. Is one of your breasts larger than the other? Also very common, for breasts. Also normal. In fact, all of these states are perfectly normal and attractive; none are shameful or ugly. If someone tells you otherwise, tell this person that (a) they don't know jack, and (b) their opportunity to learn has ended, because they are clearly not worthy of your breasts.

Take care of your breasts. Be nice to them. Buy them pleasing little bra outfits, in the correct size. Check in with them! Check them for lumps, to make sure they are staying healthy. Your breasts will thank you for your appreciation and support. They are some of the most politicized, criticized, fix-ated-upon, and misunderstood parts of the human body—the Hillary Clintons of anatomy. Would you yell at the Secretary of State if you had to carry her around everywhere? Will you ever forgive me for this mental image? Odds are, in both cases, no! So be good to your breasts, before I have to make awkward metaphors about them again.

BEING TRANSGENDER IS ALSO NORMAL.

When you're born, people usually take a quick look at the shape of your genitalia, slap an "F" for vagina or "M" for penis on your birth certificate, and expect that one letter to define you for the rest of your life. Astonishingly, despite this super-advanced scientific process, lots of people grow up to realize that their M or F designations don't fit how they feel inside.

If you get an F label, and actually grow up to feel like a girl, you're cisgender. *Cis* means "on the same side"—your body and your gender match. If you're labeled F, but grow up to realize that you're in every other way a guy, you are transgender. *Trans* means "on the opposite side"—your body is "on the opposite side" of your gender. There are trans boys and trans girls, and there are trans people who don't identify as either boys or girls. All of that is common, normal, and awesome.

But when you grow up with a body that doesn't match your gender, body insecurity can suck on a whole new level. You might be a guy born with a uterus, who gets periods and breasts despite the fact that he doesn't want or need them. You might be a girl born with a penis, who has to deal with all the unnatural-feeling effects of that. Either way, getting your body to match your gender, if you choose to do so, will take time, and often medical assistance. Since I'm cis and haven't experienced this, I asked my friend Queen Emily of the blog Questioning Transphobia about it.

"'Your body is fine' *doesn't* mean that you should never mindfully change it, as a trans teen," she said. "Cis society often holds out the idea that if you just had more self-esteem and felt better about your body, then you wouldn't be trans. But being trans isn't about low self-esteem, it's about a persis-tent sense of wrongness about your sexed body and social role, it's about knowing that you should be something other than what everybody sees…that you *are* something else. So 'your body is fine' to me means, fundamentally, it is fine to be trans. It is fine to go on blockers or hormones. You are fine, and you will be fine."

See? You're fine. The smart lady said so. Which is good, because whether you are cis or trans, you are still going to have to learn our next horrifying fact, which is:

VAGINAS MAKE NOISES AND SO DO BUTTS AND THAT'S HOW THINGS ARE.

Sorry. Take a big breath, hold it in your mouth by puffing out your cheeks, then try to expel it without opening your mouth. You hear that noise? Yep. Other parts of your body make that noise, too, under similar circumstances. Sex, for the record, can cause similar circumstances. (Also it can cause terrible diseases, so use condoms! And/or other protection appropriate to your personal shenanigans. But back to the main topic.) Yes, it's true: sex has fart noises in it sometimes. So do gymnastics routines, yoga classes, and Taco Tuesdays in the cafeteria. It's gross, it's weird, and it's how things are. So take a breath, maybe laugh if it seems awkward, then go on with your day. Because sometimes, your body really is embarrassing. Just like the bodies of everybody else, everywhere, forever until the end of time. ♦

DAYDREAM NATION

Secret magic in the middle of the desert.
By Petra and Tavi. Thanks to Dana and Stazia (Vision Models) for modeling.
All photos taken by Petra and styled by Tavi.

This past summer, Petra and I explored some of California's secrets together. This one is in the desert of Niland and called Salvation Mountain. In the 1970s a man named Leonard Knight built it out of adobe, hay, and paint to spread his message of love and God, but whether you're religious or not, it's a pretty incredible creation. Especially when you can experience the huge size of it, and the ridiculous heat, and consider that this guy worked on it every day and still has not abandoned it, decades later. I would like, make a clump of dirt with my fist, dip it in a paint bucket, and then give up. But look at this thing!

Exploring Salvation Mountain made me feel like a little kid, which is a rare and sacred thing when you are no longer one and can't figure out why you can't just LIKE stuff the way you used to. It's magically colorful, and the only sound was the wind whistling, and when we drove up, a black cat ran by, and we didn't see it again. It exists in the middle of the desert, and sort of independent of time. It's sad to say, but as someone who's been alive only 15 years, I think Salvation Mountain is one of very few things I've ever seen that haven't become a commercial opportunity or tourist attraction. Still, the best secrets you don't wanna keep, so we hope you like these. —Tavi

NOVEMBER 2011: GIRL GANG

Welcome! Our theme this month is Girl Gang. We will be talking about girl bands, actual girl gangs, and all the nuances of friendship that for some reason are so specific to girls, especially of the teenaged age. Togetherness! Rivalry! Bracelets!

The Rookie girl gang (plus Joe) isn't a bad crew to be a part of. When Rookie was but a tiny sperm in the uterus of my mind (sorry), the New York staff plus myself all had a "meeting," which quickly devolved/evolved into sitting around eating pizza and talking about how much we love Joan Rivers for four hours. Some of our rituals include Anaheed and me texting each other poop Emojis, Anaheed asking over chat that I send her a virtual pizza while I insist on a toilet because I don't feel like getting up, and Anaheed bugging me to finish this editor's letter while I ask why I still don't have that toilet I asked for. Aren't we a quirky, zany, wacky, loving bunch?

I'm so happy you're still here! This shall be a good month.

On Wednesdays, we wear pink.

love,
tavi

it's a beautiful day in the Neighborhood

Pretend it's the weekend with these sunny photos.

Shot by Petra. Styling by Tavi.

Thanks to Maddie, Amilie, and Becca for modeling.

Literally the Best Thing Ever: The Golden Girls

I relate to them more than anything I see on the CW about teens or young adults.

Writing by Amy Rose. Illustrations by Kelly. Playlist by Hazel.

What do you most appreciate in a close friend? I need certain qualities like honesty, trust, loyalty, and the ability to crack a mean dirty joke. And you know who embodies all of these qualities pretty much better than anybody? The characters on *The Golden Girls*. The show, which aired in the '80s and '90s, was about four Florida women in their "golden oldie" years living together as roommates and best friends. Despite their advanced age, I relate to them more than anything I see on the CW about teens or young adults.

The group was made up of Dorothy, a dour, intellectual woman with a sharp sense of humor; Blanche, an egotistical Southern belle with a rapacious appetite for male company; Rose, a sweetheart space cadet who could never quite keep up with the others; and Sophia, Dorothy's tiny, wickedly funny mother. Although they were all vastly different, it would be a mistake to lock them in to these archetypes as if they were frothy Candace Bushnell characters. Don't get me wrong, the over-the-top ladies of *Sex and the City* have their place and time, but it's definitely far away from the real-world scenarios that unfolded in the Golden Girls' wicker-furnished stronghold in Miami. These girls—*my* girls—were too fast-paced to pause for rhetorical laptop musings and cosmos, despite being at least a decade older. With SATC, people are quick to identify with one particular character—"I'm a Carrie," "I'm a Miranda," etc.—but you can see parts of yourself in each Golden Girl, because of their complex charms, varied histories, and perspectives on social issues.

Each Golden Girl is a life idol to me in her own specific way, from Rose's inde-

fatigable (if somewhat dopey) sweetness, to Blanche's self-confidence and refusal to be slut-shamed, to Sophia's hard-assed old-world wisdom, to Dorothy's…well, everything about her, really. Dorothy, impeccably portrayed by Bea Arthur, dominates both the house and my heart with her intelligence and verve. You know that girl in your high school who's not only waaay more well-read than everyone around her, but can also apply her smarts to the kind of impossibly perfect, well-timed quips that stick with you for days? Dorothy is that girl's spiritual grandmother. She reminds me of my best friend in the world, Lilly, despite the fact that Lilly has a mohawk as opposed to a well-coiffed silver bouffant. *The Golden Girls* made older women visible in a way they hadn't been before: as people with active social lives, beautiful clothing, fulfilling jobs, and, best of all, friendships that rang true to people of all ages. The show actually makes me less nervous about getting older, in a way.

You know how you love your best friend because he or she tells you when you're acting insane, melodramatic, or otherwise over the top? Dorothy, Blanche, Rose, and *especially* Sophia are often hysterically, devastatingly honest with one another in the same way. Nothing is off limits, and the topics range in outrageousness from Blanche's robust sex life to Rose's dimwitted stories about growing up on a farm in Minnesota. Their candidness with one another is way more affectionate than the guarded niceness of other sitcoms I've seen, or the feigned, outré bitchiness of shows like *Gossip Girl*. Also, they say shit to each other that you have to love somebody to

be able to say, or else you're just a terrible person. Don't we all reserve a special, albeit kind of awful, realness for the people we hold dearest?

These four AARP-eligible mavens focus not only on getting to know one another, but also on exploring and deconstructing just about every controversial issue of their day without glossing them over or working toward a saccharine moral. One of my favorite episodes, "Adult Education," has Blanche clashing with a professor who teaches a difficult class at her night school. She approaches the guy, asking about how to improve her grade, and, as the wink-nudginess of the title suggests, he offers to swap her a roll in the hay for a guaranteed A. When she tells her friends about it, they're justifiably outraged, and Dorothy gives Blanche the courage to report his ass. A big part of this is Dorothy sharing her own story about the importance of refusing to stand for a man misusing his privilege and perceived authority in a sexual way.

Being the queen she always was, Dorothy went to the board of education, which investigated the case and forced him to resign. "Of course, much later, I found out I was not the only person he had harassed," Dorothy tells Blanche. "I spoke out, and

Hanging Out with the

Pink Ladies

1. I'm a Lady - SANTIGOLD
2. HEY, I'm Gonna Be Your Girl - THE DONNAS
3. Crying shame - The BLANCHE HUDSON WEEKEND
4. Maybe I Know - LESLEY GORE
5. Hey! Get Out Of My Way - The Cardigans
6. I Know What Boys Like - The Waitresses
7. In the Flesh - BLONDIE
8. Take It As It Comes - Vivian Girls
9. HANG UP BABY - PLUMTREE
10. GREASE - Franki Valli

RIOT GRRRL GERMS

1. Rebel GIRL - BIKINI KILL
2. GIRL GERMS - BRATMOBILE
3. HER JAZZ - HUGGY BEAR
4. Axemen - HEAVENS TO BETSEY

because I did, a lot of other women didn't have to go through the same thing." AMAZING, IMPORTANT, TRUE. In this moment, Dorothy basically lifted the text of every feminist zine to ever exist and translated it into prime-time gold. It sounds crazy, but I actually channeled Blanche when I had to confront my own harassers at a certain point in my education.

Blanche eventually sits down with the dean of her school, and he declines to take her seriously and tries to bury her problem in the bureaucratic purgatory that is sexual-harassment paperwork. When she tells him that she won't be ignored and needs him to actually deal with the problem, he asks her if she has any witnesses, which she doesn't. He then parrots the much-beloved refrain of any and every idiot who has tried to shut up a female victim of sexual wrongdoing: "Without substantial evidence, it's your word against his, and a man's career is at stake." THIS EXACT SITUATION HAS HAPPENED TO ME. Maybe this is why I felt so gratified when, instead of standing for this tired old trope, Blanche essentially tells him to go fuck himself before storming out of his office. She wills herself to earn the grade with hard work, then confronts the dean with this beauty of a monologue: "I, sir, am a lady. Maybe not the smartest lady in the world, but I do know that my self-respect is more important than passing your damn course, and you, sir, can kiss my A!" She underscores this (admittedly corny, but still awesome) last line by shoving her finished exam against his chest, to wild cheers and applause from the studio audience and tons of melty swooning and fist-pumping from me.

The girls also had the bitchinest style around, from Blanche's low-cut sequins and kitten heels to Dorothy's swingy chiffon blouses.

Even Sophia had a fashion trademark: her wicker-and-bamboo purse can be seen in just about every episode, often blending in with the living room furniture. Their fashion sense is equal parts hysterically dated and authentically brilliant, and I'm often torn between trying to give the weighty topics on the show their due and coveting the ladies' insanely great over-size-teddy-bear-sweater-with-pantyhose outfits. Luckily, there's more than enough room for both.

Even if I weren't totally biased as a result of loving their characters so much, I'd find that the real women behind the Golden Girls are just as admirable and socially prescient as their TV counterparts. While I don't want to understate the importance of the effective, amazing work Rue McClanahan and Betty White did for animal-rights charities, Bea Arthur's lifelong devotion to working with oppressed communities is especially touching. Over the course of her career, she used her fame to champion the rights of women (duh), the elderly, Jewish people, and, perhaps most notably, LGBTQ people. The legacy of her altruism continued even after she died in 2010: She bequeathed $300,000 of her estate to the Ali Forney Center, an incredible organization that provides housing and so much more to homeless LGBTQ youth in New York City. Thanks to Bea, this is now my charity of choice.

Onscreen and off, these ladies fought hard for what they believed in, whether it came to friendship, social consciousness, or monochromatic pantsuits. Every episode was a study in girl love and strength. Plus, if you watch it with your grandma, I guarantee you a great bonding experience—when else will you both be able to giggle together and talk openly about something as serious as sexual harassment? *The Golden Girls* might even make you wish you were closer to her age, so you could run with television's ultimate girl gang. ◆

Secret Style Icon: The Ronettes

No one wore a beehive and a pencil skirt like this trio.
Writing by Leeann. Illustration by Kelly. Playlist by Stephanie.

There were a million girl groups in the 1960s, but the Ronettes were the biggest, baddest, and sexiest of them all. While Motown groups like the Supremes went to charm school to sand down their rough edges and become more acceptable to white audiences, the Ronettes did no such white-washing, and it shows. The Supremes were the prom queens of soul, poised and proper young ladies in false eyelashes and evening gowns. The Ronettes were the girls popping their gum and gossiping under the bleachers.

At the heart of the Ronettes' look was the standard-issue mascara-and-miniskirt bad-girl uniform, but taken to the most ridiculous proportions: pencil skirts so tight they made the wearer wiggle more than walk, winged black eyeliner laid on so long and thick it disappeared into their bangs, hair piled so high atop their heads you were better off measuring it in feet, not inches.

Then there was lead singer Ronnie Spector's voice. It wasn't the mannered croon of Diana Ross or the soul-deep belt of Aretha. It was *weird*: a jagged, androgynous wail as urgent as a heart attack. When Ronnie yelped at a boy to "be my baby NOWWWW," it was as much a command as a come-on. Plus, her eyeliner game was so tight—yes, that is a wing at the top AND bottom lashes.

The Ronettes' look has inspired tons of fashion editorials, but maybe it's more telling that I think of them literally every time I backcomb my hair, squeeze into a pencil skirt, or sweep liquid liner all the way up to my temples. It's such a simple look, but it always turns heads, every place you go. ◆

5. D.A DON'T CARE - TEAM DRESCH
6. NARROW - MECCA NORMAL
7. M.I.A - 7 YEAR BITCH
8. MISS HELL - CALAMITY JANE
9. I'D RATHER EAT GLASS - EXCUSE 17
10. BITTERNESS BARBIE - LUNACHICKS
11. DON'T YOU EVER - SLANT 6
12. WOULD-BE SABOTEURS TAKE HEED - EMILY'S SASSY LIME
13. FIBREGLASS - TATTLE TALE
14. PENETRATION - LUCID NATION
15. ANONYMOUS - SLEATER-KINNEY

CAMP ROOKIE

Awwww.

By Eleanor

Thanks to Georgie, Donnika, and Hannah for modeling, and
Mirren for making all the patches and buttons.

Fight like a Girl

Girls aren't supposed to get angry. Here's why you should ignore that "rule."
Writing by Sady. Illustration by Brooke. Playlist by Jessica.

A few weeks ago, I got into an argument with a guy over his politics. He was promoting an organization that had done some really sexist things. I thought he shouldn't work for that organization unless he was willing to denounce its sexism; he thought I was too angry to let him talk. We were both right. Within a week, that man and I had emailed each other and had both apologized.

Problem solved, right? Well, no. Because this guy told me that, after learning about our argument, a girl who "knew [me] in real life" and was my "friend" had told him all sorts of nasty things about me. He could tell me what she said, but not who she was.

That same weekend, I found out that a woman I'd disagreed with in the past was writing tweets about how I was "stupid" and "worthless," and alleging I had done stuff I had never actually done. This woman and I had several acquaintances in common. She hadn't tried to speak to me directly one single time.

Being upset about that took up some of my time and energy. But not all of it. Because I had also just found out that one of my lady friends was angry about something I'd said, but she hadn't told me she was angry yet, so I was worried about whether she secretly hated me—it didn't seem at all likely, but I'd just found out that someone who knew me "in real life" thought I was awful, so I really did have a secret hater—and I emailed her to see if we were OK.

None of this is unusual. And it doesn't just happen to me. In fact, I've done some of these same things to other girls. According to researchers, this behavior is a major

part of how girls (not all girls, obviously, but generally as a population) handle anger. It's called "relational aggression," a really textbooky term that just means "using friendships to bully people." The tactics of relational aggression include telling people's secrets, forming alliances to gang up on them, spreading rumors, sabotaging their projects, and giving them the silent treatment. This has just as many serious consequences as other kinds of bullying: it damages people's confidence, makes them less likely to trust people or enjoy spending time with others, and can even lead to their doing poorly in school, developing anxiety and depression, or becoming suicidal. It's underhanded, it's dishonest, and it's cruel. But it's also what lots of girls do.

Well: no more. No more, my fine lady friends! Because today, we are going to have some real talk. It's my hope that by the time you are as old and wizened as I am, girls will not be doing this to one another anymore. And neither will women. But in order to accomplish that, we have to learn how to fight.

RULE #1: BEING ANGRY DOESN'T MAKE YOU A JERK.

A lot of relational aggression stems from the fact that girls are taught to deal with problems in a really specific way. It's not that boys don't do the things I've listed; they do. But they're also likely to use direct forms of bullying, like physical fighting, whereas girls tend to stick with indirect warfare. And there's a reason for that.

Will it surprise anyone if I say the reason is sexism? No? OK, then: the reason is sexism! As Rachel J. Simmons outlines in her book *Odd Girl Out: The Hidden Cul-*

ture of Aggression in Girls, girls often find it easier to vent our anger by being passive-aggressive or talking behind someone's back, because we've been taught that approaching someone with a problem is "mean" or "rude." Girls aren't supposed to be angry; girls aren't supposed to be aggressive; girls, basically, are supposed to like every single human being on earth, and make them all gift baskets full of mini-pies just for existing. So when we're angry—and everybody is angry sometimes—we go behind one another's backs, and act like top-secret super-spies about it, because doing anything else just wouldn't be *nice*.

Look, I'm not a scientist, but I've done some research, and it turns out that it's actually *way meaner* to call someone names behind her back than it is to say "that thing you did was messed up" to her face. It also doesn't work—when you don't confront people, they never actually know how they made you angry. This method ensures that your target can never apologize or change, and that you will therefore stay angry at her for, quite possibly, the rest of your life.

It's even worse if you can never admit you're angry, and feel like the "nice" thing to do is to put up with people being cruel to you in silence. Being "nice" is great, but letting people hurt you isn't ever "nice" or necessary. Again: if you don't say you're angry, you don't give other people the chance to change. So the problem persists until you are 87 years old and in the nursing home cafeteria and your friend is still making fun of that Justin Bieber poster you used to have, and you finally just snap and hit her over the head with your cane while screaming, "HE! WAS! FRIENDS! WITH! KANYE!"

Sounds like fun! Or, you could try just saying, "That thing you did was messed up." But consider:

RULE #2: ARGUING IS NOT A TEAM SPORT

The first thing you want to do when you're angry is get other people to take your side. It makes sense. Getting your friends to say that you're right helps ease your guilt about being angry in the first place. It also helps if you can convince people that the person you're arguing with is terrible, quite possibly the reincarnation of Hitler, or Satan's baby; that gives you permission to treat her however you want. After all, she's EVIL. You're just trying to keep people away from her, before she destroys their lives. Or kidnaps Commissioner Gordon, or holds the world hostage with her Death Ray, or, uh, makes out with another person you had a crush on, or whatever: EVIL! is the point here.

Stop. You are not the Friend Police. You have no right to tell other people whom they can like. You can tell friends that you're upset; you can tell friends that you're angry; all of that is normal. If this person is physically endangering you, or is being abusive, you can tell friends (and authorities!) that you don't feel safe around her. But if you're just plain mad, you have the responsibility to go to that person first, and tell her, "That thing you did made me angry. Here is why."

Talking to someone privately changes things. It's no longer about who can get the most supporters; it's not about Team You versus Team Her, or (even worse) Team You versus one unlucky person. It's about the issue. You can talk about the problem you have with her, you can listen to her problems, you can come up with a solution that works for both of you. All of this is possible, if you don't declare war.

I once took an anthropology class. (Cool story, Me!) I can't remember a single thing I learned, except for this: in a lot of societies, exiling someone is considered a punishment worse than death. If you do something so bad that they want to do *more than just kill you*, they cut you off from your friends. People need relationships in order to be healthy and happy; isolating someone causes major pain and damage. This is also why solitary confinement is often considered torture. I'm not saying that you don't have the right to choose whom you hang out with; you do. But you might want to think twice before you *literally torture somebody* for being kind of a snot in homeroom. Also:

RULE #2(A): IF YOU CAN SAY IT TO HER FACE, DON'T SAY IT ON FACEBOOK

Or Tumblr. Or Twitter. Or YouTube. If at all possible, try to avoid making a T-shirt about how much you hate this person and selling it on Etsy.

I'm not sure how things work in this wacky digital age, but I am pretty sure that people still know how to personally contact their own friends. So taking your issue to the internet is passive-aggressive. Even worse, it's a sign that you are interested in publicly humiliating somebody. Not only do you want to hurt her, you want to hurt her on a forum where literally anyone in the world can join in. Did that person's terminally ill grandma just read your thoughts on how her granddaughter is evil? Did the boy who's been harassing her for months just read them, and get encouragement to harass her some more? Did a message forum that's known for bullying girls online and sending them scary death threats just read your post? Did a SERIAL KILLER read it? You don't know! It's the internet!

Try email first, friendo. Arguing is bad enough before Hot Teen Girl Fights Dot Com gets involved.

RULE #3: DOING BAD THINGS DOESN'T MAKE YOU A BAD PERSON

Here's where we talk about what you're actually going to say when you confront someone. In my experience, there are two ways you can begin this conversation, and they are:

EXAMPLE A: Dear Friend: It has recently come to my attention that you suck. Boy, do you ever suck. It's hard to tell why you suck so much. Maybe it's that totally messed-up joke you made about the diorama I made for science class. That diorama perfectly depicted the plight of the endangered humpback whale (*Megaptera novaeangliae*), but it's clear that you couldn't tell, because you were distracted by your own science project, "How Hard Can I Suck? Really Hard, Watch Me." But I'm not sure that it was just the joke, although you do clearly hate whales and are probably the main reason they are endangered. Other reasons why you suck might include your stupid face, or the fact that once in kindergarten you hogged all the blue crayons, even though you knew I needed them for my picture of a humpback whale gliding majestically through the vast ocean. I'm not sure, but I thought you ought to know that you suck. Signed, Your Friend Who Doesn't Hate Whales.

EXAMPLE B: Hey—that thing you said about my science project hurt my feelings. I worked hard on it, and I'm passionate about the subject, so making fun of it was uncool. It also didn't seem like you; you're normally really supportive. I just wanted to check in to let you know that that was weird, and also to see if everything is OK between us. If something is up, I'd like to fix it.

Now: the reason you want to send the second letter, and not the first one, is not "to be nice." The reason you want to adhere more to Example B is that it actually works. Example A says "You're bad, you've always been bad, you always will be bad, here's every bad thing you've ever done, bye." The person receiving this letter can respond in one of three ways: listing all of your flaws, trying to "prove" you're wrong, or staying away from you. You lose a friend or you get into an even bigger fight. That's all that letter is good for.

Example B says "That thing you did was bad, everybody does bad stuff sometimes, I want to get past this." This person can apologize, they can tell you why they did it—maybe it wasn't even about you! Maybe their parents are fighting, maybe they were just yelled at by a teacher, maybe they're getting a bad grade in that class and your mind-blowingly awesome whale project made them feel insecure—and you can both fix whatever has gone wrong. You're not stuck in the "No I'm not, YOU are" cycle, so you can move past the fight.

So simple, right? Well, not really. As it turns out, there are complications.

COMPLICATION #1: You Both Did Bad Things, Oh No!

Oh, hey, here's a shock: fights aren't usually about just one thing. Often, conflicts emerge after months or years of people hurting each other, until one of them finally blows up. Sometimes this person feels like the other bad things weren't "big enough" or "serious enough" to get mad about, so they just stay quiet and accumulate grudges, until the other person finally does something "big enough" to address. But when that happens, all of the anger that's been built up over the years comes out. So, you think this is about Suzy making fun of your whale diorama. But Suzy thinks it's about the fact that you never compliment her art projects, and you didn't invite her to your Sea World trip, and you made fun of her for liking Kristen Stewart, and Suzy is pretty clearly under the impression that you are the real jerk here.

Well, you're both jerks. And now that you're actually talking about it, you can figure out how to do better. Maybe you could make a point of asking for apologies when things actually happen from now on. Having a conflict is not the same as playing a video game—it's not like one person is going to be the winner, and the other one is going to lose all her lives and fall off the screen. You're probably going to find out that you both hurt each other, and you're both going to have to apologize. But try not to compete over who was the most hurtful. If someone only wants to talk about what you did wrong, try saying something like, "It's true that I can do bad things, but you're responsible for your own choices." And prepare for:

COMPLICATION #2: Some People Don't Want to Make Things Better

Every time you have a conflict, you stand to lose a friend. And that's really, really scary. When you're honest and open about a problem, even if you do it respectfully, the other person might just refuse to listen, and might even start using bullying tactics on you. So, given that risk, why do it?

It all comes down to how you see this situation. You could see it like this: "I told my friend that she made me angry, and that upset her, so now she doesn't like me." Wow, what a terrible story about losing a friend! But here's the other perspective: "I told someone that she made me angry, and she decided she didn't want to treat me respectfully, so that's how I found out she wasn't my friend." Wow, what a great story about how you were brave and honest!

It's great to be friends, but you do not need to be friends with everybody, especially not if they treat you badly. Your social life is like a closet. Sometimes, when it gets crowded, you have to throw things out. The first items to go should be the relationships that don't fit you anymore. You don't have to punish those people or get revenge on them; you just move on. Conflict is one way to figure out which relationships are working. If you approach a good friend with a conflict, that person will not hate you or try to hurt you. If anything, being honest with each other will make you closer. If not: good news, you just cleared out room for a new friend.

Now that we've established this, it's time for:

THE STIRRING CONCLUSION: FIGHTING LIKE A GIRL CAN CHANGE THE WORLD

So, you had a fight. Yeesh, that was draining. But let's list everything you didn't do, while you were fighting: You didn't lie. You didn't betray a fellow girl. You didn't try to expose any girls to verbal or physical harassment. You didn't destroy another girl's confidence. You didn't make it less likely for that girl to succeed at work or in school, either intentionally or as a side effect of your actions. You didn't hurt yourself, or treat yourself like you deserved to be hurt. You didn't let your fear control you. I've got to stress this: *You didn't make any girls less confident, less successful, or more endangered by harassment.* You, therefore, have taken yourself off the team that is constantly rooting for girls to do poorly in school, to do badly in life, to hate themselves, and to be scared all the time. You just scored a victory for feminism, my friend. Because you had a little honest conflict.

It is essential for girls to learn how to fight. There is a lot for us to fight, in this world! And some of it is serious! The wage gap isn't going to go away if we just tell all of the wage gap's friends that it made out with someone else's boyfriend under the bleachers. Antiabortion politicians aren't going to change their minds if we just stop inviting them to our parties. Knowing how to say "this is messed up" without feeling guilty is a huge part of being strong. But girls also have to know how to fight without destroying one another. There are too many girl-destroying forces out there; we can't afford to do their work for them.

"Fighting like a girl" can mean "relational aggression." It can mean being indirect, being untrustworthy, causing drama in order to make yourself feel better at another person's expense. But "fighting like a girl" can also mean just being honest, open, and willing to have a little healthy conflict once in a while. Girls tend to care about our friendships a lot. We do. But part of caring about our friendships is making sure that they are safe spaces in which we can tell the truth about how we feel. So here is the best part about this second way of fighting like a girl: when you do it, you show that it's possible. The world doesn't end. When you're honest, and stand up for yourself—even when that's uncomfortable—you make it possible for every other girl to believe she can do the same. ◆

Ladies FIRST!
1. Moonday School (intergalactic Church)
TheeSatisfaction
2. Shut the F up, Boy (The Declaration
of ROSEY GUNZ) • Nikki LyNette
3. The BBQ (ft. RAH DIGGA & RAGE) •
ETERNIA & MOSS
4. BANG • RYE RYE and M.I.A.
5. COLD ROCK A PARTY (BAD BOY REMIX) •
MC LYTE
6. 1980 • ESTELLE
7. DADDY'S LITTLE GIRL •
NikKi D.
8. THE LOVE OF MY LIFE
WORLDWIDE • ANGIE STONE +
ERYKAH BADU
9. PRO NAILS
(ft. KANYE WEST) •
KID SISTER
10. YOU CAN'T PLAY
w/ MY YO-YO
(ft. ICE CUBE) •
YO-YO

Candy Apple Crime

By Petra

Special thanks to Kealan from 69 Vintage and Dennis from
House of Vintage for pulling these pieces, and to Carly, Adrien,
and Maimouna at Peggi Lepage for modeling.

yay, geometry: an interview with joss whedon

Our hero on Shakespeare, high school, and his new movie. No, his other new movie.

By Tavi

For anyone who has the nerve to be enthusiastic about things, a species I believe is commonly called "nerd" or "geek," Joss Whedon is like a living embodiment of that presidential slogan about hope. A person might be laughed at in high school for reciting self-motivational mantras with rocket-ship metaphors, but these are the people who have the will and creative juices to go on to make great things, great and thoughtful and awesome things like *Buffy the Vampire Slayer, Angel, Firefly, Serenity, Dr. Horrible's Sing-Along Blog, Dollhouse, Marvel's The Avengers,* and now, a semi-modernized version of Shakespeare's *Much Ado About Nothing.* Here, Joss talks about that homemade project and things of feminist concern, helps me get over myself and my attitude problem about school, and displays the wonderful knowledge and interestingness you gain when you have the nerve to be enthusiastic about things. And so, vote for Obama in 2008! Or…what? I don't know what I'm saying anymore. Read the interview. Bye.

TAVI So **The Avengers** **was like this huge superhero production, and really exhausting, I would imagine. After making it you should've taken a vacation, but instead you made another movie. I wanna know why, and what's wrong with you.**

JOSS There is something horribly wrong with me. I admit that fully. I'm not exactly sure how it happened. I was in New York at the end of the shoot of *The Avengers,* in the beginning of September. It had been about seven months since I'd slept for a full night. I was so crazed, and Kai, my wife, and I were talking about the vacation we were gonna take for our 20th anniversary of bein' sweeties. We had October free, so we were going to Venice. Then we started

talking about *Much Ado*—neither of us can remember how it came up. And Kai was like, "You know what? Make the movie. Venice isn't sinking *that* fast." I said, "Honey, there's no way I can adapt the script and put it together in a month." She's like, "Yes, you can." So I started talking to people about it. Then I realized how much work it would be and I was like, *I have gone insane. This is a terrible idea.* But at that point I'd already started getting people to commit, so it was like, *I gotta put my head down and do it.* It's one of the weirder decisions I've ever made and absolutely the best.

That's good.

Yeah. What if it turned out the other way!

That would suck.

It was exhausting, but it was the kind of exhaustion that feeds you and makes you strong. I mean, I'm very excited about *The Avengers,* and I hope people will be like yay! for that film, but you know, you make a movie like that piecemeal, a tiny bit at a time, and then you assemble those pieces, and half of what's going to be great about the movie is not even built yet, because it's special effects. And then I get to do this other thing, where I'm shooting by necessity about eight to 10 pages a day of just… meat. All the interactions, all the dialogue, all the silly, all the fun, all the visuals— they're all there. They're accomplished by the end of the day. You don't go, "Oh, excellent! We got him walking into the room. Tomorrow he'll say a word." It's a completely different experience.

You've worked with a lot of the actors in *Much Ado* before, and you filmed it in…I believe I read 12 days? On a shoe-

string budget and in a single house. Does that kind of seat-of-your-pants spirit come through in the movie at all or will it be like *The Avengers: Shakespeare Edition*?

[*Laughs*] It definitely will come through— though hopefully not so much that people go, "Wow, this looks like they shot it fast!" But yeah, it is literally homemade. 'Cause it was my house we shot it in.

Oh, wow!

Yeah. My wife designed the house. She's an architect. That was another reason we finally decided to make the movie. I was like, I have the space, the whole movie takes place in one location. And I happen to live in it, and it happens to be beautiful. I mean, I'm in love with that house. My only regret was that we didn't have any kind of rigs or steady cams or anything like that, so I couldn't move from space to space as much as I wanted to. Because part of what's beautiful about that house—and what I like about a film—is the flow.

I heard that you used to throw these, like, Shakespeare parties at your house.

They were Shakespeare *readings.* Shakespeare parties sounds like we all get in the big collars and quilted hose and dance to a lute. It's just people showing up and reading. We started it years ago with some of the *Buffy* and *Angel* people—actors and writers and friends—and it turned into a huge monster of fun. Everybody just enjoyed each other enormously, learned about the text, got to pretend, got to show off a little, and got to make fools of themselves. Then it kinda died down for a while, because we had kids, and everything dies down when you have kids. But during its most fertile period, we did *Much Ado* with Amy [Acker] and Alexis [Denisof], and it became clear to me that if I was ever going to shoot a version of that play, this is my Beatrice and Benedick. They had both done an enormous amount of Shakespeare onstage, and they were the kind of people that even when they had tiny little parts, they would just blow it up, and not in a show-offy way. When they read Beatrice and Benedick, they were just delightful.

That's kinda perfect.

It all happened very organically.

Did filming Shakespeare feel different from your normal supernatural and superhero stuff, or did any of the super-*blank* tactics come in handy?

The most interesting thing to me was that it's not that different. When you do Shakespeare, you have the burden of trying to make it all make sense. And what I figured out was that my version of *Much Ado* is just exactly the way I make my shows and my [superhero] team movies. Everybody gets to step up and explain why they're there. They get to have their moment, you know, that explains why in their world, they're the center of this universe. Everybody gets to shine. They are all heroes. Especially Hero.

We have to read a bit of Shakespeare this year, and we did *Romeo and Juliet* last year, and I had a bit of trouble with it. It's hard to read and appreciate something when it's an assignment for school. Any ideas on making it easier? Did you like Shakespeare in high school?

Oh my god yes. Literally my favorite subject. I loved what he had to say, I loved all the darkness, I loved all the strangeness. *Hamlet* is my favorite—that would be no surprise to anybody who's hung out with me. But I also found sometimes that I needed someone to interpret it for me. The best thing is to see it. Because there are certain things that don't make sense until you really understand the context. I would always read a play before I saw a film of it, and I remem-

ber reading *Henry V* before I saw [Kenneth] Branagh's version, and going, *OK, this doesn't make any sense to me at all*. Then I saw the movie and saw, A, where it did make sense and I had missed it; and, B, where Branagh used the fact that it didn't make sense to create his own emotional through line. Both of those things were life lessons for me. He's great at making clear to an audience what he's saying and what he's feeling, and sort of going beyond the text and saying, here's why they're talking about this odd thing in the middle of this very emotional scene. And there's a good deal of that in my *Much Ado*. A good deal of finding not just the point of the scene but the life beyond it.

Your *Much Ado* is a modernized version, right?

It's modernized in the sense that it takes place today, or in a sort of nethertime. I mean, there are definitely iPhones about, everybody's dressed rather elegantly, a lot of suits. This was a purely artistic consideration and had nothing to do with the fact that we had no budget and it was BYO costumes [*laughs*]. But we decided Leonato is clearly like a politician, and he lives the life of an extremely rich politician. One of the things we added is that he has what I refer to as a court photographer, who's always just *there*, taking pictures, because everything in the play is a big event, and very important people are *always* having their pictures taken during big events. But also, the way she's looking at everyone, and the way we're looking at everyone—which is very often through glass or in a reflection or distorted—and the way they're all looking at each other and not really seeing each other is very much kind of the point of the thing.

Is there anything in it that you think would appeal especially to A Teenage Girl?

It is the first romantic comedy, in the modern sense. Two people who can't stand each other who are perfect for each other. All the greats—*His Girl Friday*, *The Cutting Edge*—all the great romantic comedies have built off of that premise to some extent. There's a lot of humor. There's a lot of romance.

I think Beatrice is one of the great female characters that Shakespeare ever wrote. She is extraordinarily witty. And generally speaking, Benedick—he may get the last word in the play, but not generally around her.

There is also an element where everybody behaves like a bunch of teenagers. Status is everything, and everyone's always forming little cliques and either turning against or trying to help other people, and gossip nearly destroys Hero and tears everything apart. It is a very fraught little world that would be recognizable to anyone who's ever been in a school.

What I'm saying is, the villain in *Much Ado* is gossip.

Can we talk about the feminist problem of this play—the fact that the plot revolves around whether Hero is a virgin and therefore worthy of the love of her father and her fiancé? Doesn't her father say he wants to kill her when he thinks she's had sex?

Yeah. But everything in the play is taken to a modern interpretation [in the movie] in the sense that, yes, they're talking about whether or not she's "a maid," or a virgin. But what [her fiancé] Claudio's dealing with is the idea that she's into somebody else and that she's made a fool of him. What [her father] Leonato's dealing with is being publicly shamed. And that the closest person to him in his life, his daughter, has been lying to him. It was very much about playing the emotionality of two men who feel like they've been made fools of. It's not about the hymen so much as it is about, uh...the human. The human, not the hymen! That's my motto.

Does he tell her she should die in the movie?

It's in the script: "Do not live, Hero, do not ope thine eyes." But in that same scene, I have him embracing her fiercely, because he's just so torn. He can't figure out what to do. What he does is I think reprehensible, and so do we all, but we worked hard to understand that in his position what had just happened was socially completely devastating, and that's what his whole life was based on. And that emotionally he felt completely betrayed. But by that same token, before that scene is done, he's holding on to her, saying, if they've done something to her, I'll kill them. We played it in such a way that he lost his temper completely, but then at the same time couldn't not hold her.

Then there's another problem, which is why would Hero take Claudio back after he's been such a dick to her?

Getting her to forgive him was important, and part of that had to do with, when she finally says to him, "And surely as I live, I am a maid," she doesn't say it like, "It's OK, I'm a virgin"; she says it like, "You were fucking wrong." She's fierce. A lot of lines that are often played laid-back and passive are her getting in his face. And I also added a bit: in the funeral scene, where Claudio's going down to the tomb to mourn for her and he's all distraught, she's actually watching. You can see her feel like, *Well, I'm still kinda pissed, but he clearly means it.*

There's been a teenage girl, or a little older, in almost everything you've done, and I wanna know what that fascination is about. Are you making up for the fact that you went to an all-boys school?

[*Laughs*] I think that obsession existed long before I went to an all-boys school. You don't really grow obsessions late in life. I think they're formed early.

I have never really known why I need to write about really strong adolescent girls. I do know that I have issues about helplessness, and that seeing [girls] portrayed as helpless, for all the years of my youth, got very old. I am much more interested in some of the older comedies, particularly the black-and-white comedies of the '30s, when most of the movie stars were female and they actually had things to do and a lot to say before they were sort of sidelined in the mainstream, in movies. And I was raised by a super strong, very interesting woman. And I was also very tiny and helpless. Those are the things that I know about. But I still don't know why my ava-

tar's a girl. But she always has been, and I've just given myself up to it.

What were you like as a teenager, other than helpless?

Um, I was annoying. But I was funny. As much as I annoyed almost everyone, I could make them laugh. I was a terrible procrastinator and, unless it was English class, kind of a terrible student, and I just…I hate that every day of my life. I regret that.

Really?

Yeah. Every day.

You should talk about that more, 'cause I'm in a really awful "I don't care about school" phase and I need to get out of that.

I don't think I ever had an "I don't care" phase, because I went to schools that were so good that you really got engaged in the process of learning. I just had a mental block against doing work, even if it was work that I loved, and that makes me sad. It plagues me. Like my girl avatar, it's something I never really understood. Why would I sabotage myself? Because ultimately, I find, the class is gonna be as good as you decide it's gonna be. You may have a terrible teacher. You may have a great teacher. But there is no such thing as a boring subject. It's just a question of whether you're going to decide to engage with it.

Math, I was good at, but I never really engaged. Literature was always the thing that had my heart. And I loved history, but I still could be lazy. I took a lot of languages—I can speak none of them now. I just really never got off my duff unless it was creating something. I always wanted to cut right to the part where you're making something. I didn't actually want to learn how. Which doesn't work, by the way.

I didn't really start writing till after college, didn't realize I was a writer till after college. But once I started, I worked as hard as I could. All the time. I didn't actually study writing, but I lived with a lot of it, and grew up with a lot of really good writers. Like with everything else, if I don't

lay the groundwork, if I don't do the stuff that seems like it's not that rewarding, I don't get the reward later on. I feel that all the time. Not to sound like the biggest old fogey in the world, but it's true.

So why do you think school doesn't matter?

Like I *know* why it matters and everything. The thing is, I feel like you have this point of view when you're a teenager that's unique, the same way that I'll never see things the same way I did when I was little again, where everything is all new. And I'm always itching to take advantage of that in ways I don't think the schooling system encourages you to do. So I'm always writing or drawing or something…I don't know. I think it's also because I've always been a perfectionist and now I'm burned out from that as far as schoolwork goes. I think I was kept under the illusion that grades in middle school were really important, which they're not, and now I'm all worn out.

You used up all your best, and now high school is gonna be a disaster. I do sometimes feel that school is a little counterintuitively designed. I don't think it necessarily takes the adolescent mindset or heartset into account enough. There is a need for exploration and change, and there are so many questions and there are so many priorities shifting and there's so much shit going down, and our design for schools is pretty much "sit them down and give them facts." I do think there are better ways to engage people in not just the accumulation of knowledge, but, you know, the desire, the habit of pursuing knowledge.

You said that you didn't really realize that you were a writer until after college. What happened for you to realize that?

A desperate need for funds. I was planning to go to northern California and make movies, but I didn't have any money at all, and I knew you could make money by writing a TV script—that's how my father made his living for many years—and I thought, well, TV is a lesser art form, but I'll just try my hand at a script and maybe

I can make enough money to get started. And the moment I started writing my first spec script, a script just to show people I could write or find out if I can, I fell madly in love with writing. And later on I fell madly in love with TV and realized, oh, most of the best writing isn't in movies. It's in this other place.

Were there any shows that made that clear to you?

Hill Street Blues was enormously influential for me. I'd never seen anybody quite do that.

Can you explain what that is a bit?

Hill Street Blues was a cop drama from the early '80s, and its tonal shifts were startling and deliberate and unlike anything I'd seen on TV. Every week, every scene, the ground would just shift under your feet. You really didn't know what kind of show you were gonna see. It was gonna be dramatic and people would cry and blah blah blah, but you also never knew when they were gonna suddenly drop something very funny or very tough or very unexpected. And that's the only kind of TV I like to make. You go in not knowing, and most TV is about knowing. Mostly people [watching TV] are like, "Can I order potatoes again? Thank you for the potatoes. See you next week." A lot of my favorite shows are potato shows. With *Roseanne*, for instance, you know what you're in for. And *Columbo*. But I just like to change it up.

I feel like I skipped over the high school stuff out of cowardice but it's weird to talk about because I'm, like, in a rut.

I've been in a rut. I was in a rut for several years. Ruts are easy to come by when you're a teenager. The ground is pitted with them. I also know that even though I couldn't articulate it, I was pretty much in control of my world in a sense that…you know, early on, I don't know, maybe 14, I realized that every year I go to school and in September I'd be like "Yeah! Let's do this! I'm very excited!" and by mid-October I'd be behind in everything. And I kind of trained my-self—I gave myself this little mantra: I was like, you know, "I'm gonna be fierce this year." I can't remember the whole mantra, but it had to do with me being a rocket ship. And it worked. I was like, *No, I'm fierce homework guy, engaged guy, doing my work, I'm a rocket ship, I'm not gonna let up.* And it was working great, and then I told somebody about my rocket ship mantra, and they laughed at it. And I just stopped.

Did you ever fall into a Lindsay Weir thing where you're less into the idea of being a rocket ship and more into the idea of being a lazy person or somebody who doesn't care?

[*Laughs*] That's a good metaphor for me, a lazy person…

No! I was talking about, OK, about my-self, because suddenly the idea of being someone who is not engaged becomes appealing somehow. Even though I know that I actually do like math and that I am a huge nerd, that idea at some point this month became appealing to me.

You know, there's two versions of that. One's "I don't want to do anything that I don't want to do." Then there's also "I wish to be this person. This person who is not engaged." Which I think are two different things.

For me it was never me-against-the-school kind of stuff, because I was raised by teachers and my mom taught at my school that I went to for 10 years, so I always sort of had their perspective in mind, and had respect for what they were trying to do, and I had some of the best teachers you could have. So it wasn't that, but there was desire to be disengaged, or at least to appear disengaged, a desire to be…dare I say bold? Which I really never even got close to. Super did not accomplish bold. It's not like I was gonna go hang out in the alley and smoke cigarettes with the "bad" kids. It's just that thing where you want things to feel easy, like they seem easy to you, like you're just sort of coasting.

Sometimes you need to get away from ordinary expectations, but at the same time it's very easy to be a lazy person and go, "I'm getting away from ordinary expectations by not doing my homework." And with the way some classes are run, all of a sudden you find that, yes, you've just become a lazy person. You actually haven't done anything awesome or disengaged or cool, you've just forgotten to do your homework. Again.

Well. I'm going to take that and do something inspiring with it. Can we know anything about what Wonder Woman was like in the script you wrote [which the world will never see because of stupid people at studios]?

She was a little bit like Angelina Jolie [*laughs*]. She sort of traveled the world. She was very powerful and very naïve about people, and the fact that she was a goddess was how I eventually found my in to her humanity and vulnerability, because she would look at us and the way we kill each other and the way we let people starve and the way the world is run and she'd just be like, *None of this makes sense to me. I can't cope with it, I can't understand, people are insane.* And ultimately her romance with Steve was about him getting her to see what it's like *not* to be a goddess, what it's like when you are weak, when you do have all these forces controlling you and there's nothing you can do about it. That was the sort of central concept of the thing. Him teaching her humanity and her saying, OK, great, but we can still do better.

Why do you think the "humanity and the world being awful" theme is something that you visit a lot? Like in *Dr. Horrible*…

Well, I think the world is largely awful, and getting worse, and eventually the human race will die out. And it'll be our own fault.

That's gonna be *my* rocket ship mantra.

[*Laughs*] "It's all futile and soon the human race will die out. And now, geometry! This isosceles triangle will save us all!" No, I can be very pessimistic on a broad scale. On a smaller scale, I love people and I'm interested in them. There are certain human truths, like death, that nobody gets to escape, and pain, which everybody not only feels but needs. You have to go through it. So for everybody, at some point—very often for teenagers—the world is a terrible place. The world is a giant, awful black hole of evil conspiracy. Sometimes that's because you have perspective on what the world's really like, and sometimes it's because you've completely lost perspective and you're having a terrible day. But no matter what, everybody shares that feeling, and life is kind of about your ways around that, your ways around certain truths. Some people combat it with faith, some people combat it with work. For me, if I'm not writing or creating something, I get very antsy. That's my little defense against darkness. Also, my kids.

If being creative is part of your work and not doing that work makes you antsy, but it can also be so exhausting, how do you make all of that work?

Well, you do have to shut down every now and then. That was hard for me for a long time. My wife kind of helped me by demanding that I do so. That worked out. And then I had kids, and everything changed. I learned to be present. I learned to stop and just do what I'm doing for a little while. And then I'm recharged and it all helps. I started doing yoga, too. There, I said it. Yes, I live in L.A. Clearly I live in L.A. Now excuse me while I have my protein shake and my chardonnay. Mixed together. No, that was a horrible idea.

It sounds awful. Even though I've never had chardonnay.

No, no, no. Stay in school, kids! Geometry!

You subscribed to *Sassy*, right?

I did, I had a subscription.

And it was for girls but you really liked it.

Yeah, I did. I liked the way they talked to girls. They talked about things like feminism, body issues, community, and diversity, but in context with teenage girls' actual life and language—not with an agenda of either dic-

tating their politics or getting them to buy more makeup. Other people weren't doing that. I liked what they had to say, and I liked the bands. Definitely some people say, "It is odd that you should have had a subscription to *Sassy*." But I don't think it needs to be explained. I get complaints about *Buffy* that, you know, "There's no strong men! Male character!" I'll be interested to hear what people say about *Much Ado* on those terms, because men are very often supremely dolt-ish in this movie, but even Beatrice herself is made a bit of a fool. I'll be interested to hear some people say, "Oh my god, this text is so misogynist," and some people will say, "No, it's a great feminist text," and some people will say, "No, it's just a funny play!"

Is it any of those things to you? Just a funny play, or misogynist, or feminist…

I think it's often chauvinist, often feminist, often funny. It's human; it's Shakespeare, you know? He has a very keen eye for who we are and he's a little bit merciless with it. That's where he gets his humor as well as his darkness. I think that's kind of what makes it art—you can't just be a political statement one way or the other. It's gotta breathe beyond those boundaries.

OK, I think we're about done. Is there anything you'd like to say to the TEEN-AGE GIRLS OF AMERICA?

Um, go geometry. Yay geometry. I feel like I gave it a bad rap earlier. Um…if there's something I have to say, it'll show up in something I create. I talk better through other people.

Well then I guess we'll have to keep an eye out for what you say through *Much Ado About Nothing*, in theaters blah blah blah!

[*Laughs*] Wow! That was segue-tastic. You just wrapped that whole thing up.

Thank you. And thank you very much.

Thank you! Nice to talk to you.

Nice to talk to you too. ♦

I'm supposed to be pretty, skinny, smart (but not too smart), cool, funny, and flawless. All without trying.

Writing by Lexi Harder.
Illustration by Emma D.

Embarrassing fact about me: I started keeping a food diary last week.

I feel OK admitting this secret of mine, because it's not really a secret anymore. Last night a few of my friends found my food diary, and at this point I really couldn't be any more embarrassed than I already am. They passed it around, reading it out loud to one another, raucously laughing. One of them pulled me aside and said, "You have a food diary? That makes you seem really…insecure." In the face of their teasing I tried to pretend I didn't remember writing it, but the entries were dated, so *that* plan backfired. In the end I laughed it off and even went so far as to make fun of myself, which finally got them to drop the subject, leaving me, my ego, and my self-worth shriveled into a ball of humili-ation. It was all I could do not to curl up into the fetal position and turn into a scrap of bellybutton fluff.

There are several things I find wrong with the entire situation:

1. Who in the hell goes through other people's things and seeks out OBVIOUSLY PRIVATE CONTENT and then proceeds to read it to an entire room? Maybe I'm crazy but I am filing that action under Very Rude, Inexcusably Impolite, and Im-mature behavior.

2. At first the friend who found the journal didn't notice it was dated, so I thought I was saved, but the next person who read it noticed and pointed it out. Ouch. Also immature, but I guess embarrassing me is that amusing—don't let me keep you from your fun!

3. Society in General. This point needs significantly more elaboration, but for now let's just say that sometimes people are assholes. (See above.)

I won't pretend I'm anything special. In fact, I'm an almost depressingly normal girl. I get OK grades, I have a pretty awesome family and a friggin' sweet boyfriend, I know a lot of cool people I can call my friends, the whole shebang. Normal Girl material. Along with being a Normal Girl I am supposed to be pretty (without trying), skinny (without trying), smart but not too smart (without trying), cool (without trying), funny (without trying), and perfect (without trying). The minute it looks as if I'm *trying* to be any of those things I am alternately pitied or ridiculed.

Now, I'm not saying that I think I should be pretty and skinny, etc. The GIRL POWER part of me is screaming that at the top of her lungs, believe me. At the same time, I see how easy it is for me to slip into that overly critical, probably insecure mode, where I make fun of girls who are overweight, on a diet, failing class, and almost any other insignificant point you can think of. Dumb things that certainly don't determine a person's ultimate value. Which makes me think that other people are saying the exact same things about me. Which leads me to record what I'm eating, which leads to shame when my friends find out I have feelings.

Still, if the worst thing I can be mocked for is the fact that I am occasionally depressed and worry about my weight and how others see me, then I congratulate myself. Congratulate myself for being human, because I secretly believe that everyone else is just as insecure. This doesn't mean I'm not angry at how unjust everything is. Why does contemporary society condemn an (oh, I might as well say it) overweight girl who one day decides to eat a salad, but celebrate a "hot" girl who decides to eat a cheeseburger? (Never mind if it's the only thing she's eaten in three days. Or she may have a balanced diet and love cheeseburgers and was just born with a conventionally attractive body. Or…WHY AM I EVEN THINKING ABOUT THIS? See what happens?)

It doesn't help that if I tried to voice these frustrations in public I'd probably also get made fun of. (You might be making fun of me right now.) People might just say I'm overreacting. I'm not. Which is why I'm wary of calling myself a feminist in public. My male friends, ill educated as to what a feminist actually is, would laugh, cease to take me seriously, and tell me to get back in the kitchen. No, seriously, sexism still exists. I have friends who think *rape* is funny.

What my point is: society sucks. It's a damned if you do, damned if you don't kind of situation. I'm not allowed to be fat, but I'm not allowed to go on a diet either (or keep a food diary, for that matter). I'm not allowed to be dumb, but I'm not allowed to be smarter than a boy. I'm not allowed to do drugs or drink, but I'm considered boring if I don't. I'm supposed to be an empowered woman, but if I ask for respect dudes will just call me an annoying bitch. Heck, if I wait to have sex I'm labeled a prude, but if I lost my virginity today there would be a lot of people thinking *that slut*.

I'm still angry, but I choose to look at it this way: since I can't win, why not do what I want? I have a right to eat salad or eat an entire chocolate cake, answer questions and ask questions in class, keep a food diary or throw it away, have sex when I feel like it. And I think everyone should, because one day I want to meet people who like my ideas and won't laugh at me because they're afraid of other people laughing at them. Who cares, anyway? I do, I can't help it, but it doesn't mean I have to let caring rule who I am and what I do with my life.

End rant. ♦

Lexi Harder is a 17-year-old part-time mermaid, part-time hibernating bear who spends her free time watching British period dramas on the internet and cleaning her room.

Home Town Heroes

Skate crew of our cotton-candy dreams.

By Petra

All clothes, Petra's own. She D.I.Y.'d the collar and crowns. Rhinestone skateboard by her and floral skateboard painted by Apple Darling. Thanks to Apple and Gwen (Peggi Lepage) for modeling.

The Old Crowd

Badass babes. By Chrissie. Thanks to Angalina Sandoval for doing hair; Angel Dorr and Lenaig Delisle for doing makeup; Elvia Carreon for styling; Hy Khong for assisting; and Justina, Raton, Tennessee, Amanda, and Jasmyne for modeling.

DECEMBER 2011: HOME

I'm excited about this month because I love winter and the excuse to stay inside all day. I love snow while it's still pretty. And holidays while *they're* still pretty, before everyone just gets sick of one another. I love forts and sweaters and hot chocolate. Actually, I'm going to take this opportunity to offer up the very helpful tip of putting fun-size Crunch bars in your hot chocolate. Just slipping that in there because it's not exactly original or clever enough to be its own D.I.Y. post.

But as much as I love my bed and family and hot chocolate, I don't always feel at home, at home. I don't always feel at home in my hometown. I was first made aware of the idea that home could be an identity you find or make yourself when I saw *No Direction Home*, the documentary about Bob Dylan's life through 1965. He was born into a small town in Minnesota that was boring and simple, and went so far as to say he could've been born to the wrong parents. And he hoped to find home through his relationship with music.

His music came to mean a lot to me. After getting through the phase where you're like, "I saw a documentary and now I'm an expert!" I actually did devour a couple more movies about him, read his book, read books about him, and of course listened to his albums until I couldn't *not* mouth the words along subconsciously. I taught myself guitar so I could play his songs, and me and my best friend performed them at a record store together. I decided I would one day write a masterpiece called "Song to Bobby," based on his own "Song to Woody." *I started carrying around a notebook every day in case inspiration were to strike.* Whenever I could, I related a school project to him. I made a little book illustrating his songs for no one to see but myself. In a night's angst, I *painted* the lyrics of "Like a Rolling Stone" on my wall. Oh, and I had a shrine at some point. A whole corner of my room: vinyl records, books, pictures from magazines, paper cutouts, candles. (The candles part was a little joking. I will give myself that.) The point is: I had found what made me feel like I was home, and I was serious about immersing myself in it.

Then I found out Cat Power already did the "Song to Bobby" thing. Then I remembered a former friend of mine who had Green Day lyrics painted on her own walls. And the one with *Rent* lyrics. Then I saw Dylan live at Summerfest and realized that as much as I believed my connection to his music was special, a bunch of college dudes in cowboy hats being way too loud and way too drunk did, too. Then my dad said casually and nostalgically one day while picking me up from a friend's that he, too, once knew all the words to Dylan's best albums, and wasn't it crazy that his daughter would go on to do the same? I realized then that I would go through many phases in my Journey as an Adolescent, and that this was only the first. That in a matter of time, I would forget what it was about Dylan's music that I thought was so great. We have no shared experiences, and his lyrics don't describe my feelings or whatever. It always just sounded right.

While this obsession was pretty angst-ridden, it was also totally sincere. And, as the process of growing to somehow understand the world has slowly made my enthusiasm for anything pretty rare, I get a little homesick for that first phase of being a person who absorbs things and thinks about them. That was a time when I was so much in my own world that I wasn't aware of what a cliché that world made me, and so in awe of it that I wouldn't have cared anyway. It was the last time I would feel totally childlike in my outlook on something. And that's, well, kind of a bummer.

The thing that had always fascinated me the most about Bob was that he was constantly changing—from a shy Woody Guthrie impersonator, to one of those musicians who somehow get away with being a total dick onstage and to their fans because they're suddenly so badass and oh my god look at those SUNGLASSES and did you ever SEE such attitude, to a recluse, to a *gospel singer*, to, a few years ago, singing about Santa Claus.

I take comfort in knowing that it's OK, then, for me to change too, and that, when I need to, Bob Dylan will find his way back into my life as needed. As long as I can put on one of his records, I can always find home.

OK, now you know I have a soul or whatever. Welcome to December.

love, tavi

field studies

You know how winter is cold but cozy and has a certain kind of smell?
By Eleanor
Thanks to Anya for modeling and Mirren Kessling for
her Dr. Martens-customization skills.

HOW TO BE A HAPPY HOMEBODY

Make your own fun.
By Hazel

There are nights when I don't feel like going to a Superchunk show or hanging out at the local coffee shop with my friends. I just want to stay in and read a book by the fireplace with my pug, Nigel. Doesn't that sound nice? It certainly sounds nice to me, because I am a 90-year-old woman. Just kidding. I'm an über-cool teenager—you know that. For some reason, people love to make homebodies feel bad for choosing to stay home all the time. I've had friends who have tried to make me feel lame for not going out more and "living life," whatever that means. They would label me a big fat ol' loser just because I loved hanging out at home! On one hand, I think: *I'm 17. I should be partying nonstop!* On the other, if being home makes me happy, then I should stay home. And on my mutant third hand, I think, *Does this make me lame?* No! And anyone who says otherwise doesn't know how much fun being a homebody can be, apparently. It's not lame if you want to stay home. In fact, staying home can be super fun! Behold my top eight suggestions for an awesome night indoors:

1. WATCH MOVIES FOREVER AND EVER AND EVER...

...or at least for a couple of hours. Sometimes I'll pick an interesting director whose films I've never seen before, like Gregg Araki or Hal Hartley, and watch one film every night until I've seen their entire body of work. I love inviting friends over for Chinese food and a Disney movie marathon or '80s movie marathon or, really, *any* movie marathon.

2. MAKE ART.

I like to create, and I don't mean in the sense of making a scene in a restaurant. I labor over paper chains and miniature Japanese fish kites. One time I had some plastic animals lying around from Walgreens so I glued bar pins to the back of them and, voilà, they were wearable. (Always have bar pins.) Hell, you can make a flower crown or just give yourself an artful Sharpie tattoo.

3. READ SUPER-SMART LITERATURE AND STUFF.

It is getting increasingly hard for me to find time to relax and read. Being home means an opportunity to fill my brain with the written word. Books, zines, you name it. I can get completely lost in a good story—so lost that three hours pass and I've finished the sucker. The last kickass collection I read was *The Girl in the Flammable Skirt* by Aimee Bender. It was trippy and lovely and otherworldly. Add it to your wishlist!

4. CAST SPELLS ON YOUR CRUSHES.

Draw a pentagram on the floor and put four candles at different points on the edge of the circle. These represent the four elements. Make sure you have some sort of offering (roses? red wine?) to a higher power and place this in the center of the star. Chant the name of the person you hope will fall in love with you 666 times. Warning: this is probably an activity best saved for when you're home alone. That way, if any demons enter the house, they'll only harm you, and not your family. Or maybe don't listen to me because I don't actually know what I'm talking about.

5. WATCH TV.

I will climb into bed with an entire Amy's pizza to watch a series—and eat the pizza, in its entirety. This is a little dangerous because, whether it's a mockumentary comedy like *Summer Heights High* or a freaky thriller like *Twin Peaks,* getting addicted to a good show will make you never want to leave the house until it's over. Do you watch *Mad Men*? You don't? Then why are you reading this? Get thee onto Netflix and glue your eyes to the computer screen.

6. DRESS UP.

You don't need to go out to dress up. I like to go through my closet and put outfits together that I haven't tried on before. I cut shirts, I shorten skirts, I stick safety pins in anything. Also, I recommend getting freaky with your makeup.

7. PLAY BOARD GAMES.

OK, I might sound like a total square, but games can get pretty intense. Especially Pictionary. It's like, "Whoa, I'm sorry I didn't know this eyeball with three dots in the center means hysterical blindness. Yeesh!" Anything can happen when you play Trivial Pursuit or Scrabble, too. Maybe you will get SO into the game that you flip the board over. Maybe you'll throw it at someone! But, hey, you won't be *bored.* Ha ha, get it?

8. GIRL TALK.

I could talk to my friends for hours and hours about school, boys, Congressional earmarks—ya know, girl stuff! But seriously, one minute it's 6:00 PM and then, suddenly, it's two in the morning and all of the takeout is gone and one of your friends just had an emotional breakthrough. Your besties can be all you need to have a good time.

So the next time someone asks you what you're doing on Friday night, you know what to say: I'm drawing a David Bowie–style lightning bolt on my visage, eating a four-cheese pizza, and watching *The Doom Generation.* Doesn't that sound like the best night ever? ♦

hanging out with Margot Tenenbaum

1. judy is a punk — THE RAMONES
2. Village green — THE kinks
3. these Days — St. VinCent
4. Fourth time around — BOB Dylan

5. Desolation's Plan — Coma Cinema
6. toi, mon magicien — CHantal kelly
7. (if paraDise is) Half as nice — amen corner
8. Other towns and cities — Camera obscura
9. the boxer — simon and garfunkel
10. christmas time is here (vocal) — vince guaraldi trio

about a boy

The attack of the Puberty Pterodactyl.
Writing by Spencer. Illustration by Brooke. Playlist by Hazel.

When I was 12 years old, I had my first bout of what would prove to be a long-lasting relationship with anxiety and depression. My grandma died, I had a panic attack, and all of a sudden the colors of my childhood paled to a lackluster gray. The wonder and excitement of playing with Legos, jumping in leaf piles, and knowing close to nothing about the world subsided, leaving behind a dull, anxious ache. I wasn't suicidal—I wasn't even miserable. Just deflated. No longer living effortlessly. I could only think one thing, and that was, *Where did my feelings go?*

The years wore on, and I kept on wondering. I was officially depressed for a while and then, after some therapy and some thinking, officially OK. But even when I felt better, I wasn't totally better. I didn't get that blissful, carefree kid feeling back. Life wasn't effortless like it used to be. I started wondering if that business back in the '08 was really just a kick-start to the inevitable, and that something else was responsible for all of this. For this hole. Then I discovered my friends felt weird, too. They didn't say so, but their newly adopted hobbies and disaffected demeanors told me enough. (I guess I didn't say anything to them, either.) Something swooped down and snatched "feeling OK" from our brains. An emotional pterodactyl. An emotional pterodactyl named Puberty.

But that didn't make much sense. I always thought that to be shafted by the process of growing up, something "real" had to happen. Some sort of bona fide suffering has to go down (maybe like the death of a grandma) before you can feel less happy. After all, discomfort doesn't grow on trees! The weight of the world can't just appear out of thin air!

Well, little did I know, discomfort does grow on trees, and the weight of the world can appear out of thin air. This is mostly because, like all feelings, sadness and unease

live inside your noggin, and as anyone who was once a child knows, anything can happen in there. I had it all backwards. I don't feel weird because my body's changing and girls are confusing and school is hard and drugs are scary. I feel weird because my thoughts are different—my feelings are different. I feel weird because I feel weird. A wispy beginner mustache, or a lack thereof, is easy to understand; feelings aren't.

And that's something no health class can teach you. It's the type of thing that has to smack you in the face, either softly, for years, or violently, on your pitifully hairless, bar mitzvah'd cheek. Or both. Your parents and the ostensibly naughty "puberty" books at the library can reassure you all day that you're 100 percent, perfectly, absolutely normal, but nothing can save you from being scared out of your mind that your mind is changing. Nothing can save you from feeling weird. Nothing can save you from not being a kid anymore.

Four years have passed, and I have yet to be Benjamin Buttoned. At the time of that first panic attack, I was like the kid in that YouTube video "David After Dentist," constantly asking myself, and my parents, and even a therapist, "Is this forever?" I used to be constantly afraid that something was short-circuiting in my brain, and that if I didn't do something soon, the damage would be irreversible. That whatever chance I had of reverting back to childhood bliss would slip away. I guess now I realize that that really *is* what happened. Life won't ever be as simple as playing with Legos and jumping in leaves again. It can't be. If it were, there'd be no friction. No yang to our yin. Without bad, there's no good, and if we all felt OK all the time, there'd be no point.

It seems like, as time goes on, every moment becomes a smaller and smaller slice in the whole pie of our life, and as that pie gets slowly eaten by time, each slice becomes more important. We zoom in,

isolate, and savor that slice for every nugget of its deliciousness. As far as I can tell now, doing that works out just fine. But I lived the first four years of my adolescence thinking "savor the moment" was a gimmick, some sort of cherry grown-ups put atop life because they believe that life is a steaming pile of shit. I thought that "enjoy the little things in life" was code for "this sucks, but we make the best of it." That scared me, because I don't want to think that life is a steaming pile of shit! When I grow up, am I gonna think life sucks? Is some inescapable, adult-making monster—that emotional pterodactyl?—gonna force me to think that life sucks?

I'm just afraid of being jaded. I'm absolutely terrified of not wanting to live. It's a reasonable concern for anybody any age, but it's especially reasonable when you've just started to realize that there's a whole, ginormous, scary world beyond your family, candy, and *Rugrats*. It's especially reasonable when you feel fucking weird. I don't know who I am. At least I think I don't. I don't know if I think I think I don't.

Maybe that's another thing they can't teach you in sex ed. You won't feel weird forever. You *can't* feel weird forever. Things change. That is the reason you feel weird in the first place; things changed! And deep down, no matter how much I wish I could go back to the wonder years, live the simple life in the ole neighborhood, play with Hot Wheels and have my birthday parties at Chuck E. Cheese, I know that's the way things should be. In all my unsureness, frustration, and feeling weird, I know it couldn't be any other way. This too shall pass. ♦

RESCUE REMEDY: AN INTERVIEW WITH FIRST AID KIT

They write the songs that make me (and Patti Smith) cry.
Writing by Tavi. Illustration and lettering by Brooke.

Things that happen when I listen to First Aid Kit:

1. I cry.
2. I can't figure out why I'm crying.
3. I deem everything I know to be meaningless and decide I need to throw my life away and go live without internet and school and…I don't know, I don't really have a plan yet, I just know there's gonna be a lot of fields and sunsets.
4. I need to know where these magical sisters, Klara and Johanna Söderberg, ages 18 and 21 respectively, come from, like, besides the literal answer SWEDEN, and beyond the fact that a YouTube video they made three years ago is why people like Bright Eyes and Fleet Foxes started paying attention to them, and why they are now about to release their second LP, *The Lion's Roar*.

If they deserved a simplified description, I would introduce them by saying they make a folksy kind of music, songs with titles like "I'm Building Myself a Boat," lyrics like "I'll be your Emmylou, I'll be your June, if you'll be my Gram, and my Johnny, too," and a bunch about railroad tracks. But they deserve a much better introduction than that. Lots of people write storytelling songs about trains and set them to acoustic music and do pretty harmonies, but First Aid Kit transcends that cliché.

Their songs sound like they've gone away and seen too much and come back tired but still alive. Their music kind of has its own way of breathing: filled with tension for a little while until it goes over the edge and exhales while the instrumental parts just seem to grow. This part of every few songs of theirs is most thrilling in concert, when Klara plays guitar so intensely you'd think it's her only way of communicating, while Johanna stands perfectly still and lets her voice carry out so that it seems kind of infinite, or like it's been waiting to come out for forever, and I kind of can't help imagining that it comes from under the ground up through her mouth, or that a little part of the sky exists in her diaphragm or something. They can sound like freaking angels, or like women demanding life's answers and who can make Patti Smith cry (which they did, when they performed her song "Dancing Barefoot" when Smith was in the audience).

But it's what their magical voices are saying that really gets to me, because it's painfully familiar. Some songs start like bedtime stories and become family secrets. Simple lyrics quietly turn dark, or dark lyrics are hidden in upbeat music—in "King of the World," there's the fear that "suddenly my fake laugh will sound sincere," or that "one day I'd wake up all alone with a big family and an emptiness deep inside my bones." In a simplified version of this intro—the one I maybe should've written, because it's getting sort of late—I would probably describe First Aid Kit's music as the way Klara and Johanna see the world around them, but the more I listen to their new album, the more it feels like it's the world around me, too. Their descriptions of strangers on the street in "New Year's Eve" and mentions of telephone calls and shopping malls in "In the Hearts of Men" feel familiar. We see the same things—and you do too, probably—they just see them differently. Isn't that a strange feeling? For something you see or feel all the time but don't think too hard about to be given right back to you, either finally making sense or just raising more questions, packaged with a perspective you've never thought of before?

For those looking for that strange feeling, prepared to find either comfort or terror; for all you lost souls, I give you: First Aid Kit.

TAVI How did you discover the music of Johnny Cash and all those very American influences growing up in Sweden?

KLARA I can say that it all started when I heard Bright Eyes when I was 12, and I was like, "Well, OK, what did Conor Oberst listen to when he wrote this music? What has inspired him?" And through that [process] I found Bob Dylan and Johnny Cash and all those amazing musicians. It's sort of been like that—through searching for their influences—and through Bob Dylan we found the Carter family and Bill Monroe and even older stuff.

Did it give you any expectations for America? How did things feel when you got here?

JOHANNA I think we had a very special relationship to America, because in Sweden (or anywhere) you're met with American culture all the time. Our TV is like 90 percent American shows. So when we came to America the first time, it was like we'd been there before. It didn't feel so new. We almost feel like we grew up in America, but we didn't. But we're constantly amazed, driving through America, seeing all these places that we've heard of in songs and in movies—we kind of feel like we're in a movie when we're in America. We're like, *America*, that's where things happen for real, like, you *are* someone if you live in America. I know that's really silly, but that's how we feel.

I mean, you totally get that feeling from movies and everything. Do you write more from instinct or from strategy? Feel it out or think about it more?

KLARA Feel it out, definitely. We really try not to stress the songwriting or think about it too much. We try to let it come when it comes. I always have my iPod or a notebook or my phone or something, so I just write down ideas that I get. They can just come from anything—like just walking down the street and seeing something that reminds me of something, and I just start writing, you know? I start writing lyrics from that. Sometimes I leave it and then find it a million years later and think it's good.

Can it ever be painful to write a song?

KLARA There can definitely be things that can be hard to write about because they're personal. But writing is sort of just like therapy, like going through what you're feeling. Writing, for me, sharing these songs, is kind of a way of saying "I feel this way," and hopefully someone will hear it who feels the same, and we'll all feel a little bit less lonely.

Is it ever hard to perform something that personal for a bunch of people? And so often?

KLARA I think you kind of become a little detached from the songs when you play them live so much.

JOHANNA They aren't yours anymore. When the record's released, it's like it's your baby in the world. You know, we share it with the world. And when you perform the songs you kind of come back to when you were writing them and how you felt. But it's never as strong as when you were actually there.

There's a storytelling element to your music. When I saw you live, you said that you couldn't figure out why you were writing about a man cheating on his wife when you were so young. So where do those stories come from?

KLARA That's just so hard to explain. It's kind of the magic of it—we don't know where this stuff comes from. It just kind of appears in your head and you're like, *wow!*

JOHANNA A lot of those stories were influenced by our mother, who's very feminist, so the feminist themes in those songs are unconscious.

KLARA I don't think "Tangerine" is a feminist song, though.

JOHANNA No, but like, those themes of "You're Not Coming Home Tonight," the housewife leaving her man—I think that one's been influenced by our parents a bit,

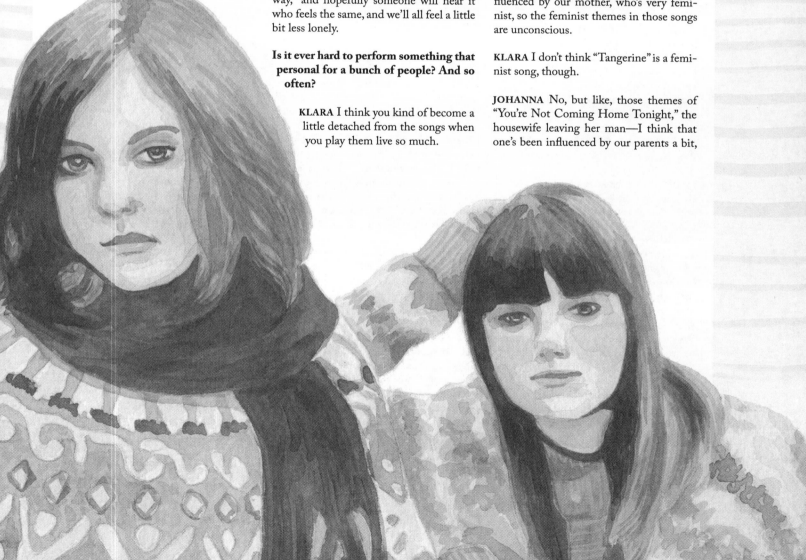

and, I don't know, like you just imagine a TV [show], like a soap, anything…

KLARA When I wrote "Tangerine" I was listening a lot to Jenny Lewis and Rilo Kiley, and I think in my head I was sort of trying to write a Jenny Lewis song. At the same time, it feels completely honest. It's not just trying to be like this other person. It's hard to explain.

She was at your show, actually, when I was there.

KLARA Yeah, I know. How crazy is that?

Did you get to meet her?

JOHANNA Yeah. She's one of our biggest female idols, role models. We really look up to her.

KLARA So it was so incredible that she came. We had met her before at a festival where Bright Eyes played in Sweden, but she'd never heard our music at that point, so we didn't have a lot to talk about because, you know, we were just big fans, and she didn't really know who we were. But she came [to our show], and that was such a huge compliment…it was just indescribable.

Can we talk about feminism more? When did you first realize you were feminists?

KLARA Well, I have a funny story. I was like six years old or something. Our mom sat both Johanna and me down and said, "I want to talk to you about feminism." Like, I was like six! We have an awesome mom—she's amazing. And she said something like, "You know, things aren't really just in this society." She just told us stuff, and the next day I was with my best friend at the time, and her mom, and I told them, "I'm a feminist, are you?" And my friend was like, "What's that?" We've kind of grown up having a feminist perspective on everything we encounter.

JOHANNA Just like gender roles, commercials, advertisements, other things where women are portrayed, I think we've had that perspective. We hope that we can be

positive role models for girls. This business especially is really discriminating against women.

KLARA And it's small things.

JOHANNA Yeah, you notice it all the time.

KLARA I've been reading this Tumblr blog; it's called All the Birds. It's about Joanna Newsom and how she's portrayed in the media, through a feminist view. They were writing about things that people have written [about Newsom] and being critical of it. And I kind of realized that it's crazy, like [people] always write about her like she's an elf or a fairy. And she's always compared to someone like Björk or Kate Bush. Just women who do stranger things with music. If they were men, they probably wouldn't be compared the same way.

JOHANNA It's hard for people to take us seriously. When we started, we were 14 and 16. Half the questions were about how young we were and how we weren't like other girls. You just felt like [people thought] girls of that age weren't capable of writing lyrics about anything other than boys and partying. It was really terrible, the view people have about teenagers—really generalizing.

There's an article I read about Joanna Newsom and it was saying that a lot of the criticism about her basically comes down to she's too girly, she's too feminine. That's really annoying. It must be helpful to have that feminist perspective if you have to deal with all that.

KLARA You're more aware of things so you're just like, annoyed with people. [*Both laugh*] But I'm really happy our mom has a voice and made sure that we were really conscious of that.

A lot of teenagers work on our site, like creative young people, and I end up talking with them a lot about how when you are young and you're still becoming a person, you go through all these phases, and whenever I grow out of a phase, I end up just hating whatever I wrote. Did you

ever feel that way—almost kind of embarrassed about music that you wrote? I mean, it's not bad, it's just kind of that feeling of growing.

KLARA Not the songs, particularly, but I think when you listen to our EP, I was 14 when we recorded that and Johanna was 16, and when I listen to it now I can hear that I wasn't really confident with my voice. I hadn't really found my voice, so I was trying to sound like other people. It's really obvious to me now when I listen to it and think, *Wow, I was really trying to sound like this person*. The songs have always been more universal than just personal things.

JOHANNA We have become more personal with time. Hopefully we weren't too personal at that age!

KLARA We aren't too ashamed of it.

JOHANNA The very first, old recordings from when we were like 10 and 11, I'm really embarrassed by. Some of it's awful!

KLARA But everything we've released under First Aid Kit we're not embarrassed about. I mean with this record now, I can still be like, "Oh, I could have done this differently." And I think that's good, because you want to evolve and have new things going on.

JOHANNA Because things constantly change. I mean, that's the point of life is to change. If you don't, there's nothing interesting going on.

KLARA And Johanna just said the meaning of life.

JOHANNA Yeah. There you go.

You have a very strong visual aesthetic, especially onstage—your dresses you had on when I saw you just moved perfectly with the music. Wanna talk about your style a bit?

JOHANNA We've also gone through a lot of phases with that. When we first started out, it was very simple, like jeans and flannel shirts. Now we've sort of…we see a lot of pictures on Tumblr and it's sort of shaped our aesthetic a lot. It's very '70s. We go vintage shopping a lot in Stockholm and when we're on tour. It's fun to go into different vintage shops—it's like a souvenir, sort of.

I'm going to throw out all journalistic objectivity right now and say that when I listened to the new album, I basically just cried and I couldn't figure out why. What kind of music is like that for you, or what kind of bands do that for you, if any?

KLARA Well first off, thank you so much. I mean that's why we make it, because if we can inspire people or make them feel something, that's all that it's about. So it means a lot to us that you say that. There are a lot of people [who do that for us]. I think recently Joni Mitchell has meant a lot to us. Her album *Blue* is just amazing, so sad and personal that it feels like she just…

JOHANNA …reveals her innermost secrets to you.

KLARA It's incredible, so moving. And especially now, during Christmastime, I always listen to "River"—that's always such a tearjerker. Bright Eyes has meant that to us too, but it's weird now that they're sort of our friends; it would be sort of weird sitting and crying to their music. It still means so much to us, but I can't listen to it in the same way that I did before. Townes van Zandt, Leonard Cohen…Johanna, what would you say?

JOHANNA You pretty much said our main three. Fleet Foxes were very important to us when we started out.

KLARA But what makes you cry?

JOHANNA Oh no, I don't really cry to Fleet Foxes. Elliott Smith makes me cry.

KLARA Oh, yeah. You play an Elliott Smith song, Johanna will literally just be lying on the floor.

JOHANNA Yeah, I can't even listen to it. It's just too beautiful and fragile and I just want to hug him, and then he's not there and, you know, it's just…aaaah.

KLARA You can't even talk about Elliott Smith with Johanna, it's too personal!

We can change the subject! It's OK!

KLARA I've also just gotten into the Mountain Goats. Have you listened to him?

No.

KLARA OK, well if you want to hear a song that's really sad, that makes me cry, you should listen to this song. Now I can't even remember what it's called…what's it called, Johanna? [*Sings*] "I wanted you to love me like you used to…" Oh, "The Mess Inside." There we go. It's so beautiful and really sad. You have to listen to it.

I will! Is there any music people might be surprised to find out that you like?

KLARA We listen to lots of Yeah Yeah Yeahs. They're awesome.

JOHANNA Karen O is a really amazing woman.

KLARA Watching her live is…she's so cool and she looks so happy at the same time. Most people look sort of pissed off and cool, but she's just loving it, and it's really inspiring to see that. We're looking through our iTunes library…

JOHANNA We're trying to think of something that's not like folk…

KLARA I like Bollywood music. Something about it is really awesome. Billie Holiday I really love as well.

What would you say to other girls who want to make music, like around our age?

KLARA I would say just do it, but I would say do it by yourself.

JOHANNA …or with your sister.

KLARA Or with your sister. People can think you need a producer and you need someone to write songs for you. We just had a little luck because we have great parents who are really supportive and really help us. Like the first record deal that we got…they wanted to give us a record deal, but we said no because they gave us this thing that's called 360 deal, which is like basically they just want to control everything. And I was 14, and I was like, "Oh my god, I'm going to release a record and this is amazing," but our parents said we can't do this because this deal is crazy. I sort of came to my senses and I'm so happy now that we didn't sign anything like that. That would have been the worst thing. Just do it…just write and don't be afraid.

JOHANNA Do it for yourself because you need to do it.

KLARA It can be so much fun.

JOHANNA Don't do it for anyone else. And I think YouTube is probably the greatest tool for spreading your music.

KLARA Yeah, and if you want to learn to play an instrument, just go on YouTube and search for a song that you like and how to play it, just play the chords.

JOHANNA We knew like four chords when we started. If you have the right feeling and the right ideas, you don't need to be a professional guitarist or professional musician, you know? If the ideas and feeling are there, that's all that matters.

I do think there's something to be said for that attitude…I think the best decision I ever made was for us to do Rookie independently. It's so nice saying what we want.

JOHANNA That's what people like, like raw emotion that hasn't been censored. The most important thing in music for us is honesty. If you feel like you can be totally honest, you'll make good music. ♦

MEMORY LANE

It's not creepy to go through your friend's mom's life memories, right? And then share them with the world in your TEEN INTEREST magazine?

By Tavi

Rookie writer Spencer has the coolest mom ever, and she let me borrow this giant chest she has of all her photos, letters, notes, diaries, and even very old pieces of gum from her life as a kid/teenager in the '60s and '70s. She kept absolutely everything, and after looking at all of it, you'll want to do the same, and write lots of letters, and write in a diary every day. THANK YOU, Sue Miller, for letting me borrow your life's work and for letting us publish it, and thank you, house, for not burning down the whole month I kept it in my room. (This is only some of it—the rest is on our site.)

Butch Wayne
Russ
P Joe
Foo

I think
Hi! I see you

Robin Manna
3900 Enfield
Skokie, Ill 60076

Write back
real soon

EISENHOWER·USA

Thursday
Aug. 12

Dear Sue,

Howdy! What's new.
I really miss ya a lot.
It was hilarious yesterday.

...and Deb R. saw it. For the picnic Saturday I might ride on the "bicycle built for two" with Bruce and Debs might ride mine. I went outside for recess today and it seemed so strange. Ice was out too. But I was running around the playground cuz I had a bite of a marshmallow treat. After school we went to my house and then the playground. Didn't do much there. Colleen & Ruth are on the grams diet. Mr. Andrews knows about my diet and he doesn't think it's gonna work. I had to pish during math and he goes "If you didn't drink so much water you wouldn't have to go potty so much." But he let me go and I nearly crashed in to B.J. on the way cuz he was coming out for his drink. Sigh. Fran's party starts at 6:00 and we're eating first and dancing till a quarter to nine. Then from 9:00 to 11:30 we're swimming and it's all over at 12:00. You get to use a hairdryer cuz she said the ones with the longest hair get to. Remember yesterday, Welsh made you strawberry shortcake? Well, Bernie made it out of the exact same stuff. So what did you do when you got to Cally? What did they serve on the plane? Tell Danny I'll probably write to him tomorrow. Ok? Ok! Did you see any cute boys yet? Did you meet any? Did you go swimming yet? Oops, I forgot. (GEORGE) Did you go to Disneyland yet? Say Hi to your Dad, Danny, + Sam. I didn't really break my diet yet but I might get a nickel thing at Sandlers tonight. Sshhh! Don't tell. Well, I have to go now, I'm going either to Brunits or the playground. I'll tell you in tomorrows letter what happens tonight. Have fun and be sure to write to me no matter what! Bye! Bye! Ok! Bye! Bye! Love, Jeanine

Dear Sue,
Hi! How's the weather out there? What have you been doing? I'm such an idiot! Last night I was walking to the phone to call you and I remembered. Last night me and Debbie S. went to the playground. The only boys of ours out were Claude and George. You'll never guess who I was by a lot! Benjamin Clark!!! He got so cute you'd die! He has a tan and his hair is a lot lighter and his hair was in a middle part and he didn't wear anything black! Sigh! Did you see any cuties yet? Guess who's going steady? Dorothy Nime! With a junior from Roosevelt. She has a gold wedding band on the baby finger of her left hand for a ring! She says he's cute. I'm not supposed to tell anyone so keep quiet. Oh, I'm sure you're gonna tell all the Californians that Dorothy Nime is going steady! I went to choir today. I don't believe that I made it there by 8:00. I didn't know any songs. De Americans have to wear a white blouse and either pants, a skirt, or a jumper. I thought you had to wear a dress so I wore my white puff-sleeve blouse and the jumper I wore to Bub's cedar. (It was dress rehearsal) Then we had indoor recess and it was so much fun! We got to go in whichever room we wanted from 10:15 to 10:40 and we wrote on the board and played piano and other junk. Then during the period after recess I cleaned the earphones. Miss Genitis didn't even let me have a helper. But a 5th grade class was in there and a girl dried for me, not that I wanted her to!!! I got a tootsie pop and 3 tootsie rolls and I had to give it all away except half a baby tootsie roll (diet, you know) Elden was so nice to the 5th graders, it...

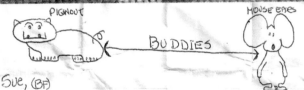

PIGNOUT   BUDDIES   HOUSE EARS

Sue, (BF)
Hi! I'm a witch! I had a dream that I went to Claude's house and there were stairs going up with white carpet and a mat for your feet by the front door and a basement and everything and I asked him and he has all that! Ain't it cool? Does Vi and Bub & Zaid remember me? I haven't seen 'em in years. I feel like an idiot! I haven't slept over in years. My mom likes you. She goes "When is Sue sleeping here?" So I go "I don't know" So she goes "She can sleep over any weekend she wants" Howard Leifman got a haircut and does he look sick! Edna Braun is gorgeous. She took all of Lynn's good looks away! (ONLY KIDDING) The only boys that didn't get a haircut are: Claude, Mark, Gregg, Cary, Steve, & Billy. Guess who I like? Not telling. Claude gets me sick. Now he's copying 257. Oh, so what. If I can let other kids. Jill's crazy. She has the most pretty, straight hair and she curls it. Same with Karen Sorenson. I brought you 2 butterscotches. Sheila Linderman looks like she's pregnant. Did you work on your newspaper? I have 3 pages so far. I can't wait til I have to make a list of what to bring to Hastings. I love lists. Jeanine (BF)

FLOWER POWER

Miss Sue Miller
c/o Wam Bolrick
5300 Oak Park Ave
Encino, California. 913

miss debbie rose
5701 n. rumball
Chicago, Illinois

IT'S SO HEAVY
I WANT IT

IT'S SO
FAT
GIVE ME
A FAT
LETTER

"hi" to your...
"hi" to da mm...

HI
HAVING
FUN
miss you

ABI SAYS "HI"

PETS I'VE HAD

2 rabbits (Fluffy & Muffy)
aprx. 20 fish (?)
2 birds (Toby & Flip)
1 squirrel (Squeaky)
1 cat (Whiskey)
1 lizard (
aprx. 10 turtles (?)
aprx. 50 fireflys (let go of course)
+ 1 DOG (P.J!!!!) (formally known
as "Millers Pride of P.J. II")

+ Neal Karbin's
June 14, 1970

NE   DEBBIE
      + MARTY

This diary belongs to:
Susie Miller

Do Not Open Without
Permission From Owner!

PRIVATE

THIS MEANS YOU!

HUH I'M A HIPPY

Boys I liked

kindergarten - Howard Ventura
1st grade - Howard Ventura
2nd grade -
3rd grade - Lenny Lowe
4th grade - Steve Skolnik, Stanley
            Charles, Irving Kolichman,
            Barry Brown
5th grade -
6th grade - Cory Skolnik, Steve Dubow,
            ~~Barry Bro~~ Brian Sherman
7th grade - Ricky Michaelis, Cory Skolnik
8th grade - none of your business

Dear Sue,
   I am in library now. We have a sub. I am so
tired. Like my bear? I think Vidor's gonna be
absent this afternoon cuz she left the work on
the board. We have gym today. Claude's cute. What
states should I wear today? Are the 6½'s
sharpened? Dorothy Nimz is wearing the tightest
and shortest sweater I have ever seen in my life. So
do you like P.J.? Do you like Ricky. Yeah, Ricky.
No, Cary. Do you? Yeah, I'm sure. No, I'm poor.
Poor! I am poor! I have no clothes! Oh, you do?
No, you have none. I wish I had your clothes.
Do you like what Debbie Rose is wearing? Do
you think Debbie Schwartz looks good with a
middle part? Do you like what Claudia's wearing?
You're right. I don't think Bruce Kramer ever
wears bells. Either does George. Either does the
new old Steve. Speaking of Steve, I hate Steve
Skolnik. Look how straight Julie's hair is! It's
pretty. Well, I have to go. Bye
                                    Jeanine

P.S. Guess what?

JULY 24   T

Apollo 11 came back
to Earth I washed
my hair.

Dear Sue,

   Hi! You are at the dentist right now and I am in your room. Hello! You just came in and you talked funny. You have to go eat now! Bye! I will keep on writing this letter. Since I am not in school, I can make it personal. But I don't want to. Well, isn't it cold outside? Yes, it is indeed! I was quite chilled when I entered your front door about ▇ minutes ago. Much to my dismay, Welsh informed me that you were not home. Now you are. Sure? Really? Gosh! Well, what are you wearing Saturday night? What are you wearing on your graduation date with Gregg? What is Debbie wearing? Where are you going? Oh, you don't know? Oh, Paris France? Oh! Well if I ever saw a sad kid I saw Fran Stein. Me and Debbie were going by Mr. Krane's room so I waved at Fran and she waved back. But she looked like she was about to cry so I go "What's wrong?" And she goes "Mark." And I go "He likes you" And she goes "No he doesn't. He's taking Debbie out for graduation." I felt so sorry for her. If I ever wanted to tell anyone a thing or two at that moment, it was Debbie Rose!!! So we did. And she said she didn't think she was gonna go with Mark. About 10 mins. before she was telling Deb S. how she couldn't wait 'til her graduation date. It's going to be so much fun. Us two couples." She knows perfectly well she'll end up going, but what could she say with me and Debbie

standing there? Well, I don't understand the math so don't do it. Did you know that Rosana bit Claude and he had to get a rabies shot? (Only kidding about the shot but she really bit him) Did you get any mail today? I didn't. I still didn't get my APRIL "SEVENTEEN" yet. I just glanced over at your mirror and UGH! There I am! I am the ugliest thing! I have a pot belly out to Africa and my face, well, my face was made for house haunting. Enuf of that! Here you are! You just walked in but you didn't say HI. You just called me a snob. I bought peanut butter kisses and a BIT O HONEY. Have to go now. You are beginning to speak. Oh, ruf, ruf. Bye.

               Jeanine

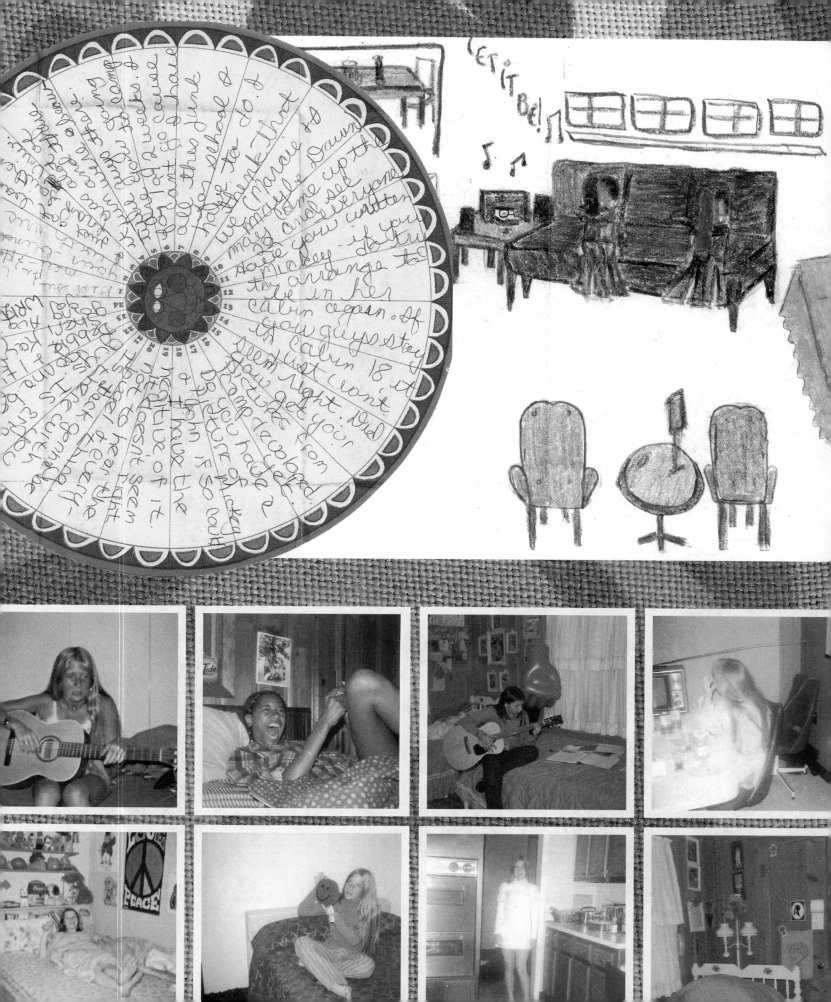

annie's room

Eleanor told us that her friend Annie's room was amazing, and she was right. Here, Annie gives us a tour.
By Eleanor

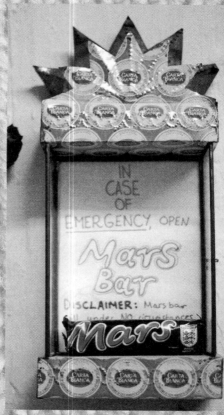

Literally the Best Thing Ever:
Joni Mitchell

I really mean it this time!

Writing by Tavi.
Illustration and lettering by Brooke.

"Literally the Best Thing Ever" is usually about not being embarrassed about bizarre fascinations with things like stickers and *iCarly* and Martha Stewart. But Joni Mitchell is no guilty pleasure. She is not a temporary obsession. She is, LITERALLY, *I REALLY MEAN IT THIS TIME*, the best thing (person) ever.

Joni Mitchell had polio as a child, which made it hard for her to form traditional guitar chords with her hands, so she made up her own tuning and chords, and sometimes played a dulcimer, which is why it is close to impossible to figure out many of her songs on guitar, and why she has had so few successful imitators!

People (like myself) write about music in the '60s like it was so PURE, but even Peter Paul & Mary were totally defined by their manager, Albert Grossman, who made them all stay inside while recording in Florida because he liked the *idea* of them all being *pale*. Joni had no contrived brand that way. She wrote her own songs; she got her own perspective of Woodstock watching news coverage in a hotel room; the song "Blue" has moments of being critical of the druggy lifestyle of her music peers. What I love is that she could be part of that music community that was so rooted in fighting against stuff, but that her own protest songs were deeply personal and less explicit.

"Woodstock" expresses unity without getting all WE'RE ALL IN THIS TOGETHER, and "Big Yellow Taxi," which starts with the lyric "They paved paradise / Put up a parking lot," somehow feels more about the *circle of life* and whatnot instead of about *society*—which, for me at least, has a more powerful effect, and hits way closer to home.

Her personal songs weren't intended to feel protest-y, but they were subversive in their own way. It's taken a long time for the romanticism of a poet or a tortured artist to stop being exclusive to dudes—and this hasn't been 100 percent resolved yet—and so some people have enjoyed the convenience of classifying Joni's work as dopey overemotional "girl" music. Which is really unfair! As much as I love Bob Dylan, it took him almost 15 years before he could take any blame for a failed relationship in his music! Joni's right there on the track "River," saying that she's "so hard to handle," that she's "selfish" and "sad," and that all this has lost her "the best baby that [she] ever had." It takes strength to admit to weakness, and to be so honest. Why, here's a convenient quote from Joni herself on the subject:

"The *Blue* album, there's hardly a dishonest note in the vocals. At that period of my life, I had no personal defenses. I felt like a cellophane wrapper on a pack of cigarettes. I felt like I had absolutely no secrets from the world and I couldn't pretend in my life to be strong. Or to be happy. But the advantage of it in the music was that there were no defenses there, either."

I think for some people the most difficult thing is coming to terms with the fact that being happy will not come as easily for them as they feel it ought to, that just smiling will usually not be enough, that being sensitive and observant sometimes makes you feel more "in touch" with "life" or whatever, but most of the time it just feels like a burden, or like everyone else is in on some kind of joke that you're taking way too seriously, and sometimes you feel like a brat because you can't just accept how things seem to be, because you have to *think* about it all and that just results in things always eventually being somewhat painful, and it sounds so pretentious, but it's not like it's *smart* thinking necessarily—it's not like you're better than anyone—it's just that you're curious about things, I guess. There has been plenty of art made by people trying to make the best out of this personal realization, from Sylvia Plath to Courtney Love to Liz Lemon. But Joni opened that door a crack or two. The range of musical artists who have named her as one of their major influences includes Prince, Madonna, Björk, Sonic Youth, Led Zeppelin, Joanna Newsom, and Regina Spektor, to name a very few.

I don't know if I think some people are more this way than others, but I do think everyone, at some point, is attacked by the monster that is puberty. Sometimes it's more than just puberty, sometimes it's depression, and often it's hard to have the articulation or awareness to create art from it. But, if there's a way to be optimistic about sadness, the thing I do like about being depressed is that that's when I get the most out of "Blue," or out of my favorite Joni song, "Cactus Tree," the last track on her first album, *Song to a Seagull*.

Each verse tells the story of a different guy trying desperately to connect with the woman he loves. I've always pictured them as multiple lovers of the same woman, though now that I think about it, I guess it could be the stories of various relationships. Nevertheless, the relationship always falls through for the same reason: "She's so busy being free." The song describes each man's story in detail—one climbs a mountain, another sails, the seventh is "bleeding from the war"— but whatever this woman is doing, it's barely described beyond that one line, repeated at the end of every verse.

The prettiest idea is that "being free" means she's hitchhiking or playing guitar in a field or some other magical 1960s stereotype thing, and travel is mentioned at some point. But one of the few hints we get about this woman is that "her heart is full and hollow," which honestly makes me think that it's possible she's not doing anything at all, except thinking and feeling and being so preoccupied with all that that it's hard to let others get too close, hard to be in on everyone's joke, hard to be satisfied with the idea of happiness all these other people created. And that makes it a little more OK to feel that way myself, because, SPOILER, sometimes people use words like "they" or "you" when they're really talking about themselves. And god, how comforting that someone else is not strong and not happy and can still get something like Joni's music out of it, and that sometimes being not strong and not happy means getting the most out of Joni's music. ♦

surviving a small town

It's not as bad as you think, we swear!
Writing by Sady. Knitting by Kathleen.

There is exactly one thing that makes Westerville, Ohio—my hometown—unique, and that is that it has no unique qualities whatsoever. It was a small town—you always ran into two or three relatives at the grocery store—but not small enough to be quaint or charming. It was Midwestern, but not Midwestern enough for us all to have super-cool accents like Frances McDormand in *Fargo*. It wasn't close to any big cities, but it wasn't in the country, either. The country would have been much cooler than what I ended up with; out there, you could farm, and get in touch with the rhythms of nature, and what have you. Maybe you could get a pony. In Westerville, we had no ponies. We just had the most boring town in America, slapped onto the side of the most boring *city* in America, which is Columbus. All of the stores were chain stores; all of the restaurants were chain restaurants; the only all-ages "punk" shows were at the local megachurch, and those were just some dudes who had grown goatees and gotten tribal tattoos so that it sounded less boring when they told us to obey our parents.

Westerville, basically, was hell. A slow, boring, Jean-Paul Sartre hell, where you are just locked in the same room, with the same people, for eternity, with nothing to do, ever. And yet, I survived. I even got to leave, eventually. But I used to feel very self-conscious about where I came from. Whenever I spent time around people with cooler upbringings—people who'd always lived in big cities, or who had grown up on vegan hippie communes, or just hipsters who had to live in the most fashionable neighborhoods at all times and who made a big point of only hanging out with the Right Sort of People—I felt like a big, boring, bland nobody. I wished I'd had an interesting life. I wished I'd been from anywhere but Westerville.

But that was before I figured certain things out. Yes, it can feel really good to get out of your small town. But before you do that, you have to live there. And there are benefits to that experience. If and when you leave, you are going to find that you are, strangely, far more interesting than many people with "interesting" life stories. Because here are some things you learn to do, living in the middle of nowhere:

1. DEVELOP UNIQUE TASTES.

For a while, it is probably going to feel as though you are alone in the world. If everyone else is into the high school football team, and you are into Lou Reed, or 20th century poetry, or (let's just say) feminist theory, well: odds are, given the small population size, that you are not going to find many other people who share your interests. And it is certainly going to be hard to find a way to act on them.

This isn't an experience that's reserved for people who have "weird taste," or even vaguely unusual taste. As it turns out, the biggest bands also skip the smallest towns. Nobody is getting Kanye West to play the sticks; his album with Jay-Z is called *Watch the Throne*, not *Watch the Delightful Service at Applebee's*. If you have a small movie theater—one town I lived in briefly only showed two movies at a time, and they were both "art movies"—then you probably miss a lot. It's easier to get clothes and books in a small town now, thanks to the internet; you don't have to rely on a single far-away mall, or the tiny local bookstore. (Yes, it's charming and independent in theory, but less so when you see that the only display table is reserved for *Harry Potter*. And has been since 1997.) But it's still hard to meet new people who can tell you about what's happening, in terms of clothes and books. In fact, it's hard to meet new people, generally. If you ever feel like you're in a social rut in your small town, well: I hope you like that rut. Because you have already met everybody, and everybody has already met you, and you are pretty much stuck with them.

But, as it turns out, a bit of isolation is a good thing. People who grow up with the option of joining whole subcultures dedicated to their tastes always have to deal with the question of whether they'd still have the same tastes if they didn't have those subcultures. They have grown up learning about this stuff from others, and have consequently learned not only *what* to like, but *how* to like it.

You, on the other hand, are free. No one is going to tell you what to like, or how to like it, or even where to find it. So you figure out how to rely on your own judgment. This is what's referred to as "taste," for the record. You're developing yours—by finding what you like, thinking about why you like it, and standing by that even when people disagree with you.

2. GET RESEARCH SKILLS.

The Youth of America have a unique and wonderful blessing, compared with previous generations. That blessing is called Tumblr. When you want to find out about things, you've got a billion people talking about what they think is cool, and sometimes posting snippets of it online for your enjoyment.

In my day, we had no Tumblr. What we had was called *Factsheet 5*, and it was a directory of every more-or-less prominent zine in America. (Also, articles with headlines like, "WILL THE INTERNET REPLACE ZINES? Ha Ha, Never," and "*Factsheet 5*: 10 or 15 Years From Now, Teenagers Will Definitely Know What This Magazine Is.") I spent weekends poring through *Factsheet 5* with a highlighter, marking zines that sounded interesting, and figuring out how I could get my allowance to cover as many of them as possible.

You guys: this was so much better than Tumblr. Granted, I'm old and cranky. But having to find cool stuff the hard way taught me so much. Aside from that whole "making your own judgments" thing we covered earlier, it taught me things like:

every piece of art has a history, and a context. If an artist that you enjoy mentions having liked something, even just in passing, track down whatever it is they mentioned. Learn the names of people who are in bands you like, and then look to see if any of those people have been in other bands; if you enjoy a nonfiction book, read its bibliography. Track down those related books, and related bands, until you have a whole world of stuff to enjoy, not just isolated pieces. And get a library card. Seriously, this is the dorkiest advice I will ever give you, but: get a dang library card! You would be shocked at how much easier it makes things. My library had an AV section stocked by someone who was really into '80s and early-'90s indie-ish stuff; I found out what Sonic Youth and Pavement were by just checking out a few CDs with interesting covers every week. That's how I found out who David Lynch was, too. Oh, and if you are into clothes, let me tell you a secret: That crappy Salvation Army nearby? It's actually better than 88 percent of the "vintage" stores in large cities. You can get a dress for $10 that would cost at least $50 elsewhere, and there is far more interesting stuff to find, because it hasn't been picked over, because *no one knows how great it is but you.*

Weirdly, it works this way socially, too. It's a cliché to say that small-town Midwesterners are "nice." I don't think we are; we can be as sexist, racist, homophobic, or just plain mean as anyone else. But we are tactful. In smaller towns, people will treat you like a huge jerk, but they usually won't *call* you a huge jerk. And this is because we know that if we give in to our natural urges and call you a stupid buttmunch, *we are going to see you again.* We are going to see you every time we go to the grocery store, and it is always going to be awkward, and even if we think we have gotten away from you it will eventually turn out that we are dating your second cousin, so *guess who is coming to our wedding, because it's you.*

I did not like being unable to call people jerks. So I moved to New York, where I can be a misanthropic judgeypants without reservation until the day I die, peacefully alone, surrounded by cats, as nature intended. But I will not deny that I made closer and more tolerant friendships in Ohio than I have almost anywhere else. Because the same thing applies: If your town has a very limited number of people, you can't just avoid people because they have unusual taste in music, or slightly different politics, or seem kind of weird. You have to learn what there is to like about their personal weirdness. And since there's nothing going on in town, and you can't just stand next to each other at a concert, you actually have to *talk* to each other.

Sure, on one hand, there is nothing cool going on in your town, no one cool to hang out with, and nothing to do. On the other hand: are you kidding me? There's decades and decades' worth of cool stuff out there, publicly available, and cheap or even free. There are some of the most unique people you'll ever meet—and you have nothing but time in which to get to know one another.

Your only problem, really, is that the new cool stuff isn't happening in your town. Which brings us to:

3. GET CREATIVE.

Oh, there are no cool bands in your town? Nobody is playing shows? You wish you were able to go somewhere and hear live music, specifically catered to your own tastes, whenever you want? I'm sorry. I couldn't hear you, over the sound of your NOT LEARNING HOW TO PLAY GUITAR.

If you want new, cool art in your life, you have three options. One, you can stand around with a bored look on your face and wait for some cool new art to fall out of the sky. Two, you can locate a supply—which is frequently hard, if you live in a small town with few resources. Or, three, you can *create* the supply. You can take these amazing qualities of yours that we've been talking about—the taste that comes from having to cultivate and rely on your own judgment, the knowledge that comes from having nothing better to do than look, hard, for stuff to like—and you can create what is literally the *newest, coolest piece of art you can personally imagine.*

I know, I know: You don't know how to play guitar yet. Or write short stories, or start a blog, or paint, or direct short films, or sew your own clothes, or take photos. Maybe you've tried that stuff, and it was really hard, and you did a bad job. You know, I had a friend with the exact same problem, once. Her name was "Literally Everyone Who Has Ever Been Good at Anything, Ever, JEEZ." It's fine to have a rough start. That's how you learn.

It might take you some time to learn your trade. You will probably be bad at first. You will create a few things you're not proud of. And no matter how good you are, the art you create as a teenager will be very different from the art you create as an adult. And that's fine. The only way a bad artist ever became a better artist was by *making more art.* Classes, feedback from your friends, editors, and all of that: they're nice. But you are never, ever going to get better at something you don't actually do. And the good news is, if you enjoy creating art, living in a boring small town gives you lots of time to practice. It's not like there's anything else going on tonight, right?

So, let's take a look at you! And all of these awesome skills you picked up, living in a terminally uncool small town. First of all, you learned to be an individual, with individual tastes—and to analyze and defend your tastes. Seems like it might be useful in conversation! Then, you learned how to dig up new, cool stuff—even stuff that's relatively obscure—so it seems like you probably know a lot. Another fun quality in a friend or companion! And then, finally, out of sheer desperation, you learned to practice an art form your own damn self. Which is relatively rare. And, given that you've done nothing but practice since forever, you're probably pretty darn good at it by now.

Yes, Small Town Girl: Hang your head in shame. For lo, due to your not having grown up on a hippie commune and/or in Williamsburg or Portland or Austin, you have turned yourself into that least interesting of all things: a unique, articulate, knowledgeable person with great taste who can spot cool things before they're popular, and is also a talented artist. DAMN! Who's going to want to hang out with you now? ◆

winter sweaters: a taxonomy

Know your knitwear.

Writing by Tavi and Anna. Illustrations by Cynthia.
Playlist by Rookie staff.

TYPE: THE COLLEGE SWEATSHIRT

DEFINING CHARACTERISTICS: OFTEN A HOODIE, WITH THE NAME OF A SCHOOL PROUDLY EMBLAZONED OR CHEAPLY EMBOSSED ON THE FRONT.

AS SEEN ON: COLLEGE STUDENTS, ALUMNI, AND AMBITIOUS HIGH-SCHOOLERS.

WHEN TO WEAR IT: A SUBTLE WAY TO ANNOUNCE TO THE REST OF YOUR GRADUATING CLASS THAT YOU GOT ACCEPTED EARLY INTO COLLEGE.

TYPE: THE COSBY SWEATER

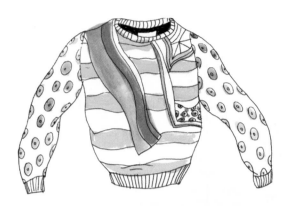

DEFINING CHARACTERISTICS:

IMAGINE THERE WAS AN EXPLOSION AT THE PAINT-AND-GEOMETRIC SHAPES FACTORY AND THE ONLY THING LEFT WAS SWEATERS. THIS WOULD BE THE RESULT.

AS SEEN ON:

BILL COSBY, HIP YOUTHS.

WHEN TO WEAR IT: YOU WANT PEOPLE TO MAKE FACES IN RESPONSE TO YOUR APPEARANCE.

TYPE: THE ARGYLE

DEFINING CHARACTERISTICS:

A PATTERN OF OVERLAPPING DIAMONDS, OFTEN IN CONTRASTING COLORS. LOOKS BEST ON A SWEATER VEST.

AS SEEN ON: PREPS, NERDS, PROFESSORS.

WHEN TO WEAR IT: TO FEEL ALL SMART AND STUDIOUS IN ORDER TO GET HOMEWORK DONE; YOU GO STRAIGHT FROM GRADUATION TO RETIREMENT AND DECIDE TO PLAY GOLF.

homeward bound

1. wake up - arcade fire
2. the chanukah song - adam sandler
3. sloop john b - the beach boys
4. make it home - juliana hatfield
5. santa claus is back in town - elvis presley
6. stand - r.e.m.
7. our house - crosby stills nash & young
8. choo choo train - the heart beats
9. care of cell 44 - the zombies
10. i ain't in checotah anymore - carrie underwood
11. place (naive melody) - talking heads
12. home - low

TYPE: THE CARDIGAN

DEFINING CHARACTERISTICS:

BUTTONS OR OTHER TYPE OF FASTENERS UP THE FRONT.

AS SEEN ON:

GRANDMAS, LIBRARIANS, MR. ROGERSES

WHEN TO WEAR IT: WHEN ACTING AS ONE HALF OF THE
BILL COSBY AND MR. ROGERS CHRISTMAS SPECIAL.

TYPE: THE CABLE KNIT

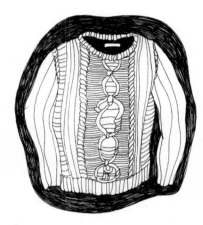

DEFINING CHARACTERISTICS:

CHUNKY BRAIDED KNITTING PATTERN.

AS SEEN ON: GRANDPAS, FISHERMEN, GRANDPAS WHO ARE
FISHERMEN.

WHEN TO WEAR IT: A GRANDPA WHO FISHES.

TYPE: CHRISTMAS SWEATER

TYPE: THE BALLERINA

DEFINING CHARACTERISTICS:

WRAPAROUND STYLE, OFTEN TIED WITH
A RIBBON AND COMING IN PASTEL SHADES.

AS SEEN ON:
BALLERINAS WARMING UP; GIRLS WHO LOOK LIKE
THEY PROBABLY NEVER POOP.

WHEN TO WEAR IT: YOU ARE AN ACTUAL BALLERINA
AND THIS ONE IS BORING TO YOU.

DEFINING CHARACTERISTICS:

SNOWMEN, REINDEER, AND SANTAS. OFTEN EMBELLISHED
WITH RIBBONS AND BELLS, JUST IN CASE WHOEVER'S WEARING
IT ISN'T ALREADY OBNOXIOUS ENOUGH.

AS SEEN ON: AUNTS, SEVENTH-GRADE HEALTH TEACHERS.

WHEN TO WEAR IT: IRONIC SWEATER PARTIES; TO TEACH
MIDDLE SCHOOLERS ABOUT CONDOMS.

ON DISCOVERY:
AN INTERVIEW WITH DANIEL CLOWES

Wherein we talk about comics, Cool Dads, Daria, *and whether there is any hope for my generation.*

By Tavi

This interview is super long, so I'll make this intro super short. Daniel Clowes is responsible for such beauteous works as *Ghost World*, *Mister Wonderful*, *Ice Haven*, *Wilson*, and, most recently, *The Death-Ray*. He's also partially responsible for comics being thought of as a real art form nowadays. Most important, he is responsible for the line "You guys up for some reggae tonight?" And, while I may not be up for reggae, I am up for you reading this interview! Haha! Haaaa. Ah, sometimes I hate myself. Enjoy!

TAVI Many of your characters are kind of pathetic and lonely, but somehow your observations seem more compassionate than condescending. Are you concerned at all with making sure you're not making fun of them, or does it just end up that way? Do you think you've ever made fun?

DANIEL CLOWES I try not to worry about that too much, but I try to make fun of myself more than I would make fun of anybody else. I try to hold myself to the same amount of scrutiny that I would any of my characters, so I would hope anything I do never comes across like I'm trying to show myself as being better than my characters or making a point about how people shouldn't live this way or anything like that.

Do you find it comforting or terrifying that people can relate to characters that are closer to you?

It is comforting. In a way that's the whole idea, I think: to try to get across things

that I feel are so personal that they actually can't be put into words, trying to create characters that will express these feelings that I can't quite articulate, and to have people actually respond to those things in an emotional way. That kind of connection with other people, I think—that's what you can hope for when you're doing this kind of stuff.

Our theme this month is Home, and Enid Coleslaw [from *Ghost World*] seems to have kind of a mixed relationship with her hometown, as do the citizens of Ice Haven, and a lot of that is about being surrounded by a kind of low-brow culture. So I was really surprised to learn that you grew up in Hyde Park, Chicago, with a professor grandpa talking with other smart people like Saul Bellow in the next room.

At the time it was just boring. It was like, *I wish he'd just shut up and come to dinner so we can eat.* It wasn't until years later when I heard other people talk about the people who had been over at my house that I realized, oh yeah, those guys are actually famous. I just figured they were other old boring professors like my grandpa.

My dad went to Woodstock, and when I was younger he tried to get me and my sisters into that music, and I thought it was really lame, and then later I liked it and I felt like I'd been cheated.

[*Laughs*] You'd been cheated 'cause you didn't get to go to Woodstock?

No, because my parents had tried to make us like that stuff first.

Oh, I see, so you didn't get the joy of discovering it on your own.

Yeah, and then I thought it was lame for a long time.

I think about that a lot with my son. I don't want to inflict the stuff I like onto him. He's only eight, so right now I could get him to like anything, pretty much, but when he's a few years older I really don't want him to respond to anything because I like it too much or not enough. I want him to sort of find his way into his own stuff, so it's something I have to constantly modulate. I don't want him to associate this music with me, I want him to discover it on his own and then I'll go, "Well, I happen to have all their records!"

That's healthier, I think. There was an article on the *Onion* that was like, "Twelve-Year-Old Girl Isolated From Peers Because of Cool Dad." Her dad makes her listen to the Talking Heads and everything, and then she can't relate to anyone else.

And now is the era of the Cool Dad. I know lots of parents who I just think, like, *God, if my parents had been like that I would've been into all this cool stuff.* Luckily they weren't, so I discovered all that stuff on my own and they sort of disdainfully shook their heads at the stupid stuff I was interested in. But there are a lot of things that I don't respond to. I'm not into video games, so I can just see my son becoming, like, a video-game tester as his job or something. Developing video games.

Nerds and underdogs are in a weird place right now where they're kind of cultural insiders. How important do you think it is for there to be outsiders and a counter-culture?

That's probably a bigger question than I can answer. I used to feel sort of a kinship with people who were into stuff I couldn't be less interested in. Things like fantasy novels about elves. I realized those people were sort of seeking some kind of comfort in fiction, in this kind of escapist literature, that I could kind of relate to as a teenager, and now those kind of people just seem like…that's everybody, you know? Like everybody is into the kind of stuff that only a very small group of damaged, shut-in nerds were into back when I was a teenager. So it's really kind of hard to understand that world. I can't quite grasp that a girl in high school would see the Thor movie. That is just unfathomable to me. When I was in high school, if I'd gone up to a girl and said, "Would you like to go read some of my Thor comics with me?" they would've just thought I was the lowest form of human life. I was actually on the subway in New York and saw this Attractive Teenage Couple, and the guy was like, "Hey, wanna go see *Thor* tonight?" and the girl was like, "Yeah, yeah." And I just thought, *That is just blowing my mind that that is happening right in front of me.*

I feel like every actor will be in an interview and be like, "I'm such a nerd secretly! I like *Star Wars!*"

Every actor! It's always like, you know, Brad Pitt—"I was a total nerd!" No you weren't!

You're Brad Pitt!

It's impossible!

You've talked in the past about the depressing strip-mall-ness and commercialization of the world, and you've talked about the greatness of discovery being kind of lost now because of the internet. So I'm wondering if people my age have anything to be happy about.

[*Laughs*] No, you don't! No, it's just a whole different apparatus for finding things. You used to be able to drive across America and every town would have a little junk shop, and you'd go in there and you could find some weird old book or something that you'd never heard of, and that would lead to you seeking out other stuff. You used to have this sense that if you just kind of drove off the freeway a little bit, you'd run into some interesting little pockets of culture. And now you're just gonna see another Applebee's or whatever. All that stuff is gone. It's been plowed over. So really the only way to find stuff now is on the internet. I could tell you right now about some obscure filmmaker and you could know more about him by midnight than I would've been able to find out in 10 years when I was your age. But I don't know that it would mean much to you unless you really connected to the guy and kept following it and doing more and more research. It'd just be like, *Yeah, I know about that guy,* and then you'd move on to the next thing. There's something about having it be a mystery that you have to solve and figure out that really connected you to this weird culture back then.

On days when I'm more optimistic I feel like then the real good stuff stands out, though.

That's certainly true. It also used to be like, you'd buy an album by a recording artist and there'd be one or two good songs on it, and there'd be all the rest that were just kind of to fill up the album, and you'd work your way through that and learn to like the other songs after a while, and then you'd wait till the next album came out. And now it sort of feels like everything is all the greatest hits. You learn about a musician and you immediately can figure out what their 10 greatest songs are, and you just listen to those and you don't experience the full breadth of their failures and mishaps and all that stuff. I feel like that's how all culture is. And I'm as guilty as anybody else now— if I hear about an author or something I go straight for their most well-known book and read that first, and, you know, I don't have that experience of kind of building up to that. You don't wanna read the rest of their books after that because you figure, *Well, I've already read the best one. It's not gonna be much better than that.*

I hadn't thought about that. Maybe we should be using this interview for a site for people who don't like the internet or something.

[*Laughs*] Like a site where you have to write a letter to somebody and they'll print it out.

Exactly. So we've had a couple articles this month about growing up somewhere boring and how to make the best of it, and Enid is kind of a reference for us for that. How would you explain her attitude toward growing up in that kind of environment?

You know, people used to write reviews [of *Ghost World*] and say, "She's cynical and depressed," and I think she was the exact opposite of that. She figured out a way to make her life more exciting just by imagining the things around her being charged with some kind of mystery and energy that's possibly not actually there, but that she's giving to them. She's able to look at people on the street and imagine these huge, important stories about them and to create drama out of very small things in her life. And I think that's kind of the best you can hope for when you're stuck like she is.

She is often lumped together with other moody young women like Daria or Margot Tenenbaum. We're guilty of that on Rookie. Do you see that comparison or no?

Daria came along after *Ghost World*, and I always felt like it was influenced by it, though I have no great specific evidence for that, so I was always somewhat resentful of *Daria*, though I've actually never watched it. But I'm sure there was sort of a zeitgeist of that type of character floating around in the air at the time. Enid first appeared back in 1993 when I did that first episode of *Ghost World* [in *Eightball*], and it really felt like you weren't seeing that type of person at all in any type of culture.

You've often used settings that are sort of boring-town-y, but it's not a Stepford, white-picket-fence, creepy-happy thing. Do you consciously avoid that?

Yeah, 'cause my comics aren't really about suburbia ever, you know. I never lived in surbubia. I lived in Hyde Park my whole life, and then I moved to a horrible neighborhood in Brooklyn, and I've lived here in Oakland, which is another urban environment, for the last 20 years, so I never lived in the suburbs at all. It's really a matter of kind of paring down the environment that the characters live in so it's not about where they live as much as who they are and how they're interacting. The places they live in are supposed to be kind of nondescript. And it's always funny, 'cause people will say, you know, "I thought that was really cool that you set *Ghost World* in North Oak, Virginia!" or some other place that I've never been in my life, just because it has something that feels like where they live. That's sort of the sign that you're onto something, when you can make people feel like it's about them in some way.

People have written that the characters of *Ghost World* and *The Death Ray* are these

average, relatable teens. Do you think of them that way, and did you set out to create characters people would relate to?**

You know, I've never set out to create a character that people could relate to, because I think people tend to flatter themselves in terms of…if you want to create a character that people relate to, it's usually a character that people imagine themselves to be, somebody who's sort of heroic and courageous but not recognized as such by others. And I always found that to be kind of false. I feel like it's sort of pandering to a certain kind of narcissism on the reader's part. So I'm always trying to create characters that seem like plausible human beings in whatever situation they're in. Which to me usually means that they're sort of erratic and scared and confused and trying to move toward their own comfort and safety at all times. That seems to be the general principle of how humanity operates.

There's a kind of anti-art-school feel to your comic *Art School Confidential* and the art-class scenes in *Ghost World*. What do you have to say for yourself now that there are comics courses in art school and people like you are so fancy?

The thing is, all that stuff [in *Art School Confidential* and *Ghost World*] is a response to being in art school in 1985. It was really such a different world. I used to tell my teachers I wanted to do comics and I would try to show them Robert Crumb and Art Spiegelman and other examples of people doing really great comics that have clear value to them, and they'd just shake their heads, you know, like, "Why would you want to do that?" And then they'd try to teach you whatever weird thing they were doing, and it was always something like neon sculpture or something. Like, that's fine for you to do that, but why would you ever presume that's what anybody else should be doing? It was really deeply frustrating. You were kind of put in a world with these people who should've been the very first people to recognize that comics could be a viable art form, and they were the most resistant of all.

What kept you wanting to do comics, despite all that?

Of course I tried to do all that stuff, but it was literally a guessing game. I would just throw some stuff together like, "Maybe this'll work?" Every once in a while it would be like, "This is great! You get an A!" and I'd have no idea why. I'd try it again the next week and it's like, "No, this is terrible, you get a D." I had no clue what it was all about. Still don't. Luckily I had a really clear sense of what I wanted to do, and I was sort of fueled by the resistance. It made me feel like I should really dig in my heels—I had that kind of adolescent thing of, "I'll show them! I'll prove them wrong!" And all these schools that teach comics, I don't know that anybody good ever comes out of any of those. I don't know, I think it's something you have to learn on your own. Pretty much any art form is like that. You can learn a few little basic tricks, but you gotta figure out your own way of doing things.

A lot of typical superhero stories have that "I'll show them!" attitude, but in *The Death-Ray* Andy doesn't really seem to want to get back at people who made fun of him.

If I think back to myself at that time, I would've felt like I was being oppressed by others, like really seriously, but if I were to look around and try to find a specific target for my anger, it would've been pretty tough. Most people don't bother with a kid like Andy. It's not like they spend time picking on him—they just don't think about him ever. That's hard to respond to. So I wanted to capture that feeling of having a desire for revenge but not necessarily having a target for it.

The book kind of loops back to that, to ignoring versus negative attention. When characters are killed there's no bloody death scene—they just disappear and aren't on the next panel.

Yeah, I find that really disturbing, too. I used to have dreams a lot when I was a kid about, like, people disappearing—like they'd just be *gone*. And I'd wake up screaming. It was extremely horrifying. Somehow a body riddled with bullets is like, *Well, there it is, and now I understand why they are no longer living.* But the thought of just *not existing* and being *gone* is really terrifying. There's something about drawing comics, too, where sometimes I'll draw a guy in the background or something and he doesn't look right and I'll just erase him, and then I'll have this feeling of *I just obliterated this human life.* Like, here was a guy who never existed before and I put him there and now he's gone, and there is something really disturbing about that.

Have any of your characters ever made their way into your dreams?

Every once in a while, yeah. I'll have a dream where one of my characters is just like, a guy.

Are they weird real-life versions or are they drawings?

The few times I can think of they're real-life versions, which is very disturbing.

You've talked about being into comedy like *MAD* magazine growing up. What comedy do you like today?

I like all the typical stuff, like Sacha Baron Cohen and Ricky Gervais and all those guys. *Curb Your Enthusiasm.* There's actually this new show on HBO by Mike White called *Enlightened*, with Laura Dern, and it's so subtle that it's not even a comedy—it's so close to just being like a really unbearable soap opera or something, but it's *just* over the edge of being comedy, and I find myself laughing my head off at it without really understanding why. It's brilliantly on that razor's edge. But, I don't know, I'm sort of a sucker for anything that's even trying to be funny.

Ghost World **the movie was nominated for an Academy Award for "best adapted screenplay." Was that weird for you? Like,** first you couldn't even get your art teachers to understand why you wanted to do comics and then you had to do Oscars stuff?

Yes, it's quite a leap. That's kind of how it is being any kind of an author, I think. You're spending so much time alone where you're just desperately hoping the FedEx guy will come so you have somebody to talk to during the day. You're just living inside your own head in this little tiny microworld in your studio, and then all of a sudden you're out speaking in front of Russell Crowe or something. There's no in-between, like where you go and speak to five people and then 20 people—it's just you're doing one or the other, so I think it's actually really bad for your mental state. I much prefer the staying-at-home part of it.

It's a very monklike way of living. Would you ever be able to share a studio?

No, I can't imagine that. I've actually always wanted to hire somebody to help me do stuff, and it would save me a ton of time, but the thought of just having someone in my studio…I'd feel like I'd have to make lunch for them and constantly entertain them. I don't have the personality to just turn everything off and ignore people and focus on my work. I have to really be completely alone.

What was influential to you growing up, visually?

Just the whole world. As a kid I loved the look of the early '60s, kind of the pre-hippie era, just the haircuts and clothes and the way women dressed—it was really appealing. And then all of a sudden people started wearing, like, filthy clothes and messy hair and stuff. That seemed really hideous and horrible to me. It definitely relates to what was going on in my life at the time because, as with many kids who grew up then, my family was just disintegrating while all that stuff came in, so it represented this chaos that was entering my life. But I still have an affection for that pre-1968 look, that kind of saturat-ed Technicolor look. That seems like the real world to me, or like the way things should be.

Say someone finishes this interview and wants to get into reading comics. Where should they start? Other than your new book.

[*Laughs*] Yes, I would start with all of my work! You know, the publishers I've worked with, Drawn & Quarterly and Fantagraphics, you kind of can't go wrong with 90 percent of the stuff they publish. There are great artists like Robert Crumb and the Hernandez brothers that have these gigantic bodies of work that could take years of your life just to get through, and then there are other artists that have much less out there that are much easier to navigate, like Chester Brown, who has made four or five books, but they're all amazing. There's lots of stuff out there. I wouldn't recommend anything specific because I feel like we're at the point now with comics where people can kind of figure out on their own what they like.

What would you say to someone who wants to make comics? Not about a career as a cartoonist, but about the actual process of making them?

A good way to start is to make comics about your own life. Sort of a good way to learn how to create fiction, if that's what you wanna do, is if you're really honest and do something that feels like you're revealing a secret to people. I've never read anything like that that isn't interesting, no matter how crudely done it was. And I would always say don't try too hard starting out. You get people who have been doing comics for two weeks and they're like, "I'm gonna do a 500-page graphic novel about the Civil War!" or something. It's like, you're gonna do three pages of that and then never ever draw comics again, because you'll realize what a horrible, boring idea that would be. I would say just keep it to two or three pages and then build up from there. But don't overshoot your abilities. ✦

HOME
IS JUST A WORD

Stills from a movie that exists only in Petra's imagination.

Photography by Petra. Lettering by Brooke.
Thanks to Eva for modeling and Madelyne Beckles for styling.

- He never returned.

- I thought no one could break me

- I think we should keep it a secret

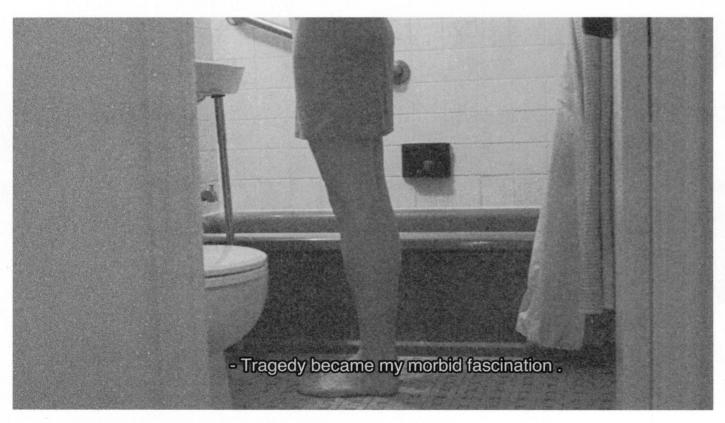

- Tragedy became my morbid fascination .

- I just had to escape.

DANCING ON MY OWN

1. Dance More · the DOGS
2. Tightrope · Janelle Monáe (ft. Big Boy)
3. Pull Shapes · the Pipettes
4. Blister in the Sun · Violent Femmes
5. Oogum Boogum · Brenton Wood
6. Super BASS · NICKI MINAJ
7. Dancing On My Own · ROBYN
8. GIRLS FM · Happy BIRTHDAY
9. My Boyfriend's BACK · the Angels
10. CHANGES · David Bowie
11. Troublemaker · Shannon & the Clams
12. HEART of Glass · Blondie
13. Huddle Formation · The Go! TEAM
14. Do You Wanna Dance? · the Beach Boys
15. Toucha, Toucha, Touch Me · Rocky HORROR PICTURE show
16. In the Sun · She & Him
17. I want you BACK · Jackson 5
18. Twist And Shout · the Cramps
19. Cruel · St. Vincent
20. Signed, Sealed, Delivered · Stevie Wonder
21. Hold Me Tight · the BEATLES
22. Dazed · Bleached
23. Crocodile Rock · Elton John

JANUARY 2012: UP ALL NIGHT

Happy New Year, Rookies! Our theme this month is Up All Night, which means the partying kind of up all night, but also the staying up late to watch TV alone or write a paper kind of up all night. Nighttime is the BEST time for the latter because the whole world is asleep (except like half the world but whatever). It's a kind of alone that doesn't feel lonely. There's a real freedom to it, actually. Nobody will interrupt your Netflix marathon. It's easier to be creative, since you're less aware of other people and their annoying *brains* and *opinions*. It is not actually that great for paper-writing. I hate myself every time I am writing a paper at 3:00 AM. I do not condone it. Here is a list of names I have saved school papers under on my desktop:

poop farts, piece of shit, i hate everything, i hate everyone, lol cry, ugh

Though I may be too busy mumbling under my breath about school and agonizing over what to call a file that would soon become "poop farts" to actually partake in club culture, I'm fascinated by it, especially all those wacky kidz who have the stamina to boogie into the wee hours of the morn. Also, glam rock! For some reason glam rock made a lot of sense for Up All Night. David Bowie is a real hero of ours this month.

And as far as going dancing goes, I can get down in the privacy of my own home just fine! Here, actually, is my bedroom-dancing playlist (facing page). Proceed with no caution, and all of the confidence of Maria von Trapp.

I'm writing this right now at night, so I'm in that weird mode I was talking about where you don't comprehend the idea of other people existing and having their own opinions, so I'm ready to write, like, anything. Actually, I'm feeling like really artistic right now. Hark! An acrostic poem just poured out of my soul onto my computer!

U is for typing "U" instead of "you" because I'm tired.
P is for "Please send pizza," an email I frequently get from Anaheed when it's late.
A is for Amy Poehler, because nighttime is obviously the best time to watch *Saturday Night Live*, and Amy is my favorite cast member of recent years. Some of my favorite sketches of hers are "Kaitlin at the Mall," "Bronx Beat," "Live With Regis and Kelly," and the Palin rap.
L is for "loser," a thing my sister might say when she comes in my room late at night to see I'm testing different cereals in a jar of Nutella while lying in bed.
L is for lying in bed with a jar of Nutella testing different cereals in it.
N is for Nutella.
I is for I don't know why the guy who invented Nutella hasn't called me to be best friends yet; I just dedicated four lines of my dang acrostic poem to his product and now I really want Nutella and like if it was free that would be really cool OK thanks.
G is for "GNO," one of my favorite Hannah Montana songs.
H is for "HNO," the working title for a song I'm writing, short for Harry's Night Out, about a middle-aged man getting up in the middle of the night and going outside to water his plants.
T is for This poem is over I am going to bed.

BURN BABY BU

Ooh, shiny.

By Petra

All clothes and styling, Petra's own. Thanks to Maimouna and Talvi for modeling and Anna Collins for doing makeup.

AN ACTUALLY USEFUL ARTICLE ABOUT DRESSING FOR A PARTY

Without any mention of your body shape or your style personality.

By Jamie

Every article about dressing for a party focuses on things that I don't care about. I mean, thanks, lady/teen magazine, it's really nice that you took the time to liken my body shape to a piece of fruit and then pick out some items that are flirty or edgy, but what I choose to wear to a party usually has nothing to do with how I am shaped or what my "style personality" is, and more to do with how I want the night to proceed. Parties are condensed pockets of potential where anything can happen if only I go into the evening with the proper outlook. Getting dressed is just one way to set the tone.

Thus, instead of an article about outfits, this is an article about strategy. I talked to a bunch of my friends about how they decide what to wear for a night out, and distilled their answers into a few tactical plans. All of these are viable party-outfit strategies, because you are a real human with a diverse range of moods, and not a pear-shaped hanger for statement necklaces under $25 that will catch your crush's eye from across the room.

"I CAME TO DANCE."

This is probably the most honorable party-dressing motive. You aren't at the party to network or hook up or cry in the corner—you're just there to have a good time. Wear flat, closed-toe shoes and clothes that won't make you overheat. Jeans are good for maximum coverage if you plan on dipping it extra low, but outside of that they don't do too much to actually enhance your moves. I like combining leggings with a fringy or twirly dress that moves when you move (just like that). A dress with pockets is doubly convenient, because it lets you leave your purse at home. If you want to wear makeup, go with bright lipstick instead of heavy eye makeup, which will run when you sweat. Ignore that advice if you are going for a "Thriller" type of thing.

SPONTANEOUS UNPLANNED COSTUME PARTY.

If you are like me, you are probably disappointed by most of the year's conspicuous lack of opportunities to wear costumes. It's like, October is a creativity feast, and then all of a sudden I'm expected to dress like myself for 11 contiguous months? No. Like most rules I disagree with, I have chosen not to follow this one. On nights when I feel like being someone else, for whatever reason, I wear a costume. A bizarre hat. A bowtie. A hula skirt. In movies, people who wear costumes to non-costume parties are always made out to be losers, but in real life, everyone loves costumes. You'll be drowning in high-fives by the end of the night.

TRYING TO TOUCH TONGUES OR SOMETHING.

About half of the people that I surveyed agreed that sometimes they are just trying to hook up. On these nights, I don my Boobs Shirt. I would describe this garment in greater detail, but you know what I am talking about, because you have an equivalent article of clothing—that thing that makes you feel confident. Wear it. I don't care if it is an oversize rugby shirt or a micro mini. If you feel sexy in a snowsuit, you have your outfit right there. Your chances of getting some at a party increase exponentially when you genuinely feel like you look sexy. Forget what some magazine or salesperson tells you is sexy and just wear what makes you feel good.

YOU CAN JUST WEAR A REALLY GENERIC OUTFIT OR SWEATPANTS.

Sometimes I just hate myself and I don't want to go to a party and I try on 500 outfits and cry on my bed a little and then refresh Facebook a dozen times in search of the meaning of life. And then I go out.

I'm not sure what happens between the breakdown and getting in the car to head to the party, but at some point I choose an outfit. This is a great time to pick something really normative. I'm a strongempoweredfeministwoman as much as the next person, but sometimes I just need to not think about things and blend in. Wear whatever you think everyone else is going to wear, or just wear sweatpants. Be a wallflower. You are already impressive because you are leaving the house while feeling crappy—bravo! You are an American hero. Now you can leave the party early if you want because I just gave you permission.

ASK ALL THE QUESTIONS A MOM WOULD ASK.

Is it raining? Is it cold? Do you have to wait at a bus stop at night? Do you have a long walk? Is there going to be a non-gross place to put your jacket when you get there? Will there be air conditioning? All of these are important questions to ask if you are trying to plan a purely functional outfit. Use common sense to solve problems! Walking far? Wear flats. Cold? Bring a coat. This gets a little trickier when more than two factors are combined. Cold outside but hot in the party room, with no good place to put your jacket? Wear two crappy sweatshirts that you won't be devastated about losing or ruining (hello thrift store). Planning a successful outfit under complex circumstances can get challenging. This is a good time to consult a friend who will also be attending.

IGNORE ALL OF THIS AND DRESS LIKE YOUR REGULAR SELF.

Nobody cares what you wear to a party and sometimes it isn't worth the energy to construct an elaborate backstory or motivation for your outfit. Just wear what you wore all day. You look fine and will probably have an OK time. ◈

LITERALLY THE BEST THING EVER:
GLITTER

It needed to be said.

Writing by Laia. Illustration by Minna.

Is there anything in this world that brings an instant feeling of elation quite like glitter does? Some people enjoy the laughter of a newborn baby or a puppy falling on its butt or whatever, but glitter is the universal symbol for awesomeness and parties and fun.

And so it is that girls in particular just love glitter. I generalize because it's true. Boys like glitter when they're little. We all do as we sit at our communal tables in preschool and draw trees and faces and monsters in white glue on construction paper, which we then douse with glitter and bring home to our parents like a treasure. Then someone is all, "Glitter is for girls!" So boys dump it aside to go play in mud and we don't even care 'cause we're all, "More glitter for us!"

But: WHY? Why is it that teeny-tiny pieces of shiny paper can be the thing that lifts us up to a higher level of sparkle-consciousness? I don't even know what glitter is actually made of, but does it matter? I just assume it's, like, tiny pieces of stars crushed and bottled for our enjoyment.

Growing up, I put a lot of effort into rejecting stereotypically girly things (mostly I was just really against the color pink), but even in my fervent feminism, glitter never offended me. I had blue glitter sunglasses that were my signature until my face outgrew them and they became part of a décor I call "crap on my vanity." Then there was my first electric guitar, a Stratocaster-style black number that found itself covered in multiple coats of silver nail polish within two weeks of coming home with me. (How else would it be obvious that it was mine?) I named her Stella as in stellar as in stars as in glitter. That very same polish was later used to coat a pair of kick-ass spectator

shoes that I purchased in the midst of a Gwen Stefani phase. I bet you didn't even know a tiny bottle of nail polish can go that far, but yes, it can.

Glitter nail polish is INDISPENSABLE. It is the *MacGruber* of your life. Never travel without it. Never live without it.

Luckily, when I was growing up, there were myriad options to glitterify our entire existence. It was almost necessary to sparkle at all times, and not because we were vampires. My friends and I stocked up on body glitter during weekly pilgrimages to Claire's, where we also picked up my favorite glitter-development of the '90s: those hair-jewel malarkies. These were tiny rhinestones with Velcro in the back

that you would put in your hair and they would stay because that's what happens when you put Velcro on hair. Maybe you think a rhinestone is not technically glitter, but if you were a giant, it would look like glitter from afar, so it stays. Courtney Love rocked the hell out of this look; she also made it rain glitter in her video for "Miss World" and, obviously, she's a good role model. Anyway, I had glitter eye shadow and glitter eyeliner, so it was just never possible for me to be matte. I never *wanted* to be matte. What was the point of wearing makeup if you weren't going to sparkle and shimmer?

Whether you wear it in your hair or on your face, glitter is infallible. It's not just something that you douse yourself in before every major (and minor) event in your life. No, it's also a substance that brings us all together. When I told my new roommate, Amy, that I would be writing about glitter, she excitedly showed me her experiment with glitter and fabric glue, which was basically a rectangle of fabric packed so tight with sparkling pieces that I almost had a heart attack because I suddenly wanted everything I owned to look like that. We ruminated for what seemed like forever about the many items of clothing we would D.I.Y., like shoes and jeans and hats and possibly even our own skin, and how we would love to leave fabulous trails of glitter everywhere we went. And glitter is the only thing that will make me willingly talk to strangers on the subway or in the street. I can admire someone's shoes, but if they're wearing *glitter* shoes? I will take off my headphones and ASK where those came from.

Glitter (and love, I guess) will bring us together. But mostly glitter. ✦

OPEN ALL NIGHT

Intense conversations happen at 3:00 AM in front of a plate of cheese fries.

By Amy Rose, Anaheed, and Lori

AMY ROSE Twenty-four-hour diners have a certain magnetism for teenagers who are out all night, as you might know from your own 3:00 AM adventures. Anaheed, Lori, and I traversed the downtown New York City diner scene to document their younger patrons.

We all met up at the first location, raring to go. We ordered tons of coffee, made a plan of attack, and psyched ourselves up. Problem was, we couldn't find many teenagers at the first two places we went (the figure being exactly zero at the second one, sigh).

After a hot tip from a friend, we were able to find tons of fascinating, hilarious, serious, silly, and occasionally wasted people at the third place: the IHOP in the East Village. Which, of course, is the real purpose of late-night diner excursions: at that hour, in front of a plate of cheese fries, the conversations are sometimes INTENSE, and sometimes have you falling out of your IHOP chair laughing.

The first place we went was Big Daddy's, one of a chain of diners in Manhattan. Lori, Anaheed, and I met at the Gramercy Park location at midnight on a Friday night. Big Daddy's is like a cartoon diner, more than a little reminiscent of Wowsville from *Ghost World*.

After ordering fries and coffee, we scouted out the two girls in a back booth:

12:34 AM

Ashley (19) and Kiara (23)

LORI What brings you here?

ASHLEY Just catching up with my girl-friend.

ANAHEED How did you guys meet?

ASHLEY High school. She was a senior, I was a freshman. We bumped into each other in a class.

KIARA I'm very friendly. Overly friendly.

ANAHEED So you made the first move?

KIARA Yeah, like, "Hey, what's up? What's your name?"

ASHLEY She's a liar. She had great shoes, and I was like, "Your shoes are amazing."

AMY ROSE What did they look like?

ASHLEY They were dark gray with a purple heel. She was like, "Oh, thanks." Then we sat next to each other and started talking, and here we are today, talking.

ANAHEED How long ago was that?

KIARA Four or five years ago.

ANAHEED What's your secret for making love last?

KIARA Be honest, and have as much fun as you can. Always keep that other person happy.

1:08 AM

Rachel (18), Jodelyne (18), and Kai (19)

AMY ROSE What brings you guys here to-night?

RACHEL We were at this karaoke bar. And we wanted some munchies after.

ANAHEED What did you sing at karaoke?

KAI I sang "Superbass." Don't judge me.

ANAHEED Can you do the rap?

KAI No, I can't rap!

ANAHEED It's 1:12 right now. What time are you supposed to be home?

KAI Two o'clock, but I'm not going to be home till like four or five. I set my own curfew by just not coming home.

ANAHEED Are you going to get in trouble?

KAI My mom's asleep, so I'll just sneak in and sleep.

ANAHEED Do you have a technique for sneaking in really quietly?

KAI I take my shoes off at the door.

ANAHEED What about you, Jodelyne?

RACHEL She's kind of Cinderella.

JODELYNE Yeah, I was supposed to be home at midnight.

ANAHEED Is there anything that you guys want to say to the teenagers of America?

KAI Teenagers, stay cool. And don't be afraid to lose.

ANAHEED Why not?

KAI Because losing helps you learn how to win.

JODELYNE I don't know, take more chances? I don't, which is bad.

RACHEL I guess for me it'd be, like, don't be afraid of taking that chance, because you never know when you'll find a good opportunity.

KAI No. That was too cliché!

RACHEL But for me that's so relevant. If I didn't take that chance, then I wouldn't have found myself in the good situation I'm in now.

AMY ROSE What chance did you take?

RACHEL Living on my own. Moving away from my parents. That was definitely a big risk for me. It was like, I have to take on that financial toll myself now. I have to start paying my bills and all of these things. So it was kind of a big chance, and I didn't know where it was going to take me, plus it put me on kind of bad terms with my parents, you know? Now I'm kind of working things out [with them].

ANAHEED What do you like about living alone?

RACHEL It's so much more freedom. The freedom is priceless, let me tell you. The downside is definitely having bills and more responsibility—that stuff is ridiculous. But things are going well for me, I can say that.

ANAHEED Anything else you want to tell our readers?

RACHEL I don't know. I feel like our generation is dying.

ANAHEED What do you mean?

RACHEL I feel like each generation is getting worse. Our generation doesn't find new ways to be cool. They just find new ways to be stupid.

After finishing up at Big Daddy's, we went to Veselka in the East Village, where we came across not one single solitary teenager. We did, however, run into a friend of Anaheed's, who, even though he is like 40 years old, knew that IHOP was a much better bet for teen cruising. As such, we basically owe the rest of this article to him. Thank you, Todd, for being a 40-ish guy who knows where to find a plethora of teens at any given moment of the night! That's not weird at all, and we love you for it.

2:13 AM

Romis (19)

ANAHEED So what brings you here at two o'clock in the morning?

ROMIS I'm out with my sisters and friends.

AMY ROSE I like your ring! Is it an engagement ring?

ROMIS No, it's my birthstone.

ANAHEED Oh my gosh, it's beautiful! And it matches your necklace.

ROMIS I'm actually like the boy in the house. My sisters are girly girls.

ANAHEED You're pretty girly.

ROMIS I didn't used to be. I've actually changed a lot.

AMY ROSE What made you change?

ROMIS I got a boyfriend.

ANAHEED What's his name?

ROMIS José.

ANAHEED Where does he live?

ROMIS He's in Queens. At the juvenile detention center at Rikers.

ANAHEED Oh wow. How long has he been there?

ROMIS Since July 2010.

AMY ROSE Do you mind if we ask what he did?

ROMIS It was a gun charge.

ANAHEED Is that hard? Do you visit him a lot?

ROMIS Well, before I'd go three visits a week, every week. Now I just go visit him on weekends.

ANAHEED How'd you meet him?

ROMIS At school. He was my best friend.

ANAHEED How long were you guys best friends before it got romantic?

ROMIS A year. Then he gave me a kiss without me actually looking. It was like, I just turned my head, and then: oh!

ANAHEED That's so cute. How long have you been together?

ROMIS Since March 25, 2008.

ANAHEED So you guys were together for two years before he had to go to Rikers?

ROMIS Yeah.

ANAHEED Do you feel like he's changed since he's been in there?

ROMIS Yeah. He got jealous. More jealous than he was.

ANAHEED Do you think that while he's in there, there are probably a lot of guys who find out their girlfriends are sleeping with other people, and so—

ROMIS That's the problem.

ANAHEED It gets back to them.

ROMIS That is the problem. He's imagining that I might be tired of going over there. And he feels that I'm not getting what I should be getting.

ANAHEED And how do you feel?

ROMIS Nothing's changed between me and him.

ANAHEED But are you getting sick of it? Is some part of you like, *I should be dating someone here on the outside?*

ROMIS No. I made a promise that I was gonna wait. And I'll stick by my promise.

AMY ROSE What does he say when he gets jealous? Does he get mad?

ROMIS Yeah, he says he's gonna let me go, because he feels I'm still young and I need to live my life. He feels I should have fun.

ANAHEED And what do you say to him?

ROMIS I tell him I'm not like other girls. I'm different. And that's the reason why he fell in love with me. That's what he likes. Me being me. So he can't compare me to someone that I'm not.

The next group we met—Monet, Sharaine, and DJ—were so pretty and done up. Monet was wearing wild multicolored eyeshadow and some crazy false lashes, Sharaine was all cleavage and red lips and braids, and DJ, a self-proclaimed Fashion Police officer, was wearing Minnie Mouse-ish polka dots. They ruled for lots of other reasons as well. They kept telling us that we should take a subway ride with them sometime to see how amazing their conversations are, and we really, really want to take them up on it. Here's why:

3:09 AM

Monet (19), Sharaine (20), and DJ (19)

ANAHEED You guys look awesome. Look at your eyelashes!

MONET Listen. I'm girly. I'm verrrrry girly. If you met me like two years ago, I would never have all of this.

ANAHEED What happened?

MONET I don't know. I just started wearing makeup.

ANAHEED Was it hard to learn?

MONET No, because you know what? I used YouTube videos. I like the ones where people really show us how to put it on. I literally watched one video five times.

SHARAINE [*Monet's best friend*] Most of the time I can't do my makeup or my hair for anything, so that's why I have these two in my life.

ANAHEED Who did your makeup tonight? It looks great.

SHARAINE My sister [DJ] did my eyeshadow.

DJ I do hair, makeup, dressing…I should be a stylist, right? I'm like my own little fashion police.

ANAHEED If you're the fashion police, what violations have you called your sister out on?

DJ You do not want to get me started on that.

ANAHEED What are her worst fashion crimes? I want to hear them.

DJ I told her today that I didn't like her earrings. I was like, "I think they're like grandma earrings."

ANAHEED These ones? They're cute. [*For the record: Sharaine was wearing really pretty dangly earrings with geometric shapes embedded with rhinestones.*]

DJ They look like what grandmas wear when they go to a funeral. That's what I think. So I told her!

ANAHEED [*To Sharaine*] But you kept them on.

SHARAINE I just bought these fucking earrings. And I think they're freaking awesome. So I'm gonna wear them.

DJ But not everything you buy should be worn! Or even bought, to begin with! I criticize everything—I don't criticize; I give my honest opinion. Because at the end of the day, everyone is judging you when you leave.

MONET Word.

AMY ROSE Do people get mad at you for sometimes being too honest?

DJ I don't keep a lot of friends, because I'm so straightforward. A lot of people can't deal with my personality, because they don't like what I say. I know that sometimes people can get hurt. Monet just laughs at me.

MONET I know I'm fly! I don't care what nobody say; I'm fly.

DJ My great-grandma always used to say you have to look a certain way even if you're taking out the trash. So when I'm in my house I'll have my hair up looking crazy, but as soon as my mom's like, "You have to take out the garbage," my hair has to come down, I have to go put on mascara, I have to put on proper pants. They cannot see me looking ridiculous. At all.

[*At this point Anaheed catches a glance at Monet's makeup bag, which is ENORMOUS.*]

ANAHEED You carry your whole makeup bag around with you?

MONET Of course!

ANAHEED Can I feel how heavy it is? This is really heavy. It's gotta be…

AMY ROSE I really want to take a picture inside of it. Oh my god, you do have a lot.

MONET [*Taking things out of the bag*] I mean, I have scrunchies, just in case, Bare Minerals, I've got my brushes, this is eyeliner, lip gloss, lip liner, more Bare Minerals, Sephora, Revlon…[*Stuff keeps coming out of this bag endlessly. It's a bottomless pit of makeup!*]

AMY ROSE Oh my god.

MONET …here's blush…

AMY ROSE You've got the Argan oil…

MONET …my lipstick…

ANAHEED Josie Maran stuff...

MONET ...mascara, another brush. Yo, these brushes ain't cheap, either.

ANAHEED How many lipsticks are in there? [*Pulling them out one by one*] One, two, three, four, five, six, seven! Seven lipsticks that she just carries with her all the time. So do you guys hang out together a lot?

MONET We could not speak to each other for a whole year, but I know that once we reconnect, it's gonna be a fun time. I know these two ain't going nowhere.

SHARAINE I've put too much money into this relationship to see it go anywhere.

MONET No no no no no no no no. Listen, listen, listen.

SHARAINE I used to always be the bread-winner in this relationship.

MONET No no no no no, hold on, hold on.

DJ I'm not involved in this conversation. I'm just gonna look the other way.

MONET She acts like I've never spent a dime on her.

AMY ROSE Did she buy you all that makeup?

MONET No! I did.

DJ It's a weird relationship. You do not want to get in the middle of an argument between them.

MONET It's like we're married. Long story short, we were supposed to hang out, but then I went to go hang out with my honey. I was wrong; I admitted it. We got past it.

SHARAINE [DJ] was like, "Are you having sex with her? I don't understand why you guys are getting into this argument."

DJ These are the questions. I have to know these things. Because you're on Facebook

like you're dying, like, "My god, she hurt me so bad!" And I'm like, "Did you just lose your boyfriend?"

SHARAINE Listen, I went a year without my boyfriend. So if I can go a year without a boyfriend and still have a best friend... even if I get a boyfriend, [Monet] better be there.

DJ [Sharaine] disappears out of nowhere. Like the other week, I'm calling her all week. I look on Facebook the next day, and she's liking people's pictures. I write a comment, she deletes it. I'm like, Oh my god, I'm going to kill this girl.

ANAHEED Sharaine, what do you have to say in your defense?

SHARAINE [*To her sister*] OK, you know the situation that happened there.

DJ Why are you liking photos if you don't even have your phone?

SHARAINE I told you where I was at the time.

DJ But why are you liking photos? You couldn't contact me, but you were liking other people's photos. And deleting my comment.

SHARAINE Your comment is still on my wall!

DJ No it's not.

SHARAINE Yes it is!

DJ No it's not.

SHARAINE Yes it is.

ANAHEED What was the comment?

DJ I wrote, "What is your problem?" And she deleted it two days later!

SHARAINE I did not delete it! It's still on my wall!

ANAHEED Can I just say, if someone wrote that on my wall, I would probably delete it.

DJ Why would you delete it? It's a legitimate question!

SHARAINE [DJ] scares the crap out of me with that crap.

ANAHEED She is scary, a little.

SHARAINE She's a little intimidating.

DJ What?! I don't get this! Why do people say this? I'm the sweetest person.

SHARAINE You're more intimidating than scary.

DJ I don't like that. I don't like that at all.

ANAHEED But earlier you were like, "I'm straightforward; if someone can't take it, then they can't take it!"

DJ [Sharaine] has anger problems.

SHARAINE You're the last person to talk about anger issues.

DJ I don't have anger issues; I have a problem with your anger issues.

MONET Man, listen. [*Pointing at Sharaine*] That's my headache. She's my headache. [*To Sharaine*] You piss me off, I swear. You get on my nerves. But I love you.

SHARAINE You get on my nerves, too. But you my ride or die.

EVERYONE Awwww.

Taniqua, Shanuys, and Dajon, all 19

AMY ROSE Where are you guys coming from?

SHANUYS The Penny Farthing. It's a bar.

ANAHEED Are you guys in school?

SHANUYS No, I'm working.

TANIQUA I was going to school, but what so happened… [*Chokes up*] Oh my god. I don't want to talk about it.

ANAHEED You don't have to.

DAJON She went to school, it wasn't for her, so now she's here.

TANIQUA No, I want to tell people this, because it's crazy. [*Tearing up*] I owe the school 7,625 dollars and 75 cents.

AMY ROSE & **ANAHEED** Oh my god!

DAJON The cops is coming for you!

TANIQUA So now I'm not in school. Every time I tell my story I want to cry.

ANAHEED How long did you go there?

TANIQUA Only a semester! Can you believe it?

AMY ROSE Where were you in school?

TANIQUA Mercy College, Dobbs Ferry. It's a private school, so it was expensive.

ANAHEED And you, Dajon?

DAJON I go to school in Long Island City. And I work to support my shopping habit. But I plan on moving on to bigger and better things.

ANAHEED What is your life going to be like, in your dreams, when you've made money?

DAJON I don't want a big house; I want a two-story condo or a loft, in Lower Manhattan. And a BMW or a Range Rover—white. It has to be white. I just want to be a socialite. I'm meant to be rich. Eventually I'm going to be. And y'all gonna be pulling up this tape like, "I talked to him at IHOP on January 28th, 2012."

ANAHEED [*To his friends*] Do you think that he's gonna do it?

SHANUYS Yes. I have faith in him.

ANAHEED Why?

SHANUYS Because he's Dajon!

This last group was really and truly fucked up, more so than anyone else we encountered over the course of the night. We gave them fake names for the sake of readability, but used their actual ages.

Li'l Arf: A wonderfully belligerent 15-year-old girl who looks and acts like a baby Lesley Arfin.

Strawberry: Li'l Arf's strawberry-blond boyfriend, 17.

Amnesia: A sweet 17-year-old who couldn't remember where she had been all night.

Scruffy: Amnesia's extremely stoned boyfriend, 17.

The Kid: A soft-spoken, butch 15-year-old wearing a baseball cap and a rugby shirt.

ANAHEED Where were you guys before this?

LI'L ARF We were at [Strawberry's] house, and [before that] we were at a party.

ANAHEED What kind of party was it?

STRAWBERRY Kind of like a rave.

ANAHEED Was it fun?

AMNESIA I don't remember.

ANAHEED And from there you went to [Strawberry's] house. What did you do there?

AMNESIA I really don't remember.

AMY ROSE What'd you do at the rave?

STRAWBERRY Got drunk.

LI'L ARF All you need is a beer and a Xanax, if you're trying to get drunk.

ANAHEED What did you order to eat here?

LI'L ARF I got off the kids' menu. Can you pass my crayons?

ANAHEED What did you get?

LI'L ARF A funny face. Where's this going? Like, your little website?

ANAHEED Yes, to our little website. It's called Rookie.

AMY ROSE You guys look so stoned. Did you smoke a bowl?

STRAWBERRY I smoked some bong, yeah.

LI'L ARF Wait, are you gonna arrest us?

ANAHEED No.

THE KID We smoked a few Js.

LI'L ARF What did I do today?

THE KID We went to that party.

LI'L ARF No, I mean like to*day*, day.

THE KID I came over to your house.

AMNESIA What day? Oh, I slept all day.

SCRUFFY Tonight's our first night of being second-term [seniors]. We just finished our first term of senior year today.

ANAHEED Congratulations! How was your first term of senior year?

AMNESIA Awful.

ANAHEED Why was it awful?

AMNESIA Schools, colleges, all that.

STRAWBERRY What's the spin of your website?

ANAHEED It's for teenage girls but it's not stupid.

LI'L ARF Like the Vagina Diary? What is that thing?

ANAHEED Yes, it's basically a vagina diary.

LI'L ARF No, but you know what I'm talking about?

AMY ROSE Yeah, The Vagina Monologues.

LI'L ARF Yeah, that thing. So…what do you need? What are you, like, interviewing us for? Don't you have questions?

ANAHEED Sure, we can have questions. [*In serious-journalist voice*] What do you feel is the greatest challenge facing teenage girls in America today?

LI'L ARF Wh…what?

ANAHEED What's your favorite food?

LI'L ARF Pickles.

ANAHEED What's your favorite color?

LI'L ARF Purple.

ANAHEED What do you look for in a man, or a woman?

LI'L ARF I like a big bush. Is my funny face coming? Oh shit, if you guys wanted to kill us, you have all this information on us now.

ANAHEED We have so much dirt on you.

AMY ROSE What about you, [Amnesia], what's the hardest thing about being a teenage girl?

AMNESIA I want to have sex without a condom.

STRAWBERRY I finished, like, second semester today.

ANAHEED Congratulations.

STRAWBERRY Oh, no, I finished first semester. Into second semester.

ANAHEED Did you guys all grow up in New York?

SCRUFFY Yeah.

ANAHEED I feel like kids who grow up in New York grow up faster. When you meet kids from other places, do they seem really different?

SCRUFFY We know how to handle our shit better.

STRAWBERRY Yeah. I don't suck.

LI'L ARF I don't know what I would be like if I grew up somewhere else. Oh no, I would probably be so weird. ♦

Special thanks to Todd Barry for location-scouting help.

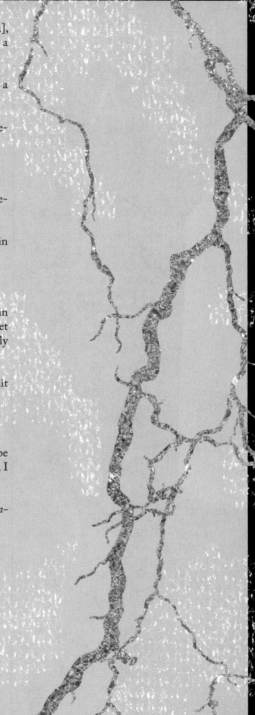

MIDNIGHT SNACKS: A TAXONOMY

Sophisticated gastronomical musings.
Words and drawings by Amber

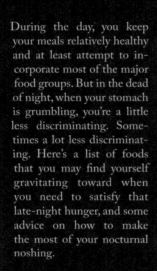

During the day, you keep your meals relatively healthy and at least attempt to incorporate most of the major food groups. But in the dead of night, when your stomach is grumbling, you're a little less discriminating. Sometimes a lot less discriminating. Here's a list of foods that you may find yourself gravitating toward when you need to satisfy that late-night hunger, and some advice on how to make the most of your nocturnal noshing.

1. COLD LEFTOVERS

We should be thankful that, even in a recession, we Americans have the kind of financial situation where leftovers are even a possibility. Nevertheless, there is something inherently unappealing about all of the plastic, airtight containers and Saran-wrapped casserole dishes that always seem to be occupying the refrigerator. In the daylight hours, you'd be hard pressed to find anything less enticing, but come nighttime that amorphous blob of peas, carrots, and mashed potatoes, that greenish roast, that week-old Chinese take-out, all call to you. Suddenly, they're no longer leftovers, they're a "super yummy remnant," and all your misgivings melt away. In fact, you become so convinced of the integrity of this food that you don't even warm it up.

Tips and Tricks: If you don't know exactly how long the food has been in the refrigerator, stay away from it. Food poisoning is a very real thing.

2. EASY CHEESE

By day, upper-class sophisticates may spread their Cheddar 'n Bacon–flavored Easy Cheese on crackers, but after dark it's safe to assume that even they are tossing etiquette aside and squeezing that golden, processed goodness directly into their mouths. Easy Cheese is the ideal snack—it doesn't require any preparation, it tastes enough like actual cheese to satisfy your late-night lactose longings, and because of its pasty form, you really don't need to chew it. Some people see this canister o' cheese as evidence of the dumbing down of society—they call it the epitome of low culture and the harbinger of end times. They might have a point, but you can use Easy Cheese to draw little happy faces on other foods, walls, or sleeping family members, and that's kind of cool, no?

Tips and Tricks: Squeeze a bit of Easy Cheese onto your cold leftovers.

3. THE BOWL-LESS SUNDAE

Step 1: Put a scoop of ice cream in your mouth.
Step 2: Don't eat it.
Step 3: Spray some whipped cream into your mouth.
Step 4: Drizzle chocolate syrup over the whipped cream.
Step 5: Eat the mixture.
Step 6: Feel awesome and satisfied.

The beauty of the bowl-less sundae is that there's minimal cleanup. You also get all the flavor of a sundae without having to make an actual sundae. But beware, this isn't for amateur midnight snackers. In order to pull the bowl-less sundae off successfully, you're going to need a really solid understanding of your gag reflex and a good sense of the radius of your mouth.

Tips and Tricks: The bowl-less sundae is the perfect sleepover snack both because it's fun to eat and also because, if things go awry and you start to choke, you'll have someone to perform the Heimlich Maneuver on you.

4. SANDWICH FILLINGS

It's one or two in the morning, everything is kind of hazy, you're hungry, you kind of want a sandwich, but you definitely don't have the energy to fiddle around with that tiny wire twist tie on the bread bag or even to walk over to wherever the bread is kept. Sandwich fillings—that is, the ingredients that usually make up the business part of a sandwich—might be exactly what you need. Lunchmeat, tomatoes, Kraft cheese singles, pickles, peanut butter straight from the jar—any of these are suitable after-hours treats. Yes, that's right, sandwich fillings can be quite filling. (You get it? Because they're fillings, like, they're inside of something, and then they're also filling because if you eat them you won't be hungry anymore because they're filling and they're filling.)

Tips and Tricks: Be a courteous snacker. If you do choose to eat peanut butter straight out of the jar, you might as well take that jar up to your room and make it your own. No one should have to eat peanut butter that you've put your finger in.

5. POTATO CHIPS

Chips (or crisps, as they're called in some parts of the world) are the classic late-night snack, and because there have been so many great innovations in chip production, they now come in a variety of sizes, textures, and, most important, flavors. They can taste like tacos, hamburgers, hot dogs, BBQ ribs, and chicken tikka masala. There is a chip to satisfy your every craving, and that's just beautiful. The well-known drawback is that it's almost impossible to eat only one of these savory treats. Even if you don't have a problem with that, you should remember that people can be very territorial about their munchies and if you weren't the one who purchased the wasabi-flavored chips, you may have to deal with an angry family member or housemate in the morning. It's always important to weigh how hungry you are against the inevitable repercussions of eating the entire bag of chips. Because you will eat the entire bag of chips.

Tips and Tricks: If you do have the energy to make a sandwich, add a layer of potato chips on top of your cold cuts. You won't regret it.

6. HALLOWEEN CANDY

Even if you stopped trick-or-treating years ago, you probably have a sack or a ceramic dish filled with Halloween candy somewhere in your home. Maybe you just couldn't pass up all of the fun-size Snickers and M&M's that the supermarkets start peddling at the end of October, or maybe you didn't get too many trick-or-treaters on Halloween. Either way, it's January, February, or possibly even March, and you still have all of this candy. While some people might advocate throwing it out, you're no fool—those Tootsie Pops, Nerds, Smarties, and Now and Laters can be a godsend at midnight.

Tips and Tricks: As every Halloween candy hoarder worth her Jolly Ranchers knows, it's important to stay away from chocolates that are several months old, because they taste weird.

7. COOKIES

If you know that there are cookies in your home, you're going to be thinking about them before you go to sleep, while you're dreaming, and then of course when you wake up in the middle of the night for a snack. If you're simply rummaging through cabinets with no specific craving and you happen upon a bunch of cookies, it can feel like you've hit the mother lode. When it comes to late-night snacks, cookies are the bee's knees, the cat's pajamas, the dog's bollocks.

Chocolate chip, oatmeal, Oreos, gluten-free, they're all wonderful. At nighttime, even those kind of hard, questionable ones that are packaged in a tin—your grandmother probably has some at her house—taste all right.

Tips and Tricks: Packaged chocolate chip cookies aren't the greatest, but if you put them in the microwave for a few seconds, they're slightly better.

8. RAMEN NOODLES

When you need something more substantial, you're going to want to go the ramen-noodle route. The preparation time is longer than it is with most midnight munchies, but there's a big payoff—not only do the noodles taste delicious, but you'll feel the sense of accomplishment that comes with cooking your own food. Ramen is also perfect if you want to carbo-load before an all-night marathon study session.

Tips and Tricks: After you've finished the noodles, you can drink the noodle-flavored water that's left in your cup or bowl. So you basically have two meals in one. ◆

ZIGGY PLAYED

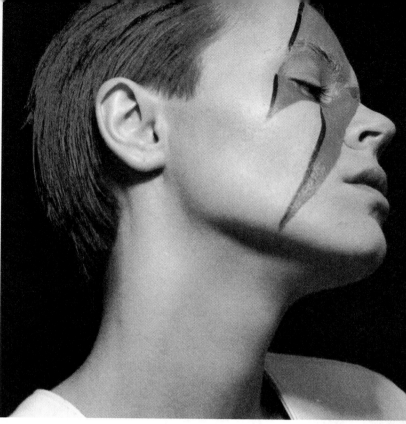

GUITAR

Jamming good with Weird and Gilly. By Petra
Special thanks to model Adrien at Spot6 and Peggi Lepage, stylist Bryanna Brown,
stylist's assistant Chloe Wise, hair and makeup artist Brianna Bission,
and Jason for helping out and letting us use his space.

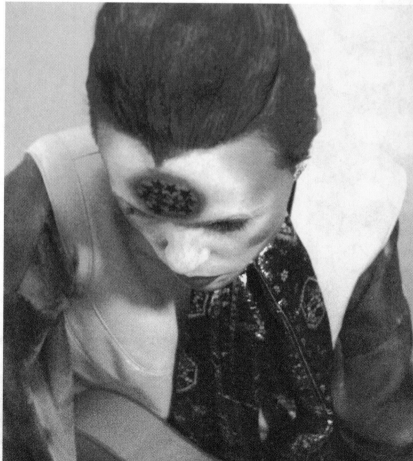

HOW TO NOT CARE
WHAT OTHER PEOPLE THINK OF YOU

I don't know why I haven't gotten my own show on the Oprah Winfrey Network yet.

By Tavi

Not caring what people think is the hokey pokey to getting through each and every day—it's what it's all about. (GET IT?) I don't know if not caring what people think comes before or after liking yourself, but I think learning to do either will help with the other.

I don't feel like the most qualified person to talk about this, but I don't know what it would take to be the *most qualified*. Self-esteem is the kind of thing that sucks basically for every girl, no matter what your circumstances, probably because you are constantly told you can and should *be better*. We get a depressing number of questions from readers about this, but I have too much to say to condense it to a couple paragraphs for a Just Wondering article. "Be yourself!"-type stuff isn't effective without the exhausting breakdown we're about to get into. I've split this up into three sections: wearing what you want, your physical self, and your *internal* self. Damn, I don't know why I haven't gotten my own show on OWN yet.

1. WEARING WHAT YOU WANT

People respect people who wear what they want because they wish *they* could be that courageous. The problem is that in order for this to work, you have to *be* courageous. Or at least, at first, appear to be. You don't have to walk around singing "I Can Go the Distance," but if you feel insecure, you can't show it. That sounds unhealthy, but this is one of those situations where you have to *convince* yourself you don't care before you start actually not caring. You have to, like, *brainwash* yourself a little bit.

Read interviews with people like Lady Gaga and cool old ladies who don't give a shit if someone thinks what they're wear-

ing is weird—in fact, they invite it. Certain mantras will stick with you, and you'll just have to repeat them to yourself throughout the day, on the day you choose to wear something "weird." *Healthy* brainwashing, right? Here's a gem from the late Isabella Blow, fashion editor and muse to Alexander McQueen: "My style icon is anybody who makes a bloody effort." I typed it from memory, because this is one of my arsenal of phrases that go off in my head whenever someone is being a tool.

You have to challenge anyone who gives you a funny look with a look of your own. Or don't acknowledge them at all, because they're not worth it! What will happen is that you will walk by and go on with your life feeling good that nobody's got you down, and they'll stand there a little dumbfounded. Maybe eventually they will grow up and realize how stupid it is to care about how other people look, and to expect people to care that they care, or maybe they'll stay an asshole forever. You'll probably never see them again. If you do see them again, because they're a classmate or friend, their opinion might not be worth valuing. I get that it's hard to just cut off communication with someone, and no one wants to do that over a single incident, but you just know now to be a little more critical of their opinions or views when they offer them. You don't have to take what they say personally.

I think most people are afraid of dressing a little stranger or cuter because they're afraid people will think they think they're so great. Like people will be like, "OH, SO YOU'RE ALL ARTSY NOW?" Nobody will say this if you act like it's no big deal, as opposed to constantly checking yourself in trophy-case reflections or whatever. If

anyone *does* say it, you look at them, give a subtle "you are an idiot" bitchface, and say, "…No?" And they will feel like a *dumbass*.

What such people don't get is that most people who like more obscure music or wear vintage clothes don't think of themselves as *artsy*, they're just exploring and trying to define their taste instead of being someone who likes whatever is handed to them for fear of being mistaken for pretentious. I don't like the term *hipster*—I think it's become so broad as to apply to basically everyone—but the defining quality is that a hipster thinks and cares about what their tastes *say* about them, instead of just *liking what they like*. And so there is nothing more hipster than a person who decides that the only reason another person is wearing a colorful dress is that they're concerned with what that dress means for their image. It's hipster to give a shit if other people are hipsters or not; this is why people who claim they're not hipsters are the most hipster of all, because they're *thinking that hard about it,* and *caring that much about what other people think*.

People are afraid of trying to be creative because they're afraid that they won't succeed, but who said your "success" in getting dressed has to be evaluated by other people? As long as you're into what you're wearing and it makes you more comfortable with yourself, it doesn't matter if someone else thinks you've put together a perfectly composed outfit. Actually, the effect of your confidence will only add to how stylish your outfit seems. It's like the best catch-22 ever.

Also, some people think that once you start dressing "weirdly," you have to keep it up. My middle school reputation was based on wearing really crazy stuff, and whenever I went to school in PJs, some people thought I'd given in to the naysayers. If anyone said anything, I just had to shrug and be like, naw man, I'm tired today. Again, it's about the whole people-deciding-your-image-for-you thing. **Don't let them.** Make them feel *stupid* for trying. This might feel cruel at first, but have no shame or guilt. You have every right to wear whatever you want, and if someone is so narrow-minded that they need to get on you about it so that the world is easier for them to understand, they might need a reminder that it doesn't work that way. *They're* the ones who think so highly of themselves that they expect you to care what they think of your shoes. You're just trying to have a good time. (Oh, and this strategy is not reserved for people who have reputations for being obnoxious and opinionated. It is not a contradiction to be nice or shy or whatever you think of yourself as, and still have to be like, every once in a while, *Relax, bro, I'm just trying something different.*)

It comes down to this: if you dress "weird," kind old ladies will come up to you on the street and tell you that you made their day. And that will make *your* day. It's the most delightful thing.

2. LIKING YOUR BODY/FACE

One of the most insightful things I've ever read about eating disorders and body esteem in general was a comment on my blog a while ago that I regret being unable to find now. The writer was saying that most people think girls want to be skinny because of Hollywood and *Vogue*. This girl wanted to be skinny because she wanted to be a *protagonist*.

She didn't expose herself to mainstream fashion magazines or TV; she was interested in art films and books and indie music. But no matter how alternative the movie, the protagonist was almost always skinny. And wanting to be a protagonist means wanting to *be someone*, as most people do. Apparently, your story is only worth hearing, you're only *someone*, if you're skinny—it's like, the *blueprint* of a human. Once that's down, you're allowed

to be as interesting and protagonist-y as you want! Apparently.

No matter how much people our age have been raised on *girl power* and *believe in yourself* and *you are beautiful*, ignoring the beauty standards of the culture we live in is close to impossible. And as this lady pointed out, these standards and expectations exist outside mainstream culture like reality TV and tabloids; they exist in punk and indie cultures, and in "artsy" Tumblr cultures that are all about looking like a fairy, but only if you're a skinny white girl. I often find myself guilty of the "Everyone should love their body!...EXCEPT ME" mentality, where you believe in body acceptance on a theoretical level, but are still hard on yourself about conforming to those standards. You know they're bullshit, and you know you're worth more than your looks, but you still can't help feeling guilty or anxious over something like your weight or proportions or whatever thing is left on the constantly updated to-do list handed to us monthly by way of magazine headlines. Like, OK, say I got my "bikini body"—next month I'm going to learn that my eyes are way too far apart, then that my chin is a little too floppy, until I need to start ranking my earlobe shape on a 1–10 scale.

I think a big reason many girls shy away from calling themselves feminists is that they're worried they won't be able to live up to this idea of a Strong Woman, and that there's no room in this club for anyone who isn't 100 percent comfortable with herself all the time. You can totally be a feminist who has insecurities. Feminism isn't about pretending we all feel like Wonder Woman, it's about being honest when we don't, and having the conversation on why that is.

Thankfully, lots of this conversation is online, along with lots of just general support and inspiration and whatnot. Yeah, I'm talking about not caring about what people think, but it is comforting to know that some group of people somewhere will welcome you for dressing in weird clothes. The "body acceptance" tag on Tumblr will bring you to lots of body-acceptance blogs and fashion blogs. They're for everyone,

and I think it's healthy to check in whether you feel like you really need it or not.

Also, now that we're all teeeeeenz, it's a bit late to undo some of the Photoshoppery we've been raised around and grown to see as normal or desirable. But it helps to surround yourself with images of women who aren't like the ones you typically see in tabloids or on TV. Images are powerful, and it's only when I find myself looking at certain fashion magazines or Tumblrs that I feel myself once again grow insecure about how I look. Most of the time I'm in my little bubble of Enid Coleslaw, Frida Kahlo, Lena Dunham, Patti Smith, Cindy Sherman, JD Samson, Grace Jones, Fairuza Balk, Gabourey Sidibe, and Kathleen Hanna. It is so, so important that influential female people and characters who are not conventional, in their looks and/or personality, exist. Pop culture, and just *images*, make a huge difference in how people think, and watch the documentary *Miss Representation* if you're not sure you believe me.

But what if you don't want to live in a bubble? What if you don't want to totally reject the majority of our culture and spend all your time in a John Waters gang of outcasts, forever plagued by your secret desire to read *Cosmo*? What if you want to enjoy tabloids and reality TV and looking at shows from Fashion Week and photos in *Vogue*, but without letting the beauty stuff get to you? I think as long as you are discerning, you can totally be a part of that. But when you catch yourself thinking, *God, I wish I looked like that*, you have to remind yourself that the person in that ad is heavily Photoshopped, or sat in a makeup chair for three hours, or both. It's not about pretending you don't feel that way and keeping it all down and putting on a Strong Woman face, it's about being honest with yourself when you start to feel this way.

And, the disclaimer: I am thin and white and able-bodied and I generally fit our culture's beauty bill. My confidence, self-esteem, whatever, still goes up and down. (THANKS HORMONES, AND NO YOU WILL NOT BE GETTING A BASKET OF MINI MUFFINS FROM ME ANYTIME SOON.) Which brings me to...

3. LIKING YOUR BRAIN/PERSON-ALITY/SOUL/THAT STUFF

Prettiness is not only about being physically attractive. There's a prettier kind of *personality*, you know? More smiley, more agreeable, charming, less likely to challenge someone on what they say or call them out for being an asshole. And because our culture, for a long time, associated *girl* with *feminine* with *pretty*, but not with *smart*, there's a message out there that you can only be one or the other—pretty or smart, feminine or funny, Sarah Palin or Hillary Clinton. In her book *Is Everyone Hanging Out Without Me?* Mindy Kaling wrote that she has dealt with having to decide whether to be pretty or funny her whole life. There is an episode of *30 Rock* where Liz is upset that Jenna, the prettier/thinner/blonder/dumber actress, gets all the attention for a line Liz wrote. Pete reminds her that Liz is a writer, not a star, and this is what she agreed to.

In reality, of course, plenty of women are both smart and pretty, funny and feminine, etc. This is why pop culture needs more strong female characters. Not like, *I'm a superhero and I'm supersexy and STRONG and my boobs look really good in this catsuit but oh wait I'm totally two-dimensional.* Like, multifaceted, with many layers. Like, you know, human. *Mad Men* is great because its women are just as multidimensional as the men. I love Lena Dunham for writing characters like this. I love the characters of *Ghost World* and *Dreamgirls* and *The Royal Tenenbaums*.

When it comes to becoming the person you want to be, you have to know who you want to be first. And it's hard to know what we, as girls slash women, *really* want. I may want to look a certain way because I know it will get me respect and people will pay attention to what I have to say. But *I* don't really want to look that way, I "want" to look that way because it's what *they* want, and I'll benefit somehow, but I don't know who comes out on top in the end.

The root of your confidence in all three of these not-caring-what-people-think subtopics is knowing that you, ultimately, believe in everything you look like or do

or say, whether someone else challenges you on it or not. But that is a lot of pressure and responsibility! Because you probably don't know what exactly *you want*—and we're all young and human, so there's no rush—you will probably find that you *don't* believe in everything you ever look like or do or say. Someone might criticize you, and you'll think about it, and you'll agree with them. This is fine. It's all part of figuring out what makes you feel most like yourself and, in turn, most comfortable with yourself. Nobody is perfectly consistent, and anyone who expects people to be that way is just trying to make the world easier for them to understand. This is what we call *laziness*, and not the awesome kind where you eat a lot of stuff and watch TV.

Just be wary, when you get down on yourself, of where the negativity comes from, especially if that place might be society or culture or whatever. I mean, I can't even get *started* on all the mixed messages we get about sexuality. We've all seen *Black Swan*, right? Trying to be *innocent but sexy but purity rings but grinding at homecoming* will make a lady bonkers. You'll have visions of Winona Ryder hiding in your kitchen. I am a big fan of Winona Ryder, but I don't need her hiding in my kitchen.

Besides: everyone else is too busy worrying about themselves to worry about you, so you don't need to be concerned with what they might think. If you're worried because of what *you* think of yourself, that brings us back to two paragraphs ago, to *self-respect*. Again, you don't need to be a completely complete human right now. Or ever! That's what makes you human.

There will be bad days, where you feel like complete shit. Eventually it gets easier to recognize—somewhere between the point when you've been following a fight in YouTube comments and the point when you cried because you saw the VHS of *Aladdin* that you walk by every day sitting on top of your TV—that you are having one of these days. When you recognize this, spend the rest of the day being nice to yourself. There's nothing you can do but get through it and know that you'll wake up tomorrow and it'll just be different.

These are the days when you need to have some humility about the fact that you're sitting in bed watching pirated episodes of *Sonny With a Chance* and eating peanut butter out of the jar.

"Self-esteem is for sissies. Accept that you're a pimple and try to keep a lively sense of humor about it. That way lies grace—and maybe even glory." —Tom Robbins, *Fierce Invalids Home From Hot Climates*

This mindset is comforting to me in a way "everyone is beautiful!" is not. I don't want to believe that I should be concerned with being beautiful, I want to believe that I can be comfortable with myself even though I'm also the kind of person who follows everything that comes out of my mouth by cringing and questioning my own mortality. Yes, I get a little sad when I remember I'm too neurotic and too sarcastic, and that I choose to be loud or quiet at all the wrong times to be a Sofia Coppola character, but also too vapid, too easily amused, to be as cool as Daria. But I'm not a Sofia Coppola character, and I'm not Daria, I'm me, and I want to look and act like me. And I'll define *me* for myself, and it can be, like, this whole other thing that exists outside of body types and comparisons and references. I just wanna like what I like and do things I enjoy and have solid friends and be too busy experiencing this *grand old thing we call life* (holy SHIT where is my call from OWN) to worry whether I'm allowed to or not.

It's easy to let your mouse slip to your webcam in a moment's boredom and start wondering what's so wrong with you that you can't even get your eye makeup right, or realize you've been brushing your teeth for 10 minutes because you started staring at a blemish in the mirror. It's inconvenient to seek out communities and role models who make you feel good about yourself when there's all this other crap all around you.

It will always be harder to get to be someone who doesn't care what people think, but that's why you're a tiny little awesome warrior for even trying. And isn't that kind of exciting? Go forth, tiny warrior, and conquer. ♦

DAVID SEDARIS IS AS AWESOME AS EVERYBODY HOPED

One of the greatest writers of our time weighs in on eating buttons and dispensing free condoms.

By Tavi

David Sedaris is one of the funniest human beings on the planet, one of the greatest writers of all time, and the neatest member of my Sims family of favorite writers that I once made (WHILE SURROUNDED BY MY MANY FRIENDS AND BOY-FRIENDS.) I mean, have you heard him on *This American Life*? Have you read any of his books? *Holidays on Ice*? *Me Talk Pretty One Day*? *Squirrel Seeks Chipmunk* (original title: *Let's Explore Diabetes With Owls*)? Because if not, please do. But first, read this interview. He talks about growing up and writing and all that "life" stuff, but also about his favorite Japanese clothing designers and giving condoms to teenagers. He also mentions—multiple times—that he doesn't know how to drive a car. I think it's a plea of some kind. In the future, people will look back on this interview and say, "If only we'd gotten him that car, his would've been the BEST Sims family ever."

TAVI Do you ever find yourself playing up a certain side of your personality to get a better story later on?

DAVID SEDARIS I was just thinking about this the other day. I never learned how to drive a car. And so I never really developed aggression skills. And so I'm not very good at saying no. I think that saying yes, or being afraid to say no, leads to a lot more stories than playing up a side of myself. Most people, something starts to happen and they're able to say, "No, I don't want this to happen," and, "No, you're going too far," and, "No, I don't like the way you're talking to me." But I'm afraid to say that.

You write a lot about your family, and your childhood sounds unpleasant at times. But you and your sister Amy obviously turned out great. How did that happen?

Amy and I are not exceptional. I think the only reason that things worked out for us the way they did was because we were ambitious, whereas some other people in my family weren't. I just spent some time with my sister Gretchen and I thought, *How could I have ever forgotten how funny she is?* And I saw my sister Lisa earlier this month and thought the same thing. Lisa writes too, but she's never been interested in showing it to other people. The only difference with me and Amy is that Raleigh [North Carolina] was too small for us, and we wanted to get out of there as soon as we could. Whereas my brother's content to just be a funny guy at a party.

What compelled you to share your writing, unlike the other members of your family?

I don't know, I've always wanted everyone to pay attention to me! When you come from a big family, you're always competing for attention. In our case, we were always competing for our mother's attention—our dad's attention was negative. Nobody really wanted it. In high school, I was in the drama club, but I have all these nervous tics, and so when I got a part, all my tics went into overdrive. It was just horrible. And I realized, *OK, that's out.* So then I tried visual art. That was OK, but that wasn't right either. And then I started writing, and it seemed right. When I'm writing, I'm just alone in a room, and then going on tour is my reward for spending all that time alone in a room.

Have you gone back to Raleigh? Is it as bad as you remember?

Yeah! [*Laughs*] I never learned to drive a car, so my world there was very small. And I still don't know how to drive, so when I go back, my dad picks me up and gives me rides. I'm still 14 in that regard. And so I still have a 14-year-old's view of it. And Raleigh has grown a lot, but it hasn't grown in a way that interests me. It's another Target, another T.J. Maxx, another P.F. Chang's. And I could never live with that kind of heat again. So I think I made a right decision.

Are you ever surprised by the kinds of people who come to see you on your tour?

Yeah, I am. I went to 42 cities in 43 days on a lecture tour and, in that case, people are buying tickets, so you're getting people who can afford a 50-dollar ticket. Now, I'm on a book tour because I think people should be able to come for free, so that introduces me to a completely different kind of person. A truck driver came to one of the readings, and that made me feel really good. Last night I met a nurse and she had just that day had a patient who defecated a button.

Oh my god!

Yeah! A button came out! And I said, "But did he eat it off his clothes?" And she said, "Yeah, I think that's what he did." Every now and then, someone comes down the line and I think, *God, I'm so grateful to have you as a reader.*

Are you ever perplexed when certain people like your stuff?

Well, I imagine it'd be the same for you. Whether you have a book or a blog, the audience is kind of invisible, for the most part. I'd like to think that I could stand in front of these people, and talk to each one of them, and know how to make them happy. But I would have no idea how to make them happy. The crazy part is realizing that being yourself is the key. For some insane reason, people like you.

I just realized my question was basically, "Are you surprised that people even like you?"

No, but I am! I actually am! I wanted to give something away to the audience, so I thought I'd print up a joke book and give it to people as a little souvenir. It was gonna cost me $20,000. Instead, I decided to print up these postcards. One was a photograph of the skull of a Pekingese. One was a book cover that I'd hired a designer to make when I was going to title my last book *Let's Explore Diabetes With Owls*. And then the other just said, "Abortion, $3." I got to this theater in Memphis and they said, "You can't put this card on your table. The people who come to this theater are very conservative." And I said, "But it's a really good price for an abortion!" And they said, "No, you don't understand." And I said, "I would be ashamed to look a child of mine in the eye and tell him or her that I passed up a deal like this." My whole schtick was that it was just a really good price. I said, "I really need those cards on the table." And not one person complained. A couple of years ago, I offered priority signing to smokers because smokers never get anything. Everyone's down on them all the time. And a man filed papers to initiate a lawsuit saying that I was discriminating against non-smokers on California state property. To me, that's like, *What are you doing in my audience? I don't want you.*

Do you see a lot of teenagers at your shows?

Yeah, I do, and I always have gifts for them because I'm always so honored that they come. If I run out of gifts, I give them money. A couple of years ago, I gave condoms to teenagers because I wanted something that was light and easy to pack. Perfect, right? And then I got a letter from a woman in Chicago who said, "I came with my daughter to see your show and she's 15 and you gave her a condom and told her you didn't want to be responsible for her losing her virginity so she could only use it for anal sex." Yeah, that's exactly what I said! I don't know how she could've been offended by

it. I mean, I was nice to her daughter. And then I wrote about it and people would come up and say, "Where's my condom?" And then that kind of ruined it. So now I take like the shampoos and conditioners from my hotel. And I have these little cards that I got at the Museum of Contemporary Art in Chicago, the gift shop there, which I think is fantastic. They're these little cards and they're really beautifully printed on nice paper and they say, "STOP TALKING." They don't say, "Shut up," so they're still polite, but they have a trillion uses.

What's so special about when teenagers come see you?

Everybody *says* that they have better things to do, but teenagers are the only ones who *really* do have better things to do. When I meet a teenager, I think, *They could be getting high in a car.* And instead they came to hear a middle-aged man read about going to China. I'm just so honored. And I always write teenagers back. But I don't like it when they put their school address as the return address. Like, if they give me their home address I'm gonna stalk them or something. Or when they say, "Thank you in advance for answering this." I still write them back, but I scold them for saying that because that sounds like something a teacher told them to do. That's a dumb person's idea of how to get somebody to write them back.

Were there any people like that that you wrote to or admired as a teenager?

There was an author I started writing to—I wasn't a teenager, but I was in my early 20s—but I would just write him anonymously, and when I look back on it, it must have been…he just must have taken those and thrown them straight into the trash can. [*Laughs*] And he's somebody who I always admired and who I still admire and when I was in California a few weeks ago he introduced me. And I've never told him that I used to write him anonymously.

I heard that you wish someone would ask you how much money you make. So how much money do you make?

[*Laughs*] Whenever I go to a school group I'm always surprised that no one asks that question, because that would be the first question I would ask! So I can't answer it, but I always thought someone should *at least* ask. I'm so surprised it took somebody this long!

Is it weird having to answer people's questions about work you've written about yourself?

I never read anything about myself. Anything. So I think that really helps, in a way. Because I think if I did read things that came out of my mouth, I would never open it again. I would think, *Oh my god, I can't believe how stupid I sound.* Like my brother was interviewed one time, and he read it, and he said, "That's it, I'm never doing another one." If you really wanted to be that much of a control freak, that's a full-time job. You wouldn't be able to do anything else!

Even if you heard a review was positive, you won't read it?

Nope. I feel like if you read the positive ones then you have to read the negative ones, too. So I just don't read any of them.

You write about some weird people. Are you concerned with not making fun of them, or trying to keep it fair?

I always think that if you're going to make fun of somebody, it helps to make more fun of yourself. I was reading something from my diary recently: I was in a hotel and I ran in [to the coffee shop] to get a quick coffee, but I hesitated for a moment and this woman got in line in front of me. And she looks up at the board and says, "A latte. Now, is that the same thing that Barbara likes to get? The one with the whipped cream?" And I'm behind her thinking, *Oh, fuck.* That's the last person you wanna be in line behind! And so I do kinda make fun of her, just because she's one of those people that ask the guy at the counter, "So, did you go to college? Where did you go? 'Cause my son went here, but he's not working yet, but

I tell him, 'Rome wasn't built in a day!' Are those lids different sizes? How do you keep them straight?" And I've got steam coming out of my ears. But, in the end, it's just about what a complete jerk I can be.

This is a stock teen-magazine question, but that's why I think it can be very telling: if you could tell your teenage self anything now, what would it be?

I would tell my teenage self, "You were right!" You know? Whenever a story comes out in *The New Yorker*, I'll open the magazine, put it on the table, walk by it as if I just happen to be walking by, and I'll think, *Wait a minute! Is that my name? There's my name on the cover of* The New Yorker! *And it says—oh look! Table of Contents, my name is there! And—oh look! On page 43, oh, there's my name!* And I always want my teenage self to see that. But, of course, my teenage self never will. But I guess all the advice when I was a teenager—well, not all of it, 'cause my mom was a pretty great person—was like, *Don't be yourself. Fight your instincts. Become somebody else, because what you are isn't good enough.* I mean, every young person goes through a phase of trying on different personalities, but I think in the end I came back to myself. And I think that I was right to do that.

I read that you keep a diary every day. Do you ever reread it?

I've been keeping a diary for 35 years. At the end of every season, I print it out and make a cover for it and I put pictures in it—it's pretty elaborate for something that no one's ever seen. I go back to the diaries all the time. If I'm working on a story, it really helps. I can go back and look things up and look up names and details. Writing in my diary is a compulsion at this point.

Are you ever worried that you'll run out of stories and weird things that happened to you?

No, because all you really have to do is be alive and be observant. When I first started

writing, it was a question of writing about big things. My mother died—that's a big thing. I was a really horrible performance artist—that's a big thing. My grandmother lives with us, that's a big thing. But as I get older, it's more like making something out of nothing, and I actually think those make for better stories.

The story "SantaLand Diaries" is like, you worked as an elf, and in *When You Are Engulfed in Flames* it scales down so much it's about a spider.

Yeah! I guess that's the thing. It just all depends on how you write about it. I think I'm a better writer now than I was when I wrote "SantaLand," because that's so choppy to me. The last time I reread it I was mortified.

Well, I think we're about done. Thank you for doing this.

May I ask you a question?

Yes.

I love your blog. [It said] you went to Japan. Are you familiar with 45 RPM?

No!

It's a Japanese clothing company. They have like 12 different stores in Tokyo and each one sells different things. And it's Japanese, so everything is really nicely made and it's crazy expensive. It's not as bold as Comme des Garçons, but it's almost like hippie clothes. Anyway, I didn't know if you had ever written about or seen those.

When we went there, I was really homesick. I had never had Subway before in my life and then we got it twice in one day. It was really pathetic. But we did go to one store that was tiny and it was all imitation '50s Americana.

There's a lot of that there. Did you meet Rei Kawakubo?

I met her when we went there a couple years ago. She's terrifying.

Is she?

Yeah. I'm just intimidated by her because she's one of my heroes. Where does your interest in fashion come from?

My sister Gretchen has always had a good sense of style. It was never prescribed. She never looked like anyone else, and I always admired her confidence, and the ease with which she combined things. When she was a teenager Gretchen subscribed to *Vogue*, so that was when I first started reading about fashion. This was in the mid-'70s, when Yves Saint Laurent was doing his gypsy thing. I always liked to keep up, but after leaving my parents' house I was too broke to afford magazines, so I'd read them at the library. Then I moved to New York, and on recycling night I'd go through the trashcans in my downtown neighborhood, and come away with all sorts of things: *L'Officiel, Harper's Bazaar*, the now defunct *Mirabella*, British and Italian *Vogue*s, you name it. [My boyfriend] Hugh and I moved to Paris in the late '90s. We had a friend who worked for Givenchy, and she'd sometimes give us tickets to the shows. This was back when Alexander McQueen was the designer, and it was like going to a fantastic circus.

I've just always liked knowing what's out there. Clothes are interesting to me in the same way that buildings are. Most interesting, I think, are the Japanese designers. I like looking at things at the Dover Street Market in London. It's mainly Comme des Garçons, and every-thing appears to have been made by elves. In Tokyo I love a company called Kapitol, and another called 45 RPM. It's basically hobo clothing, but with nicer fabrics. What I like about Japanese stuff is that it's generally not about looking sexy. It's good clothing for older people who like having a little secret: special lining inside their pockets, or really big buttons. ♦

First let me say this: I am so, so sorry about what happened to you. What might still be happening to you.

If you have been sexually assaulted—recently, or a long time ago, when you were little, or this year—then I'm writing this piece for you. And, like many people to whom you may speak about this, my first response is that I honestly don't know what to say. I can't tell you that I know what you're going through: I don't. Your experience is yours, not mine, and I can't assume that I know all about it. You get to have your own feelings. And I know that I, personally, really hate it when people tell me that some awful feeling or situation of mine is "going to be OK." Because, sure, it's *going* to be. But right now, it's not. I don't know when the "OK" starts, so don't talk to me about it, because right now I want to talk about *right now*.

So, I'm definitely not going to tell you that. What I can tell you is that I am so, so sorry that it happened to you. And I can tell you that it happened to me, too. I was sexually assaulted. And in this, I am not unlike many, many other women, including many of the women I respect and admire most, and many of my friends. (It has happened to a lot of men, too, but a lot more women.) And, having talked to those friends a bit, and having gone through some of this myself, I know that there are a few things nobody talked me through, and that I want to talk through with you.

It is, actually, going to be OK. But it's probably not OK right now. And right now, you probably have no idea when the "OK" is going to start. So you don't have to be OK right now. You are going to get yourself there, eventually. Here are a few of the things you will walk through, on your way.

1. SOLITUDE

You are not alone in this. But for a while, you will probably feel as if you are. I mean, why wouldn't you? What your attacker did to you was completely outside the range of what we think of as "normal human behavior." Or even *cruel* human behavior. When cruel people dislike somebody, they normally just curse, or yell at them, or something. They don't *force sex* on that person. But someone forced sex on you, and maybe that person has done it more than once, or maybe more than one person did it; that's an experience that's completely outside

WE'RE CALLED SURVIVORS BECAUSE WE'RE STILL HERE

A few of the things you will walk through on your way to "OK."
Writing by Sady. Illustrations by Leanna.

of anything we think of as "normal." You may even think that you must have done something bad to make it happen, or that you are a bad or weird person because it happened, or that it couldn't possibly have happened to anyone else.

Well: it could have. (It has.) None of this had anything to do with you personally. The most important thing, for me, when I needed to understand this, was looking at statistics. If you are a girl, you're not alone: one in four girls is sexually assaulted before the age of 18, and girls between the ages of 16 and 19 are four times more likely than the general population to be sexually assaulted. And if you are a boy, you're not alone, either: up to one in six boys reports being sexually assaulted before the age of 16. If your attacker was or is someone you know, or a family member, that can feel uniquely terrible. And it *is* terrible. But it's not unique, so you're not alone there, either: most rape victims know their attackers, and child sexual abuse is perpetrated by family members about 34 percent of the time.

These facts are very scary for a lot of people to think about. But they will keep you from feeling like a freak, or like you—and you alone—"deserved" the sexual assault. Sexual assault is very common. One-in-four-girls-level common. I'm guessing that if you gave a plane ticket to one out of every four girls in America, and made them all fly to some desert island so that you could see what they all have in common with one another, you wouldn't be able to find a single universally shared factor. So, no: this was not about you. And no: you are not alone.

2. CONFUSION

Right now, you may have some trouble believing that what happened to you was sexual assault. You may feel that it was "not violent enough," or that you "didn't fight back hard enough," or that it didn't look like the kinds of sexual assault you've seen on TV or in movies. This is an extremely common reaction, even among adults, and even among people who have actually experienced very violent assaults: forced sex and molestation are so scary that your brain often refuses to fully acknowledge them. One woman I spoke to described her experience, and then told me that "if it had happened to anyone else, I would call it rape." That's not an instance of this woman being wrong; that's a demonstration of how shock works. Over and over, it has been shown that people who experience overwhelming, frightening, shocking events—soldiers in war time, people whose relatives die suddenly, sexual assault victims—feel, at first, as though what has happened is somehow not real.

Let's make a deal, you and I. I'm going to describe a few common forms of sexual assault. In exchange, you will follow the very simple advice I have for you at the beginning of the next paragraph. Sexual assault can consist of any of the following things: If someone touched your genitals or your anus with any part of their body, or any object, without your permission, that's sexual assault. If someone touched, kissed, or fondled any part of your body without your permission, that's sexual assault. If someone threatened to get you in trouble

or hurt you unless you did something sexual with them, that's sexual assault. If someone did something sexual to you when you were unable to resist—if you were trapped, or unconscious, or very drunk or high and hence not able to understand or control what was happening—that's sexual assault.

That list is incomplete. But here's the most important part: if you think you *may* have been sexually assaulted, or if you think you were *probably* sexually assaulted, or if you would call it sexual assault *if it happened to somebody else*, you need to talk to a doctor about it, and ask her/him to call the police. Call a rape crisis hotline—RAINN (1-800-656-HOPE) is the biggest and most easily accessible—and ask them what to do and where to go; if letting your parents know about this is dangerous (for example, if you were attacked by a parent) remember to ask the hotline if the hospital is required to notify them. If you're really concerned about privacy, don't give your name or phone number when you call. Seriously. They might be required to tell authorities what's happened to you if you're under 18, but they can't if you don't tell them who you are.

If the assault happened very recently, if it is at all possible, go straight to the hospital and ask for a sexual-assault forensic exam, so you will have proof against your attacker. Don't shower, don't change, don't read the rest of this article: GO. If it happened a long time ago, then go to a therapist. This, again, can be complicated when you are young; therapists normally can't tell anyone else what you say, but if they think you're in danger, especially from your parents or guardian, they might be required to notify someone. So ask the therapist which information they can share, and what they *must* share, and with whom, before you start talking. Get an honest, plainly worded deal you can both agree to. When you talk, you don't have to call what happened "sexual assault" if you don't want to. Just describe what happened as best you can, and then you and the therapist can decide what to call it afterward.

This is all a bit scary, but I recommend that you talk to these people for two reasons. First, I don't know who your attacker was, so I don't know who else you can talk to. And second: no matter what your situation, you need support from people who understand sexual assault and can help you heal. Sometimes people don't understand sexual assault, or are cruel about it, so you absolutely do not have to talk about what happened with people you don't trust. But therapists and rape-crisis counselors are hired to understand. Right now, you are dealing with something that can have a lot of long-term consequences, and you can't always see those consequences clearly when you're living through it. You need to be in touch with at least one person whose first priority is keeping track of you, and making sure that you are OK.

3. PAIN

Pain is a message. You are probably going to experience a fair amount of it, so it's important that you know this. No matter how bad it is, pain is not a judgment, or a punishment, or a weakness: pain is a message, from the part of you that wants to live, telling you that something is wrong.

After a sexual assault, pain can take many different forms: You can be overwhelmed with emotion, or you can be completely numb. You can be angry all the time, or sad all the time, or scared all the time, or all three. You can have vivid flashbacks about the assault, or you can have trouble recalling it. Sometimes all of this happens to the same person. Consensual sex can become scary or complicated in ways it wasn't before—some people start to have a lot more sex, some people have a lot less, some people can only have it in really specific ways for a while, lots of people just feel differently about or during sex, even if it doesn't seem like anything has changed. Some people seem fine unless they're exposed to one specific thing that reminds them of the assault: a touch, a joke, a song, a place—for someone I knew it was a day of the year. No matter what form your pain takes, it often looks really messy. But don't let anyone tell you that it's wrong. I don't care which jerk told you to "handle it" "better"; you are receiving a message, right now, from a very necessary part of yourself. The message is, "I want to live. Get me some help." It's urgent. That is why it hurts.

The problem, with this kind of pain, is that it can last. It can follow you around, wake you up at night, and not let you sleep. All you can think about is the pain, and you start to forget what it's like to *not* be in pain, and you will try anything, *anything*, to make it go away. Here's the problem, though: when all you can think about is pain, you are not going to be making the most clear-headed decisions. And when you will try *anything* that promises to make the pain go away, some of the available solutions are really stupid. People who have been sexually assaulted are more likely to become alcoholics, or to develop an unhealthy relationship with drugs. So if you're not sober or drug free right now, try being sober. Get help to do that, if you need it. See how things change. I don't say this to be judgey, and I did in fact drink before I turned 21, so I'm not saying it because I'm an old-timey schoolmarm who doesn't get the kids and their parties. Drugs and alcohol are just very bad for people in crisis. You really need your whole brain right now, so that you can get better. Anything you use regularly can create long-term changes in how you process emotion—pot is bad for some people's anxiety, alcohol exacerbates depression—and it's all really easy to overuse when you're freaking out. Also: getting wasted doesn't take away the pain; it just makes you temporarily unaware of it. So if you have serious problems to deal with, and you're putting drugs or alcohol on top of that, well: it's sort of like turning on the television to distract yourself from the fact that your house is on fire. The fire will only get bigger. You will only get hurt. But you won't notice the danger, for a long time, because you're watching the show. Try being sober, if you're not already, and see if you get better at putting out fires.

I am assuming that you already know about the *even worse* option, for making the pain go away. This option is not an uncommon way for survivors to try and resolve their pain: in a study of rape survivors specifically, one in three had considered suicide. So it's not strange if you've thought about it. But if you are thinking of killing yourself, or if you are hurting yourself in any way, you need to talk to a therapist about this, or (again) call a hotline, *right now*. Those people can talk through your specific situation with you, and I can't. They have years of training, and I don't. I will just tell you this: no matter what is happening, the possibility of change exists. Most people who want to die don't actually want to stop existing; they want the pain to stop existing. They feel powerless over the pain, and they

think it will never end. But there is literally no one more powerless than a dead person. As long as you are alive, there is something else you can try; there is some new way you can try to take your power back. Dead people can't try anything.

4. BEING OK

One day, you're not going to think about this every day. It may be hard to believe that. I know that whenever something really bad happens to me—not just big traumas, like sexual assault, but also relatively normal but awful things, like losing a job or a relationship—I'm convinced that I won't ever get over it. And in some ways, I never do. I'll never have that job again. I'll never be loved by that person again. For the rest of my life, my life will be different, because something was lost. And I'll never go back to being someone who hasn't been sexually assaulted. That's something else I lost. A big something. My life would be different if that hadn't occurred.

These things still hurt, sometimes. All of them do, the little ones and the big ones. They all still sometimes break my heart. But I'm older now than I used to be. So I know, now, what happens when the heartbreak is over.

The end of heartbreak is not, generally, big. It doesn't announce itself. No one comes to your door with a brass band and crowns you King of Over It and plays the Glorious Anthem of Recovery. It's just this: one day, you'll be sad about what happened. You'll sit there, with the sadness, expecting it to break you; you'll expect to go right back to the heart of the pain, the messy animal howling part that you were always so sure would never go away. And then you won't go back there. And in that moment, you'll realize something: you haven't actually been there for a long time.

"Being OK" isn't a celebration. "Being OK" isn't a guarantee that you'll never feel the pain again. "Being OK" is summed up in six words: that happened a long time ago.

This has changed you. It is always going to be something that has changed you, for the rest of your life. It will pop up in ways that surprise you. There will be days when the pain is back. If you have post-traumatic stress, you are not going to have an easy time of this. You are going to have to walk through more than most to get to "OK," and you may have to keep walking back to it, over and over. But you are not alone, and help exists, and "the rest of your life" is hopefully going to be a very long time. One day, all of this will have happened a long time ago. That's what I can tell you, about being OK.

And the fact is, you are not ruined. You are not broken. You are not forbidden to be OK. I actually felt guilty about this, when I realized it was happening to me—I thought there was some rule that meant I would only ever get to be bravely suffering and sort of all right, and that if I were actually happy, it would mean that I had betrayed myself and my experience. But this is not a 19th-century novel about a fallen woman; this is your actual life. No rule or event can forbid you from being happy. You can get past "OK." You can get *way* past "OK." You can actually get to "great." That's where a lot of the sexual assault survivors I've met have ended up: GREAT. So I'm not telling you that you have to be happy now. I'm telling you that it's possible, and common. And one day, you might end up there, and not even realize it until you take a second to look around.

No matter where you are, though, you are not drowning, right now. But you are in the water, and it's dangerous. So you have

to grab the rope that leads you back to the boat. I am not the rope; I am talking to you so that you know the rope exists; I am talking to you so that you have a few ideas of how to make it to "OK" again. You're out there in the water, and I'm just telling you to look around for something that's going to save you.

Because primarily—here is the big secret, the part I wish someone had told me—*you* are what's going to save you. Doctors can help you, and you'll be the one who visits them. People can be trustworthy and capable of helping you heal, if you reach out—you'll be the one who reaches. You may need to get past a bad relationship with a chemical, or a bad relationship with yourself—you'll be the one who gets past it, the only one in the world who has that power. And maybe, on some days, you are going to literally save your own life.

I know you can do this. I know it. Because look at what happened to you. Look at what you've been through. And then, take a second to notice this part: it happened, and *you are still here*. Not just here, but reading an article about how to save yourself! And you've made it to the second to last paragraph! And it is a LONG article.

We call one another "survivors." We don't often take the time to think about what that means. What it means is "the people who are still here." What it means is that you faced down something that no one should ever have to. And that even this terrible thing was not enough to stop you. What it means is that you are incredibly strong, even in the moments when you don't know that. What it means is that you are not drowning—there is a rope, a lifeline, and it will bring you back to the boat, and back to safety. What it means is that you are the rope. Grab on. ◆

THE DRUG DIARIES

THREE STORIES BY GIRLS ABOUT THEIR RELATIONSHIPS TO DRUGS AND ALCOHOL.

ILLUSTRATIONS BY KELLY

ME, ON DRUGS

By Lexie K.

I was 15 when I got drunk for the first time. I went to Hayley Anderson's* Halloween party dressed up as Beelzebub (we had just finished reading *Paradise Lost* in English), took probably four sips of Hayley's parents' vodka out of a water bottle, and promptly declared myself "schwasty," at which juncture I proceeded to stagger around proclaiming my drunkenness to the world until I found a boy who would hook up with me. We kissed on the dance floor for a little while before he took me by the arm and pulled me outside.

On the swings in Hayley's backyard, he told me, "I don't want to make out with you."

"Oookay…" I said, wondering what in the hell he thought we had been doing for the past 10 minutes.

He took a deep breath. "Do you want to give me head?"

At that point in my life, I thought a blow job entailed pushing hot air out of my lungs, through my mouth, in the general direction of someone's penis. While it's actually a lot more up-close and personal than that, I found the mere notion of putting my face anywhere near this stranger's crotch deeply disturbing. "No thanks," I said.

He stood up and brushed off his jeans. "Bye, then," he said. He turned around and went back into the house. It wasn't until one of his anonymous goon friends whistled at me as I slid off the swing that I realized the kid hadn't even been wearing a costume, and that I was dressed up like some kind of Wannabe Devilish Sexual Predator.

I loved it.

You have to understand: at the time, it seemed like I was eons late to the whole make-out scene. (Later on I'd find out that this was just patently untrue, as a good 60 percent of my friends—girls and guys— were still card-carrying lip virgins at that point. On a similar note, most of them had yet to touch a drop of liquor, contrary to my firm and unquestionable belief that everyone was partying like crazy without

MEDIUM COOL

By S.U.

I've always been a quitter. There are very few things that I can say I've stuck with for more than a few years—my brain just seems to get bored after a little while. Smoking pot was the same way. I started smoking occasionally with my friends during my sophomore year of high school.

For us, it was easier to get weed than alcohol, and since we weren't really going to any parties, smoking just seemed to make more sense. We would use a little bowl or a crushed soda can (TERRIBLE idea, I have no idea what we were inhaling) to smoke bad, cheap weed in somebody's basement or the park. Was it fun? Sort of—we'd laugh like crazy about random things and eat tons of food, which is pretty much what we would do even if

MISSION CONTROL

By Emily D.

It was ninth grade. The moment had come. It was the kind of thing huddled girlfriends talked about in middle school at sleepovers but no one had actually done, at least in my school. We were in the backyard, in a tent. It was my best friend's birthday party, but I

wasn't exactly friends with the other people there: the infamous "popular girls." Partially filled water bottles went around the circle, suffusing the tent with sickly sweet smells. I was handed a pink Nalgene half-full with clear liquid. Everyone turned to me, waiting. That was the first time I decided to drink.

The second time was in tenth grade, on our way to a homecoming afterparty, inside a limo. I was with a large group of my friends, and a few boys I didn't know. A couple of my friends wanted to indulge in me. So much of what I did in my teenage years was contingent upon stuff I thought other people were doing that they weren't actually doing.) I'd had my first kiss only a few months before, and it had been averagely sucky in the way of too-much-braces and not-enough-tongue, but the overall awkwardness of the situation had been considerably augmented by the fact that it had taken place in an old folks' home. A fellow volunteer and I set our charges up with a Fred Astaire video and snuck off to go make out in the hallway, which smelled like adult diapers and vitamin smoothies. I guess I should've closed my eyes, but something about the DROP SOILED LAUNDRY HERE sign just to the left of my make-out buddy's head had me mesmerized. The whole thing was just too embarrassing to handle, and so it didn't really count.

So as much as I knew that I ought to be offended by this thing that had happened at Hayley's party, I actually felt…validated. This was how making out was supposed to go down—fueled by alcohol on a sweaty dance floor, not out of boredom in the

we weren't high. The next day, I'd go home bloated and tired, feeling like my mind was working just a bit slower than usual.

Around junior year, I began drinking more than smoking, preferring the way that alcohol turned me into a more outgoing and confident version of myself. I was under pretty strict parental supervision, but still managed to do a couple of ridiculous, irresponsible things. I went home with a complete stranger (and let

back hallway of the dementia ward at 10 o'clock in the morning. For a long time I had tried so hard to have a normal, functional teenage existence—to get on the map as somebody who goes to parties and gets attention from boys and knows how to have a good time. And it turned out that the whole time the key was right in front of me, in a bottle, 80 proof.

of my abstaining friends contributed to the acidic churning in my stomach. In other words, I felt like an asshole. I felt like I had done something very, very wrong.

That moment was the end of my alcohol usage, and I'm proud to say I've never actually accepted any drug offers at this point. Why I don't use drugs and alcohol is a very personal decision. I can't say it's because of the videos from health class, my mother's lectures, or a religious deal. It doesn't even come chiefly from those two previ-

But people don't just jump from zero to 60 with this stuff; gradually, concessions are made, standards eroded, expectations allowed to shift. A lot of the time, you enter high school as innocent and sweet-smelling as a baby's bottom and you tell yourself, *I'll go to their parties, but I won't drink their alcohol.* And then something happens—maybe you're desperate for some-

ous experiences. I suppose my philosophy toward using is that I don't understand why some people believe they need such things to have fun. Yes, I know, "o reason not the need" (in the words of King Lear) (yes from Shakespeare) (deal with it), and I'm not trying to make a Puritan argument, but why would you need to change yourself, change how you think and how you act, change the way your senses work, change even the way your brain works—why would you need to make alterations

some drinks on the ride, and, being infatuated with one of them at the time, I did not hesitate when offered, even though I could feel the glare of my other friends, the ones who disapproved of this illicit behavior. I can't remember how much I drank, and I didn't exactly know what being drunk was supposed to feel like, so when I was accused of being such, I denied it. I still don't even know if I was. I was confused; the fun of being bad was fading quickly, and the searing guilt sparked by the looks and comments one to kiss you, or you get curious to see what all the hubbub is about, or you're bored and it's there—and you take those first sips and secretly want to yak but you keep it together and in your head you know something's changed. So then maybe you say to yourself, *All right, I'll drink their alcohol, but I won't smoke their weed.* But then you make up some kind of bullshit in order to break that promise (really, what's the difference between an actual high and a contact high? [answer: a heckuva lot]),

to your personality, your own self, to have a nice night?

But: I know that teenagerdom is a time when the idea of changing your personality can be really appealing. I know that a lot of us (myself included) are searching around for an identity, something that will give us confidence and make us feel like "ourselves" (because most of us don't know what our "selves" are, and we are changing day to day and minute to minute). "Stoner" or "party girl" or whatever can seem like a really easy

and from there, it's only a matter of time before you're snorting bath salts in a hovel somewhere.

Of course, that whole slippery-slope argument is ridiculous, and anybody who tells you that is probably either a neurotic parent who's watched a few too many SUPER IMPORTANT REPORTS ABOUT THE CRAZY SHIT YOUR KIDS ARE GETTING UP TO RIGHT THIS MINUTE (jenkem! toad-licking! Smarties-as-gateway-drug!) or on crack themselves. But I

identity to grab hold of and just be, for a while. I get that. But my own sense of identity and self-respect comes, in large part, from sticking to my morals, which include being sober.

I also understand that the sensation of using the common stuff—booze, weed—is something completely different from the regular world, and that that's the primary source of its appeal, but when someone I really care about gets numb to those sensations and wants to move on to something

think it's true that a lot of teenagers think they're invincible, and that their beliefs are set in stone, immovable. Some people's are, but a lot of people's aren't, and I don't think that's necessarily a bad thing either—the world is really complicated, value judgments one way or the other are inherently dangerous, and the people who know exactly where they stand on every single issue are more often than not closed-minded morons—but when drugs and alcohol are involved, it becomes surprisingly easy to give relativism a bad name.

I know, because I went a little crazy. The summer before 11th grade, I moved to the East End of Long Island, where it was a lot easier for me to get my grubby little paws on alcohol ET CETERA than it had been in my suburban town back in California. The Hamptons were full of cool, creative, wealthy people who partied all summer and really partied all winter, when there was absolutely nothing else to do. My new school was the kind of place where a kid could be expelled one week for snorting coke in the bathrooms and invited back the next be-

him drive my parents' car), I passed out in a friend's bathtub, and I drank until I puked. More than once. Looking back on this time period only three years later, I hear the old woman in my head go, "What the hell were you thinking?" I don't have too many regrets about the things that I've done, but it doesn't take much thinking to realize that my actions were incredibly risky. My friends at the time were, quite reasonably, pret-

bigger, something worse, I try to talk them out of it. My arguments are pretty generic; I simply remind them of the health issues or the potential punishments they could receive if something were to go wrong, but sometimes—usually, in fact—that person doesn't let me in. And I don't blame them—we've all been hearing those arguments since we were in seventh grade, so their effect is gone.

Let me make this clear: I don't shun people who smoke or drink—several of cause his parents were, you know, important like that. I'd never experienced such culture shock in my life. It was all well and good to flounce around tipsy and giggling at a Hayley Anderson–type (i.e., very classically high-school-ish) high school party every once in a while, but in New York, the stakes were higher; everybody seemed so much older, and so much more adventurous. And somewhere along the way, I made the decision to become like them.

It might not have happened like that if I hadn't developed a huge friend crush on a pretty, popular senior who happened to live on a winery. I've always wondered what it was that Cecilia saw in me—one theory I can't bring myself to dismiss is that there was something semi-charming in my naïveté—but we became incredibly close dizzyingly fast. I spent almost every weekend at her house, where I learned to taste the difference between the Pinots and the Sauvignons and eventually developed a taste for rosé that occasionally veered off into dangerous territory. I also acquired the vocabulary of an accomplished pot smoker,

and I trained my tiny asthmatic lungs to cooperate accordingly.

See, there are a few distinct phenomena that tend to accompany that initial foray into the oh-so-scintillating world of drink and drug. The first one is that a lot of these contraband activities are going to be wholly unenjoyable the first time you try them. Like a lot of 16-year-olds, at first I found the taste of wine revolting (and don't even get me started on vodka). The difference between me and a lot of other people is that I was just a little more willing to push through that discomfort. At first it was a social thing, but once I finally broke through to the high of whatever I was doing and was able to enjoy myself, I started to develop an insatiable curiosity, and I really did become a lot more adventurous. Friends of those beginning to experiment, be warned: as annoying as novice sub-users are (and we're all annoying when we start out, because we generally either follow more experienced users around and copy every single thing they do, playing lush puppies to their booze hounds; or try to

appear confident by pretending that we invented drinking/smoking/snorting/whatever else, which is particularly unattractive), it's this stage that's the real concern. Thing is, once somebody actually starts to like messing around with these substances, they often forget how to have fun without them (never mind the fact that they spent their first 16 or 18 or however many years doing just that). And they start to lose the healthy fear that stops them from getting into too much trouble.

My first strike, for example, was entirely my own fault. I took shrooms with Cecilia one weekend and then wrote something about it and left it lying around the house. Of course, my parents found it. Naturally, they worked backwards to deduce that I'd been drinking and smoking, too, and they were none too pleased. The confrontation that followed was messy and painful for everyone involved, and, from my 17-year-old perspective, One of the Worst Things That Had Ever Happened. I listened as they berated me with the possible dangers of "experimenting with psychedelics," and

ty concerned with what I was doing. Lucky for me, this period lasted only six months or so until I made some older friends and learned the value of drinking in moderation. Who knew that other people actually drank while playing games or dancing, rather than simply for the goal of being shitfaced? It was a valuable lesson that kept me (mostly) out of trouble for the rest of my high school career.

Directly above and below this piece are accounts about the extremes of the substance-use spectrum: people who've done lots of different drugs or who abstain from everything. I'm here to present a different path—a middle path, if you will. I drink, but not in excess. I go out for drinks on weekends with friends. That's all I do. I've never even tried anything harder than liquor and weed, and I have no desire to. Marijuana was never a

"gateway drug" for me. In fact it's lost all of its appeal for me.

The ironic part is that I'm in college now, in New York City, and I have never had such easy access to good-quality weed, and so many people offering it to me for free. My closest friends all smoke cigarettes and pot, and constantly ask me—or rather, jokingly plead with me—to join them. I never do, mostly because it's been over a year now and I'd like to keep the streak going,

my good friends smoke together, but that doesn't stop me from worrying about them. I know the immediate effects of weed aren't very taxing on a person, and you can't exactly become addicted to it—but I really do fear that it can be a gateway drug, and excessive use of hard drugs and alcohol can change a person. Not that change is always bad, or that it isn't inevitable—but I get a little uncomfortable seeing someone I used to hang out with telling stories of their Friday-night run-ins with cops, carrying

handles through the park, or smoking in their bedroom. I don't want anyone getting in trouble.

I'm aware that I sound a little hypocritical right now—on one hand I don't want to judge people who use substances; on the other I'm all worried about their "long-term damage" and "negative consequences." But I do genuinely feel both of those somewhat contradictory things at the same time. I don't support my friends' using, but I still love them all and enjoy hanging out

with them…when they're sober. Being around drunk/high people when you're not that way is a little awkward. It's like hearing someone tell a hilarious inside joke that you're not part of. All of my friends understand my stance on all this, and if someone doesn't accept my not wanting them high around me, they're not worth my time.

I live in a well-off suburban community outside Chicago, where drugs are readily available. Navigating through this kind of town as a straightedge isn't as hard as you the fact that they even called it that made me hate them. How could they claim to understand me or my actions if they were so clearly stuck in the '60s? A lot of what I was feeling was humiliation and genuine self-loathing, too—in case you haven't tried it, it's pretty traumatic to go from being the picture-perfect daughter to the wayward disappointment in one afternoon—but part of the problem was that I was being bombarded with mixed messages. My grades were excellent—I kept up with my responsibilities at school and at home—and I wasn't exactly a junkie, and yet here I was being told that I had put my life in jeopardy, and violated the sanctity of parent-child trust in the process.

Even worse, my whole relationship with Cecilia got messed up. She barely spoke to me that whole summer, and a lot of that had to do with other stuff she was going through, I think, but still, riding on the coattails of One of the Worst Things That Had Ever Happened, it was pretty devastating. I remained pretty confused throughout 12th grade, and angry at

everybody involved, so naturally I started ingesting just about anything I could find.

I took an entire bottle of Robitussin gel-caps, which fucked with my vision for a good 20 hours but put me in a hell of a good mood, and also made me believe I'd never said the words *Buffy*, *dad*, *hungry*, *girlfriend*, *Stickies*, or *parents* before in my life (I still have the list on my computer). Taking the whole tube of Dramamine the night I had to watch Terry Gilliam's *Brazil* for school was such a disturbing experience that I don't even want to get into it. By far the most intense was salvia, after a hit and a half of which I was parading around my backyard and I felt like a triangle? and I was convinced that I was on a Nickelodeon game show being pushed along a track by invisible shamans (if you thought Miley Cyrus was exaggerating, let me assure you, I have been to that headplace and she was not).

If it sounds like I was desperate, it's because I was: desperate for escape from the reality of senior year, desperate for any small act of rebellion, and—maybe above

all else—desperate for a good story. Problem is, there's only so much within the realm of the socially acceptable. Apparently, getting smashed with your friends is cool; swallowing an entire bottle of Robitussin on your own time just to see what will happen is pathetic. I'm not denying that it's stupid as hell—and whatever you do, if you're going to prove the news reports that your parents watch right by abusing cough medicine, stay the hell away from Coricidin Cold & Cough, because that shit can kill you—but it just bugged me, hearing people criticize me so harshly when they were going out and getting shitfaced and driving around. Just because that was more mainstream didn't make it any more benign, and there was so much hypocrisy involved that I started getting even angrier, and going even harder whenever I got the opportunity.

I realized something had to give this past August, when I went down to Celebration, Florida, with my mom for a family funeral. Celebration, for those that don't know, is the Disney Company's own

but also because there's just so much more stuff to DO here in New York. Not only night things, like clubs or bars or parties, but tons of museums, concerts, themed parties, and so on, to the point where I actually feel like I'm wasting my time by not being busy exploring the city 24/7. And yes, I'm sure there are plenty of people who do all of those things while high, but when my friends smoke pot it usually leads to them spending the night in bed

ordering a delivery of 20 cookies for three people (happened), or passing out and being taped to their own bed (also true). I love my friends dearly, but if I have to be completely honest I love them a lot more when they aren't high.

Last spring, I started getting horrible side effects after drinking even small quantities of hard alcohol—horrific stomach cramps combined with the other lovely side effects that one would typically asso-

ciate with food poisoning. (I don't think I need to get into details here.) I'm still not sure if this was caused by having one too many shots of cheap vodka, or my body was simply rebelling against me, but I eventually made the connection and switched to drinking only wine and beer. I also started drinking a bit less, partly out of stinginess (drinks can cost $10–$16 each in NYC) and partly because I realized how annoying it can be for other, more sober people

might think. I'd say a majority of the 800 students in my grade have used alcohol or drugs at least once, me being one of them. The percentage of consistent users hovers around 30, which includes a portion of my close friends. During my underclassman years I did feel a lot of pressure, which led to the tent incident, but as time passed, my need to participate subsided. Freshman year, everything was sloppy, full of raiding parents' cabinets, and power was handed to those willing to do so. From junior year on,

it was barely discussed. It wasn't something you needed to prove anymore, just something you could do if you wanted.

Staying sober does make me feel somewhat accomplished—it's not a big shiny medal of willpower, just a small pleasant feeling I can tap into when necessary. I don't view myself as better than people who aren't sober, but breaking through my generic teenage self-conscious shell and going against the general trend of high school social behavior was a tiny personal

victory. Abstaining keeps me out of trouble—not just with the police or my authoritarian parents, but also with my friends, and even myself. Sure, I'm left out of the occasional fun-weekend story, and I'm not in the Facebook smoke-ring album, and no that concert wasn't actually that good, but when I weigh all that out in my head, I feel all right about it.

I'm not planning on abstaining from alcohol for the rest of my life. Hopefully I'll skip out on the usual college spree, and

Stepford, master-planned to have the look and feel of the happiest town in America (I should have known this was a recipe for disaster going in). The minute I walked into the deceased's house, I thought I was absolutely going to fall down and die, because the place was chock-full ceiling to floor with Disney memorabilia. This, combined with the unbearable awkwardness of having had relatives I hadn't seen since I was two cry on my shoulder all day, proved too much for me to handle, so I made a beeline for the minibar. I probably had six glasses of red wine in total before I ran into the widow.

She caught my arm as I was drunkenly staggering into the kitchen, and complimented the one Disney accent in my entire wardrobe, a small Piglet decal on the underside of my iPhone. "I play Piglet!" she exclaimed brightly.

I was happy that she was happy, but I didn't quite understand. "Excuse me?" I slurred. I then listened for 10 minutes as this tiny 70-something-year-old woman told me how she worked at Disneyworld

to have to take care of you when they just want to enjoy their night out. But I never saw a reason to stop drinking altogether.

My recent stint of near-sobriety (in comparison to the past, at least) has taught me a couple things. One is that many people will not stop asking you to smoke or drink with them, even if you tell them that it will make you disgustingly sick. I've had to give graphic descriptions of vomiting while on the toilet in order to convince

people that I really don't want to take a shot of Smirnoff with them, thanks. For those who don't want to imbibe, I've found "I'm allergic to hard liquor" and "I'm driving tonight" to be the most effective ways to get others off your case. But once you get your point across, people will usually respect you and include you in whatever they are doing, even if you aren't as wasted as they are. Watching drunk people say and do absurd things can be either truly hilari-

ous or insanely boring depending on your mood. The good news is that this helps you figure out which people you actually enjoy being around. Some people are fun all the time, drunk or otherwise. Some people are not. When you are actually able to observe this with some degree of sobriety, you can make the distinction more quickly.

I still drink because I like to drink. Having a few drinks on a weekend night is fun. It's sort of the cheap(er) version

take things in at a pace, and at a level, that's comfortable for me. What that level will be, I'm not quite sure yet. My parents don't handle alcohol well, and I predict I'll be the same way. But in my fantasy, I would be one of those chill young adults who nonchalantly carry around a bottle of beer at a party or baseball game—this may be totally unrealistic, but I'll find out in good time. As far as drugs go, I've considered trying weed before, but I never found my reasons good enough other than just for the sake of

trying it; at the rate I'm going, the chances that I ever will are slim.

I worry my current resolve will crack upon entering college, and that if it does I will lose part of myself in the process—that some big part of me will dissipate, and I'll come out as some new person. But I also know that everyone changes when they leave high school, and I will too, and if it happens without drugs and alcohol, I'll have something more to be proud of. I like feeling in control of myself. Right now I do that

by staying sober. If I can retain that feeling while using alcohol or drugs someday, that'll be OK, too. That's how I'll know what I'm doing is right for me. ◆

Emily D. is a senior in high school fervently awaiting replies from the colleges she applied to. When not drooling at the mail slot, she spends time either trying to communicate with her dog in a language they created, belting songs from the musical Cats, *or daydreaming that Jack White is her brother.*

as a cast member (i.e., one of those people in costumes).

"Is that why you moved to Celebration?" I asked warily.

"Well, no," she said. "Mostly we moved to Celebration because it's the ultimate Disney souvenir!"

"Excuse me," I said again, and found my way to the guest bathroom, where I proceeded to vomit all over the tub. The next thing I knew it was two in the morning, and I was back in the hotel room with my mom.

It was so much more embarrassing than the old-folks'-home incident—who gets blackout drunk at a funeral reception? As horrifying as it was, I kind of needed something like that to show me that my priorities were way out of whack. Some things are just not OK, even when you're a relativist.

I'm now in college, where it's easy for people who are particularly susceptible for whatever reason to the allure of drugs and alcohol—people like me—to get a little carried away. It's particularly challenging because here, the party never has to stop.

There are about a hundred things going on any given weekend night, and they're all within walking distance, so you never have to worry about your parents driving you around (or even knowing where you are or what you're doing). You can keep booze and weed and whatever else your little heart desires right there in your room, and as long as you're not a loud idiot about it, nobody in authority ever has to know. It might sound like paradise, but it can easily turn into hell. (Because you know that whole higher-learning thing? You also kind of have to save some room for that, too.)

The Celebration Affair had been a wake-up call, and so, when I got to college, I decided I might as well head the whole descent-into-hell thing off at the pass; I started seeing the drug and alcohol counselor of my own accord. And you know what? It was awesome. She was really cool and she listened to what I had to say and didn't judge me and laughed at stupid things I'd done that were funny, because she knew that I was smart enough

to know that they were stupid. She helped me to make sense of the chain of events that led up to my puking in a newly dead man's bathtub. And she worked with me on harm reduction, which I'd never heard of and which I thought was especially cool because it meant that I could still drink (and smoke weed, I'll admit it) on occasion and in moderation.

So, if I could go back in time and stop little Lexie from sipping those sips at Hayley Anderson's party, would I? Probably not—I might stop her from going outside with that jerk, but, hey, we all have to come up against some jerks sooner or later—but I would definitely give her some advice:

1. Don't be afraid to ask for help. You can have concerns about your lifestyle (or anybody else's lifestyle for that matter) without having a "problem," and you can have a "problem" without being an alcoholic or a drug addict. And should you find that you are an alcoholic or a drug addict, that's OK too, because it doesn't mean that your life

of having dinner with friends, and the relaxing effects of alcohol make it easier to socialize with new people or go out dancing without feeling awkward. I've also reached the point where I sort of enjoy the taste of a good beer or wine. I, like all under-21 college students, have a fake ID, and with easy access to alcohol, drinking has become less of a competitive sport performed at frat parties (or so I hear from my friends at other schools)

and more something to go out and do at an interesting restaurant or bar. Drinking is definitely not something I feel 100 percent compelled to do—when I'm busy with work or with friends who don't imbibe, I can easily go a month or so without it—but as long as I don't have to go out of my way for a glass of wine, why not? So, see, I'm not always a quitter. ♦

S.U. is a junior in college.

is over and you can't ever have fun again. There are people who can help you deal when stuff gets a little hairy, and these people include drug and alcohol counselors, friends who are smart and not unduly judgmental (but also not crazy party animals who can hardly take care of themselves let alone advise you), and (le sigh) even parents.

2. Try not to lie. I ended up spending the better part of three years lying about who I was with and what I was doing, and let me tell you, it is a job of work; your energies are better spent elsewhere. If you're doing something you have to lie to your parents about, you would probably be better off not doing it, at least until you're out from underneath their All-Deciding Parental Thumbs. Which brings me to my next point…

3. Slow your roll. There is plenty of time to throw caution to the wind and experiment in all kinds of ways. I've just realized by the time I become "legal," it will have been six years since I started drinking. Again, I could definitely have used those six years to try other stuff that might have been more constructive. Like reading up on what can happen to you when you're under the influence of alcohol so that I wouldn't have had to find out what a blackout was the hard (read: funereal) way.

4. Do your research. I CANNOT stress this enough! If you are determined to do drugs, go online and find a number of reputable sources with information about what you should do to minimize the risk. Anything with a .gov or a .edu is likely to have some good scientific information, but obviously a lot of it is seriously biased in the don't-do-drugs direction, which is only going to piss you off if you've already set your mind to it. For something a little edgier, try erowid.org. They have great information about history, legality, dosage, and long-term and short-term effects. The experience vaults (aka "trip reports") are useful too, but bear in mind that they recount the experiences of randos and that you should take them all with a grain of salt.

5. Watch *Brazil* sober. Really, it's a good movie, and you will just not understand it if you try it any other way. I mean it. ♦

Lexie K. is in her first year at an imitation East Coast liberal arts college in Southern California, where she spends most of her time playing Scattergories with the campus cat, snorting crushed-up little pieces of Goldfish crackers, and lamenting the fact that she has no future in the current economy by repeatedly banging her head against various hard surfaces.

All names have been changed.

BLUE THUNDER

What goes on between dusk and dawn.

By Eleanor

Thanks to Mirren for glitterfying the photos, and to Baitong for modeling.

FEBRUARY 2012 OBSESSION

Welcome to February! The theme this month is Obsession, and so we are indulging all of our creepy, only half-ironic interests in the sickeningly girly and sweet. Do not be fooled, however, by all the pink and hearts—there's something really creepy about obsession too, you know? When I emailed our staff about what they wanted to write and take pictures of this month, lots of them were interested in stalkers and hoarders and *Toddlers & Tiaras*.

I would say we are a pretty qualified group to talk about obsessions of all kinds because most of us are bloggers, and I know that feeling the obsessive need to record everything is probably my biggest reason for using the internet as I do. I feel slightly less pathetic about it when I can assure myself that I am true to my obsessions in real life.

Sometimes I worry about this passion I have for the ever-glowing flame of LIFE, though. I can only think of the part in *Ghost World* when Enid compliments Seymour's room full of records and antiques and he says, "You think it's healthy to obsessively collect things? You can't connect with other people, so you fill your life with…stuff?" I have chosen to pretend it was a technical error in the movie's sound, and we will put off discussing what obsession means for a social life until we're on our next month. I'm sure what Steve Buscemi actually said was, "It is really good to be a hoarder and, Tavi, you are the best of them all. Please be my wife." Speaking of, yes, this month will have quite a bit of the love stuff going on, too. May as well start that now. Along with acrostic poems, I write love songs. It's a little embarrassing, and maybe I'll regret putting myself out there later, but here goes anyway:

> *Why does glass cut through our love?*
> *Why do you insist on [mumble]-ove?*
> *You said to call, you said to beep*
> *Now you're not there, even though I've reached*

It's about one time when I was walking my dog and a house on our block had *Kim Possible* on their TV so I tried to watch it through the window without volume while my dog was pooping (and for the rest of the episode after that).

love,
tavi

CARTE POSTALE

Miss World

Meadham Kirchhoff and tacky school dances and lots and lots of candy.
By Eleanor

Thanks to Ayesha, Frenchie, Monica, Sophia, Azura, Simone, Caitie, and Lucy for modeling, to Mirren Kessling for her wonderful set designs, to Rachel Hardwick for doing makeup, to Oscar for assisting, to Issy for letting us shoot in her beautiful home, and to Meadham Kirchhoff for designing the most gorgeous collection ever, and then letting us shoot it.

All clothes by Meadham Kirchhoff, apart from the stockings, socks, and Simone's tutu, which are Eleanor's own.
Headbands and pom pom tights made by Mirren.

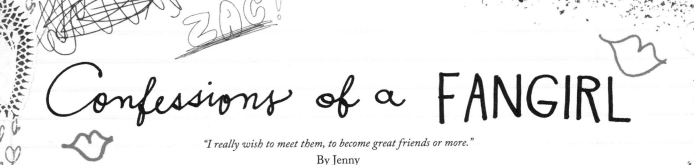

Confessions of a FANGIRL

"I really wish to meet them, to become great friends or more."
By Jenny

During my first year of college, I wrote poetry about "enlightened twats" and short stories named after Smiths songs, which of course I thought was the most obscure and artistically genius thing I could do. I wore vintage wedding gowns from the '20s that I bought off eBay for $2.99 plus shipping—this was in the early naughts, before eBay exploded with vintage sellers charging a fortune for a polyester crapsack—and listened to the kind of music that my friends said sounded like "weird noises." I was anti-pop. I was anti-establishment. Anti-everything. Whatever.

The week before finals, I stayed up for 30 hours straight working on papers, and when I was done, I went with my friend to the local Safeway to get some snacks. While I was waiting in line, I picked up a weekly gossip rag and flipped through it. I came across a short article reporting that 19-year-old Taylor Hanson—'90s heartthrob and the group Hanson's singer-keyboardist—had tied the knot with his 18-year-old girlfriend. This is the part where I avert my eyes and hang my head in shame: I immediately started crying. I was no longer an enlightened twat. I was a 13-year-old fangirl.

I was crying when the cashier scanned my one-liter bottle of ginger ale and my bucket of Planters Cheez Balls. I was crying when she asked me if I wanted the magazine. I was crying when I told her that I would put it back. And I was crying when I didn't put it back and just stood there instead. I only stopped when I realized that my friend was eventually going to find me crying in the supermarket and he was going to want to know why. When that happened, I would either have to (a) lie to him or (b) explain that I was crying over the guy who sang "MMMBop" when we were in seventh grade and, oh yeah, I still secretly believed that I would one day meet him and he would fall in love with me and confess that when he was a shy, lonely 13-year-old boy writing love songs for *Middle of Nowhere*, he always imagined someone exactly like me, but never thought in his wildest dreams that she was actually out there.

But there's more. And after I show it to you, I'm going to have to burrow my way into the mines of Moria where the freaking Balrog lives. The summer before ninth grade, I sporadically chronicled my love for the Hanson brothers in my diary. I present these entries to you, in all of their manic, misspelled sincerity.

6/22/97
Dear Diary,

I read in a magazine that June is the month of making dreams come true for Capricorns, meaning me. I usually don't believe in these things, but lately I've been having this feeling of unsettlement that I know won't go away until I fulfill my dreams of becoming a widely acclaimed singer/songwriter/keyboard player. I know I won't feel complete until I'm sitting there at the Grammys with small beads of sweat forming at the anticipation of finding out whether my name is in that envelope.

Another dream of mine was to meet Bush, who are four incredibly talented men in their 20s. But as shallow as I am I decided I would trade them in to meet Hanson. I secretly think Taylor Hanson is like my soulmate or something. Even though this means nothing, he's 13 like me & plays the keyboard like me. I just don't know if he writes the majority of the songs. Hanson are incredibly talented too. *I seriously am serious about meeting them.* Taylor has inspired many of my songs. (Isaac also did. I just thought I should mention him.) I really wish to meet them, to become great friends or more with them, to live a long full life, and to become a top-of-the-charts musician with a great band that I will stick with. I really hope my new band will finally be formed & come together & start performing this summer. Please God, if you are up there, listen to me & help me out.

7/3/97
Dear Diary,

I got my period the 2nd time & it's horrible timing. Tomorrow is the day there is a party at one of my parents' friends' house. The only thing I'll do that day is jump in the pool. Do you think I still can do that if I have blood dripping? Probably not. Oh well.

I think I am officially obsessed. Obsessed over the Hanson brothers. Every other minute is concentrated on them, their good looks, their funny personality, their great hair, great songs, music, lyrics, etc. I can't get them out of my head, no matter how hard I try. Ugh! One of my dreams would be to meet them and become great friends with them or even more. Pretty dumb, huh? Actually it's not. They are my idols, practically my role models. They've inspired me & I really look up to them. Who knows? Maybe miracles do happen! Bye!

8/16/97
I got my hair cut real nice & contacts. Funny how a lot of things are based on looks, huh? Sometimes, I feel like there isn't a single person out there who will understand or get to know me. Feels like I'm alone in this world. I'm always constantly helping others through sticky situations, consoling, giving advice. Then I present my life to be flawless. And yet, it feels like I'm screwed up the most. Seems like I can't get

JUNE 20 Dear Diary, July 3

I got my period the 2nd time to it's horrible timing. Tomorrow is the day there's a party at one of parent's friends' house. The only thing I'll do that day is jumpin in the pool. Do you think I still can do that if I have blood dripping? Probably not. Oh well. I think I am officially obsessed. Obsessed over the Hanson brothers. Every minute is concentrated on them, their good looks, their funny personality, their great hair, great songs, music, lyrics, etc. I can't get them out of my head, no matter how hard I try. Ugh! One of my dream

would be to meet them and become great friends with them or even more. Pretty dumb huh? Actually it's not. They are my idols, practically my role models. They've inspired me to I really look up to them. Who knows. Maybe miracles do happen! Bye!

an hour with my parents without feeling like I'm gonna break down. Sometimes, they make me think & feel like this world we live in is all about money. Being some hot-shot doctor. Making my dreams die instantly. Like I never could accomplish them. Everyone, even my best friend Diana, thinks I don't have what it takes to be a famous, talented musician.

I want to make my dreams reality. I want to fall in love, get an albumn out, and tell my parents "I told you so." Prove to the world that maybe I'm not another mistake, another immigrant. Sick of feeling savage. Feeling in second place, sick of obsessing over Hanson. Sick of daydreaming, fantasies, and cute guys who break hearts. Sick of being underestimated. I need someone so desperately to hold on to. To love me & understand me. Please I need someone to help me.

[no date]
Dear Diary,

I don't know what's wrong with me these days. These past few months, come to think of it. One minute I'm so happy, the next I'm breaking out into tears. I feel like I'm destined to become my parents. Shrewd, bitter people. I want to follow my dream, which is music. How can I do that if my parents expect me to become a Harvard grad? When everyone sees me as a shy egghead. When even my best friend doesn't understand.

Sometimes I look at the Hanson brothers & I think what it must feel like to be them. To have talent, skills, supporting parents, money, a nice house, and good looks. It's like a packaged deal they were granted. I feel so foolish for thinking these stupid thoughts. Wish me luck & 3 miracles or at least the first miracle.

1. Very successful career in singing, songwriting & keyboard playing
2. Meeting the Hanson bros. & becoming friends or more
3. Getting the chicken pox scars off my body

8/20/97

Just a few minutes ago, I was angry & so sad. Now I feel like a giddy little kid again. Trying on a new coat & hugging my mommy & daddy. Felt like I was 7 again. I only feel remorseful that I may never meet the Hanson brothers or have a record deal & a CD that will be chart topping. Too bad. But thank you God, for blessing me with a semi-charmed life.

8/21/97

Well it's final. I won't see Hanson perform. So what? I don't know. But I feel like

I was so mad that I should probably never meet the Hanson bros

MMMBop!

I hope that my dream, that one with music will not be just a stupid dream.

I ♥ Hansen

there is no reason for me to live anymore. No purpose left in life. Isn't this sick?

8/24/97

Hanzhi's mom & Jing's mom called me pretty, should I be proud? Just a few days ago I was so mad that I would probably never meet the Hanson bros. or get a record deal. I feel only sadness now. Oh well. I will try as hard as I can to achieve success. I won't let anything get in my way. I swear.

10/11/97

I feel pretty darn ugly now. Hanson is the farthest thing from my mind. Just a few hours ago, I had a conversation with my mom. A real one, one that I haven't had in years. I told her so many things that I've kept bottled up for years. I don't know if she heard all I was trying to say, but at least she listened this time. I still have so many things that I could never tell her in this lifetime though I hope that my love of music will not be just a stupid dream. I need it to become a reality soon, before, I fear, it's too late.

And now, before I show you my last diary entry about Hanson, I should explain a couple of things. At some point, I decided I was going to make one of the Hanson brothers fall in love with me by writing them the most brilliant, witty, intriguingly dismissive letter I could possibly write. When I didn't hear back from them, I started writing letters addressed to their parents because I figured, *Well, they probably have waaaay more free time to spend carefully reading fan letters!*

Here's one such letter:

9/26/97

Diana & Walker Hanson & co,

First off let me warn you: don't you dare send me some silly fan club form! Secondly, I want to congratulate your boys on finally achieving their dream, and you, for helping them to do so. Also, the point of writing to you was that I figured Ike, Zac & Taylor would never get the time to read my letter with their insane schedules. Of course, they should feel free to read it at

their heart's desire. (Being sarcastic.) Besides, I've already written a letter to them & I'm expecting a fake autograph sometime soon.

Anyway, I just wanted to let you know that I completely respect & admire your sons for their musical talent & their dedication to family and God. They have deeply inspired me to try & work hard at my own dream of musical success. However there are 2 things about your sons that bother me & I greatly resent. First of all, what's with their one-too-many love songs? How old was Zac when he decided to write a song about pining for a girl? When he was 10? Are they writing fiction stories? Isn't music all about writing from the heart & being in touch with your soul? How could your sons possibly grasp the idea of falling in love at their delicate young ages? The fact that they dedicate most of their songs to girls sickens me beyond belief. Second of all, I don't want to offend anyone or put you down, but I so completely & sincerely think there are another group of Hansons in this world who have the same talent & ability, but may be too "ugly" or don't have the money or support that you've given your sons. I pity those who struggle whenever I see your sons on TV or hear their song on the radio. Not to say that your sons haven't struggled for fame & recognition, but I guess we oughtta face facts. Those screaming girls aren't screaming at the concerts because they are so overwhelmed by that "great song 'MMMBop.'" They're going crazy because they are in bliss from seeing the long blond hair & sparkling eyes. I mean, you stick your sons there a year later with a pot belly & a shaved head & I promise they won't need to fear getting mobbed again.

Before I end this "cruel" but honest letter, I really want to tell you how lucky your sons are for having such great parents. It is incredible how supportive & flexible you are with your children. Encouraging them to believe in God & following their dreams. I wish my parents could be half as supportive as you are to your sons.

I hope that this letter will be read by someone, anyone. I hope I will have made at least a little difference & impact in

that person's life. I hope, if this is Diana & Walker Hanson reading this, then you can urge your sons to tell all their obsessed fans to get over it. Hanson, or any other group for that matter, is not worth being obsessed over because you can't spend a part of your short life devoted to some cute stranger. Lastly, I wish you & your family luck in future albums, friends, obstacles, and even girls.

Forever & Always Truthful,
Jenny Zhang

You see, in my calculating little brain, I thought, *Hey, if I insult the Hanson brothers to their mother, she will show them my letter and then maybe they will become intrigued by my hot, hot insolence and become obsessed with me.*

I waited for a reply. The days were not days, but like endless stretches of unorganized time that existed solely to stop me from becoming Taylor Hanson's girlfriend, Zac Hanson's fun older sister, and Isaac Hanson's confidante. And then, like every rabid, uncompromisingly obsessed fan at one time or another, I was betrayed.

I came home one afternoon to find a letter from the Hanson Fan Club. Even though I knew in the back of my mind that the "Hanson Fan Club" meant I was probably getting some kind of generic form letter, the part of me that believed in miracles, that believed great things could happen just because you want them to, still believed, as I tore open the envelope, that I would find a handwritten letter to me from

Taylor, Ike, and Zac telling me how their mother had told them to read my letter and, boy, were they glad they did, because I was the most interesting person they had ever heard from and, P.S., was I as physically gifted as my BEAUTIFUL MIND had led them to believe?

Then I opened up the envelope, saw it was a generic form letter, and the part of me that believed in everything started to die. I kind of lost it. I went into my mom's room and stole a tube of lipstick from her makeup bag and drew penises over all my Hanson posters. I drew Xs over their eyes and wrote "I HATE YOU" across their faces and then I drew some more penises. Then I tore it all down, crumpled it into a big ball, spit on it, stomped on it, and even considered pissing on it, but I lived in a carpeted room and I knew that I would suffer way more than the Hanson brothers would. Then I proceeded to write the most spiteful, rage-filled letter I've ever written to anyone, including people who have ACTUALLY wronged me.

I'm not sure I can replicate what was in that letter, but be assured that I used every single insulting variation of "penis," "vagina," and "asshole" that I could think of. A sample sentence likely included phrases like "you worthless sacks of shit" and "you sicken me to my core."

This is what my diary entry looked like that day:

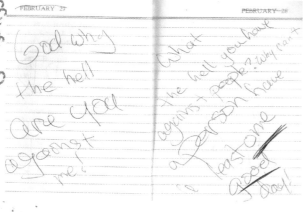
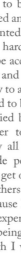

And then I finally got it. I was in love with a manufactured product, and it wasn't OK anymore. I made that manu-factured product my own, the way we all do, and my love for it wasn't any less real or meaningful, just in the same way that you can read a book or see a movie or hear a song and feel like it was created just for *you*, so *you* could be forever changed. But I got to a point where I wanted more than just a relationship with a product, and that frightened me, because it meant I wanted real relationships with real people, and real people are fucking flawed! They will sometimes disappoint you or even hurt you, intentionally or unintentionally. And they belch and fart too much.

Which is what's so fun and intense about obsessing over famous people: they aren't real. Taylor Hanson was whatever I wanted him to be, and what I wanted was for him to never marry anyone (except me, OBVI). So when the reality of his life finally intruded on the fantasy of mine, I cried. I wonder if that isn't partially why Beliebers cry when they finally meet Justin in the flesh—the collision of fantasy with reality is just too terrifying. I cried because I loved my fantasy too much. It gave me so much pleasure to imagine how lonely Taylor must have been, and it gave me pleasure to imagine being the one to unlock that loneliness. I cried because my first celebrity obsession manifested itself at the same time that I was trying to articulate what I wanted in my life, which was to be adored and tal-ented and adored for being talented. I cried because it was hard to figure out how to be accepted by my family and my friends and how to assert my profound need to be my own person. I cried because I found it easier to fantasize about how all of this would be made possible if I could just get one of the Hanson brothers to love me. I cried because I wanted so badly to experience the feeling of being in love. I cried because, even though I was no longer 13, I was still susceptible to comparing my life with what little I knew of other people's.

Though I am way too old to believe that my teenage fantasies will save me, I still find myself taking comfort in them. A few weeks ago, I stayed up all weekend watching Hanson videos on YouTube, and I came across a clip of Taylor forgetting the lyrics at a concert and then endearingly asking the audience to help him, and suddenly I was all, *What a magnificent person, I wonder if he and his wife are going to get divorced, even though they have four kids. He would probably be more intrigued and fulfilled by someone really creative and unhinged like, um, me.*

When I told my roommate that I was writing an essay about Hanson—in case she was wondering why I was blasting their music every morning—she told me that her friend had interviewed Zac for the A.V. Club a few years ago. Immediately, I thought, *I am only two degrees of separation from Hanson!*

You knew all along I was going to do this, but to quote from "MMMBop":

"Can you tell me who will still care?"

I can tell you who—ME. I still care. I will always care. ◆

Literally the Best Thing Ever: HEART

I love the Wilson sisters so much that I almost cannot bear to share them.
By Sonja

Where do i start? i think HEART is the best band name ever. I also believe their cover of Led Zeppelin's 'The Battle of Evermore' is better than the original and that LED ZEP should have been covering HEART. I named a book after them — it's called I LOVE HEART. Two words: THEY SLAY.

Once upon a magical night in 1996 — a pretty uncool time to get into an album from 1978 — I was sitting on the doorstep of my apartment listening to A cassette tape of DOG AND BUTTERFLY (on my walkman). IT was almost a surreptitious act; I was defying my then-current state of punkdom. The tape wound its way to the 7-minute opus MISTRAL WIND, at which point the music entered my orbit, shifted my AXIS, and took total POSSESSION. HEART MOVE MINDS. This epic track encompasses all that is great about HEART: it starts off with an acoustic guitar, slow and pretty, before the mystical lyrics wend their way to a KILLER drum fill and possibly the heaviest electric guitar riff known to humankind. IT was like the universe was speaking directly to me, whispering secret solutions to all my problems. my love for HEART was carved in a tree.

The band is essentially the WILSON SISTER ANN and NANCY. In 1963, 13-year-old Ann came down with MONO and missed three months of school. HER mother bought her an acoustic guitar so she wouldn't go crazy (until she went 'CRAZY ON YOU' much later). BUT it was 9-year-old NANCY who picked it up and checked it out. Later dubbed "WHIZZ FINGERS" by her older sister Lynn, NANCY was a natural. She would often fall asleep with the guitar beside her. Meanwhile, ANN was having a rough go of it. A debilitating stutter made her painfully shy. IN VH1'S BEHIND the MUSIC, she said that by the time she hit puberty, she felt "totally ugly, totally unpopular, totally gross." Her classmates were brutal about her weight and gave her awful nicknames. Singing became her salvation. IN fact, her stutter disappeared. Probably my favorite thing ever is when people find a way to be in the world and fully express themselves through their art.

HEART'S magnificent debut album, DREAMBOAT ANNIE was released in the U.S. on Valentine's Day in 1976. "They were the first band that was led by women, the songs were written by women, and all the decisions were made by Ann and Nancy," said Pearl Jam's manager, Kelly Curtis.

BUT beyond the wind chimes, the cowbell, the "sad faces painted over with those magazine smiles," the gong, a song for every mood possible, BEBE LE STRANGE, the operatic caterwauls, LOVE RULES, Ann's flute solos, metal, mandolins, the blood, the album art (especially on their 'forest album' LITTLE QUEEN), their outstanding GET-UPS, and their huge hair, it's their SISTERHOOD that makes their music so magical. I spent my childhood wishing I had a sister, specifically a twin, to share the load with me, to talk to and understand me. As someone who grew up in fantasyland, it was affirming to see that this was possible in real life and, as a result, I've created a similar sisterhood with my friends.

In 1999, I was jealous because Sofia Coppola scored her Virgin Suicides with two HEART songs. HEART were mine and they were all i had — OR so i thought. IT was a time in my life when I was still gouging out my own identity. I was consuming books, music, movies, art, and poetry in an endless quest of identifying SELF. It was hard not to take ownership of this band that meant so much to me. BUT Sofia was right. HEART should be shared.

P.S. Don't ever do a HEART song at karaoke. They are inimitable.

How to Approach the Person You Like Without Throwing Up

Advice from a 10-year-old girl, a 52-year-old man, and lots of people in between.

Writing by Amy Rose. Playlist by Tavi.

By far the most common question we get from readers, for our various advice columns, is some variation of "I like this person. But I'm scared to talk to them. How do I let them know I like them?" So, while articles on "How to Make HIM Notice You" aren't really our style here at Rookie, we also couldn't ignore this trend, and we sure don't have anything against crushes and love and turning your make-out fantasies into reality. So we thought about this question and realized that there's no one good answer. How best to make a move on the person who occupies your brain space during the majority of your waking hours depends on what you feel comfortable with; it's different for everyone. So we thought about it some more, and talked about it as a group, and asked some of our friends, and finally came up with a few ideas to help you out, you little vixens to be.

"Flirting," as we see it, doesn't have to be as overt and corny as, like, the ol' Elle Woods "bend and snap" method from *Legally Blonde* (on what real-life planet would that work?). It's more about being at ease while interacting with people in a way that's a little more suggestive and fun than your average conversation would be. Flirting isn't necessarily about engineering the perfect situation that'll make somebody want to jump on you—it's about teasing, joking, laughing, touching (sometimes!), and complimenting. And being comfortable doing those things.

Again, not all of these methods will apply to every person. These are just some techniques that we've found useful when we're feeling crushed out and nervous and excited and shy.

1. EASE INTO THINGS.

Start small—as much as you might want to share with your crush object the Helga-from-*Hey-Arnold!*-style closet shrine that you've made in their honor, it's a lot more fun, and usually more successful, to make conversation and build attraction (not to mention sexual tension, aka the best thing ever) over time. Says Hannah, "The more often you talk and hang out, the better you'll be able to judge if there's chemistry and whether it's going somewhere. Trust your instincts!" If you're reading this and inwardly going, *UGH, how am I even going to have the courage to approach this person more than once without completely bugging out and proposing marriage?* don't worry. It's totally OK to be a little more direct. To wit:

2. JUST BLURT IT OUT.

Anaheed shared this tactic: "In college, I was SO shy and awkward, so I would counteract my inner desire to flee and hide with the most aggressive approach possible—I would go up to a boy that I liked and say, 'Listen, you don't have to do anything about this, but I just wanted to say I have a crush on you,' and then I would RUN away. And it worked. Probably because I liked boys who were just as shy and awkward as I was." I think this sounds pretty adorable without seeming skeevy—because even though you're putting your feelings out there, it's not in a way that puts your crushee on the spot (well, not too much). You're giving them space to think about it and then respond to you when they have their thoughts in order, although I wouldn't recommend physically sprinting away from them. Instead, once you've put it out there, just say something like, "I just wanted to let you know I was interested. I'll see you later," and calmly go about your business while freaking out and congratulating yourself inwardly. This technique works on Arabelle, by the way: "Confidence," she says, "is the only way to get in my pants. I'm always attracted to supercute shy girls, but I'm way too unsure of myself, gamewise, to approach them. I'm way into when a girl approaches ME and is like, 'So, I don't know if you're into girls, but I think you're really cute and here is my number OK bye.'"

3. ASK.

Krista says that if she could do high school over again, "I would GO FOR IT if I was fairly certain a girl was being more than normal-friendly with me. It's all right to ask people, 'Hey, is this OK?' if you feel like holding hands or putting your head on a shoulder." This approach is so respectful, and I recommend it, because, again, it's giving people room and permission to say they're not interested, and you don't look like a creep.

4. BE OUT.

For those of us who identify as LGBTQ, it can be tough to meet people you want to date in high school, or to even feel comfortable trying. But, conversely, says Krista, "If you're out (WHICH IS SO BRAVE), it's sometimes EASIER to get girls, as they come to you. The only lezzer at school = lots of curious friends." Krista has these further tips for queer kids:

♦ Widen your net. Join a club, team, or group that isn't through your school. You'll meet new girls, and it's nice to have a lot of options, community-wise, when you're first coming out.

♦ If you're attracted to one of your friends and she has told you that she's curious about girls, go for it.

♦ BRAVE STEP: Join or start an LGBTQ group at school. Even if you don't find love (or sex), you'll have created a new community and made new allies. Always cool.

5. COLLECT REJECTIONS LIKE BADGES OF HONOR.

It's OK if your crushee gives you a weird look and quickly scuttles away after you approach them. You are REALLY RAD for making a move in the first place, and this experience, however disappointing it might feel in the moment, will help you with future crush situations. The only way to stop fearing rejection is to have it happen and

realize, whether it's an hour or a week or a month afterward, that it didn't kill you. In fact, you're just fine. You can do it!

6. SHARE SOME PITHY OBSERVATION.

The key to having a nice conversation with not only a person whom you want to french, but basically anybody in the world ever, is observing and building on a common experience. If the person is someone you see often, like in class, in your youth group, or at play rehearsal, you have time to create a friendly rapport with them that has the potential to get them just as interested in you. Since you've both already shared some experiences from this thing you both do, like the weird, overzealous way your band teacher pronounces *staccato* or how tough it can be to memorize a Shakespearean monologue, you have things to talk about that aren't just "I LOVE THE WAY YOUR PANTS FIT YOUR BUTT, WHICH IS INCIDENTALLY A VERY CUTE PART OF YOUR BODY." If you can tear yourself away from mooning over being near the person for a few seconds (and I know this can be tough, of course), you'll notice the funny, weird, and specific things going on around both of you and be able to make a little joke about it. And here's a major life truth: inside jokes = foreplay. Having a secret little something between you (a) is hot and (b) will come in handy later on—you can reference it to start another conversation with this person later.

Even if you only see this person in passing, I guarantee you can find something to work with. Anna's advice can help you with this: "Whenever I see a guy wearing a T-shirt for a band I like, I have to comment. It's a good go-to because then you have something to talk about, and everybody wears band T-shirts. Generally, finding any sort of common ground works: 'How 'bout that pep rally today? That sure is a thing that happens in contemporary high schools attended by the youth of North America!'" It sure is! You can talk about basically anything, as long as you're not trying to mold yourself into someone's OMGDREAMGIRL based on what you already know about them, or what you learned from snooping on their Facebook info page. Emulating what you think they want never turns out the way you want it to; instead, it usually seems transparent and weird, even if your intentions are good. "Anonymous" (IT'S TAVI SHE'S JUST SHY EVERYONE MAKE FUN OF HER) says, "In my experience, people who aren't so self-serious *like* being challenged about the things they like, like if you have some kind of playful argument over a band or how to feel about the new season of *30 Rock*. People generally think it is cool when other people know about things and have opinions about them. They are impressed, and then curious as to how you feel about other things, and then you have more reasons to talk to each other."

Some crushes, of course, are more spur-of-the-moment, so you might be wondering how to talk to someone whom you don't know. If this person is someone you're seeing for the first and possibly only time, like from across the room at a show, it's OK to be a little more forthcoming with your attention. Again, you're in a situation where you're having a common experience, so muster the courage to stand up as straight as you can if you're able (it sounds silly, but confidence is sexy), casually walk over to the person, and say something like, "Wow, that last song was amazing. Have you seen them play before?" during a break in the set. Or if you think the show sucks, say that! Then see where the conversation goes.

7. BE AN INTERVIEWER.

An actual professional interviewer, Ira Glass (friend of Rookie, husband of Anaheed), has this suggestion: "I don't know if this is just a cliché, and I fear that it is, but the main flirting technique I know is just to act very very interested in the other person and ask lots of questions and just talk to them about *them*. Try not to seem desperate when you do this. I was very awkward around other people when I was little, and I remember consciously developing the technique of asking lots of questions to get any conversation going. Only later did I learn the importance of also talking about yourself. But asking questions and giving opinions about their situation is pretty straightforward, even for a spaz like I was."

8. LOOK THEM IN THE EYE.

If you're in a situation where it's not really appropriate to start talking to a cute somebody without seeming intrusive, like on a bus or subway, eye contact goes a long way. You don't have to STARE at them like a gross person, but flicking your eyes over to them and keeping eye contact for a few seconds will give you a clue about whether they want you to approach and have a conversation with your voices and not just your *sensual gazes*. (If they hold your gaze for a few seconds and/or smile and/or keep looking back at you, those are all good signs.) Then ask them what they're reading or listening to, and work from there!

9. TOUCH THEM.

Here's Ira again: "[Touch them] on the arm, on the knee, wherever. Their response will often tell you if they're interested. At the very least: if they don't move away from you, you're still in play. If they reposition, you're doomed."

10. DON'T SUCK UP.

Once you've gotten to the point where you're speaking to your crush object semi-often and everything is going well, first of all, that's awesome and I'm proud of you, and second, there are a lot of different tactics you can adopt now to keep things cool (and by cool I mean HOT) (ugh, sorry) while simultaneously building up to the result you're looking for—whether that's a relationship, something sexual, or just someone snuggly to argue with over what to watch on Netflix. Personally, at this point, I always stepped off a little. It's hard to keep someone wondering about you when you're always RIGHT THERE, so it always seemed better to let them IM/text/call/whatever me first. Jessica can back me up on this: "The only sure-fire things I know for getting a boy's attention are: (1) Confidence. (2) Ignoring them rather than trying to engineer yourself into being whatever you think their 'type' is. (3) This certainly barely applies to only a really tiny subset of girls, but if you write a review about how much you hated his band's record, all he will want to do is find a way to get you to like him." That last thing happened to me a ton when I was a music writer. We're not saying go out of your way to be mean (doy), but if you don't kiss the ass of someone who's used to being treated that way, they notice. This comes in handy especially if you're lusting after someone who gets a lot of sexual/romantic attention from others. If you don't suck up, and maybe even back away a little once you've established a connection, the person will be wondering where you went and possibly even start fiending you.

11. JUST BE HONEST.

There are some Rookies who frown upon method #10 and avoid what they call "game-playing" and I call "ssseduction." Here's Emma S.: "I try to follow the controversial rule of talking straight." And Hannah: "I don't believe in acting uninterested when you're actually interested. I don't like the idea of playing games." And Eleanor: "Acting uninterested actually just makes the person think you aren't interested." I've only used that method to avoid coming on too strongly after initially showing interest, and it's always worked great. So, go with whatever feels most natural to you.

12. PRACTICE!

There are ways to have fun with flirting even if you don't currently have a heart-searing crush. Although high-schoolers, especially boys, are sometimes (OK, most of the time) pretty bad at wooing the people they like in a suave way, you'll still be able to tell what it means when he or she does things like suspiciously pop up at your locker even if his/hers is across the school. Depending on what this person is like, you will find this (a) totally irritating, (b) kind of cute but ultimately misguided, or (c) endearing enough to entertain the idea of flirting back. If it's this last one, great! This is a great person to practice on, to figure out what kind of flirting you're most comfortable with. Important note: I'm **not** suggesting that you fuck around with someone's emotions or make them believe that you're more interested in them than you actually are, but, as you know, you're probably not about to get married, so it's OK

to have sexually or romantically charged interactions with somebody without getting more involved. It will definitely help to build your confidence.

13. THE SECRET WEAPON.

If all else fails, you can always follow the advice of Maura, my friend Bee's 10-year-old cousin and, seemingly, a direct descendant of Elle Woods herself. In a recent Facebook chat, she had the following advice to give her lovestruck older relative:

MAURA pretend you dropped your pencil during class and bump into him so u meet eye to eye, then he will kiss u, it will work

BEE but what if we aren't in class? what if we are at a bar?

MAURA drop something like a cherry out of your cocktail

And there you have it. Now get out there! Good luck, and have fun! ♪

High School Sweethearts

1. Playground Love ♥ AIR
2. The Concept ♥ Teenage Fanclub
3. Wouldn't IT BE NICE? ♥ The Beach Boys
4. Maybe ♥ The Chantels
5. Rebel Girl ♥ Bikini Kill
6. Thirteen (live) ♥ Big Star
7. Red ♥ JORDAN CATALANO
8. Magic Man ♥ HEART
9. Leader of the PACK ♥ the Shangri-Las
10. Dirty Boots ♥ SONIC YOUTH
11. Fourteen ♥ Beat HAPPENING
12. Perverted Girl ♥ HAPPY BIRTHDAY
13. Too Young To BE in Love ♥ HUNX & HIS PUNX
14. One Summer Night ♥ that dog
15. Society's Child ♥ JANIS IAN
16. Lady L ♥ NICK ANDOPOLIS · 17. Gigantic ♥ PIXIES
18. Sunshine, Lollipops & Rainbows ♥ Lesley Gore
19. POP QUEEN ♥ BEN Lee
20. TONIGHT you BELong To ME ♥ Steve Martin & BERNAdette Peters

196

American Dream: An Interview with Sky Ferreira

The pop-musical rule-breaker talks about music, fame, Ryan Gosling, and the pleasures and perils of being a girl.
Interview by Tavi. Illustrations by Minna and Sonja.

I always feel weird and intrigued seeing photos or videos of Sky Ferreira doing her job of being a pop star, because she feels like *one of us*. She's obsessed with pop culture and fascinated by the corner of humanity she's become a part of since she was first noticed online at the age of 16 for her cover of Miike Snow's "Animal" and her own song "One." Sky just feels like someone I follow on Tumblr who also marvels at the humor behind celebrities' ways of publicly presenting themselves, but she is also really good at performing and has to publicly present herself, too. And so I wondered, how does such a gorgeous teen-dreamdancemusicmelodymaker remain true to herself when she is aware of the traps of insincerity in the WILD WORLD OF POP MUSIC? I stroked my beard and met her for an interview.

She apologized for being tired—she'd been up until 6:00 AM the night before watching *Weird Science* and videos of Whitney Houston on YouTube. She seemed eager to talk but chose her words carefully, aware that taking control of your own identity is no joke, and that the stakes are high when you're in a position like hers. She seemed still a little skeptical about her

place in a world of publicists and photo ops, but glad to know how to be skeptical. Now 19, and coming out with a very personal debut album after a string of dance singles, Sky Ferreira knows she doesn't need to fit into a mold of one type of artist or another, but is free to be one of those "human" people who have different phases and facets.

TAVI Do you want to introduce yourself to our readers?

SKY FERREIRA I'm Sky Ferreira. The Great and Talented Sky Ferreira. [*Laughs*] No, I'm kidding. I don't know! I'm the worst at that type of stuff.

Is it ever hard riding the line between full-out bubblegum-popping teen-girl pop and being so interested in music that would be considered more alternative?

I know exactly what you're talking about. It's almost a problem. I'm in this weird thing where I'm not Katy Perry but I'm not like Kim Gordon either, so I'm in this weird, hazy…I would say it gives me more freedom, but it also really restricts me. There's this rule that, like, if I do pop music,

I'm never allowed to do anything else, or since I did dance music, I always have to do dance music, but someone like Beck can do whatever he wants. I appreciate pop music, but that's not really what I plan on doing for the rest of my life.

Is it hard wanting to do so many different things at a time when it seems so important to have a consistent personal brand?

Yeah, it's ridiculous. The whole thing is ridiculous. My record label told me a year ago that only two girls were allowed to come out and be on the radio for the next three years. Everyone thinks there's this, like, movement with girls, because there are all these girls dominating the pop charts, but there's actually a very calculated formula to all of it, and they don't like people that they can't completely control.

I was sitting in a meeting the other day and they were telling me how to get a song on the radio. They were like, "You have to remind someone of something." You can't make something new. They were like, "How about you make, like, a Blondie song, but a new version?" You always have to be the new *someone*. I could be the new

Lana Del Rey, and she came out like six months ago. [*Laughs*] They really don't do that to guys at all. "He's the new Justin Timberlake!" You never hear that.

Even though someone like Justin Bieber could be considered the new Justin Timberlake.

The way female musicians act towards each other is so weird, because I think we get pitted against each other. It's really competitive, but in a passive-aggressive way, because you can't really get into a fight. There are so many rules—which I haven't really been willing to follow; maybe I would've been way bigger a lot faster if I did! [*Laughs*] But I don't really care, it's not really my goal, anyways, to get *big*.

If you're doing your own thing, you don't have to feel like you're competing with other girls. Is it weird, as someone whose version of pop is very ironic and self-aware, that people who are non-ironically poppy, like Miley Cyrus or whoever, are your peers? You see them at events, pose for pictures…

I actually like Miley Cyrus more than a lot of them because at least she's not trying to be edgy—she's still Miley Cyrus. I appreciate that. That's how I felt about Britney Spears, too. She always stuck with—I don't want her fans to go crazy on me—but her bad jeans and stuff. She didn't try to get edgy.

It became a bit of a burden, too, for her, I think. People wanted her to stay innocent, and when they found out she had had sex, they got mad.

Right. But what do you expect? You had her in a schoolgirl uniform when she was 16! And the thing is, every woman is supposed to look like a little girl now, which I find so weird and disgusting, because I never thought of being a teenager as sexy. I never felt that whole Lolita thing, but [adult female pop stars] are way past the age to be singing about it…it's sick.

In what way?

I don't know, I feel like they make music that sounds like ringtones for people to jerk off to. It's so gross. [*Laughs*] That's how I feel about it! I kind of don't want to be involved in it. I'm not trying to be an indie artist either, but I don't want to be involved in that.

The Lolita fantasy is confusing to me, because teenagers are actually really sweaty and we have acne.

I know. I'm already pretty awkward-looking in general, but I had such a terrible awkward-looking face until I recently started growing out of it. I got braces when I was 15 or 16. Like the worst time to get them! I was permanently awkward for about four years, and I didn't feel sexy at all. I was just trying out things. I was writing songs not really based on me, but just ideas, the way I watch films—like telling a story. But that didn't come across so well. People were like, "That's who she is." Like the "Seventeen" video. That wasn't some weird pedophile anthem type thing. Also, "Sex Rules" wasn't directly about sex—it was a bit of a joke

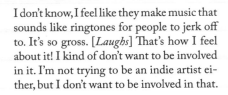

when I wrote it. I wasn't like, "Yeah, sex is awesome," because I'm not really a sexual person to begin with. It was more an ode to songs of the '80s, like Prince and Vanity 6 and even Madonna, 'cause it was just so blatant. Everything is so overly sexualized now, but it's all hidden.

Yeah, that's why it's so weird when a girl pop star is trying to show she's "grown up" and is expected to act sexual, but is then ridiculed for it.

And young girls aren't supposed to be like that, either. There's an unspoken rule. You're supposed to be sexy, but not in a very forward way. It has to be in a cutesy way.

You're supposed to look sexy, so other people can benefit, but you're not supposed to actually *be* sexual so that *you* benefit. Anaheed told me she had a professor in college who was like, "I don't understand why women don't try and look sexy all the time—if you have that power, why wouldn't you?" But being a girl isn't about being sexy all the time or getting your strength from that.

But that's what people think it's about because that's what we're told. I wouldn't say we're forced, because a lot of girls want to do that. But it doesn't mean every single one of us wants that, or not necessarily all the time. And it's hard to balance it out, because there are times I do wanna be [sexy], but there are times I don't. But it always has to be one way or the other.

I'm amazed when I look at stars who have a very consistent image growing up, because when you're young you go through so many phases.

That's the worst part. People can look at photos of me on the internet from when I was 14, or find, like, my cousin's Facebook and put pictures from it from when I was eight on Tumblr. Then they're like, "She's changed since then." Duh! And it's weird when you're young, because older people get really pissed about [your success]—they get really negative and weird.

Yeah. They belittle you with "Oh, she's just a kid." But it's like, well, you're getting really mad about someone who's "just a kid"!

Yeah, "She's just a kid but I'm still gonna pick on her for no reason." Choose one or the other! You just can't win with a lot of people, I've realized. There are too many expectations, especially of pop musicians who are girls.

It's hard to be taken seriously.

It's *so* hard to be taken seriously, because you're automatically stupid. But you can't be stupid if you're that successful, you know?

So now that you don't care what people think and you have a clear head and are able to see all these inequities, how do you think about yourself, and how do you want to present yourself and your record?

I want to be honest and make a record that speaks to people. All of my music is really honest, but this [new album] is more straightforward. I just wanted to make something different, I guess. And I did want it to speak to younger women. I don't really feel like there's anything new at the moment that does that for me personally. That's not about going out or being sexy. This record's not about that at all. I don't know how well it'll do, but personally I'm gonna be really happy with it.

What I like about the song "One" is it sounds like dance music, but the lyrics are sad.

It's a sad song. It has a lot of weird hidden messages. There's a song called "108" that's kind of about how I was exploited by some people. I watched this weird Swedish silent film when I was in Sweden about this girl in this mental institution who's in love with this imaginary man who's a thousand years old. I mixed both of them together. It was based a little on Laurie Anderson too, with the effects. The Auto-Tune wasn't a crutch, it was an effect. I can sing without Auto-Tune! I'm making sure my voice

is actually showing on this record, because that's the number-one thing that bothers me, is that people say I don't sing. But you don't have to belt like Adele to sing.

Your cover of the song "Animal" is similar. The Miike Snow version always sounded way too casual for the lyrics, to me.

The lyrics are so powerful compared to the rest of the song, and I feel like when I did the cover, people actually paid attention to the lyrics. It's obviously a great song, people know it's a great song, but [my version] got the message across clearer for some people.

What do you like about writing lyrics as opposed to poetry or prose or whatever?

I've always written really simple lyrics; it gets the point across stronger. Once you start overthinking it, you get crazy.

What artists would people be surprised to find that you like?

I kind of love everything. I love Laurie Anderson, but I also love Britney Spears, but I love Sonic Youth too, and April March, and the Shangri-Las…all that music. I love Brian Eno. The dance music I really appreciate is disco, but it's more like Chic, like Nile Rodgers. I love bass line. I love live music. That's what I'm trying to achieve on my new album—to make it something that can be played live. I mean, there'll still be some dance music, but the majority of it I'm doing with Jon Brion, who did all the Aimee Mann records, the first Fiona Apple records, the *Magnolia* soundtrack. Working with him is almost therapeutic, because he's not trying to make a hit—he wants to try something new, which is really exciting, because a lot of producers are just trying to make money.

The other day I put a demo up on Soundcloud, and someone said, "Oh, she's working with Jon Brion? Well, if she wants to be Fiona Apple maybe she should get raped."

That is a fucked-up thing to say.

I know. That isn't who she is.

And then people looked at her "Criminal" video like she had no clue what she was doing because she was so wounded, but maybe it was her way of trying to take back her sexuality.

Yeah, her way of reacting to it. Sorry to get all heavy or whatever, but I was so painfully shy when I was younger, until I was about 13 or 14. And something happened. I got sexually abused, twice, by two different people, when I was a teenager, from 12 to 16. And I went to the cops, but not right away, because I was scared to, like I didn't know how to tell my mom. The first time, I didn't tell anyone for a very long time. And [the police asked me] why I didn't come to them earlier. And they told me that because I was quiet I kind of caused it. "You're prone to it, you're an easy target because you're quiet." So one day I made myself really loud and obnoxious, and stayed that way for like three years. I went to court with the guy, and they didn't do anything to him. He had to move 15 blocks away from me. He was never allowed to be closer than 15 blocks away from me. I was like, that doesn't mean anything, he's gonna do it to someone else.

Oh my god. I'm so sorry.

It's fine. I've come together with it. It didn't define me. I kind of had this year to think about it while I was writing this record, just thinking about how people are treated. People expect things to just define you. Like, "She was raped, that means she's a victim forever." Or "She should be ashamed." Obviously it's not something I'm proud of, but it's not something I'm gonna hide for the rest of my life. That's the problem: a lot of people don't say anything until they're way older.

The fact that going to the cops "too late" could mean anything is bizarre to me, because there's no "right" way to deal with it.

Exactly. They were like, "Have you had sex before?" That doesn't matter. The whole thing was insane. None of it makes sense. Luckily [the second] time I knew what to

do. They found the guy because I scratched him across the face. I was sleeping, and he broke into the house. I remember this night so clearly. It was only 11 o'clock at night, and my mom was out. I was sleeping, and I thought I was dreaming—I felt something for two seconds and then I was like, *Wait*. He was rubbing my leg or whatever. So then I scratched him across the face.

He tried to say I assaulted him, but it was self-defense. He got arrested, but that's it. This guy has kids. It's so disturbing. And they don't do anything about it. I guess you can go on a website and see if anyone who lives by you has a [criminal sexual assault] record, but what does that mean? They said, "He didn't penetrate you. He didn't have sex with you, so it wasn't sexual." It's like, he was touching me in my sleep. He broke into my house and touched me in my sleep. A stranger.

The fact that the legal system can deal with it so irresponsibly…

Or they wait three months to do anything about it. You go to the police and they'll arrest him for like a week and he'll go out on bail or whatever. But it takes months to go to court. The whole thing is so sick and disgusting. And a lot of people are scared to say anything for those reasons, but also they don't want to be known as a slut or ashamed of it—that's traumatizing, too.

Did you have that on your mind with the new record?

A little bit, yeah. On some of it. I've never said anything 'cause I don't want it to define me, but I feel like it's appropriate to say something here. Because people feel like it defines you, and it doesn't. It's really unfortunate and disgusting and traumatizing, but it doesn't make you who you are. That's kind of what some of the songs are about.

That's the thing with Fiona Apple: people assume that's what her life is about, and it's not. They can't just give her the fact that she made great songs that were powerful, it has to be something else.

Yeah, they can't just give credit to a young woman for being a genius. Nicki Minaj said something like "All these producers come to you and want to play daddy and pretend that they're making you."

They forget that they wouldn't have the songs if it wasn't for you, either. Like with Lana Del Rey. [People are] like, "Everyone's made her." But it's her decision at the end of the day, what she's doing. No one's forcing any of these girls to do anything. And everyone talked about Lana's [*SNL*] performance and how bad she was, like it was proof that she was man-made, but then why was it so bad? I'm not saying it was bad—it wasn't great—but if [she were man-made], wouldn't it have been the most amazing performance, or with lip-synching and fireworks or whatever? It was the most honest *SNL* performance in a long time!

A lot of pop music is repetitive, and I just think there needs to be new things out. Some of my stuff is really referential, but I don't want it to be nostalgic. There are references and I'm inspired by a lot of things, but I live in 2012. I always find fake nostalgia really weird.

I feel that way about fashion.

Me too. I know everything kind of repeats itself in a cycle, but some things I think I've just seen too many times. We're both really young, and if we've already seen it a ton of times, I can't imagine how many times everyone else has.

That's why I like Rodarte, 'cause their version of '70s nostalgia is like, they'll embody their friends' basements from when they were growing up instead of re-creating vintage clothes exactly.

Yeah, I love their clothes. I can't afford any of it though.

Who else do you like?

Givenchy's probably my favorite. [Riccardo Tisci's] stuff is sexy but not too sexy; but it's not too elegant, either. It's a bit dark, which I like. And he makes giant T-shirts with panthers and crazy prints, but not too insanely bold, either. It's not wearing me. That's what I like about his clothes. Because often when I wear a lot of high-end clothes I feel like they're wearing me, I'm not wearing them. Some of it's too elegant for me. I'm feminine in a lot of ways, but I can't ever wear a full-length dress or a gown. That's how I feel about a lot of high fashion, so I like to mix and match it. I'm not a model, so I can't wear it the same way anyways. You know who wears clothes really well? Elle Fanning.

I love her so much.

She's so young, but it looks age appropriate. It doesn't look like she's dressing too old—it looks like she chose it. She probably did! She actually has taste. The worst thing is when I see a celebrity wearing clothes and know it was a stylist being like, "Honey, you should wear this, it's fierce." I think Elle's aware.

I like reading interviews with her where she talks about how she looks at Style.com and fashion blogs, because to me the people who end up with the best taste are the ones who absorb everything and are curious, because then they come back with what they know they like. Way better to be obsessed and geek out than pretending to be cool for not knowing who someone is or whatever.

I totally know all the models' names and everything, and I'm not ashamed of it. And I love watching shows. I enjoy fashion in general. Not necessarily because I can wear all of it, but because I like it. That's how I am with pop culture. Tumblr is a blessing and a curse, 'cause there's some weird, foul shit on there, and you can lose so much time! I can procrastinate forever. They have every still and quote from every movie possible. It's just an archive of never-ending visuals.

I feel like being a nerd in that way pays off though. Not nerd like, "I like *Star Wars*!" But if being cool means being uninter-

ested, then being a nerd is being obsessed with and appreciative of everything.

That's how I was with music when I was younger. Not just with indie music blogs—I would read a lot of Italian disco blogs all the time, and I had all this weird music I probably wouldn't listen to now, but I have no shame in liking all that stuff. And I don't think people should [feel ashamed], or that it has to be ironic. I genuinely just, like, love everything.

Amy Poehler said she doesn't believe in ironic TV watching, like you're obviously drawn to that show for some reason.

Exactly. I watch, even though it's disgusting and it's sad, *Toddlers & Tiaras*. If it's on, I don't see how any human being can not watch it. I saw this lady [on there] crying because she was a good Christian, but she had entered her stepdaughter in a beauty pageant and the stepdaughter only got second place. She was like, "I guess God didn't want her to have it." I was like, *Oh my god, this is so crazy, these people are nuts.* The Kardashians are a whole other thing where I lose my mind. And Heidi Montag should've had her own show. And I love Rebecca Black too.

The intro to Rebecca Black's song is actually so good to me.

People were acting like it was so weird that there was this fake record label where they paid a thousand dollars to make a video. But you go to a mall and people are asking if you want to join a fake modeling agency. Like, it wasn't that weird. And they delivered!

What are some other things you're obsessed with right now?

I'm obsessed with Courtney Stodden, because it's the most bizarre thing I have seen in a long time. She blows my mind. Barbara Walters should interview her for "the 10 most interesting people of 2011" or whatever, 'cause it is so bizarre and weird. There's something really honest, I don't

think she…well, yes, it is an act, but there's only so much she can act.

I've also been watching a lot of *Weird Science* for the past month.

Really?

Yeah. I saw the TV show in the early 2000s like on UPN or one of those channels during the day, when I was home from school sick. That and *The Secret World of Alex Mack*. How does [Alex Mack] do that? I never understood how…I think I missed the first episode where she started turning into liquid for no reason. I remember watching *10 Things I Hate About You* and I could only think of [Larisa Oleynik] as Alex Mack, and I was like, "Why isn't she turning into liquid and wearing a backwards cap?" I was so confused by it. I also watched *50/50* the other day with what's his name, Justin…

Joseph!

Joseph Gordon-Levitt! It's like this generation's alternative *Beaches*, with dudes. Like Seth Rogen is Bette Midler in that movie. I love Seth Rogen. I'm also a big *Freaks and Geeks* fan. And *Daria*—I have it on DVD, and I just rewatched the whole entire series in like two weeks straight. It's still so funny and so relevant. I wish there was a show like that now. It really speaks to girls at that age. The writing is so good in that show, it's amazing. It has some *Mean Girls* but it's also really *weird*, like Gregg Araki, too. So strange, that show.

Anything else you'd like to say to the TEENAGE GIRLS OF THE WORLD?

Eh…Kanye shrug. Oh, I loved that Feminist Ryan Gosling blog. It's the funniest thing ever. Now I actually think he's a feminist.

I didn't really get his appeal until I saw that and I was like, "How charming!"

Me neither. I remember seeing him in *Remember the Titans* and being like, "Oh, maybe." ♦

P.S. I LOVE you

Every now and then Erica sends us an unsolicited photo album from out of the blue with some really sweet description. She said this one is of "two dandelions in love." We'll take it.

By Erica

Thanks to Cristina and Kimberly for modeling.

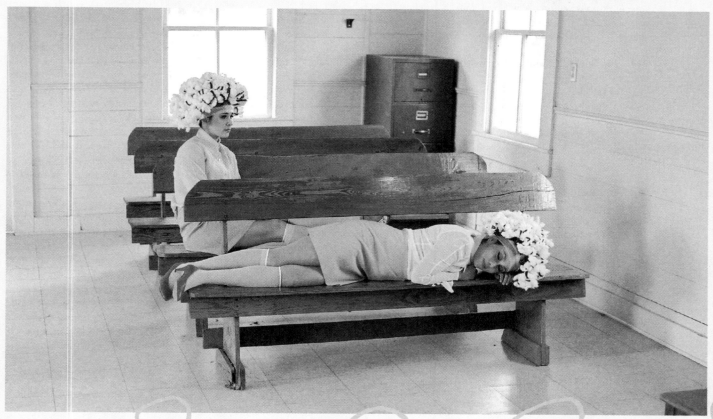

The Year of My Eating Disorder

I wanted to be the best at something, even if it landed me in the hospital.
By Charlotte S.

I used to think it was my friend Alli's* fault that I was admitted to the hospital in seventh grade with a heart rate between 40 and 50 beats per minute. A normal resting rate is between 60 and 100—mine was so low that I had passed out in school after an anxiety attack. This happened during orchestra. I don't actually remember passing out, but my friend Erica said that when she followed me into the hallway, I was hyperventilating. Then I fainted and became unresponsive for a couple of minutes. Soon after this, I was hospitalized. I weighed far below what I should have at the time.

Why was it Alli's fault? Because she could still starve and I couldn't. I was forced to eat. I was forced to spend six hours a day in group therapy while she was in school, and her parents didn't suspect a thing.

I've struggled my whole life with low self-esteem, anxiety, and a warped body image. Though I did not realize it at the time, part of the reason my parents sent me to a therapist in the third grade was that, even at nine, I was restricting my food intake and obsessed with being thin.

Then, in sixth grade, I met Alli. She was a dancer and she was told she *had* to be thin to do what she loved. We began "supporting" each other by counting calories. We brought salads for lunch, and when we changed for gym, we did so next to the mirror so we could clearly see who was thinner. Alli always was, so I made up my mind at the end of sixth grade to lower my intake. She followed suit.

We saw each other almost every day that summer, swimming together, eating frozen mangoes, and tossing out the sandwiches our parents had packed for us in the woods near the pond. Sometimes we would go to the library and look at *Seventeen* or read diet books, which inspired me to read cookbooks with nutritional information to find things I "could" eat.

When school started, I saw my life slide sharply downhill. Alli and I had only orchestra together, so all but one of my core classes were lonely affairs. I trashed my lunch every day save for an apple that I cut into tiny pieces. Alli and I further limited our caloric intake. We talked about "fat" girls on the way home, many of whom I now think of as beautiful. We told each other everything about our days while comparing the number of fingers we could fit between our thighs when our knees were touching.

OK, I know you might be worried that this is going to be a pro-ana, "thinspiration" piece now, but it's not. This is the story of my 2011. But if I'm going to tell you what happened next, I need to tell you everything I thought and felt at the time, which is not at all pretty and definitely unhealthy.

I will start on Valentine's Day of last year. About two weeks after passing out, I checked into Bader 5, the wing of Children's Hospital Boston that treats psychiatric disorders. I hated myself and everyone there. I hated the food most of all. Every day I counted calories until they went over my head and I felt like I was going to

drown. I was sure—absolutely sure—that I would starve again once I was released.

At first, I had no friends and sat in silence, shaking and lost. Every day I woke up at 5:00 AM after a restless night. I ran in place silently in my room with the door locked—this was the only time I was allowed to close my door. At seven, I would take a shower, which humiliated me because I hated being naked, but also gave me a sick thrill because I was still "thin." At eight, I had breakfast, which was supposed to be finished in 30 minutes, but I prolonged it to 40 or 50. At 10:00 AM, I had a snack. At noon came lunch, 3:00 PM meant another snack, dinner was at five. I looked forward to visits with my parents every evening from five to eight, but I didn't talk about my recovery. Instead, I talked about sadness, and how I missed my friends, and when I would get back to school. Also, my therapy was not very productive. I tried hard to block out all of the reasons I was anorexic: my need to beat Alli at being thin, a desperate desire to get guys to look at me, the urge to be the best at just one thing. I did not share any of these thoughts with my therapists. I did not tell them how, once I was home again, I would go right back to counting every calorie that passed my chapped lips.

Then my luck changed. A girl came to Bader 5—I will call her Amanda. She arrived on my one-week anniversary there. She made my days bearable because she was like Alli, only younger and more soft-spoken. We talked about our habits. We

204

talked about this other girl on the unit who scared us with her loud voice. We talked about television, family, friends, everything. Mainly, though, we talked about starving. And slowly, more girls like us arrived: Kelly, Coco, Lily. And I began to feel a little happier. I had people who understood me, people who hated it there as much as I did, people who didn't want to get better. However, as everyone saw my mood change, they assumed my recovery was working. My team at Bader—which included a therapist, a nutritionist, and a case manager—decided, along with my parents, that it was time for the next step.

On March third, I was let out and sent to a day program at the Cambridge Eating Disorder Center (CEDC). The program was scheduled from 9:00 AM to 3:30 PM, meaning I could go home, but not to school. Every day was spent in silence.

Inside my head, I was still anorexic. I ate like they wanted me to, but I was always judging the other girls on how "skinny" or "fat" they were, and I was always counting the calories or sneaking to the bathroom to check myself in the mirror, which was unsuccessfully covered up with motivational quotes. The people there tried to talk to me, but I refused. Group leaders would ask for my ideas on issues and about my life at home, but I would give one-word answers, all the while staring at the ground or at my thighs. I was scared they would reject me and I would be even more of a loser in my own eyes, rejected even by freaks. Freaks like me.

The only time I talked to anyone besides my parents was when Alli came over to my house. She told me about her life and asked about mine. We drew the "fat and ugly" people that we would never be. I asked her about Andrew, the boy I liked, and she said everyone missed me. She told them there had been an issue with my heart. She also told me that her ballet teacher complimented her on how skinny she was, and how her children's-size jeans were so big that she could fit a couple of fingers between the waistband and her abdomen. Every time I saw her I loved her. Every time I saw her I hated her—because she hadn't gotten caught and I had.

At this point in my life, I also had two other close friends: Erica and Christie. Erica and Alli were already friends, but Christie and Alli had never been close. Then, somehow, after I landed in the hospital, they were best friends. Christie had no idea that Alli was anorexic. At first I felt happy when Christie and Alli visited me together because we were like a group, but it also made me uneasy because, slowly, they were getting closer and closer. I felt like each was stealing the other from me.

Still, I started to feel a little better. Maybe it was because I was well nourished and thinking more clearly. Or maybe therapy really was helping. I became more open and talkative at the day program. I still

didn't talk about my recovery—the original reasons for my eating disorder, how I was still counting calories, my horrid body image—but I began to talk about other things, like my mixed feelings about Christie and Alli's growing friendship and my inferiority to Erica, with her perfect grades and cello playing. I was surprised that people didn't completely ignore me.

In April, things were looking up. I had the best 13th-birthday party ever! It was Oscars themed and everyone dressed up, me in a genuine '20s flapper dress with red-beaded fringe. We went to the auditorium of the college that my father worked at. Everyone drank mocktails and played with balloons. I stopped caring as much about what people thought of me. This manifested in different ways, the most visible of which was that I started to wear vintage clothing. This was important because I became more confident that I could be good at something other than starving—dressing. I was slowly becoming friends with people in the CEDC and I finally had people to talk to at lunch, people whose phone numbers I could ask for, people who liked me even though I was messed up. I was really happy for the first time in more than half a year. Things were going better, but I still had not recovered. I still filled in

"yes" on the paper we filled out every day that asked if I had "used behaviors," which refers to counting calories, self-harm, throwing up, weighing oneself, etc. I was still judging foods based on their calories. Meals were hard, and sometimes, at home, I did not finish within 30 minutes and had to drink Ensure. I still heard Alli's voice in my head asking how many calories I had eaten today, and I wanted to go back to a time when I could tell her that I had only chewed a piece of gum.

I'm sorry to say that I think my methodical eating triggered bad behavior in other people. I know that if I had seen someone eat like I did, cutting peas in half, I would feel horrible. I'm sure my eating provoked in other people what talking to Alli provoked in me, the "you are soooo fat, you eat waayyyyyy too much" voice. For some reason, I was surprised that I was still in treatment while others filed out and into the evening program and new ones took their place. Why wasn't I let out? It was, of course, because I was still unhealthy, both mentally and physically.

Then I made a mistake. I started lying on my check-in papers. I said no, I had not used behaviors. No, I was *fine*. All because I wanted to starve again. Looking back, I don't know why, because I was happy and I was on my way to having healthy thoughts. Weirdly, because I wanted to starve again, I ate my meals without problems.

My release date drew nearer. Everyone was happy for me. Happy for a liar. And it made me sad. I was released into the evening program on April 14th, which meant I had to go into the CEDC three days a week, from five until eight at night. But this time, I had no trouble making friends. People from the day program who had graduated before me were there, and I talked to them. They were some of the nicest people in the world. They accepted me and we laughed together during the 10-minute breaks after

meals and snacks, getting shouted at by the counselors for being too loud. Yes, I still lied about behaviors and I had unhealthy thoughts. I never reached the point with my therapist where I told her about the issues leading up to my eating disorder or how I would still look at the backs of food boxes to check the fat content. But I did talk about Alli's disorder, and I felt like a huge weight had been lifted from my shoulders. I graduated in July.

Fast-forward to the present day. I regret lying to get out of the day program, because the treatment was necessary, but I still see my therapist two times a week. I am only now trying to get rid of my ED voice. I can go a few weeks without counting calories or looking at nutritional information. I am no longer friends with Christie and Alli. I tried to tell Christie about Alli's anorexia and how she always asked me when I was going back to starving, but Christie didn't believe me. She told me that it was good for girls to be conscious of their weight and that she would be happy if she lost 10 pounds.

However, I am happier than I have been since the sixth grade. I may never feel 100 percent recovered, but I know it's an ongoing process. This year is going great. My relationship with my parents has improved because I'm no longer lying to them. I'm doing better in school now that I can actually concentrate. I have new friends, ones who don't make me feel insignificant. I have a semi-boyfriend. We went to Cambridge a few weekends ago. We walked past the CEDC together, and he held my hand, and I was inspired to contact my old buddies. I hope, by reading this, others can see how important it is to open up about their struggles and not lie to the people who are trying to help.

I am counting down the months until May, when I can return to the CEDC as a recovery speaker. ♦

Charlotte S. is an eighth-grader living in the Boston area.

*All names have been changed.

Other Girls

I loathed and envied the kids in my class who reminded me every chance they had that I was not like them.

By Jenny

Here's how the first half of seventh grade went down: I was living in Queens, New York, in a neighborhood that was once the residence of white, working-class folks who, in the six years that I lived there, all moved away, one household at a time. They were eventually replaced by Latin American families, whose children played soccer in the street, and Korean families who were seemingly always getting into minivans that took them to church, and Chinese families, like mine, that I can't quite reduce down into an easy, tidy description because when you *really know* something, when you've *lived* it and *are* it—whether it's being a girl or a teenager or a person of color or trans or queer or identifying as a wallflower or an outcast or whatever—you know that there's nothing tidy or easy about it.

My parents and I lived in an old-school colonial house with another family, sometimes renting out the attic, sometimes not. There were rats in the walls, and when we boiled water in the kettle to make ramen, we would often find flattened cockroaches floating among the dehydrated peas and carrots. My next-door neighbor, a retired third-generation Italian guy in his 60s who had an outdoor pool that I stared at from behind the wooden fence that separated our backyards and a German shepherd he loved to death, who once asked my dad, "Is it true—do you eat dog in China?"—this man, who was the last remaining holdout of a bygone era in which everyone who lived on my block was a third- or fourth-generation Italian, once let me hold his daughter's pet snake, and another time, he told me that he liked me because I spoke English so well, because this is America after all, and if you're going to live in America and reap the benefits and services that were built on the backs of hard-working taxpayers like him, then you could at least learn to speak the language properly.

"I learned English in six weeks," I told him gleefully, wanting his approval the way I wanted my English teacher's approval, the way I once wanted the approval of this girl in my fourth grade class who had platinum-blond hair and promised me that she would be my best friend if I would bring her 20 perfectly sharpened no. 2 pencils every day, which, of course, I did.

"Good for you," my neighbor told me. "They should all be like you." *They?* I thought. That wasn't my first taste of feeling like the "other," and until the day I die, there won't be a last.

When my friend Joy invited me to ride horses with her out in Montauk, I begged my parents to let me go, only to call them desperately from a payphone the first day, pleading with them in my I'm-gonna-cry voice to make the two-hour drive to Montauk to pick me up and take me home because the riding instructor mistook my crippling shyness for not knowing how to speak English.

"Can someone translate for her?" he asked whenever my horse stopped in his tracks, exasperated with me for holding up the group. I was upset with myself too for playing along—I became mute, the enforcer of my own silence, unable to explain that my horse just would not stop pissing and shitting and bucking, unable to say the words I wanted to say: "I'm doing everything you told me to. I'm pulling on the reins like you said, but my horse just wants to stop and poo every two minutes. And by the way, I speak and understand English perfectly, you waste of a bunghole."

Most of the kids in my elementary school were Latino, Asian, Middle Eastern, or black. In my sixth grade class, there were two white kids—one of them smelled like Cheetos, and the other had recently moved from Ohio and got his kicks by going around calling Farshid, the Persian kid in my class, "Fartshit," and trying to come up with other ways to insult my classmates who had names and faces that revealed they were "not from here," even when they were, and even though I knew that it was all bullshit, I struggled to articulate why it was just as right to point out that someone with a last name like Smith, or Henderson, or Romney, was also someone who was "not from here."

My friends spent the summer before seventh grade, the first year of junior high, plotting which gang they were going to join. Maybe it was nothing more than some kind of "I'm tough now, fuck you" act, and maybe for some kids in some neighborhoods in some parts of the world, the act *is* the reality, because how does one get to be tough as shit without having to pretend, at least a little, at first? All I knew was that I wasn't tough as shit. I was weak as a dead flower, ready to crumble at the slightest touch and fearful of everything, of going outside and being laughed at, of walking to the public library lest some older girls follow me and throw their McDonald's french fries at the back of my head (which happened quite frequently). I was afraid of having to always prove to people that I could, in fact, speak English, afraid of not knowing how to respond whenever someone casually mimed exaggerated kung fu moves in front of me, or whenever someone asked, "Are you Chinese or Korean? I'm not trying to be offensive, I just can't tell you apart."

I wanted to live in a place where I didn't have to remember to check the kettle for cockroaches before making ramen. I wanted to live in a house that I didn't have to share with another family. I wanted to live in a neighborhood where it was unheard of that someone could be robbed at gunpoint on their way home from the subway, because I wanted to live in a place where there were no subways, just shiny cars that took bored, beautiful-looking teenagers everywhere. And oh yeah—that summer, I was slowly easing into becoming the classic textbook case of a moody teenager who was unceasingly dissatisfied with herself. I felt hideous, stuck in a body that made me feel vulnerable, like at any moment, someone was going to point at me and say, "HA HA HA HA HA HA HA HA HA HA! Look at her!" And sometimes someone did.

My family finally splurged on a basic-cable box when I started seventh grade, and I sustained myself on a steady diet of puffy Cheetos and MTV music videos. I obsessively studied and desperately envied the girls in those videos—sulky rather than aggressive, oblivious to their own beauty, effortlessly cool, dreamy but put together, wild but not disturbingly so: it was a standard of perfection that I thought maybe I could rise to if only God or whoevs would send me a pair of tits already and make my voice less squeaky and annoying-sounding and give me bigger, rounder eyes, and longer, fuller eyelashes, wavier hair, a more mysterious, intriguing personality, and so on and so on.

Here's how the second half of seventh grade went down: I moved to a suburban town in Long Island where there were no subways or soccer games on the street. The streets were empty. The kids in my classes seemed perky and untroubled. Most of them didn't need to take the bus to school because they had parents who could drive them everywhere—to the movies, to their extra-curricular activities, to sleepovers and hangouts and all the things that I was beginning to want but didn't know how to be part of because most of the kids I had known were immigrants or children of immigrant parents who worked long hours, sometimes more than four jobs between them, but still couldn't afford a car, and lived in apartments that were too small and cramped to host slumber parties.

If I had been lightly bruised by my previous brushes with racism—and no matter how well-meaning the perpetrator's intention(s) might have been, being on the receiving end of racism will always hurt—then I was fully getting my ass beat after transferring to my new school in the suburbs. I went from a school where there were two white kids in my class to a school where the vast majority of the students were white. I was one of a handful of Asian kids in the whole district and one of two in my grade. When we did a unit on World War II, the boys in my class took to calling me a "Jap," even after we spent an entire class session talking about the war crimes the Japanese committed against the Chinese during the Nanking massacre. There was a girl who loved to tell me that I looked exactly like this one Korean girl, T., in the grade above us. Every time we passed each other in the hallway, she'd stop in her tracks and put her hand on my shoulder and say, "Wait, are you Jenny or T.? No offense, but it's fucking hard to tell you apart." And then she'd pat me on the back and continue on to class.

I loathed myself and I loathed the kids in my class who reminded me every chance they had that I was not like them, that I was this monstrous, appalling "other," a comical source to be objectified for their amusement. My powerlessness depressed me. I hated and envied these kids for having been born with the power to say something cruel to me. I hated how easily a "ching chong chang" joke or the ol' PULL YOUR EYES BACK TO SHOW HOW ASIANS HAVE SLITS FOR EYES! joke could bring them instant, unspoiled mirth. It sickened and drained me to think that long after their enjoyment had faded, I would still be trembling, still sick to my stomach. And worst of all? I was *ashamed* by how deeply affected I was by all this. Not only was I experiencing racism on a daily basis, but I actually had the gall to feel sad about it.

By the end of seventh grade, I was bursting with hatred and envy for the white kids in my class, whether they tormented me or not, because either way, they would never experience what I was experiencing. There was no "ching chong chang" equivalent for white native-English speakers. There was no "y'all look the same" equivalent. When the white girls in my class dressed up like hippies for 1960s Day during Spirit Week, no one said to them, "WOW! I'VE NEVER SEEN A WHITE HIPPIE BEFORE," or "YO, THAT LOOKS MAD WEIRD." But I couldn't escape those kinds of comments if I tried.

And I tried. When I asked my sorta-friend S. if I should audition for the school play—it was *The Crucible* that year—she said, "I don't know. It might be kind of weird to see an Asian person as a Puritan," and I thought, *Well, crap, that rules out all of Shakespeare and, um, every single play in the English canon unless there's one about*

Ms. Ching Chong Chang and her slanty slit eyes. Another time, my friend K. told me that it was all but *scientifically proven* that people with European features were more physically attractive than people with Asian features, which sounded suspiciously similar to the kind of scientific racism that justified the Holocaust, slavery, and the murder of, and stealing from, Native Americans in America. But, as always, when confronted with moments like these, I always reverted back to the deaf and dumb mute I was that day in Montauk, sitting on a horse that wouldn't stop crapping.

As preoccupied as some of my classmates were with my otherness, I was just as consumed, if not more so, with their whiteness. I began to obsessively observe how the white girls in my classes carried themselves. I gazed at their curls and asked my mom to buy me hair rollers. (They didn't work on my fine, limp hair.) I eavesdropped on their conversations to find out where they bought their clothes and shoes and then I pestered my mom to buy me the same exact clothes and shoes (example: black-and-white sandals made of foam with a wedge heel that made my feet smell like the butthole of another butthole). I watched how they spoke to one another, what gestures they made with their hands, how they held their pens, how they dotted their *i*'s and crossed their *t*'s, whether their *y*'s ended with a serif curl or if they were arrow-straight, and I attempted to mimic every detail, even the unimportant ones. I attempted to erase all signs of the "other" from myself. I feared that if I didn't, I would be forever unlovable, and I didn't want that. I wanted to be loved. But as it turns out, bowing down to racist ideas of normalcy, acceptability, and beauty didn't bring me love. My obsession was destroying me bit by bit, and I was exhausted, and I wanted to stop. So I stopped.

I washed and scrubbed the first layer of butthole smell from my shoes (it was the best I could do) and gave them away. I gave my copycat clothes to family friends who were younger than me. I discovered the band Bush (I NEVER SAID I WAS COOL), who eventually became my gateway drug to Radiohead, which was my gateway drug to punk music, which became my gateway drug to adopting the "I don't give a shit" approach to life. I wore Dracula capes to school over short skirts and platform combat boots. I tied my hair into little knots the way Gwen Stefani wore her hair in the '90s, and I smeared black lipstick on my mouth and perfected my bitchface. I washed my hair in sugar water to get it to stay spiky (I don't recommend doing this in hot weather unless you want to be chased by eager swarms of bees).

When it was all the rage to get Chinese characters tattooed onto your body, I suddenly became the go-to translator for the newly inked. The same kids who ching-chong-chang'ed me two years ago were now the ones who wanted to know if the character they had emblazoned on their neck truly meant "love and peace."

I didn't know how to read Chinese characters, so I made it up as I went along. "That one says *dickbag*, and the one your arm says *I farted*," I told them. I licked sugar from my spiky hair, told a girl that if she made fun of my last name one more time that I was going to "slam your head into this wall, and I'm not bluffing, BITCH." I had no idea where it was all coming from. All I knew was that I had suddenly swung from one extreme to the other—from obsessively trying to cover up my "otherness" to obsessively flaunting it every chance I had.

There's a slimy, uncomfortable truth about obsession that I find hard to talk about. I'm not quite sure how to think about and tackle the power dynamics between the worshipper and the worshipped. Society tells us that worship is a distinctly feminine act—I'm thinking of the image of the teenage fangirl, overcome by rapture and ecstasy when in the presence of the ultimate godhead (I'm talking about BIEBER, DUH), overcome with emotion, crying, screaming, fainting, overrun—and I want to reject that shit as much as I want to embrace and repossess it, because there's nothing shameful about this kind of collective religious experience. But at the same time, it was awful to worship at the altar of self-loathing, of wishing I was a different ethnicity, of wishing I had a different face, a different family, a different life. The white girls in my seventh grade class had an immense power over me that they never asked for and were most likely never even aware of, but it was given to them because that's how privilege works—you don't have to ask for it; you already have it.

There are obsessions that might literally collapse onto you and destroy you (see: hoarders who live amongst heaping piles of rat carcasses); and there are obsessions that inspire a magical transmogrification of feelings into actual, physical things, like when you transfer your love for the English comedian Stephen Fry into a beautiful shrine; and there are obsessions that bring you into a world of beautiful things, like when you suddenly discover a band or a writer or an artist and it's like everything they've ever created was created just for you, and their music/writing/art makes you want to live a longer life just so you can spend more of it listening to/reading/looking at what they've created.

And then there is the kind of obsession that hurts you. It won't physically impair your ability to breathe or move (once again, see: hoarders), but it robs you of something so essential that sometimes you wish you *would* stop breathing. This is the kind of obsession that doesn't inspire you to be anything or create anything. Instead you find yourself kneeling at the altar of an idol who does not care about you, all the while berating yourself for not being born some other way. And as someone who has known this kind of obsession all too well, I sincerely hope from the muddy depths of my heart that you have never experienced it, and never will. ♦

Teenage Girls Assaulted By Wild Animals!

An interview with John Waters.
By Hazel

John Waters is one of my favorite people in the world. As the writer and director of such outlandish films as *Pink Flamingos*, *Polyester*, *Cry-Baby*, and *Hairspray*, he has made a career out of celebrating crazy delinquent teenagers, making the weirdest things the coolest things, and choosing bad taste over socially approved taste every single time. He's the Pope of Trash and is pretty much obsessed with everything from Justin Bieber to schoolgirls gone bad to wearing Band-Aids as jewelry. I hope after reading this interview you all get inspired to dress as dirty as possible, drop out of high school, and take every risk you can take while you're young! Please get crazy in the name of John Waters! It's the perfect way to honor him.

HAZEL You once said, "Life is nothing if you're not obsessed." Why is obsession so important to you?

JOHN WATERS Well, obsession can be good or bad. I mean, obsession can be the reason you wake up every day and love your job because you love what you're doing, if you're an artist or if you're into something. But then there's bad obsession! Like if you're a drug addict, I guess you're obsessed with heroin, aren't you? Or a bad love affair, you know, where you can't get over somebody — much later in life hopefully you look back and say, "God, why was I thinking about that person?"

But you can use that. You can use all kinds of obsession. You can use obsession for humor, you can use it for style, you can use it for fashion. Obsession is great if it brings you pleasure and helps you make your living doing something you love. It's only bad if you make the same mistake over and over with some obsession that brings you unhappiness.

What are you currently obsessing over?

Whatever project I'm doing is what I obsess over. Right now I'm writing a book; obsessing over it is what gets me up in the morning to work on it.

I'm always obsessed, really, with culture and the news. I read five to six newspapers a day and I get over a hundred magazines a month and I read blogs. I just like to know what's going on. I think it's very important in my age to have "youth spies." You could be a youth spy.

Oh my gosh! I wish! What's the book you're working on?

It's sort of an undercover travel adventure, but I can't really talk about it. I never talk about something before I do it; it's bad luck. This is a secret book. But I just wrote an article for *Playboy*; I just wrote the introduction to Ricki Lake's new book; and I wrote something for *Vogue Hommes* on my obsession, actually. I wrote about these sleazy soft-core porn paperbacks. There was one title called *Teenage Girls Assaulted by Wild Animals!*

That book sounds amazing. Speaking of assault, I know you're very open about your love of and obsession with serial killers and crime.

"I have a lot of fake food around the house." Why do you have so much fake food? "I dunno, I guess so I won't eat it all?"

I don't love serial killers. I taught in prison for a long time, I still have friends that I visit in prison, and I wrote very seriously in my last book about my plea for parole for one woman [Leslie Van Houten] who had been involved with Charles Manson. I follow

"This is my favorite book title of all time." What's it about? Have you read it? "No! I just love the title!"

some serial-killer cases, but it's not like I collect stuff about them. I mean, I do have a John Wayne Gacy painting because someone gave it to me, but I collect contemporary art, I don't collect that kind of thing.

But: I'm interested in extreme human behavior. The reason I was so interested in Leslie Van Houten was because she did something so terrible and so notorious, and how can you ever make up for that in life? How can she get beyond something she did when she was 17 years old, under the control of a madman? Just be glad *you* never met him.

You have always been drawn to these sorts of strange stories and weird obsessions, but have you been judged for them? Especially when you were younger?

For your whole life, people are always going to give you grief. Nobody who turns out to be great had an easy time in high school. People in the arts always have trouble in school. The prom queens and the football stars, their lives went downhill after they graduated. It was over.

They peaked too early.

Yes, exactly, those types peak too early. Look them up in your yearbook after you graduate. Look in your parents' yearbook for those people, and you'll see that they have pretty dull lives. But anything can happen to anybody; you don't really know what's going to happen. One thing you have to learn early on is that you can't judge people until you know the whole story about what causes them to act like they do. In high school, everybody judges everybody. They're the meanest they could ever be in high school! But things change, and I think high school probably is better than it was when I was young…

Eh, well…

Well, at least they have schools you can go to for art and that kind of stuff. But certainly how you look in high school is incredibly important, because you identify what type [of person] you are. Usually you hang around with people who wear the same kind of fashion. Which I never quite understood, because I can hang around with any type of person, and I don't pick friends by how they dress. I mean, they all have a style, but it doesn't have to be mine.

If I was 15 today, I'd probably have my whole face pierced. Parents should be more relieved if [their kids] do that rather than tattoos, because [piercings come] out. Tattoos don't!

That reminds me, when I saw you speak in Philadelphia a couple of years ago, you said something that really spoke to me about parents and kids. It was something along the lines of "Parents should be so happy that their kids are sort of weird."

Yeah, because kids need encouragement. You can't order up your kids, and you can't order up your parents. Whatever you have, you gotta deal with. I always tell parents who come to me with their daughter and her whole face is tattooed, "Let her open a tattoo parlor."

Yeah! Let her channel her obsession into a career.

[Parents] need to think of it in the best way. All of that anger and craziness when you're a teenager and all those hormones going through you and everything—it does make you crazy! And how can you forget that if you've lived through it? But it's tough when it's your own kid, because you're afraid for them. You're afraid of what can happen.

"These are two tabloid moments captured by, I don't know—we ordered them online—but this is Michael Jackson dangling his baby, the moment that caused the scandal, and this is Britney getting out of the limousine showing her private area!"

211

Waters pulled out some of his favorites from his book collection. This one is Dad's in Prison by Margaret Speed.

Why do you love Justin Bieber so much? "Just 'cause he makes me laugh so much."

Single and Pregnant

But you *have* to take some risks when you're a kid to find out who you are. You just have to learn which risks are safe and which are self-destructive. Everybody does weird stuff. As you get older, I believe if you've never been allowed to do all that weird shit, then you make it into some kind of obsession that you're too old to have!

You seem to be drawn to those risk-taking teenagers—the juvenile delinquents or the schoolgirls gone bad, like Dawn Davenport in *Female Trouble*. What do you find so fascinating about them?

Dawn Davenport was how the trashy girls looked when I was that age. What's the look now?

Probably like really poker-straight ironed hair that's been fried and tons of eyeliner all around the eyes.

Too much bronzer?

Yes! Well, I mean, I live in New Jersey, so there's A LOT.

[*Laughs*] Everybody loves to write about the bad kids from their youth. It's fun to be a juvenile delinquent, but it's not fun to be an adult delinquent.

Why weren't you ever a juvenile delinquent?

I was never a real juvenile delinquent, because in the '50s they were in gang fights! I would have lost. But I love the bad boys. Johnny Depp's character in *Cry-Baby* was based on this boy who lived across the street. I thought he looked great, but all the parents hated him. He fixed his car in the driveway and was a high school dropout. I don't know what happened to him—he's probably dead. But I made that [character] on my memory of somebody. I exaggerated it and idealized him and made him Johnny Depp.

Memories from high school are so strong when you're older that when you create anything you can play with those memories. If someone hassled you, you could make them the villain. You can mock them.

With your unique personality, I don't even understand how you survived your suburban high school experience. How did you?!

Well, I wanted to get away from it. I wanted to go downtown and be a beatnik and find bohemia. I hung around with other kids—not always from my school, but from my neighborhood— that didn't fit in either. It was a very mixed group, though. It was straight, gay, rich, poor, black, white. We hung around together and built our own little family. We had fun together and protected one another. We didn't care what the other ones thought! That's the thing: there's all those people in high school, and you have to endure them, but you don't have to hang around with them.

I didn't have a good time in school because I was bored. Boredom is the worst, because it turns into anger. I went to a Catholic high school, but you didn't have to wear the school coat, so I wore hundreds of different ones. I never cut my hair, either. Hairdos and fashion are always what make teachers crazy.

I always used fashion to rebel and make people crazy, because you can sort of protect yourself with fashion. I wore ludicrous outfits that I would think back on and go, "Oh my god, I'm so glad there weren't pictures."

I wish there were pictures! I want to see them!

I'm glad there aren't. Fashion can certainly help you identify yourself. It is your advertisement; it's what you tell the world. Not "I'm goth," or "I'm this, I'm that," but, "I have my identity." That's why kids are obsessed with fashion. It's what makes their parents crazy, because usually it's against what [the parents] want to wear. Who wants to go shopping with their mother when they're 16? Unless your mother's Betsey Johnson. Like Madonna's daughter: I'm surprised she doesn't dress like Barbara Bush, just to rebel!

I always say to kids, with fashion, that they shouldn't be wearing designer clothing—they should copy it. Go to the thrift shop and buy the worst thing that the coolest kid in school would never wear. It'll be the thing that's the most "out." Buy it and turn it into something that's funny and witty. Fashion is confidence. If you can get away with wearing it, it's a new style.

Fashion always pisses people off. The designers look to kids to do something that nobody's done. Like boys wearing their pants so they're almost falling off—who thought that up? It's hilarious! They're really walking and it doesn't fall down! But look how long it's been around. It lasts forever. I mean, hippie clothes are still around, and punk clothes too. I see kids with a mohawk and I think, *That's not real new!*

I know you also believe in fashion rules.

Diana Vreeland said, "Bad taste is better than no taste." It's true. You have to take risks with fashion. But I do have all sorts of rules, like I still believe you shouldn't wear white after Memorial Day, no velvet before Thanksgiving, no patent leather before Easter, no leather pants ever, no skinny jeans for anyone over 30, and no "belt abuse," where the first thing you notice about an outfit is the belt. But that's a lot of rules, and you can make up your own rules, with humor. I like when you notice someone for their fashion—you know they at least attempted to create a look.

Band-Aids are a good fashion accessory for teenagers, in inappropriate places for no reason. Rubber bands look really good, just 50 of them around your wrist. Looking dirty is also good when you're young—looking dirty kind of works when you're cute. But you have to be young to wear certain things. One thing I've always loved—and I think Tavi might have done this when she dyed her hair gray—is the "faux old" look. I say draw on crow's feet and Ruth Gordon lips! Mock every generation's fear of getting older.

We've been talking a lot about fashion, but what about film? One part of your book *Crackpot* that I really loved was when you say that you have guilty pleasures but "in the reverse"—your guilty pleasures are art films. You talk all the time about how much you love trash, but are reluctant to let anyone know you love art films.

Yes, that's my guilty pleasure. Certainly not *Final Destination 3*, which I loved, or *Piranha 3D*, which I loved. My guilty pleasure would be, like, *The Tree of Life*. I do like those art movies for real, but people don't expect me to.

But do you think anyone should feel guilty about their pleasures and obsessions?

I'm not guilty about pleasure. I guess if I ever had a real guilty pleasure it would maybe be if I loved *The Help*. Which I didn't hate, and I thought I would. When I love something that is mass-loved, that's probably the only time I'm hesitant to admit it, because it goes against my image. However, that can happen to me. That's why I love Justin Bieber.

But *The Help* is my number-one guilty pleasure. Even though they copied *Pink Flamingos*. They eat shit in that movie.

And that was a very mainstream movie.

It's just not dog shit, though.

What's the difference between good bad taste and bad bad taste?

You have to know the rules of good taste to have bad taste. With good good taste, you just know the rules. You like something not because it's worth money, but because you know its value, and you don't care if anyone else knows it. You pull it off seamlessly without looking down on anybody.

Good bad taste is celebrating something without thinking you're better than it. You think it's so amazing, and you could have never even thought it up. But the people who have [this thing] have it without irony. And so you're stupefied by it and you have to respect it because it is so peculiar and so weird and much crazier than you could ever think, but those other people think they're normal.

Bad bad taste is condescending, making fun of others. An old plastic pink flamingo on a lawn that two older people have had forever is just good taste. But a plastic pink flamingo on a yuppie's front lawn is bad bad taste. It's not even the original—it's mass produced, and they're way too late on the joke.

So that's the difference for me: if you're celebrating something or you're looking down on something.

My generation is also really into liking things ironically, and I read somewhere that you think irony has ruined so many things—how not everything is supposed to be "so bad that it's good." How do you think irony has ruined everything?

"This is my bulletin board where I put things that inspire me. I think it's just such a good idea and everybody should have one in their house, just a place where you can put images."

The last line in *Pecker* is "To the end of irony." Because, yes, I'm an irony dealer. But irony is snobbery. If you're really poor in a country where there's famine, is there such a thing as irony? Is anything so bad it's good? Usually irony is for the wealthy. It's snobbism, in a way, because you're saying something is good *because* it's bad.

Irony, sometimes, if you're trying too hard—like forced grossness in movies—can be tiring. Fashion is perfect for irony, but I think that's more wit. Wit is different from irony. I think fashion needs wit.

But now, with kids my age, it seems like *everyone* goes to thrift stores and buys the ugliest sweaters and wears them ironically.

They always did that. When I was young and went to thrift shops, it was stuff my parents had given, so it was all '30s clothes. Now it's '90s stuff—you know, it's what your parents threw out. But if you buy the ugliest sweater and it's funny, I think that's fine. You still look hot in it. You don't wear it to look ugly. You wear it because you're so hot an ugly sweater can't make you look bad, and that's a great look.

Being the outsider and "the different one" is becoming more and more mainstream. You always read interviews with celebrities and they're like, "I was weird and I didn't have a lot of friends" and I'm just like, "You're lying!" But to have a counterculture you have to have a strong group of outsiders. You once said, about rebellion, "When I was younger, it was being juvenile delinquents and beatniks and hippies and punks, and then grunge and rappers, but now what?" How can someone be a rebel today?

Be a hacktivist. That's how you rebel today. Sit at home on the computer and shut down American Express. Hacktivism is juvenile delinquency. That's how you do it. And nobody sees each other, so you don't have to wear an outfit. Just a T-shirt. Bad posture. It's the first rebellion where there is no look.

But how important do you think it is for kids these days to have a counterculture?

It may be less important these days. Maybe the way to rebel is to be an insider. Now *outsider* is a hackneyed term. But you can [rebel] with music and you can do it with fashion. You'll always find a way to get on people's nerves. And with art.

I know you're a huge art collector.

Art usually makes me angry at first. Over there I have a Peter Hujar picture of a pile of trash, which is the best thing in this house, because trash paid for it. I have a painting that's all just mold. I believe that art, in the beginning, should kind of make you angry, because that's what's going to change things. It's the same thing with clothes. You think, *Oh, I would never wear that to my own funeral it's so ugly*. But then you think, *Wait a minute, it's so ugly*

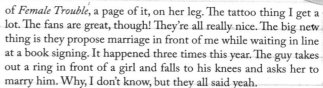

it's almost cool. And then it *is* cool! You decide it's cool by picking it up and putting it on. It isn't cool lying there in that bin. As soon as you curate it, like art, it makes it cool. That's the difference.

I kind of love it when art makes people angry.

All contemporary art does, if you think about it. You know, abstract expressionism, with Jackson Pollock, made people furious. Then Andy Warhol put up the soup can, and in one night [abstract expressionism] was over with. Then Minimalism infuriated people. It always works like that. The next generation pisses off the one before.

What about your obsessions with music? I loved the part in your book *Role Models* when you talk about shoplifting a Little Richard record when you were 11 years old and putting it on full volume and scaring your grandmother half to death!

Well, that was a long time ago, and I paid it all back, because I ended up paying $30,000 each to put those songs in the movies later. So I don't feel guilty about it. I listen to new music, too. Let's see, what am I playing here [*flips through CDs*]…Yelawolf! Eminem…Zola Jesus… That's young-people music, but I listen to all kinds of music. Here I have some Peggy Lee and Harry Connick. I listen to everything.

Who was the first musical artist that you were REALLY obsessed with?

Elvis. When I first saw him twitching when he was 18, singing "Baby Let's Play House," I thought he was a Martian. He was like a space alien. You can't imagine—in the boring, straight '50s, to see that was like, *Oh my god.* He was like possessed by the devil! And if you still go back and look at the early shots of him, they're still shocking. When he's twitching and moaning…it's still radical.

Especially when you think about, like you said, the context of the time. That conservative era. Were your parents always supportive of your work?

My parents were very conservative. They were not hippie parents or liberals. But they saw early on that I knew what I wanted to do. I had a puppet-show career when I was 12 years old. They knew that I was driven and that I wanted to do something. So they wisely chose to let me do that, even though they were mortified by it. Mortified by the films and the bad reviews and the censorship bust and all the stuff that was written about me. So they were supportive *and* frightened. They had no reference guide to know what to do about it.

You have some pretty obsessive fans, right?

Nowadays I always sign their bodies and they have my name on their ass or something. They get it tattooed. One girl had the script

of *Female Trouble*, a page of it, on her leg. The tattoo thing I get a lot. The fans are great, though! They're all really nice. The big new thing is they propose marriage in front of me while waiting in line at a book signing. It happened three times this year. The guy takes out a ring in front of a girl and falls to his knees and asks her to marry him. Why, I don't know, but they all said yeah.

Parents now bring me their fucked-up kids, which I like. They're very sweet when they come to my book signing or a spoken-word thing. I can see that it's a last-ditch effort for the parent to sort of bond [with their kid]. I treat them nicely and say, "How nice that your mom brought you here." Then to the really crazy fans I say, "Call your parents." [*Laughs*] They always look really uptight! When I see drag queens I say, "Call your parents," and they always look *so* shocked, because that's the last thing they expect me to say. They don't know what to say to that. Their entire drag persona crumbles.

It's like, "Why is John Waters asking me to call my parents?" But do you think any of your fans are *too* obsessive?

No, because they never bother me, you know? They never come to my house. I don't get stalkers. The people who get stalkers are the ones that are in the most innocuous TV sitcoms and stuff. The weird people in show business actually don't get stalkers. Well, Madonna did, but it's more like the [celebrities] you watch on TV and you think they're talking into the house or something.

Finally, do you have any advice for your teenage fans?

Choose your friends wisely, read as much as you can, and, it comes a little later in life, but make a deal with your parents that you can get on their nerves and they can get on your nerves, so think before you say something, and they have to do it too. If they don't, pull out a verbal-abuse whistle and whistle when they don't. But if you think before you say something, maybe you won't get on each other's nerves, especially in the hardest time, when you're a teenager dealing with your parents.

Ask for what you like, and get used to being turned down. Rejection is hard, but to get acceptance you have to put up with a lot of rejection. If you really like something, don't ever think, *Can I do this?* If you think *Can I?* you won't. You have to say, "I'm gonna do this, and nobody's gonna stop me!" But you have to believe that, you can't just say it. It might take really a long time, because people never say you're good at first. Or if they do, you're a flash in the pan and it's over. ♦

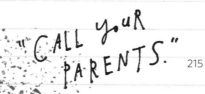
"CALL YOUR PARENTS."

Bad Romance

If you're caught in one, here's how to get out of it.

By Sady

One summer, a long time ago, I found myself carted into a therapist's office so that I could talk about my ex-boyfriend. It was very embarrassing. I had gone to a doctor for insomnia and he asked me when I had stopped sleeping well. I told him I'd had this bad break-up recently and that I was just, I don't know, upset? And I started talking about it. And crying. He looked at me like, *OK, no drugs for you*, and walked me downstairs to a therapist's office, where he booked me an appointment for the hour.

So I told the therapist my story, which I was quite convinced of at the time. It went like this: I met this guy and he was really smart and I wasn't. I knew that because he told me so and, since he was really smart, it had to be true. Also, this guy was really cool and I wasn't. I knew that because he told me so. Also, this guy really knew how to have fun. I didn't know how to do that—he'd told me I was always getting in the way of fun. Also, this guy had a lot of problems and I didn't do enough to fix them. I mean, I tried. But I was actually the reason he wasn't getting anywhere in life. How did I know that? He told me so.

I felt so *lucky* to be with a cool, smart, fun guy. He was so *generous* to date me, even though I wasn't cool or smart or fun. And then we'd broken up, and it was all my fault, and now I had a new boyfriend, but I didn't deserve one because I was awful.

The therapist looked at me. She spent a while looking at me. And then she did me the biggest favor that anyone ever has: she cracked up laughing.

The story I was telling did not make sense. There was no reason I should believe it. And once we'd established that, we could talk about my actual problem, which was not that guy, and it wasn't that I was awful, either. My problem was that if someone told me I was awful, I would believe it. And I would reorganize my entire life—including my feelings, thoughts, values, tastes, clothing, habits, and personality—and sit there wondering why I wasn't happy.

People do this all the time. Every friend I've ever had has done this, at some point, to some extent. There are a lot of intense feelings—often sexy feelings!—that go along with first relationships. There are lots of stories about what it means to love someone, and when you haven't loved many people, you tend to believe them.

You tend to believe, for instance, that being in love is the most wonderful and important thing in the world. That being in love means you are pretty, even if your partner is unkind about your appearance. That being in love means you are likable, even when your partner doesn't honor your thoughts and preferences. That being in love means you aren't alone, so you want to stay with someone even when you feel lonely in the relationship.

And girls? Girls are supposed to play it cool and not be clingy, so I never asked for more when he didn't bother to call me on my birthday. Girls were supposed to have a good sense of humor and not be nags, so I didn't object even when he insulted me to my face under the guise of "constructive criticism" or "just joking." Girls are supposed to be sexy, so I was endlessly responsive to his sexual needs even when that included denigrating or neglecting mine.

These notions are harmful. Lots of them entail losing yourself, or hurting yourself, or giving away your own power. But we tell these stories all the time. There's a part in every *Twilight* installment where someone is like, "So, Bella, can we talk about how your boyfriend's plans entail literally destroying your soul and sucking the very life out of your body?" and she's like, "But he's the sparkliest boy in school! I will love him forever."

I get it. I've done it. And so have a lot of people. But if you're in that situation, or if you've just gotten out of it, there are certain things you need to know to make sure it does not happen again.

1. LEARN THE TERM "GASLIGHT"

The first thing to know about relationships is that they should never be about control. There are lots of ideas about what constitutes a good relationship, but, for the purposes of this article, we're going to define "bad relationship" in one way: a bad relationship is one in which someone else attempts to control how you behave, think, and feel about yourself.

Sometimes, a controlling partner may be very obvious and extreme. They may keep track of how much you spend or tell you how to dress or tell you to stop hanging out with family or friends. They may threaten you with punishment if you don't obey them. If any of this is happening, you need to walk away. This is abuse and it has to end.

But many controlling people aren't obvious or extreme. Some relationships exist on the continuum between "abusive" and "great." They're codependent or toxic or they rely on what is called "ambient abuse"—not overt, visible forms of harm, but subtle ones that gradually take away your ability to function. If people overtly harm you, you might leave them. Many controlling people know this, and have figured out ways to make their behavior seem like your fault, which is called gaslighting. It's presenting someone with false information in order to make them unsure of what is happening and unable to respond correctly. If you've ever said something like "What you said really hurt my feelings" and the other person responded with "I didn't say that" or "You're too sensitive" or "It hurts my feelings when you say I've hurt you," you've experienced gaslighting. You're being manipulated into thinking you can't remember things, or respond appropriately, or that you're a hurtful person, so that someone else can avoid apologizing.

The gaslighter may change the "rules" of the relationship very rapidly or create a no-win situation in which you're told to do two contradictory things and will be punished for failing to do either. This can be overt: *You're lazy, so you should work harder on your homework, but you're also uncaring, so I need you to pick up the phone when I call you during homework hours.* Or it can be subtle: *I need my girlfriend to have a good sense of style, so never wear a shirt that I don't like, but also, if you have a good sense of style, you shouldn't have to ever ask me which shirts I like.* No matter what you do, you fail. And then this person punishes you for failing.

And here's the thing: Gaslighting, the tactic, is named after *Gaslight*, the 1944 movie, which is about a guy who tries to get his wife *diagnosed as incurably insane* by doing this. It's not always fully intentional, and it's not always done primarily to harm you—alcoholics, for example, are almost invariably gaslighters, because that's how they get people to enable or overlook their drinking—but it causes real and profound damage. It erodes your sense of reality, destroys your self-esteem, and reduces you to a depressed, fearful, self-loathing, hysterical person. At which point, the gaslighter tells you that they treat you badly because you're hysterical!

2. DON'T BLAME YOURSELF

Your first reaction, when you realize you're being treated badly, may be confusion. You may spend a long time trying to figure out why they did it. So I'm going to do you a favor. I'm going to tell you why: because you are awesome. These relationships do not happen because you are a bad partner. They happen because you are a good partner and someone else used that against you.

As discussed, people who treat you badly often say you deserve it because you're not giving enough, or you don't care about their problems, or you're too demanding. But here's the rub: people who date mean or controlling people, or even overtly abusive people, don't do it because they lack empathy or forgiveness or patience. People date mean or controlling people because they have *too much* empathy, forgiveness, and patience. You can see a good person in your partner even when other people wouldn't, you can exercise an unusual amount of compassion, and this partner noticed that you would put up with things that other people wouldn't. It's awful. And now, it's done. Because you are leaving.

3. DO NOT RIDE THE ESCALATOR

You can't make this person be fair to you. I repeat: *you cannot make this person be fair to you.* And you do not have to try. You need

to have your self-respect, your dignity, and your own firm belief in the fact that you are kind, fair, and trustworthy. I've lost that a few times. But I have never lost it more profoundly than on the occasions when I tried to get someone who was toxic to treat me nicely.

The fact is, people call these relationships "toxic" for a reason. They make you sick. And the longer you keep yourself entangled in one—whether that's by forgiving the person, or by trying to get even with the person, or even just trying to get that person to understand the impact of his or her behavior—the sicker you become. I'm not trying to say that you should walk away from resolvable conflicts. We've talked about how there are good and necessary ways to resolve conflicts. You should try those. If you're old enough, and this relationship is very serious, you can even ask that person if they are willing to get help with you to work through the relationship's problems. (Although you should also get independent help to take care of yourself.) But if that's not working, you need to leave before you start acting out.

It's very hard to respond in a healthy way to an unhealthy situation. If someone keeps twisting your words, or blaming you, or manipulating you, eventually you're going to start thinking that word-twisting and blaming and manipulation are the way to win an argument. If someone wants to prove you are a mean or weak person, they're going to do and say things that would cause any reasonable person to feel upset, so that they can watch you fall apart or lose your temper. You'll become the one escalating the fight. You'll scream awful things, you'll cry for days, you'll do mean stuff to even the score, and you'll lose yourself completely—all because you thought there was some way to make this person be fair.

You cannot justify being cruel or inappropriate because of someone else's actions. So you need to have rules for what you will let yourself do or say, and you need to stick to them. You can't make this person do, feel, or say anything, not even "sorry." All you can do is believe the following:

When I was little, I loved the movie *Labyrinth*. This was because my grandparents told me it was made specifically for me. It was about a girl who picked on her little brother. I also picked on my little brother. Clearly, this was an instructional film about how, if I were not nice to my little brother, he would be taken away by goblins. I tried to get my little brother taken away by goblins like 14 times after I watched it. Sometimes my grandparents' plans backfired.

But *Labyrinth* is a very instructional film—it just happens to be about dating. The girl, Sarah, clearly has a crush on the David Bowie character, because who doesn't? And Bowie clearly has a crush on Sarah. Because of this, Sarah gets dropped into this complex and dangerous maze. There are rules, riddles, bogs, monsters, and awfulness, and David Bowie just stands there and says: "I ask for so little. Just fear me, love me, do as I say, and I will be your slave." That's the actual line! That's the line every toxic partner will always feed you. And that's why this is so instructional.

Because it turns out that fearing him, loving him, or doing as he says is not necessary for Sarah. She didn't even have to walk through the maze. What she has to do, in the end, is look him in the eye and say one thing. There's a whole big build-up around it involving how much he's put her through and how awesome she is—"through dangers untold and hardships unnumbered, I have fought my way here," blah blah, "my will is as strong as yours and my kingdom is as great"—but that's not it. That's a waste of time until she says the one thing that counts: "You have no power over me." She has to say those words and know how true they are. And then *the whole maze falls apart.* And she's home.

You are going to get home. You already are: you are in control of your own life. All you have to do is remember that. Granted, in order to realize that, a professional therapist, who is hired to hear people say nonsensical and unhealthy things without reacting judgmentally, may have to actually laugh right into your face. Or not. Maybe you just read an article and things started to make more sense to you. ♦

We lived happily forever, so the story goes.

By Petra

Thanks to Anna, Fox, Jacqueline, Feli, Aurora, Allegra, Kim, Jacob, Ikoro, Sean, Blaze, and Chloe for modeling, and Chloe Wise for styling. Special thanks to Rosedale Heights School of the Arts, the Drake General Store, and 69 Vintage.

airplanes to help
aight ine.

ou how to make a drinking straw
the air in a straight line.

blimp

Leptoceratops
length 6 ft

MARCH 2012: *Exploration*

Hey, Rookies! Welcome to March. Do you have your PHYSICAL ACTIVITY HATS, GOING OUTSIDE SHOES, and DOING THINGS TAPE MUSTACHES all ready and set for this month of EXPLORATION? I do! For March brings spring fever, and with the third quarter of school dragging along, I am ITCHING to get moving on things—on LIFE. I just spent the past three months holed up in bed on Netflix, debating every night whether to rewatch *Sharpay's Fabulous Adventure* or *Bratz Kidz: Sleep-Over Adventure*. Now that I feel educated on adventures, I just want to go out and have my *own*, you know?

We'll save the rest of this issue for college and careers and outer space and the deep sea, though. Right now, school doesn't end for months, and the ideas of *the outside world* and *life after youth* feel so abstract. At this moment I would like to deem spring fever as the time to explore the surroundings you've got. There's something to be said for nights spent alone in your room listening to music and sulking; for Friday afternoons that somehow pass both too quickly and too slowly, when you and your friends walk around waiting for a new street to appear where you're sick of seeing the same ones you've passed every day. 'Cause you might go home for dinner and realize that you guys didn't do anything, but you talked a lot and found yourself relating to people in a way you hadn't for a long time. You might start watching a movie alone at night because you feel distant or lost, and realize by the end that you've found a little piece of yourself in the characters, and feel connected to the world for a brief moment.

There's something magical going on when your own world might be the only one you know, and you hold on to the things that you love extra hard, the bands and movies and books and friends. *Hating everything* (euphemism for "hormones") makes every emotion and experience more intense, and it means you'll identify with a band or movie or book or friend in an especially strong way that I am told there's not enough time for once you're an adult.

If you want a change of scenery but summer camp won't start for months, you have to create it yourself. Take different routes to and from school; seek out places that don't look like your own town. If you walk along the patch of grass by the highway, you might be able to convince yourself you're anywhere else, or in a place you've created far from the neighborhood you know.

Try to keep a diary. Keeping up with it is easier and less daunting when you remember that not everything has to be super-good writing or incredibly profound—just try and keep an unedited stream-of-consciousness going throughout it. No formatting necessary, just throw everything in there, wrappers and clippings and napkins and notes.

A more convenient way to collect clippings, photos from magazines, and other random things you enjoy, might be to start a Tumblr. Just don't get sucked in to spending all your time on it—you gotta DO something with the inspiration you accumulate, or else you'll feel all groggy and lazy again. If you're sick of how you dress, keep an eye out for clothes that remind you of the images that have caught your eye and your heart, and you'll create your own style by feeling like you've internalized and made part of yourself all the things you really love.

Absorb everything and go through phases of different interests and identities and come back to yourself with whatever stayed in your mind all along. It's scary and exciting and through this next month it might feel necessary. Then, once the time comes for the final frontier, you'll have an especially unique way of taking it all in.

To quote the dog from *Sharpay's Fabulous Adventure*: *supposedly cute head tilt to the side.*

LOVE TAVI

ZION

NATIONAL PARK · UTAH

844

LITERALLY THE BEST THING EVER: DEEP-SEA CREATURES

Sometimes terrifying, sometimes ridiculous, always CUTE.
Writing by Amy Rose and Rachael. Illustration by Leanna.

When I was very little, I would introduce myself to strangers as "Ariel," as in the Little Mermaid, and insist against my mother's corrections that, no, that was in fact my name. "Amy Rose who?" I've always really loved the ocean, a fact which is still truer than true today, even if I don't actively identify as a mermaid anymore (in public, anyway). As much as I adore the sea, Rachael has one-upped this passion by actually working full-time for an ocean-conservation group. Obviously, we can both agree that marine life is Literally the Best Thing Ever. Here are some fantastic aquatic fauna that illustrate just why we feel this way. —Amy Rose

SHARKS

Sharks are cool. We all know this. But some sharks are cooler than others. Take the goblin shark. Its mouth is DETACHABLE. When it closes in on a tasty fish, it SHOOTS ITS OWN JAW at the animal to catch it.

Goblin sharks live near the ocean floor, so deep that we rarely get to see them alive. They eat squid, crabs, and fish—basically anything they can catch with their terrifying shooting jaws. Also, their skin is so thin that in the light, they look pink. On another animal, that might be cute. On a goblin shark, it just adds to the terror.

On the other end of the shark spectrum is the tasseled wobbegong. This animal is like, anti-shark. It doesn't even TRY to be scary. To begin with, it has the most ridiculous name of all the sharks. Just try to say it without laughing. WOBBEGONG.

But the ridiculousness doesn't end there. The tasseled wobbegong is camouflaged. AS SEAWEED. What's more, that seaweed disguise hides the face of an ASSASSIN. Get too close, you're dinner. One specimen recently made the news for eating another shark whole. Take that, Jaws.

FISH

First, because I know someone is going to say it, yes, sharks are fish. Whatever, we're writing the article, and we choose the categories. This one is for the OTHER fish.

Like the coelacanth. The coelacanth is an ancient fish, with weird tubelike organs and bone structures that tie back to earlier days in evolution. In fact, for a long time, as far as we knew, coelacanths existed ONLY as fossils. Then we found one alive.

This was a BIG DEAL. This would be like finding a wooly mammoth wandering around the Arctic. Scientists figure coelacanths basically stopped evolving about 400 million years ago. We discovered the coelacanth when someone accidentally fished one up, and that's pretty much the most contact anyone has had with one. They can't survive the pressure change when we try to remove them from the deep, so we have to study them in the wild, which takes a lot of work. We think they give birth to live young, but we're not sure. Only one baby has ever been photographed.

If you google it, the fish itself appears to be rather…hideous, but that's because the only clear pictures we have are of old dead corpses. Apparently when they're alive, they're actually a very pretty shade of blue.

These fish can be SIX FEET LONG. Also, they live up to 60 years and give birth to live young. They're basically HUMAN, except underwater and without opposable thumbs. In fact, one theory says that these fish are closely related to the species of fish that grew legs and gave birth on land to life as we know it. THIS THING IS YOUR GREAT-GREAT-AND-SO-ON-GRANDPARENT.

OK, you're saying, coelacanths are really cool, but mostly for historical reasons. This is the ocean we're talking about—there's got to be some fish that are indescribably weird.

How about the barreleye? The barreleye fish is one of the WEIRDEST fish in the sea. They compensate for the darkness in the deep by growing gigantic barrel-shaped eyes, set deep in their heads. Their TRANSPARENT HEADS.

Apparently these eyes are super-sensitive to light, and the fish spend most of their time staring into the water above them waiting for silhouettes or glowing creatures to swim past. Then they swivel their eyes forward and take chase. It's speculated that they also steal fish from jellyfish's stinging tentacles, which they can do without fear because their eyes are safe behind a transparent shield.

CEPHALOPODS

Cephalopoda is the class of animals that encompasses all the coolest, strangest, and prettiest creatures of the sea, including octopi, squid, nautili, and cuttlefish (which you basically must refer to as "cuddle fish," it's the law). The name of the class originally comes from the Latin for "head-feet," which aptly describes the weirdo bods that these guys all have—tentacles that are attached to their cute little faces. They also all share a supreme intelligence—they are said to be smarter than every other species of invertebrates. Seriously, go to YouTube and search "octopus opening jar." We'll wait.

We should have figured that octopi would be intelligent and dexterous enough to put their many tentacles to good use, but we still found that kind of astonishing.

Squid are also incredibly smart, and this can be awesomely terrifying when a person realizes that, oh, that enormous, mythical-seeming giant creature that can grow to almost 50 feet? It's also an evil genius. Humboldt squid, which are slightly smaller than the full-blown colossals (they grow up to six feet in length and weigh around

100 pounds, so, like, still quite frightening) have been known to rip bite-size chunks of flesh from divers.

We guess there's a good reason why squid are the main enemies in underwater *Super Mario* levels after all.

Squid are fascinating for so many reasons besides their scary-cool intelligence and deep-sea gigantism, though. Have you ever heard of chromatophores? They're incredible—definitely one of the most beautiful natural phenomena out there. Basically, what they are are color-changing cells on the outside of the bodies of most cephalopods that allow them to communicate, although many scientists believe they have other, as-yet-unknown biological usages as well.

The circular units of chromatophores can also get bigger and smaller in size—like the pupil of an eye reacting to light. Cuttlefish (remember, CUDDLE FISH, or "sea snugs," if you will AND YOU KNOW WE WILL) also have them, and are similar in structure to squid, the only difference being that they have a slight variation in their internal structure. Where squid have a thin internal support called a "quill" or a "pen," cuttlefish have a stronger, bonier "plate" support. Also, cuttlefish are said to look slightly angrier expression-wise, which Amy Rose can personally verify, having seen one snorkeling once. She was on a family vacation in the Caribbean and encountered a tiny cuddler guarding a cement block attached to a buoy floating on the surface of the water. Thus began one of the cutest encounters of her life: she tried to swim up to it to get a closer look, at which point the five-inch-long babyguy started meanly darting at her to protect its turf!! It looked so mad. It was the best.

CRABS

Although no aquatic creature can match the love we have for cephalopods, we also kind of have to give it up for crabs, especially the yeti crab, also known as the "Hoff crab" because of its Hasselhoffian hirsuteness. When it was discovered in 2005, we became totally obsessed with it—a weird sea bug with the hairy arms and legs of an '80s sitcom hunk? YES PLEASE! The Hoff crab lives in huge, crazy clusters surrounding hydrothermal vents.

Hydrothermal vents are caused by cracks in the ocean floor where lava heats up the surrounding water. The sulfur in these vents attracts weird sulfur-eating bacteria, which in turn attract animals that can eat sulfur-bacteria. Since the yeti crab is such a new discovery, scientists aren't entirely sure how they fit into this ecosystem, but they have a wild theory: these crabs have been witnessed waving their hairy arms over the warm vents, and it's speculated that they are actually FARMING BACTERIA in their hair to eat later. Sounds delicious… All in all, it is a really intriguing species, and you have to love the well-humored scientists who gave it its Baywatchian name.

We could go on all day talking about ocean creatures, but we'll shut up now. But if you know of any really cool or weird ocean animals, please share! There's no such thing as too much ocean trivia! ♦

Freak Like Me

What I learned from Lindsay Weir.
Writing by Tavi. Illustration by Brooke.

On the show *Freaks and Geeks*, it's never clearly explained why the main character, Lindsay Weir, *my personal hero*, traded in her cardigan for an army jacket and started ditching class to hang out with stoners. At one point, her little brother Sam comes into her room and asks, abruptly but not out of nowhere, "Why are you throwing your life away?" Lindsay pauses before telling Sam that she was alone with their grandma when she died and had asked her if she saw anything right before it happened, "a light or anything," and her grandma, someone who'd been "a good person all her life," said no.

Maybe Lindsay, a star student and life-long rule-abider, figured then that all of her efforts to do right by her family and her teachers had been for nothing, that if there was no reward at the end like she'd thought, she might as well try to have fun. Or maybe she was just exploring.

These here precious (groan) teenage years are meant for change and for testing out being a human in the microcosm that is school and your friends and your house before you have to go be a human in the world outside. It's natural and healthy to try out different identities and go through phases. What worries me is the resentment with which I look back on the person I *used* to be. These multiple previous versions of myself, they're everywhere. They're at family gatherings and the houses of old friends, in photos on our fridge and online, in my closet and in my now-embarrassing collections of books and movies and music.

And at *school*. Oh, god, school. As you navigate the halls during those first days of a new school year, eager to adopt a new identity, you're instead met with sad, bitter reminders of your old one, and as you recognize people who knew you at a time when you were less nice/cool/interesting/smart/attractive, you panic a little bit. They do the same, and so an unspoken pact is made through uncomfortable glances and half-smiling nods. It is understood by the time October rolls around: we will never talk about who we used to be.

Which is kind of sad, and scary. None of those old versions of myself, when I really think about it, were nearly as mortifying as I make them out to be, and I'm sure my classmates' weren't, either. But it terrifies me to think that if I felt as sure in who I was a year ago as I do about who I am now, it means that, in another year, I'll be sure about some new version of myself, and everything I'm currently latching onto—all of the songs that I think I could listen to forever and all of the friends whom I deeply trust—could mean nothing.

"It all comes back. Perhaps it is difficult to see the value in having one's self back in that kind of mood, but I do see it; I think we are well advised to keep on nodding terms with the people we used to be, whether we find them attractive company or not. Otherwise they turn up unannounced and surprise us, come hammering on the mind's door at 4:00 AM of a bad night and demand to know who deserted them, who betrayed them, who is going to make amends. We forget all too soon the things we thought we could never forget. We forget the loves and the betrayals alike, forget what we whispered and what we screamed, forget who we were."
—*Joan Didion, "On Keeping a Notebook"*

Lindsay Weir's geek hammers on her mind's door multiple times throughout the rest of the series, but the finale (SPOILER ALERT!) is so good because Lindsay doesn't end up fully falling into the freak role or going back to the geek role, but instead gets into a painted van to follow the Grateful Dead with a group of friends, most of whom she's just met for the first time. And for a moment you're like, "DID THE PAST 18 EPISODES NOT MEAN ANYTHING TO YOU?!" And then you recognize the maturity with which she says goodbye to her family and Sam's friends, and you realize that she's shaken hands with her former geek self. You see her approach the van with the same uncertainty that she had when she started hanging out with troublemakers Kim Kelly and Daniel Desario, but also with a confidence that took her the whole series to find. And you realize that this show wasn't about a good-girl-gone-bad either losing or finding her true identity. It was about a girl realizing that she could give herself permission to explore and change, and as the van drives away and the show's credits start to roll for the very last time (*tear*), you know that this was only the beginning.

"You know, Lindsay, when you started hanging out with them, I felt kinda bad for you, because I thought you were gonna turn into a dirtbag. But then I realized that you were just exploring, and now I guess I'm kind of exploring, too."
—*Millie Kentner*, Freaks and Geeks

That's what it is. It's *just* exploring. Hanging out with different friends, taking different classes, joining different clubs, getting into different music, or wearing different clothes: the important thing isn't figuring out who exactly you are and your sole purpose in life THIS VERY INSTANT. It's just knowing that it's up to you the same way it was up to Lindsay Weir. In the meantime, all you can really do is find the things and people you relate to at the moment, and hold them close. Somewhere, among the hair dye bottles and sleepover souvenirs and doodled-on paperbacks, you'll find parts of yourself that you know will be sticking around. ♦

FIELD TRIP

An afternoon at the dinosaur park.

By Eleanor

Thanks to Nao Koyabu for styling, Chisako Iwanari and Tanya Ling for assisting, and Evangeline Ling at Storm for modeling.

CHOOSE YOUR OWN ADVENTURE

Sexual experimentation doesn't determine anything. It just helps you figure out what you want.

By Krista

"KISS! KISS! KISS! KISS!"

The sound echoed down the hallway. My kindergarten class was in the bathroom. I had let them go by themselves for the first time ever, figuring that, in the three months that I'd been an English teacher in Taiwan, they had successfully gone to the bathroom about four hundred times *with* my supervision. I desperately needed to wolf down an energy bar. They would be fine in the bathroom for two minutes alone, right?

Wrong.

I raced from my classroom. I tore open the restroom door. There, in the middle of 20 tiny toilets, were all 10 of the boys in my class. They were standing in a circle with their pants down around their ankles and holding their tiny little-boy penises, trying to touch each tip to the other, shrieking, "KISS! KISS!"

The penises were kissing. The girls were standing in a circle around the boys (it was a unisex bathroom), gleefully clapping their hands. "TIGER CLASS!" I shouted. That was their class name. They turned and looked at me. It went quiet. "Tiger boys," I said, very calmly. "We don't touch our penis to our friend's penis."

Louis,* the undisputed ringleader, looked up at me, his jeans and underpants in a heap around his ankles. "Why?" he asked. "Because, um, *because*," I said. "That's rude. We don't ever do that." "Oh," he responded, and pulled up his pants. The rest of the boys followed suit. We all trooped back to the classroom together. Using puppets, I started a lesson on the sound the letter R makes, and my kids promptly forgot about their adventure in the bathroom.

But I didn't. I was wracked with guilt. I was a horrible teacher. I had obviously fucked these kids up for LIFE. I had taught them that it wasn't OK to experiment with their bodies, that curiosity should be stifled! In 10 seconds, I had instilled in them fear and negative feelings regarding their bodies, and I would never, ever forgive myself for it. NEVER. Tearfully, I told another one of the teachers at my school, a middle-aged lady, what had happened. She laughed: "Kids will be kids, honey. They'll be fine."

But would they?

I couldn't stop beating myself up. At 23, I had had a typical, knee-jerk adult reaction to something that all kids do: **experiment with one another.** I took something natural and treated it as though it were distasteful, and I had put a stop to it without ever giving them a reason why. I hadn't even been able to *think* of a reason! Who was I, my mom???

It was a helping-kids-grow-up-in-an-open-minded-supportive-environment-where-they-love-their-bodies FAIL. I still feel crappy about it. But maybe my kindergarteners won't remember the incident at all. I mean, I know lots of childhood experiments like this got lost in my memory. It was only later, in my 20s, that I looked back at some of the experiences I had and went, "Oh wow, I can't believe I *did* that."

For instance, when I was six, I can remember taking all of my clothes off with my friend Emily* to prove to her that she was *so wrong*, that Barbie couldn't possibly pee, because "Barbie doesn't have a pee-hole, and I do."

As little kids, lots of us played with our friends and neighbors in a way that our parents would have found *profoundly* disturbing. We played doctor. We examined one another. Some kids do that. It's part of growing up. Human beings are sensual creatures, and never more so than when we aren't old enough to attach meaning to these experiments and explorations of one another's bodies. Years later, in our teens, experimentation continues, but it's, um, more advanced.

In eighth grade, a friend of mine yanked off her swimsuit bottom in the locker room to show off her newly grown pubic hair to the rest of us. There was a crowd of about five girls looking at her crotch. I was shocked. I couldn't look away.

Freshman year of high school, my best friend decided that we should compare our boob growth by keeping a chart. Every week we either earned a smiley-face sticker or a frowny-face one. This involved a lot of us standing in front of her mirror, topless, with measuring tape. Uh…I really liked it. I really liked looking at her boobs. They were really nice.

At 15, I was kissing boys. Oh my god, I liked that, too. I liked kissing boys *a lot*. At 17, I had my first girl-kiss, and I loved it, but it took me years of kissing and sleeping with boys *and* girls to understand that I maybe liked girls better. These days, I'm a happy homo, but you know what? None of the experimenting I did as a kid or as a teenager "made" me that way.

What's an experiment? It's a trial without an answer. We're venturing into the unknown. We can't be certain of the outcome—that's why we're experimenting in the first place. Nothing can "make you" gay or bisexual or straight or trans. You don't get "turned" by incidents in your life. These exploratory adventures help you figure it out, but they don't determine your sexual identity.

You could be a girl who says she wants to marry her girl friend at the age of four, who fools around with the neighbor boy at eight, who practices kissing her best friend at 12, who kisses boys at 14, and who develops a totally consuming crush on a cool girl at school at 15, and what are you?

You're you.

Anybody walking in on you at any one of these moments might jump to conclusions and make a snap judgment about your sexuality, but they'd be wrong. Liking boys now doesn't necessarily mean that you'll be straight forever (although it might). Jesus, I identified as totally straight until I was 20.

On the other hand, liking girls now doesn't necessarily mean that you're going to be bi or a lesbian. A friend of mine had only girlfriends for 32 years of her life, and then she dated and married a guy this winter, surprising *everyone*.

Only you know what you like. Only you decide if you're straight or bi or gay or queer or asexual—or whether you want to label yourself at all. Some people know what they are right away. Some people take years to figure out what they like. Some people are 65 years old and still figuring it out. It can change. You can spend your life learning about your preferences.

Nothing that you do now locks you into a label. All right? All right. ✦

* *These names are not real! But the people are.*

LIVING ROOM SPACE TRAVELER

How to make a cardboard-box rocket ship.

By Amber. Illustrations by Leanna.

When I was in elementary school, I loved space—specifically Pluto. I watched *Star Trek: The Next Generation* every weeknight. My idol was Sally Ride, the first American woman in space. I ate freeze-dried space ice cream and I went to the planetarium at least once a month. At nine years old, I'd made up my mind: I was going to be an astronaut. But then someone told me that you had to be good at math to work for NASA. Since I can barely add two-digit numbers together, I abandoned any dreams I had of one day orbiting the Earth. I don't regret this decision, though, because (a) I eventually went on an extraordinarily terrifying motion-simulator ride at Epcot in Florida called Mission: SPACE and had an unsimulated panic attack that showed me that even if I'd excelled at math, I wouldn't have enjoyed actual space travel very much; and (b) cardboard-box spaceships exist.

What is a cardboard-box spaceship, you ask? A cardboard-box spaceship is a spaceship made out of a cardboard box. It is powered by imagination, and you don't have to know math to operate one—in fact, they work better when you force yourself to forget absolutely everything you know about integers, decimal points, and the like. While it would cost the government millions of dollars to launch a real shuttle into space, it doesn't cost anything to fly to the moon and back in a cardboard-box spaceship. Plus, they're eco-friendly—real shuttles leave behind all kinds of debris.

The only requirement is a you-sized box. Hop inside of that thing and allow your mind to boldly take you where no card-

board box has gone before. If you have the time, though, and don't need to be out in space immediately, you might want to spruce up your ship a bit.

Everything you need to make your interplanetary vessel the envy of the neighborhood can be found around your home—this is one of the major reasons why these things are so great. I added two photon torpedo launchers to the front of my ship—you can never be too careful—which are actually toilet-paper rolls wrapped in aluminum foil. The control column is two paper-towel rolls cut up, reassembled, and covered with duct tape.

For windows, I cut out rectangles on the sides of the box and then put two pieces of plastic that I found in the recycling bin over the holes. The aluminum foil on the wings makes the craft more aerodynamic and, of course, provides some protection against enemy photon blasts.

Because I am a proponent of interstellar time travel, the back of my ship is the TARDIS. For those who don't watch *Doctor Who*, TARDIS stands for "Time and Relative Dimension in Space" and it allows you to travel through time and space. So yeah, these days I'm traveling through time and space.

When you've completed your design, take the ship for a test ride. Say things like, "Engage," "Raise shields," "It's a trap," "Houston, we have a problem," and "Curse your sudden but inevitable betrayal." Rock back and forth to simulate navigating through an asteroid field. Make a swooshing "I'm flying at warp speed" sound.

With a cardboard-box spaceship, you can go on an adventure without leaving your living room, so they're perfect for rainy days. And when you get tired of making *pew-pew* noises and fighting alien hordes, you can just sit in that box, chill for a bit, and watch some TV. If someone walks in on you while you're sitting in that box, they will think that you are the coolest person in the history of life. At least, that's what I would think if I saw you.

I found the box that would eventually become my spaceship while walking around town. Someone had left it out on the curb in front of their house with the recycling. My boyfriend said that I was weird for taking the box and then carrying it all the way home (that's a mile walk). But I have a spaceship and he doesn't, so who's weird now? ◆

HOW TO LOOK LIKE YOU WEREN'T JUST CRYING IN LESS THAN FIVE MINUTES

Sometimes you need your tears to be a secret.
Writing by Krista. Illustrations by María Inés and Sonja.
Playlist by Naomi (lettered by Suzy).

I've always been a crier.

Not like a crybaby, exactly, but…from the time I was a little kid to right now when I am supposed to be an adult doing adult things like going to work and being responsible and having my shit together, I don't hold in my feelings—I still cry whenever I'm sad. I cry when I'm really really happy. Or when something is super beautiful and there's nothing left to say.

I cry when I'm angry and fighting with someone and can't think of exactly what to say to make them see how *wrong* they are. And then I get furious at myself for crying, and then I cry harder.

And it's ooooooook I just have a lot of feelings. It's fine to cry! Let it out! There's nothing wrong with crying.

But…sometimes you need it to be a secret that you were just bawling. Sometimes you need to make it look like you totally were not just crying. Um, RIGHT AWAY.

Guuurl lemme get you a Kleenex. Here we go.

PRE-CRY

Uh-oh. You're getting teary? You think you're gonna cry?

The most important thing at this point is to *just let it happen*.

Don't fight crying—this makes it worse. When you try to hold it in you end up making weird gasping noises and your face turns red and everyone in the nearby vicinity is alerted to the fact that something's up with you.

You're *going* to cry.

Walk calmly (don't run—it'll give you away) to a bathroom. *Immediately*. I cannot stress this enough. Get thee to a lonely bathroom. Lock yourself in a stall.

WHILE CRYING

This part is easy. Just start sobbing! It's OK! Let the tears flow! No one can see you! Put your feet up on the toilet seat if you're concerned someone will come looking for you.

There's only one thing to keep in mind while crying, though, and that's: REMEMBER TO BREATHE. This is the #1 key to your after-cry recovery. In order to prevent extreme facial redness and splotchiness later, breathe evenly through your mouth (your nose will be too stuffed up) as you cry. Holding your breath and letting it out in little shuddery gasps and hiccups is what gives your face that telltale I-was-crying red color.

IMMEDIATELY AFTER CRYING

Take a few really deep breaths. Steady…steady…
Blow your nose lavishly. Do it again.
Check for other people if you're in a public bathroom.
Once the coast is clear, c'mon out.

If you're wearing eye makeup (or *were* wearing it), fold a piece of toilet paper in half and dab daintily (DON'T WIPE) underneath your eyes.

Now, in movies, this is where the main character splashes cold water on his or her face. That's fine if you're not wearing makeup, but hello? Those of us wearing makeup can't be splashing water all over ourselves. Here's what you do:

Run cold water, stick your fingers under the tap, and then gently pat cold water underneath your eyes, where it's all puffy. This cools you down and constricts the blood vessels under your eyes that are causing tattletale swelling. Splash some cold water on your wrists, too. It helps, I don't know why.

OK, your nose is red and shiny, I know. DON'T POWDER IT. I know you want to, but really don't. It will look so much worse, you won't even believe how much worse—like you're trying to cover something up and it's not working at *all*. If you powder it, you will have a red powdered cue-ball nose. Just leave it—it'll go away in a minute.

A few more deep breaths, and now it's time to leave the bathroom.

You still might look blotchy. Much, *much* better, but still a li'l… cry-y, right?

HERE ARE YOUR TWO
FINAL WEAPONS

1. Flip your hair over your head and rumple it up, like you're trying to add volume. Then flip it back and fluff it out. I learned this trick from my expert stealth-crying friend Alison, who says: "This will make you look like you are only flushed because you are so windblown and carefreeeee."

2. Juuuust as you're about to walk back into a room with people in it, do like my sneaky friend Jen does and pretend to sneeze, loudly. That way no one will think, *Oh, she's crying*—they'll think, *She just had a sneeze attack, that's why her eyes are watering and her nose is so red.*

And finally, if you're me? Visine in the purse and waterproof mascara on the lashes. Every day. You just never know. ◆

SONgS to walk TO
1. Nightcall — kavinsky + LoveFox
2. Haiti — ARCADE fine xx
3. genesis — grimes
4. i walked — sufjan stevens
5. still life — the Horrors
6. walk in the park — BEACH HOUSE
7. THE SOUND of silence — SIMON & garfunkel
8. Don't Let it Bring you Down — Neil Young
9. coming Down — Dum Dum girls

LITERALLY THE BEST THING EVER:
OUTER SPACE

(Also literally the scariest and most beautiful thing ever.)
Writing by Hazel. Illustration by Minna.

Far beyond Earth exists a void of never-ending darkness and celestial bodies. It has the potential to be the scariest place ever or the most amazing place ever. It's called outer space, and it's fucking awesome.

Outer space is so beautiful! It's filled with misty plasma clouds, swirling galaxies, and millions and millions of stars. Space is so mesmerizing that it's served as the muse for some of the greatest directors, writers, and musicians of all time. What would musical artists like Air, the Chemical Brothers, and M83 be without outer space? It's been explored in classic movies like *2001: A Space Odyssey, The Fifth Element,* and *Star Wars.* Designer Christopher Kane made outer space the theme of his 2011 resort collection, spawning dozens of knock-offs.

It's not surprising that so many people are inspired by space. It's a blank slate for our imaginations. We have no idea what aliens or planets beyond our galaxy look like, but ever since the Renaissance humans have been dreaming up all kinds of possibilities. Haven't you been dreaming about space too?

Think of all the planets we haven't explored yet! The Kepler spaceship has spotted 2,321 potential planets in our galaxy so far—that's just a fraction of the hundreds of BILLIONS of planets that scientists believe are inside our ONE GALAXY. And these same scientists say there could be 100 billion galaxies! Are you really freaked out yet, because I am, like, really freaked out.

But just think of all the aliens we haven't met yet! Why haven't they contacted us? Forty-six of the potential planets Kepler's seen are in the "habitable zone," meaning liquid water could exist on them, which means, who knows, ALIENS!? And 10 of those habitable-zone planets are near-Earth-size. What if each of those 10 planets is an identical copy of Earth and, like us, they don't have the technology to call up another planet? Or maybe those planets support bloodthirsty monsters who have been plotting their attack on Earth for centuries! Or, like the History Channel show *Ancient Aliens* explains, aliens descended on Earth thousands of years ago and helped the Egyptians build pyramids and the Aztecs build temples and, essentially, were the inspiration for all religious icons that descended from the sky? I know that sounds totally ridiculous, but you have to watch *Ancient Aliens* to understand that it's TRUE, IT'S ALL TRUE.

Outer space really is the greatest. Sometimes I'll look up at the moon and get this intense realization that humans have walked on it. I mean, seriously?! We, HUMANS, have traveled to space! It is an accepted fact, old news, stuck in the history textbooks. But when you really concentrate on that idea, the idea that we have the means to travel into outer space and are working on traveling farther and farther into it, it is just mind-blowing. Wow. Now that is literally the best thing ever. ♦

THE MONSTER MASH

Eleanor visits the Meadham Kirchhoff studio once again for a look at the inspirations and processes behind their fall 2012 show. This time, with googly eyes!

By Eleanor

THRIFTING: THE MASTER CLASS

God, you're good at this.
By Krista

Everyone relaxes in different ways. Some people bake cookies. Some go for a run. Others take a bubble bath.

I go thrifting.

To me, there's nothing like wandering the aisles of a thrift store, idly letting my fingers brush the racks of sweaters, feeling for wool and cashmere and fuzzy angora. I crave the thrill of the hunt, the adrenaline rush of a major score, the pair of really odd shoes from the '80s that no one else will have, ever.

Shopping at a thrift store isn't easy like going to a department store—it's work. That's what I like about it. I like the digging. I like leaving with something special that was really cheap and looks awesome,

then having someone freak out on me, going, "OMIGOD your shirt, WHERE did you get it???" and casually tossing out, "Thrift store," and have them frown and go, "Oh."

You paid $30 for your vintage-look '80s band T-shirt? Too bad, sucka…the one I'm wearing is real, came pre-softened, and was 90 cents.

But listen, frowning person and fake-vintage-T-shirt wearer: I'm not here to feel smugly superior to you. I'm here to help! Never been thrifting before? Not sure where to start? NO WORRIES. Me and my two skilled thrifting friends Jen and Kate will be your Guide to All Things Used.

But! Before we get down to it, there are a few things I want to cover.

1. WHAT IS A THRIFT STORE?

It may seem obvious, but not all thrift stores are created equal. Here is what is NOT a thrift store:

A place that sells upscale secondhand clothing. Places like Plato's Closet, Buffalo Exchange, and Crossroads are NOT thrift stores. They sell name-brand, imperceptibly used clothing. A dress will probably run you $14–$35. Cheaper than a regular clothing store, but definitely not a thrift store.

A vintage store. Vintage stores are cool as hell, but they're also expensive and pre-thrifted. Someone with a great eye for design went thrifting for absolutely everything you see in a vintage store, then carefully cleaned each item, sewed up the rips,

and is now reselling it for upwards of quadruple what they paid for it. Vintage stores are full of awesome, high-priced stuff because they know full well what they have, and they're banking on the fact that you don't have the time or energy to go out into the thrift-store world and find that awesome stuff for yourself. That's where they'd be wrong.

Now, a real thrift store is really cheap. We're talking $3-or-less T-shirts.

A real thrift store sells clothing that comes directly from the bags that people have dropped off for donation. The clothes aren't checked for rips, holes, missing buttons, or stains—they're sold as-is.

A real thrift store is often large and only loosely organized. It sells clothing with handwritten tags stapled onto it. Sometimes those tags are color-coded, because the thrift store has days where, say, all the orange tags are half off, or days when the pink, white, and blue tags are all half off.

Real thrift stores have little paper calendars up by the register that tell you when the big half-off sale days are. Make like a crafty hoarder and grab one of these for your fridge.

Often, real thrift stores are dirty, with clothes strewn everywhere. Don't be alarmed. Be thankful for the mess—it scares away the shoppers who aren't as adventurous as you are. The truly brave are always rewarded with the most outrageous finds.

2. IT DOESN'T MATTER WHERE YOU ARE. THRIFT STORES ARE EVERYWHERE.

Now, I live in Chicago, which is blessed with some of the best thrift stores around, but if you live in a small town or rural area, don't fret. Amazing thrifting is to be had in small towns. The best thrift store I've ever been in was on the outskirts of Appleton, Wisconsin.

Iowa, Nebraska, Montana, North Dakota—less-populated states and small towns are fantastic for thrifting, because the stores haven't been picked over by hordes of hipster kids. You know why? 'Cause thrifting

ain't cool there yet. Sure, it's cool to live in a big city and go thrifting—it's a fun way to spend an afternoon. But in places like Fargo and Sioux Falls? You're competing with almost no one for great stuff. Grandmas clean out their attics all over the country, not just in big urban areas.

The smaller the town, the more likely you are to make out like a bandit.

So. It's 11:00 AM on a Saturday, and you wanna go thrifting. Let's get down to it.

Above all else:

3. EAT SOMETHING FIRST. THEN CAFFEINATE YOURSELF INTO A FRENZY.

You are about to deal with an insane barrage of clothing—thousands upon thousands of items—that are not arranged by size and are jammed onto racks higgledy-piggledy. You will be there for hours. Do NOT go into a thrift store hungry or tired. There will be shoes and purses and racks of shirts and toys and furniture and housewares and books and a jewelry section, and you're going to need energy to get through it all.

Thrift stores, with their mess and noise and pushy old ladies and faint musty smell and squalling babies, can sometimes overwhelm you with their sheer disorganization and sadness, like Atreyu in the swamp in *The Neverending Story*. Don't give in to the sadness! You must enter that store with

enough energy to make it out alive and victorious, loaded down with finds.

Wear the right outfit. You're going to be trying on lots of clothing, and you'll have to try most of it on *over* your clothes, as there probably won't be a dressing room. Wear something simple. A stretchy one-piece dress. Skinny jeans and a T-shirt. No weird necklines or giant sweaters.

4. KNOW YOUR SHOPPING COMPANIONS.

I like to thrift alone. I like to look where I want, pore over the jewelry case, thoughtfully purse my lips as I flip through endless racks of dresses.

But if you're not thrifting alone, bring only friends who won't drag you down. The worst thing is to bring along a friend who shops exclusively in malls, who will trail behind you going, "I'm bored. This is boring. I can't find anything. This place smells. Ewww, who would buy that? This is gross. I can't find anything." This is the person you leave at home. Or bury under a pile of battered children's books in the toy department.

What you want is a crew of *skilled thrifters*, tried and tested in the battlefields of the biggest thrift stores in town. The very best scenario is to thrift with friends who are cheerful, adventurous dressers, and not your size. That way, everyone can shop in the same sections at the same time,

and there are no "I saw it first" awkward moments with your soon-to-be-ex-bestie when a pair of size-seven Jeffrey Campbell chunky heels is sitting on the shelf.

5. DIVIDE AND CONQUER.

When entering a thrift store, don't get overwhelmed and start wandering around aimlessly. Grab a cart, home in on a section (e.g., skirts) and dive right in. Look over the entire rack, pulling out anything that looks immediately interesting, then shove all of the hangers as far over as they can go and start flipping through the skirts one by one. This gives you much-needed space on jammed thrift-store racks.

Look through everything. Throw absolutely anything that looks approximately right for you (in terms of shape, cut, size, color) into your cart and forget about it. Have one big try-on session at the end with all the stuff you piled into the cart.

No dressing rooms? No problem. Many, if not all, of the best thrift stores don't have dressing rooms. (We will never know why.) Instead, there will be several mirrors scattered around the store, with groups of people gathered around them trying things on. You wore a simple outfit, so it's not a problem. Don't be shy—hustle up to that mirror and try on all clothes in your cart quickly, pulling them on over your current outfit, making sure to share the mirror with everyone else.

6. MAKE RAPID DECISIONS— DON'T HEM AND HAW.

It's cute? You'll wear it for sure? It's $1.80? Buy it.

It's kiiiinda cute? You're not sure what you'll wear it with? It's $8? Don't buy it.

Wait, though…what if you want to try on jeans? Not so easy, now, is it? You're in public! How are you gonna take off your pants in public?

Here's how: Go to the skirts section. Find the biggest, roomiest, elastic-waisted, floor-length skirt you can find, and put it on over your jeans. Then drop your jeans, grab the new pair you want to try on, and pull them on under the skirt. Then drop the skirt. Ta-da!! God, you're good at thrifting.

7. LOOK THROUGH ALL THE SECTIONS.

The bedding department often holds other linens, like adorable vintage aprons. The man-sweater section is a treasure trove of giant cashmere sweaters that women have given their husbands and their husbands have refused to wear.

The kids' section has hoodies and T-shirts, the sleepwear section has vintage slips, men's shoes has great cowboy boots hidden among all the loafers. The underwear section has silk camisoles from the '40s, the furniture section has awesome '60s luggage sets, and the books have bestsellers you've been meaning to read and weird teen-girl novels from the '50s.

Look up high and down low—the best stuff is hiding out of eye range...sometimes hidden by other sneaky thrifters in the hopes that no one else will find it before they return. Poking through random sections of the thrift store is incredibly rewarding—you never know what you'll find.

8. KNOW YOUR WEAKNESSES.

My weakness is tall leather boots. I have an entire closetful of them, none of which cost more than $10 and each of which I was certain I needed at the time.

Maybe you love, say, hand-knitted fisherman's sweaters. But you already have five of them—do you really need another?

Thrift stores are full of bargains, but remember: **you're not saving money if you're not going to get around to** *wearing* **that $4 sweater**.

That brings us to...

9. ARE YOU REALLY GOING TO WEAR THAT?

Learn from me, y'all. No matter how cool something is, do NOT buy it if it "needs some work" and you're not actually going to fix it up.

My drawers are a graveyard of blouses I think I'm going to sew buttons onto, sweaters whose sleeves I'm going to cut off for legwarmers, dresses I keep meaning to have hemmed.

I've finally learned something about myself: I'm not going to do it. I am not going to take things to a tailor; I'm not going to make things out of cool old T-shirts. Only buy "project pieces" if you're really going to spend time with them; otherwise you're throwing your money away.

10. YOU GUYS, THRIFTING IS ABSOLUTELY FABULOUS.

It requires energy, determination, and a laser-like focus. It's a way to level the playing field for those among us who can't, um, always afford the newest things in magazines. Twelve-hundred dollars for a pair of elbow-length leather *gloves*? PLEASE. Thrift until you find $4 leather gloves just like the ones you saw in *Vogue*. Wear them to a party. Everyone will be jealous, and you'll be the cleverest girl there. ♦

ON TAKING YOURSELF SERIOUSLY

If you were my middle school health teacher, you'll want to read this.
Writing by Sady. Playlist by Laia (lettered by Suzy).

When I was in seventh grade, I had the worst health teacher in the entire world. I find it important, at this juncture, to tell you his actual name, which was Mr. Dusenbury. Because here is the truth about Mr. Dusenbury: he was mean and sexist, and during every single class, he would launch into a tirade about how women were worse than men.* We were smaller, we were weaker, we had terrible hormones that made us crazy, and we would never be able to compete with men professionally, because we were all going to get pregnant and stop working to raise our babies, which was what nature intended us to do, and, and, and...

I tried to fight him on it. But he would just tell me to DO SOME ONE-ARMED PUSH-UPS THEN IF I WAS SO EQUAL TO MEN; HE COULD DO ONE-ARMED PUSH-UPS, COULD I??? So I just started tuning him out. I don't recommend this strategy, generally; I believe you should always pay attention, in every class, unless "paying attention" means dealing with *one more second* of Mr. Dusenbury. And, in my case, it did. So I would show up for the part where he told me how intestines worked, and when the "Ladies: Actually Terrible at Having Intestines" portion began, I would start writing in my notebook or reading a novel.

When Mr. Dusenbury caught me, he took the book I was reading, held it up in front of the class, and ripped it in half. I told him he had no right to do that; he did the one-armed push-ups speech; I told him that maybe he should have spent some time learning to teach instead of perfecting his one-armed push-up skills; he sent me to the principal.

The principal asked me why I had this terrible habit of writing instead of listening to misogynist rants. And I told him that I wrote because I was going to be a writer, in New York, and I was probably specifically going to write about how sexism was wrong. And he said this:

"The thing is, that's just extremely unlikely to happen. And you're going to have a really hard life, if you just decide not to listen to people that you personally feel are sexist."

"When it happens," I said, "I'll send you the story about Mr. Dusenbury."

Which: what a ridiculous thing for a 14-year-old to say! So immature! So grandiose! Such a typical, adolescent fantasy! I am sure my principal laughed himself to sleep that night. *Yes, yes, you're going to become a writer, and tell everyone how awful this school was, and then we'll be sorry. Good luck, little girl. I am quaking in my sensible shoes right now!*

Dear Mr. Dusenbury and the principal: My mother will be mailing the school a printed copy of this article, along with my C.V. and a list of the awards and recognition I have won for (a) writing, and (b) writing specifically about sexism, and (c) not listening to sexist authorities when I wrote about sexism. I will be happy to accept either your signed apology, or the school's apology on your behalf. You may also consider making me a big, festive banner, reading "OK, You Win." Although, should you wish to send this victory banner to me directly, you will need to ask my mother for my precise address. BECAUSE IT IS IN NEW YORK CITY, THAT IS WHY.

There is a point to all this, besides the fact that no competent professional would ever hire someone like Mr. Dusenbury and put him alone in a room with small children. The point is that, for anyone—but especially for girls—it can be very hard to hold on to your ambition. Even now, when it's pretty much taken for granted that most girls will grow up to have jobs, girls are still discouraged from taking their desires for accomplishment too seriously.

Because accomplishment is hard. And accomplishment, on some basic level, is pretty selfish. To really devote yourself to achieving something—anything: becoming a writer, becoming a lawyer, becoming the world's best mini-golf player—you have to have a vision of what you want, and you have to want it fiercely, and you have to be able to throw your whole weight behind getting it. But girls aren't supposed to care that much about what we want for ourselves. Like my awful, awful health teacher used to say: we're supposed to put our own ambitions aside, and focus on other people. And those other people don't even have to be babies! Consider the difference between a guy who stays in every weekend to practice guitar, and a girl who does the same thing. The guy is a brooding, intense, passionate musician. The girl is just unpopular.

That's all a load of crap. Ambition is great. Wanting things is great. Being willing to work hard to get what you want, being willing to make sacrifices in order to fulfill your own dreams: that is all super great, and admirable, and you are going to need it. Because here's the thing: your ambitions and desires for accomplishment are what allow you to have a sense of self. If you don't have a sense of what you want from life, it's easy to just define yourself around other people, and to do whatever they seem to want from you. And other people can take away their approval at any time. But when you provide your own approval—when you know what you want, and know you have what it takes to get it—you have a basis for feeling good about yourself that doesn't go away.

Right now, you are in one of the world's most enviable positions. You are a teenager. What that means is that you are smart enough and mature enough to start thinking about what you want to do with your life, but you are also young enough to consider many different possibilities.

You don't have to commit to anything on a permanent level right now. Everything is about exploration.

But while you're exploring, it's a really good idea to get in touch with what makes you the happiest. Take a look at everything you really enjoy doing, and every future you sometimes like to think you'll have. Try to envision yourself actually occupying those futures; ask yourself what would fulfill you about each one. Or what fulfills you the most right now: which hobby or action or mode of operation gives you something that nothing else can.

It doesn't have to be a big, grand, noble answer. I didn't decide I wanted to be a writer, and to write about sexism, because I wanted to Change the World. I decided that I wanted to write about sexism because I was shy and weird and wanted to find a way to communicate with people—a way to show them how I saw the world. And one of the ways I felt most misunderstood was around being female—I didn't line up easily with what people expected girls to do or be, so I figured unpacking the world's expectations about being a girl might be a good place to start.

It *was* a good start, but it was also something that other people could use. And that's the way it is for most people: if you examine your own needs, you're going to find that somewhere, somehow, somebody else needs you to fulfill them. Do you personally need to help people who are hurting? Good—the world needs therapists, doctors, and human-rights advocates. Do you need to explore, to figure out something new about how the world works? Good—the world needs scientists and investigative journalists. Do you need attention? Yeah, well, so did I, and the world needs loudmouths in every single creative field. Do you need to prove yourself through competition? Good. Find a place where you can compete, and start winning. If I ever need a lawyer, I may end up calling you.

I recommend that you start here—with what you want—because the rest of it is pretty hard, and requires a lot of strategy. Once you've figured out what you want, you have to figure out what you need, and

that can be a good deal more complicated. Fantasies are good, and so are goals, but to move forward, you're going to actually need a plan.

The first step is actually not that hard. To realize a dream, you only have to break it down into its most basic components. To be a writer, you need (a) the ability to write, (b) somewhere to publish your writing, and (c) people to read it. Open an account on Tumblr; you're a writer now. To become an activist, you need (a) a cause to rally your community around, (b) a community to rally with, and (c) a way to communicate your concerns to the public, and especially to people with the power to change whatever you're concerned about. Start talking to people, find out what they think the problems are with your school or with the world, and then figure out how you can ally with them to make an impact. Simple. Other ambitions are more complex, and harder to realize. To become a therapist, or a scientist, or a lawyer, you need many years of specialized training. To become an athlete, you need a lot of physical conditioning, and, often, a team to join. But still, in order to do any of those things, you need to break them down to basics. What are the core resources that you need to do this job? What can't you ignore or skip, if you're going to do this right? And where can you locate those resources? Answering those questions is your first step.

The second step is actually accessing the resources. This is key. It doesn't take much to be a published writer, but to be a good writer, you actually will need some training—people to give you feedback and guidance. It's pretty simple to be an activist, but to be a good one, you have to be able to educate yourself on the issues, and understand which tactics work, or don't. But this is where the whole "girls are supposed to make people like them" thing actually comes in handy. The simplest and easiest way to locate resources, to be directed toward the sorts of education or training you need, or to learn about a field, is to ask people. Somewhere, someone is doing what you want to be doing. You need to talk to that person.

Obviously, in the age of internet, it's pretty easy to find people with your dream job. But it's usually better to start with the people in your own community. If you want to be a musician, for example, you don't necessarily want to send a letter to every musician on your iPod. "Dear Kanye West, please teach me how to produce records??? Love, [YOUR NAME HERE]." Even if Kanye does write back, you're going to get a pretty weird answer. And people who get a lot of attention are far less likely to respond personally—or at all—to attention from people they don't know. It's a volume thing; when you get five emails a day, you can respond to them all, but when you get 50, or 500, you might not even have time to read them. You're better off looking for local musicians and producers whose work you admire: people who are nearby, and accessible, and far more likely to appreciate a girl who wants to listen to them talk about how they make their art, and how they learned to make it. (Oh, and by the way: try to actually admire their work. They can tell if you don't, and it makes them a lot less friendly.)

Ideally, you will find someone who can really guide you through the field, and promote you within it—a good, close, one-on-one relationship. A mentor. This is the part that every "career guide" for girls stresses—find a mentor, love your mentor, learn from your mentor—but the fact is, if you don't find one, it isn't the end of the world. I, for example, never had one special mentor. I've had about 15 mentors. My friend who ran a feminist blog full-time taught me how to make a sustainable wage from blogging, and told me about the importance of reader donations, and where to find feminist-friendly ad support. My friend who has extensive experience in political reporting taught me how to report a story responsibly, and gave me reporting assignments when I'd had very few of them, so that I could learn under her guidance. Even now, when I have a tricky question about a piece, I go to her. My friend who writes a lot about how the internet works and how it relates to the publishing industry told me how to transition from blogging to writing for other people, and introduced me to other people who knew a lot about it. All of these people were mentors. And that's why it's important for you to have done the breakdown: there are about a thousand things you need to know in order to really pursue your ambitions, and there are about a thousand people who can teach you. Your job is to keep your eyes open—to notice the gifts in the people around you, what they're great at, and learn how they got to be so great.

Because here's the thing: while you're looking around for people who share your passions, and noticing what makes them great, you're going to discover a few other things. You're going to discover what you are great at—what makes you unique, what you can contribute that no one else can. And that's how you find out who you are, and what gives you the basis to care about yourself and your ambitions. You also discover that pursuing your ambitions doesn't have to be lonely. You don't just find yourself, when you take yourself seriously. You find your community. And that can be the greatest feeling in the world.

Well. Second-greatest. Because here's the other thing: Your personal Mr. Dusenburys? The people who told you that you couldn't, you can't, you won't, you have to settle? If you really go for this—take yourself seriously enough to put your whole weight behind what you want—you are going to be able to prove them wrong. Not just say they're wrong, not just think they're wrong: get the proof, and *know* that they were wrong. It might take a while. But it can happen. And it probably will. And even 15 years later, that feels pretty awesome. ♦

As you might imagine, when we fact-checked this article with Mr. Dusenbury, he disputed a lot of what I say. But I stand by my memory.

OUTER SPACE

1. Space Oddity — David Bowie
2. Across tHE universe — fiona Apple
3. kelly watcH tHE stars — Air
4. the fleeting Skies — Samara Lubelski
5. Laika — Mecano
6. He's Simple, He's Dumb, He's tHE Pilot — Grandaddy
7. Vacuum — Gang Gang Dance
8. Sadness Licks tHE sun — Anika
9. Here Come the warm Jets — Brian Eno
10. How Does it feel — Spacemen 3

ABSOLUTE BEGINNERS

Some of our favorite grown women on the first time they had sex—with a couple of first-kiss stories for good measure.

Illustrations by María Inés. Flowers by Leanna.

LENA DUNHAM

When I was about nine I wrote a vow of celibacy on a piece of paper and ate it. I promised myself, in orange magic marker, that I would remain a virgin until I graduated from high school. This seemed important because I knew my mother had waited until the summer after she graduated, and also Angela Chase seemed pretty messed up by her experience at that flophouse where high school kids went to copulate. If my relationship to liver paté was any indication, and I had recently eaten so much that I barfed, then my willpower was very bad, and I needed something stronger than resolve to prevent me from having intercourse too early in life.

Turns out, this was an unnecessary precaution. The opportunity never arose in high school, nor even during the first year of college, save for a near-miss with a stocky kid I knew who was home visiting New York City from the Air Force Academy—that encounter went far enough that I had to fish a mint-colored, never-used condom out from behind my dormitory bunk bed the next day. I transferred to Oberlin my sophomore year, a small liberal arts school in Ohio that was known for having been the first coed college in the U.S., as well as for its polyamorous, bi-curious student body. I was neither, but it did seem like a good environment in which to finally get the ball rolling. I really felt like the oldest virgin in town, save for a busty riot grrrl from Olympia, Washington, who was equally frustrated; she and I would often meet up in our nightgowns to discuss.

I was pretty sure I had already broken my hymen in high school, crawling over a fence in Brooklyn in hot pursuit of a cat that clearly didn't want to be rescued. So the event would only be psychologically painful.

I met Jonah* in the cafeteria. He was roommates with an emo kid who worked at the video store and had a crush on my best friend, Audrey. Jonah didn't have a very specific style beyond dressing vaguely like a middle-aged lesbian. He was small but strong, with floppy hair and warm eyes. He reminded me a little bit of that Air Force kid, who had rejected me in a saga too long to recount here. Something primal kicked in, and, like an Alfred Hitchcock character hell-bent on replacing his dead wife with a lookalike, I resolved to make him mine.

The best way was obviously to throw a wine-and-cheese party, which I did, in my 8×10-foot room on the quiet floor of East Hall. Procuring wine entailed a sub-zero bike ride, so it ended up being beer and cheese and a big box of Carr's assorted party crackers. Jonah was "casually" invited in a group email that made me sound a lot more relaxed than I actually was. And he came, and he stayed, even after the entire gang had packed up and gone. We talked, at first animatedly and then in the nervous generalizations that substitute for kissing when everyone is too shy. Finally, I told him that my dad painted huge pictures of penises for his job. When Jonah asked if we could see them online, I grabbed him by the scruff of the neck and just went for it. I removed my shirt almost immediately, and he seemed fairly impressed. Wearing just a too-tight slip-skirt from the local Goodwill, I hopped up to get the condom from the "freshman survival pack" we had been given (even though I was a sophomore).

Meanwhile, across campus, Audrey was in a private hell of her own. She had been waging a cold war with her roommate all semester: the busty, ren-faire loving Philadelphian was the lust object of every LARPer and black-metal aficionado on campus. Audrey just wanted some quiet time to read political texts and iChat with her boyfriend in Virginia. Audrey's roommate was now dating a kid who had tried to bake meth in the dorm kitchen, warranting an emergency visit from men in what looked to be space suits. Before going out for the night, Audrey had left her roommate a note: "If you could please have quieter sex as we approach our midterms, I'd really appreciate it." Her roommate's response was to burn Audrey's note, scatter the ashes across the bed and floor, and leave her own note: "U R a frigid bitch. Get the sand out of UR vagina."

Justifiably distressed, Audrey headed back to my room, hopeful for a sleepover. She was sobbing and disoriented, and also pretty sure I was alone finishing the cheese, so she flung my door open without knocking. There she found Jonah on top of me doing what grownups do. She understood the magnitude of the occasion and through her tears shouted, "Mazel tov!"

I didn't tell him I was a virgin, just that I hadn't done it "that much." It hurt a little more than I'd expected but in a different way, and he was nervous too and he never came. Afterwards we lay there and talked, and I could tell he was a really nice person. I commended myself for making a healthy, albeit hasty, partner choice. I really couldn't wait to tell my mom.

Jonah wanted to date, and I figured out pretty quickly that I did not. I went over to his dorm and broke up with him in the laundry room, sitting on top of a running washer. He seemed genuinely hurt and perplexed, and I told him I'd been a virgin because I thought it made me seem like less of a she-devil. Later that year, Audrey saw him in the student post office picking up a package with a pair of used Merrills to replace his *really* used Tevas, and we laughed about it like mean girls.

Jonah and I only had sex once, but it was enough to convince me that it wasn't that hard to make it happen. I had, for the past few years, set my sights quite purposefully on boys who weren't interested, because I simply wasn't ready (despite all the movies about wayward prep-school girls I liked to watch). I had been waiting because I wanted to, and then suddenly I was ready for the change in identity I was sure would come with no longer being a virgin. But afterwards I still felt very much like myself. Although it's amazing how permanent virginity feels, and then how suddenly inconsequential. I barely remembered the sensation, the embarrassment, and the urgency. I passed the riot grrrl arm-in-arm with her boyfriend senior year and we didn't even exchange a nod of understanding.

Later, I wrote that virginity-loss scene almost word for word in my first feature film, *Creative Nonfiction,* minus the part where Audrey busted the door down. When I performed that sex scene, my first, I felt more changed than I had by the actual experience of having sex with Jonah. Like, that was just sex, but this was my work.

* *Name changed to protect the truly innocent.*

Lena Dunham is creator, writer, director, and star of Girls, *on HBO.*

LIZ PHAIR

Here's a story for you: I was terrified to have sex. When I was young, some pediatrician had told me that I was very small "down there" and that "intercourse might be difficult." Though this turned out to be completely untrue, it stuck with me for most of my adolescence, like a chastity belt locked around my brain. It wasn't just the fear of feeling pain that held me back; it was also the fear of a boy discovering something wrong with me at my most vulnerable moment. It didn't help that my physician father happened to be working at the forefront of the AIDS epidemic during my teenage years and I had a front-row seat to the early ravages of a poorly understood and, at the time, deadly STD.

Romance, for me, became all about creativity. How could I keep my boyfriends happy, but not die, and not be labeled a freak? One solution that worked amazingly well was to date a boy who was grounded for the duration of our relationship. I worked on the yearbook committee my junior year, and we would meet in deserted corridors and unlocked classrooms after school and fumble around until he came in his jeans. I have very fond memories of that. ;)

Not so fun was the weekend I tried to break my own hymen. I had become ashamed and desperate to fix this (nonexistent) problem, and wound up in the emergency room with a serious infection whose origin I was too embarrassed to explain to the nurses or my mother, who had to cancel a trip to stay home and take care of me.

I had a lot of experience with the other three bases by the time I finally lost my virginity in the fall of my freshman year of college. I was the last one of all my friends to do it, and I tried to pick a really good guy. He was a senior and captain of the soccer team as well as sitting chair of the Student Honor Committee. I had ceased to think there was anything anatomically wrong with me, but I was so nervous that I actually said these words to him: "If you're not nice to me, my ex-boyfriend said he would beat you up." I actually said this. I cringe to this day. Luckily, he saw through my Lisbeth Salander routine and was very

sweet and gentle with me. When the deed was done, I felt tremendous relief.

Even with my newfound freedom, it still took me a long time to learn to have sex without hang-ups and WITH orgasms. A few tips: you have to feel safe, you have to enjoy your own body, and you have to have the time to experiment with each other. You want the kind of trust that leads to lots of playful, spontaneous opportunities with a guy or girl who really turns you on. Obvious, I know, but somehow it's still rare to find.

The good news is—and truer words were never spoken—you were born to do this.

Liz Phair is a singer, songwriter, and writer.

BETHANY COSENTINO

I was a pretty awkward teenager. I grew up in a suburb outside of L.A. called La Crescenta, where all the girls were skinny and tan and played soccer. I was chubby, wore braces, and had no talent at playing sports (well, I did play softball for a few years, but quickly realized I hated organized sports, so I quit just before ninth grade). I had this friend: Sara Stone. She was like the epitome of perfect in the eyes of every guy in La Crescenta. Tall, thin, blonde; played soccer, softball, and water polo. She lived in a big house with a pool and a hot tub, and had the kinds of parents that let her do whatever she wanted, including having coed birthday parties.

I was the last of my friends to ever kiss a boy. I was so embarrassed about this that I would make up stories that I had kissed a guy at Christian summer camp—I made sure to lie that he lived in Palmdale, which was far enough away that no one would ever find out he didn't exist. I continued to make up story after story of all the boys I kissed. I don't think any of my friends believed me, seeing as how every kissing partner was always some mysterious boy I met at church or at an airport or somewhere totally unbelievable.

Sara had this birthday party in the summer after seventh grade at her parents' perfect house in the mountains. It was coed, and everyone was swimming and eating hot dogs and drinking soda and having so much fun. My friend Jessica and I sat awkwardly by the side of the pool watching, but not joining in, the fun. Jessica, who is still to this day my best friend, had kissed a boy—but she wasn't like Sara and didn't have every guy pining over her. We were sarcastic and cool for seventh graders—much cooler, we believed, than everyone else we knew. We sat there and watched and wondered when something cool was actually going to happen.

Suddenly Sara suggested we all get into the hot tub together and play a game. I had no idea what she was talking about. About 10 of us piled into this tub and started to play truth or dare. Since truth or dare with a bunch of hormonal teenagers pretty much always becomes dare or dare, there was a lot of kissing going on in this hot tub. I was so nervous that someone was going to tell me I had to kiss someone, and I was scared they'd be able to tell it was my first time, but I kept telling myself, *It's now or never.*

Finally it was my turn, and I was dared to kiss Michael Humami. A really short boy who was mildly popular and always wore this gaudy gold watch. I was so mortified that my first kiss was about to take place in front of a group of my friends in a lukewarm hot tub, but I went for it. I had always imagined my first kiss would be something truly special. I closed my eyes and moved toward Michael, and we kissed, and before I knew it, it was over. I was glad to have finally gotten it done, but still sort of let down that it wasn't as magical as I'd expected.

A few turns later, someone dared me to kiss Justin. I can't remember his last name, but I remember he had red hair and freckles. I kissed Justin and then felt like a pro. Two boys in one day, I was on a roll! I think we eventually got caught playing truth or dare in the hot tub and Sara's parents got upset and made all the boys leave and then the girls had a slumber party. We all talked about the kissing we'd done in the hot tub, and everyone was asking me, "What was it like to kiss Michael? He's so cute." I'm pretty sure my response was, "It was pretty whatever. I've kissed tons of guys, and he wasn't the best."

Bethany Cosentino is the frontwoman and songwriter for Best Coast.

Kevin Brennan was the emcee on open-mike nights, Mondays, at the Boston Comedy Club in the West Village of Manhattan. I had a job passing out flyers for the club every Thursday, Friday, and Saturday from 4:00 PM to 2:00 AM, and besides my 10-dollars-an-hour payment, I could go up on open-mike night without bringing two friends (a prerequisite for open-mikers was that they had to bring two paying customers).

Kevin was tall, with dark brown hair and a white-and-red blotchy Irish face. He wore a long army-green trench coat and carried a briefcase, which, at 19, I found very impressive. And he was 30—a grown man. He stood outside the club smoking a Merit Light. I went outside and bummed one.

KEVIN: *So, you go to school?*
ME: *Yeah. NYU.*
KEVIN: *What—are you a freshman?*
ME: *Mm-hm.*
KEVIN: *What—are you, like, in a sorority?*
ME: *Yeah, but you can only be in it if you're really cool.*
KEVIN: *Yeah? Who else is in it?*
ME: *Just me.*
He laughs.

Let me take a moment to describe myself here: big curly perm, black polyester shirt with long sheer sleeves, black miniskirt, and Doc Martens with thick black soles. It was 1990.

I did my five minutes and stayed for the rest of the night until the show was over and Kevin was going home.

"You wanna see my apartment?" He chuckled, I assume at his paper-thinly veiled offer. "It's in Queens."

"Sure. Yeah."

And off we cabbed to Astoria. We walked up a stairwell and through a hallway to his apartment. It smelled good to me. It smelled like first grade for some reason. Something industrial but sweet, like old paint and licorice. Inside there was a small living room, a bathroom, and two bedrooms—one his and one his roommate's. On the coffee table was a *Best of Chicago* tape. He also had a stack of records, with the Go-Go's *Vacation* on top.

"Wanna see my bedroom?"

"OK."

He led me to his bedroom—a bed, a dresser, and an ashtray. He kissed me while he laid me back in his bed.

"Have you ever had sex before?"

"Yes, I've had sex before," I said, insulted.

Here's the thing. I thought I *had* had sex. My senior year of high school I visited my sister Laura at Boston University, and she fixed me up with a friend who was from all accounts very good-looking. I knew he was the kind of guy girls in my school would think was really hot. He was in college; he was tall and lean and had long hair and a long beard—like a sexy Jesus. We sat on my sister's tiny living room couch and watched *Dead Ringers*, a creepy Jeremy-Irons-as-twin-gynecologists thriller, and fell asleep before anything really serious happened. The next morning my sister and her roommate left early for the AIDS Walk, and this guy and I—yipes, I can't remember his name, maybe Brooks or something like that—moved into my sister's bedroom. He put on a condom and pushed against me, but there was honestly no hole there. I figured that was it. The guy just pokes hard between your legs for a while. Sex. When he finally gave up, he said, "It's not like it is in the movies, Sarah. Is that what you thought?" Which was a weird thing to say right after watching *Dead Ringers*.

"No," I said defensively.

So when Kevin asked me if I was a virgin, I answered honestly: no. Somehow I think he knew better than me, because he pretty much instructed me through the whole process. He talked me through my first blow job (that, I admitted I had never done before), what to do with my tongue, what not to do with my teeth, and so on. And then, slowly at first, he pushed inside me. All the way inside. And all I could think was, *Holy shit, THIS is sex, dummy.*

He sat up on the side of the bed to smoke another Merit Light, carefully ridding the end of any excess ash, molding the red tip of it into a constant point. He put out his cigarette and pulled back the sheets to get up, revealing a Rorschach-like pattern of blood. Like a red butter-

fly stamp, getting lighter and lighter with each imprint.

There was a long moment of silence before I worked up the moxie to say, "That came out of you."

"Um. No it didn't."

Another long pause, broken by him: "It's OK. Just buy me new sheets."

Kevin didn't have much time for me, but I took whatever I could get. I couldn't wait to have sex again and again and again. It was awesome. I was in love.

The feeling wasn't mutual. As it turned out, there's a reason 30-year-olds sleep with 19-year-olds, and it's not because they're looking for something real. I beautified myself in my dorm room, checking the time and myself alternately all night for a date with him that never happened, and when I saw him next and accused him of sleeping with someone else that night, he just said, "It wasn't my fault, she tricked me," with an *I don't give a fuck* half-smile.

After six months of being his if-he-couldn't-find-anyone-better fallback sex, I gave him a letter with the ultimatum that he had to be nicer to me or it was over. He opened it immediately and read it in front of me, and said, laughing, "Then I guess it's over."

Not long after that my friend Kerry came to visit me from Washington. She asked me how I was and I told her that I lost my virginity but the guy dumped me and I was devastated.

"Fuck that shit," she said. "I'm a female chauvinist."

"Um…huh?"

"I'm a female chauvinist. I tell a guy, 'When I'm with you I'm with you, and when I'm not with you, you don't worry about where I am.'"

I was inspired. Kerry changed my perspective—changed the way I saw men and changed the way I saw myself, transforming me from prey to predator in one weekend visit. For the next two years I was on a rampage. I was a monkey swinging from vine to vine. I kept Noxzema in my bag because I never knew where I'd end

up sleeping or with whom. (Another rule from the Book of Kerry: never go to sleep with a dirty face.)

Excerpted from The Bedwetter: Stories of Courage, Redemption, and Pee *by Sarah Silverman. Copyright © 2010 by Sarah Silverman. Used by permission of Harper, an imprint of HarperCollins Publishers.*

Sarah Silverman is a comedian, actor, and writer.

MIRANDA JULY

I was 17, a senior in high school. He was 27, a grad student at UC Berkeley, the local college. He was actually my friend's boyfriend before he was mine—I guess he just really loved girls from this one particular prep school, and the feeling was mutual. My friend was somehow not really mad. I remember her describing birth control to me, which was "the sponge," a chemical-soaked sponge that you stuffed up your vagina. He was from Detroit, kind of a big guy, looked a little like a boy from *The Brady Bunch* gone bad. He was so poor that he did not even have a bed, just a blanket neatly laid out on the carpet of his friend's living room. So that's where we did it.

I visualized outer space to block out the pain, a fact I only remember because I included it in a story I wrote afterwards.

I typed it up on the family computer and stupidly named the file "The First Time." Later that week my mom took me out to a special lunch where she asked me if I'd had sex. I think she was surprised it had taken me so long. A few years later, she casually suggested that I had a lover I was visiting on my "long walks." But they really were just long walks.

We went out for a few months. It was an intense, formative time for me. I was thinking very hard about everything, including, but not only, feminism. One night I suggested we drive up to the hills overlooking the city. We parked and stood together on the edge of a cliff. I asked him to go down on me while I looked at the view. When he stood up again, I broke up with him.

A version of this piece originally ran in Dossier.

Miranda July is a filmmaker, artist, and writer.

SHANNON WOODWARD

I'm not quite sure how I missed the boat, but the boat was missed. By boat, I mean the kissing boat. The seven-minutes-in-heaven canoe. The spin-the-bottle pontoon. The make-out-party ocean liner. While all of the teenagers I knew were out honing their kissing skills, I was most likely home watching reruns of *I Love Lucy* and trying to figure out how to effectively blow-dry my terrifyingly wooly hair. In hindsight, this hair quagmire might have genuinely contributed to my late-blooming debacle. I digress. Suddenly, more people were making out in the hallways during passing periods than I believe actually went to my school. I was desperately behind the learning curve of love. I was doomed.

After giving my predicament a lot of thought, I came to the conclusion that the only acceptable thing to do to ensure the stability of my reputation as a relatively cool human being would be to somehow kiss a boy who was separated from my school life by at least 500 degrees. That way, if our makeout ended in some kind of terrible explosion, death, or hostage situation, I could easily pretend it never happened.

Enter Trent. Trent from my high school. Trent from almost every single class I was enrolled in. Trent who was surely my soulmate. Trent with his Johnny Depp hair, his ability to play nearly every Goo Goo Dolls song on his guitar, and his keen instincts as to exactly what methods of ignoring me were sure to make me swoon. Oh, yes, Trent. We were destined to be in love. Because, above all else, Trent was in a BAND.

My ingenious plan for learning how to kiss in secret was immediately abandoned. I had a target. After weeks of shameless flirting on my part (asking sporadically to borrow notebook paper and saying hello at a volume audible only to baby cats), Trent finally asked me to hang out with him outside of school. His band was playing at the community center at the local park. Please keep in mind that at this point, playing the community center was, to me, the equivalent of gigging at Madison Square Garden. This guy was my Mick Jagger. But, shorter.

I dressed up in my coolest outfit: a pair of leather pants from the Gap, and some kind of ratty lace tank top that I was convinced made me look like Courtney Love, and certainly not like some kind of sad homeless child (it made me look a little bit like a sad homeless child). I spent the entire day studying Rayanne Graff from *My So-Called Life* and methodically ripping off her "cool girl" expressions (these mostly consisted of raccoon-like stares with the occasional ironic eyebrow raise sprinkled in). With my newly acquired repertoire of faces, I set upon my mission to persuade my future husband to love me.

Everything happened like in a dream. Trent and his band performed: they were transcendent. I was convinced he was the next John Lennon. He glanced at me while he sang, and I practiced my unaffected "this happens to me all the time" half-smile, while in reality I think I blacked out for a sliver of a second more than once. He even played my favorite song, and dedicated it to me ("If You Could Only See" by Tonic—don't judge me).

When it was over, I went backstage (a.k.a. the bathroom area of the community center)

to find him. He was putting away his Yamaha and running his fingers through his glorious teen-heartthrob hair when he noticed me.

"Hey Shan, what'd you think?" he said.

"You were all right," I said, praying that he understood my sarcasm.

"Yeah?" He stood up and moved very, very close to me. I'm dead. Paralyzed. Surely not capable of speaking English at this point. I remembered the advice that my earth-science teacher, Mr. Finney, gave me should I ever find myself in a confrontation with a T-rex: don't move. They can't see you if you don't move.

Trent put his hands on my hips. "Wanna be my girlfriend?"

He said that. He really said that. Things like that NEVER happened to me.

"Sure."

That was it. It was going to happen.

It happened. He kissed me.

IT WAS TERRIBLE. Terrible isn't even the right word. It was completely disastrous. My moves were all over the place. Imagine someone blasting the "The Hokey Pokey" and "Smells Like Teen Spirit" at the same time in a very tiny, claustrophobic space. Like, say, a doghouse. That is what this kiss felt like to me—all wrong, and rhythmically a mess. Except, throw in wet and spitty. I couldn't wait for it to be over. Humiliated and panicked, I tried to come up with something to say that would save me from being awarded the title of Most Likely to Never Be Kissed Again in the yearbook. I opened my eyes. Trent looked at me, obviously a little confused by what had just happened, if not rightfully concerned about my mental health.

"Don't worry," I said. "You'll get better." I patted him on the face, and I walked away.

This stunt may the most insane thing that I have ever done (aside from sleeping in my parents' backyard for a week and ordering pizza to "tent guest house"). I had tried to make this poor boy believe that HE was the terrible kisser because I couldn't live with the idea that I might not inherently be God's gift to every teenage boy's lips. After all, I was wearing my ultra-cool leather pants and using my brand new as-seen-on-TV facial

expressions! How could it possibly have gone wrong?!

I'll tell you how: I was so caught up in the anxiety of never having been kissed that I forgot to pay attention to my partner in this kissing escapade. He actually wanted to kiss ME, not my newfound neuroses that had become a monster of their own! See, kissing is kind of like a… conversation. It takes two human beings, and it can be an incredibly engaging and memorable experience, or awful and terrible and something you never want to mention again. Kissing is an exchange of spit and tongues and lips that is different with every person you encounter (romantically!) based on their very own humanishness (look it up). You've gotta *feel* it out to figure it out.

I was a crappy, self-involved conversationalist, metaphorically. That realization in itself enabled me to slowly but surely improve upon my makeout instincts as my angst-ridden teenage years went on. I assure you, plenty of those other moments weren't pretty either, but a few of them were incredible. Movie-like, even.

In case you're wondering, the following morning at school, Trent and I couldn't make eye contact. I couldn't bear to face the shame of my own kiss-tastrophe. Our beautiful relationship ended sometime before the third or fourth passing period, through a game of human telephone. He also eventually found out through one friend or another that our community-center rendezvous was my first kiss. To be honest, it wasn't so bad when he found out. He never mentioned it to anyone. I think he had a little sympathy for me. Not enough to kiss me again, but enough to keep my secret safe.

I'd be willing to bet that Trent had had a first kiss of his own once, too, and most likely his wasn't so great, either. In fact, I bet nearly everyone at my high school had a similar story. That "learning curve of love" that I was so panicked about? It never really existed. Unfortunately, the hopeless war with my wooly hair does. It's an uphill battle.

Shannon Woodward is a writer and actor.

KRISTA BURTON

I wish this were going to be a wonderful first-time-having-girlsex story about trust and softness and exploration and naked boobies, but my first time sleeping with a girl was…awful. And it was all my fault.

I was so ready to have sex with a girl that I would have done *anything* to finally do it. You know when King Arthur pulls the sword from the stone and realizes he's the boy king and that his *whole life* has been gearing up for that exact moment? That's what my first time with a girl could have been like. A sudden realization that FROM NOW ON, LIFE WOULD BE DIF-FERENT. But instead, it was dreadful—I couldn't enjoy a minute of it. Couldn't relax for even a second.

Because I lied. I lied to my first girl-friend. I told her I had "done it before."

I told her this because I was so, so, so ready to sleep with her (dying for it), and I knew she was nervous to have sex with another girl and she wanted someone to "show her the ropes" so she didn't "do it wrong." I was terrified that she would change her mind and not sleep with me if she found out I was a virgin, so…I lied. I said I had experience.

And I *did* have experience! With my own hand. *How different could it be?* I reasoned. *She's got what I've got. I know my way around MY stuff.*

My girlfriend believed me, and trusted me, and…it could have been beautiful. It could have been two girls being a little nervous together and learning from each other and sharing each other's first time. Instead, I was in a cold sweat and panick-ing because I couldn't get her bra undone and her down-there parts, mysteriously, seemed to work *differently* from mine.

I hate to even say this, but I don't really even remember the actual sex-having. All I remember is worrying about whether or not my girlfriend was buying my act, and concentrating very hard on whether or not she was having a good time. I know it didn't last very long. It was panicked groping, it was utterly unromantic and awful, and it was all my fault for being a lying asshole.

I think your first time is important, and I would do it all over—start from scratch—

if I could. You guys, don't be like me. Don't lie about having experience when you don't. It's OK to be nervous about having sex. It's OK to admit you don't really know what you're doing. Having sex with a girl is lovely, and I promise, it's not really that mysterious. Enjoy it.

Krista Burton is a blogger (effingdykes.blogs-pot.com) and Rookie staff writer.

PAMELA DES BARRES
(as told to Anaheed)

The first man I ever had sex with was Nick St. Nicholas. But before that I performed many oral favors. My first boyfriend, Bob-by Martini, had introduced me to the joys of oral when we were still in high school. At that point I was saving my virginity to marry him. Then I went to Hollywood and got all wrapped up in the crazy world of rock music, and musicians. I was a very sensuous girl, and I fooled around with a lot of boys, including Jimmy Page, Robert Plant, Keith Moon, Captain Beefheart, Noel Redding from Jimi Hendrix's band, and all the members of Iron Butterfly.

It was a very free-spirited time—there wasn't a lot of pressure to go all the way. Guys were content to just hang with you, make out, give head, all of that. Like with Jim Morrison—I just made out with him for hours. But I was saving the big moment for someone I really believed I loved.

Nick was the bass player for a band called T.I.M.E.—Trust in Men Every-where. He later became the bass player for Steppenwolf. He was this gorgeous blond German beauty, and a real cuckoo bird—he had his own language. He tried to get me several times before I finally let it happen. I waited for a long time, because he was engaged to one of my best friends, Randee. She was waiting for their marriage day to give it up to Nick, but she approved of my being with him in the interim. It's such a '60s flower-child kind of story; it probably couldn't happen now.

I was 19 when we finally did it. I was in love, and I decided that it was time. It was at my friend Sparky's parents' house—I hope they're not reading this. Her parents were away for the weekend, and we invited Nick

over to hang out, and that's when it hap-pened. It wasn't what I imagined it would be, with all of the explosions that you hear about. The whole time, all I could think was *Oh my god, I'm doing this*. I could hardly believe it.

It was kind of like the first time I had sex with Mick Jagger. I just couldn't get over the fact that it was *Mick Jagger*. He's an incredible lover, by the way. Amazing at oral—he loved it. What a mouth! The first few times we were together I just made out with him, and he gave me huge purple hickeys up and down my thighs.

The day after my first time, Nick and I went to the beach. I remember lying in the sun thinking, *Oh my god, I did it. I did it. I did it.* I felt changed, like I had become a woman—all those corny feelings.

Luckily, after that underwhelming first encounter, I gave sex another chance. The second, third, fourth, fifth times were *amazing*. And then I became addicted to it.

Nick didn't fall in love with me, which is what I had hoped would happen, but we kept seeing each other, and then he mar-ried Randee, and I was at the wedding. We're all very good friends now.

I think a lot of girls rush into sex, just wanting to get it over with. That's not the way to do it, though. I think you really need to feel luscious about somebody, and want them, and know that they feel the same way about you. And that they respect you. ◆

Pamela Des Barres is a writer, clothing de-signer, and legendary groupie.

APRIL 2012: **TRANSFORMATION**

Happy April! Our theme this month is Transformation. The concept came to me after I spent a weekend watching and rewatching the *Transformers* movies, locked in my room, in the dark, with no food or water, so as to get rid of all other variables and fully commit to absorbing the art alone. Perhaps you've heard of this trilogy—nay, triple-scoop sundae of Jesusness—created by one of my favorite directors, Michael Bay. If not, it is about Louis from *Even Stevens* fighting robots while a hot girl cheers him on. I'm pretty sure it's a metaphor for the ways in which corporate greed has corrupted our eyes, and also it's a metaphor for violence, and also politics, and also rights, and also, too, though.

I finally emerged from my room at the end of the weekend, wondering why none of my friends had called to see if I was OK since I hadn't been posting any links on Facebook to websites about poop in three days. But I also felt, well, *angry*. Angry that it was over. Angry that this beautiful world that Michael Bay created could not exist in real life, and angry that I could not be a part of it.

Then I heard a voice. "Who says?" asked Little Kevin James, the thumb-sized version of Kevin James that started sitting on my shoulder somewhere between the 34th and 35th hour of staring at my TV in the pitch-black with no nourishment. "Who says that you can't re-create *Transformers* in real life, complete with former *Even Stevens* stars, robots, and [a bunch of other shit that I don't know about, because I've never actually seen any of the *Transformers* movies]?"

Maybe it was the casual tone of his voice. Maybe it was the wiry hair on his knuckles, the knuckles that helped him complete a half-shrug, half-butt-scratch. Or maybe it was the fact that he was too hopeful about the potential for life's greatness to care about the stain on the front of his *Paul Blart: Mall Cop* sweatshirt. Whatever it was, I felt it, and I knew that Little Kevin James was right. Why *not* try to model my life after the *Transformers* movies?

But stopping there would be selfish of me. I know that I have found life's light in the room where I sit now, surrounded by Legos and the Shia LaBeouf lookalikes that I picked up from the local community college's fraternity, Boys in Middle School Who Would Have Been Cute If They Weren't So Annoying Kappa Beta Delta. But I need to share this light with all of *you*. I need others to be happy the way I am. "I agree."—Little Kevin James.

And so, this month's Rookie theme is all about *Transformers*. I don't want to give too much away, but let's just say it will include an Ask a Grown Man by Michael Bay, a D.I.Y. on how to be the most boring protagonist ever, courtesy of Shia, and a photo shoot by Petra of robots modeling flower crowns in dreamy fields.

ALL RIGHT, YA GOT ME. Happy April Fool's! In all seriousness, this month will be about SPRING and COLORS and THE 1960S and CH-CH-CH-CH-CHANGES. Not about Michael Bay. I would like to get some *Even Stevens* in here somewhere, though. Anyway, I really hope you like it.

LOVE,
TAVI

ON CONTAINING MULTITUDES

A conversation about growing up biracial.

By Leeann and Marie

MARIE Throughout my life, people have assumed that I am Mexican or Latin American. One time, this lady came up to me in a store and immediately started speaking Spanish, then got pissed off and started yelling at me when I told her—in my extremely limited español—that I didn't speak it. (I've also been mistaken for Japanese and, a few times, Chinese.) I am actually Filipino and Italian.

Growing up, I often felt confused and alone because there weren't many kids who looked like me, but I recently read that, among children, the multiracial population has increased 50 percent since 2000, which makes me wonder if those kids are experiencing the same frustrations that I did, or if people are less obsessed with checking just one box these days. (I hope so.) Either way, I wanted to talk to my fellow Rookie Leeann about what it means to be biracial and how it's shaped the women we are today.

LEEANN I'm half Irish and half Puerto Rican. My mom is an Irish-American from western New York. My father, who passed away when I was very young, was born in San Juan and moved with his family to the South Bronx. But all my life people have thought I was Asian. There were a lot of Asian immigrants in my hometown of Rochester, New York, and I was close friends with a lot of the girls. Teachers were always calling me Anh or Thuy or other friends' names. We spent a lot of time joking about our clueless white teachers, because to us it was SO OBVIOUS that my Cambodian friends didn't look like my Vietnamese friends, and that I didn't look like any of them! I used to chalk it up to overburdened teachers in crowded city schools, or the fact that I had the classic Asian girl haircut: long dark hair with blunt bangs. But as I got older and became more politically conscious, I realized this is a really common frustration for Asian people: being lumped into this one category when there are actually a ton of different ethnicities and identities that are invisible to a lot of non-Asian people.

My mother came here from the Philippines in the early '70s and my dad is second-generation Italian by way of Massachusetts. I just found out today that I have English, Scottish, and Irish blood. I AM A HUMAN GLOBE. There weren't many Filipinos at my elementary school. I felt a bit lost and alone, which sucked balls because I was already awkward as it was. I was one of the smart kids, which was not cool, and I was chubby and cripplingly shy. In high school, I FINALLY met a couple of other cool half-breeds like me and we became BFFs. But at some point came the anger and frustration. There was this one instance in high school where I was trying to enroll in a class at a community college during the summer and had to fill out some paperwork asking for my ethnicity: Caucasian, Asian, African-American, and so on. I told the lady in charge that I wasn't sure what to do and she responded, "You can only pick one!" My face got hot and my eyes got all watery. I think that specific incident, along with people assuming I was Mexican, fueled some sort of *Where do I belong?* rage, which resulted in a few angry rants to unsuspecting people soon afterward.

Having to constantly assert your identity is annoying. I think the point might be especially sore for me because my father passed away, and I'm not in touch with the Puerto Rican side of my family. It feels like my race is the only thing that connects me to this really important part of my past. I'm really proud to be Puerto Rican and really proud that everyone says I look eerily like my father, 'cause that's all I have of him, you know? I don't have to be proud of my Irish-American heritage in that same fierce way.

Do you find that some people will be like, "What are you?" You look "exotic" or whatever, but they can't put their finger on it. When someone finds out I am Filipino they usually just ask me to cook them pancit or adobo. I can't blame them, because dat shit is good.

Oh my god, I've gotten some really interesting reactions. From white folks, there's usually A LOT of surprise, because I "read" as white or Asian to them. The surprise itself doesn't bother me if it's just matter-of-fact, getting-to-know-you type stuff. But then there's the offensive kind of surprise, where it's clear that this person is just struggling to put me in an appropriate box. The most common examples are people going, "No! Really?!" Like, OK, you wouldn't be this surprised if you weren't carrying around very rigid ideas about race. What really bugs me is when people say, "But you're not *really* Puerto Rican," meaning that I don't fit their stereotypes of a Latina. Or this question: "So do you put Hispanic on applications?" I'm always like, "Yeah, because otherwise I'd be lying." I love (meaning hate) the implication that I'm only mentioning a fundamental part of my identity to gain some imaginary advantage. Only white people are under the impression that being Puerto Rican has ever gotten anyone anywhere in this country! I think it shows what a fucked-up relationship people have to race here. If your race is not immediately apparent, or doesn't conform to certain stereotypes, people immediately start policing it.

What's the reaction been like among other Puerto Ricans?

They're so refreshingly no-big-deal about it! They seem happy to know another Puerto Rican, and this is true of everyone I've met from a Spanish-speaking country. There's a real solidarity there, which is nice, because sometimes I do worry that I'm not "culturally Puerto Rican" enough.

Filipinos always seem happy to meet other Filipinos! It's always cool to meet another Italian, too, but there's not a bunch of them in one place on the West Coast. L.A. doesn't even have a Little Italy, which has always BURNED MY BRUSCHETTA.

Have you ever been a victim of racism?

One time I gave a dollar to a homeless dude, and his form of gratitude was yelling, "Gung ho, la choy!" Another time, I was at Magic Mountain, and a group of older kids started doing that racist hand gesture where you stretch the corners of your eyes with your fingers. They yelled "chink eyes" at me and my friends. I was 10 at that time, but not so naïve that I didn't notice that these kids weren't white. They looked like the latest incarnation of Menudo. (I loved Menudo.) So it was not only my first experience of racism, but also the first time I realized that people of any ethnicity can be racist.

This is complicated, because I have white skin, and I "pass" as white, and there's a huge amount of privilege that goes along with that. So the racism I've experienced is very small compared with what other people go through. It's shocking when that curtain pulls back—and even my shock is a privilege! The most blunt example of racism I've encountered was when a former boyfriend mentioned to his mother over dinner that I was half Puerto Rican. Now, I loved this woman so much, she was wonderful to me, but it was so clear that this information, like, rocked her world. She put down her fork, looked at me in this weird, appraising way that she never had before, and said, "No way. But your features are so refined. You must be more Spanish than Puerto Rican." She said it with this kindly tone, like how you would reassure a friend if they said they were ugly. It's clear from her statement that she thought that being Puerto

Rican was not beautiful or "refined," and she wanted to reassure me that I looked…white, basically! This was her idea of a compliment.

Did you have any celebrity role models that you looked up to?

Man, I really didn't have too many! I always felt a little bit (OK, a lot) of connection with J. Lo, and I thought it was awesome when I found out Joaquin Phoenix was "sorta Rican" like me. But for the most part, it was reading people like Malcolm X, bell hooks, and Angela Y. Davis that resonated so much with my experiences and beliefs and gave me a framework for how I think about race. Reading about the history of the Young Lords, the United Farm Workers movement— all these things made me really proud of the history of resistance among Hispanic people and determined to embrace it.

You know, I wish there was a Cool Mestiza Chicks newsletter back when I was growing up, but I wasn't aware of one. (Though some internet research just showed me that there was a zine called *Bamboo Girl*, and probably more like it. Listen, we didn't have the internet back then.) And half-Filipino celebrities were almost nonexistent, though I was REALLY excited to find out that Lou Diamond Philips (from the movie *La Bamba*) had Filipino blood! Outside of school, I hung out with kids who were like me, daughters of my mom's friends, so I did get to experience that kind of common bond. How do you feel about being mixed now versus when you were growing up?

I'm just sort of over denying a part of myself for other people's comfort. If people think I'm mentioning my race to get a pass, it no longer makes me question my right to identify as a Latina. I am who I am, I'm proud of it, and if somebody has a weird or racist reaction to it, that says a lot more about them than it does about me. Also, I'm a helluva lot more mouthy than I used to be, and I am not afraid to call someone out for a racist

comment. I'm a big believer in handing it back to them.

I definitely am proud of being Filipino and Italian. I've embraced growing up in two cultures, because that's what makes me ME! Also, I have learned that my surroundings were just as much as an influence as my actual ethnicity. I joke that I am the Number One Fake Mexican because, growing up in Southern California, I was so immersed in Latin culture. I probably understand more Spanish than I do Tagalog or Italian. Do you think things have changed since we were kids?

I honestly don't feel that things have changed much! I've gotten the "you're not *really* Puerto Rican" as recently as this year. The best-case scenario is when someone seems to know that they SHOULDN'T make a big deal out of it, but even that seems awkward. For me, the matter-of-fact response has just never been the norm, from white folks anyway. It's usually either awkwardness or prurient, exoticizing interest. There's still an incredibly backwards attitude toward race in this country, and attitudes toward multiracial people are so telling, because they get at the heart of how people really feel about racial boundaries. What do you think, M?

I think there's two sides to the coin. On one hand, the statistic regarding the increase in America's mixed-race population gives me hope that the little half-Filipina girl sitting in class right now doesn't experience those feelings of strange isolation and prejudice that I did. On the other hand, I agree with you that racism is still very much alive and thriving. And I don't understand how the entertainment business is still extremely lacking in racial diversity. There are more famous Filipinos on the big screen nowadays, but my people are still so underrepresented. Lemme get a shout out to my fellow mestizas Hailee Steinfeld, Cheryl Burke, Shannyn Sossamon, and Nicole Sherzinger! Vanessa Hudgens, you will probably have to play me in the Lifetime Original Movie. ♦

HOW TO CLEAN YOUR ROOM IN 10 MINUTES

Emergency protocol for even the most serious of slobs.
By Krista

Oh no, no, no, no, no! Your room is a HUGE disaster: clothes all over the floor, books in your bed, hair ties and necklaces and chargers and cords snaking around everywhere, empty Peach Snapple bottles, hairspray-sticky surfaces, snot-hardened tissues, and a dresser buried under a mountain of crap.

You were supposed to clean your room all week but you DIDN'T, and now the very cool person you like-like/want to impress is coming over in 10 minutes to study/hang out for the first time and you just got home from school and OMG YOUR ROOM IS SO GROSS THEY WILL NEVER LIKE YOU AND YOU'LL DIE ALONE IN A PILE OF JUNK AND GET EATEN BY THE CAT.

OK. Deep breaths. Do. Not. Panic.

I've been a secret slob all my life, and no one but my family and close friends knows. At one point during college, I was picking my way, barefoot, along the tiny path to my dorm room door in the middle of the night, and I tripped. A huge pile came tumbling down. My roommate, Cayla, woke up to the sounds of my low groans. When she flipped on the light we found: the paper I had printed out and then lost and then had to frantically reprint and turn in late, the extra set of dorm keys we'd been charged $50 for losing, the scissors Cayla had accused me of moving and we'd proceeded to have an epic fight about, a half-eaten block of cheddar, 14 soda bottles, *live ants*, an open container of pink glitter (you can't get rid of glitter), and my passport, which I had been tearing the room apart looking for because the study-abroad office needed it, like, now.

I know about messes. And I am here to help you. Let's get to speed-cleaning. Ready? Go!

Here's what you need to do immediately:

1. PRIORITIZE.

Take a step back and reaaaaally look at your room. What is the biggest offender? Shoe piles? No visible floor space? Crusty old dishes? Crusty old dishes and half-empty glasses of curdled milk under the bed that are creating a sour odor? Crusty UNDERWEAR? Try to see your room for the first time, treating a shared room as if it were completely yours. What's most immediately shocking? What's the first thing that might snag someone's gaze? (Hint: it's the underwear.) **Time spent: 10 seconds.**

2. GET RID OF THE MAJOR OFFENDER(S).

Refer to the Priority Messes identified in step one and TAKE CARE OF THEM. If it's clothes and shoes all over the floor, run and get the laundry basket, pile everything into it (shoes at the bottom), and set it against a wall. Oh, ha ha, you were just about to do a load of laundry! Alternately, you can grab a garbage bag, stuff everything into that, and throw it in your closet. It's just a bag of stuff you're donating and, no, they cannot look through it. **Time spent: two minutes.**

If it's books and papers, fly around your room, picking up every single book and sheet of paper, regardless of what they are, and put them all in two tidy piles on your desk or on the floor by your bed, with the smartest/trendiest books and magazines on display. *The Hunger Games* and *On the Road* can go on top of the latest issue of *Highlights* (still a really good magazine). Look how much you read! You're so cultured! **Time spent: one minute.**

3. HIDE ANYTHING SUPER-PERSONAL.

We all have crap we don't want other people to see, especially the first time they come over. Scan the room for potentially embarrassing items, such as dental headgear, wart-removing cream, the Justin Bieber singing toothbrush (gag gift, right?!), prescription bottles, the notebook in which you've practiced writing your crush's name linked with yours, Vagisil, Monostat, foot fungus spray, the neti pot, Preparation H, used Q-tips, and anything aiding digestion. None of these things are shameful, OBVS, but they're not exactly things you need your new friends to be intimately acquainted with. **Time spent: 30 seconds.**

4. OPEN ALL THE WINDOWS.

Seriously, even if it's freezing. Air the cave out! Now spray one (ONLY ONE) squirt of your perfume right in front of your door, close to the ceiling, and fan it around with your hands. Perfect! Now anyone walking in will have a first impression of a good-smelling room. And your crush will get a waft of your scent, which is always good. **Time spent: 30 seconds**.

5. QUICKLY MAKE THE BED.

The bed is the biggest thing in your room; making it will give the impression that the room is a lot more tidy. Don't spend too long on this, just pull the sheets up and drag the coverlet over the top. Tip: if you want it to look like you definitely did not just make the bed, lie down and then get up again to leave an I've-been-sitting-on-this-bed body imprint. Place the one item you were obviously just engaged with (e.g., laptop, book of poetry, collage) on your now-neatened bed, next to your pillows. You were totally just lying here a minute ago, doing something awesome! You are always doing cool shit. **Time spent: one minute.**

6. GET RID OF ANYTHING PERISHABLE THAT HAS ALREADY PERISHED.

Grab all crusty dishes/water glasses/Tupperware from old lunches and run them to the kitchen sink. Then take the overflowing trash out. Remember: there's a HUGE difference between "messy" and "gross."

Clutter = messy. Anything that mice and roaches might like to make a nest in = gross. **Time spent: three minutes.**

7. PUT A CLEAN GYM SOCK ON EACH OF YOUR HANDS.

Get one wet. Now you have a scrubber and a duster. Use the wet one on anything sticky, like rings from juice glasses. Run the dry one over all surfaces at eye level and anything truly, horribly dusty. **Time spent: two minutes.**

Great! Your room is now passably neat(ish)! If Cool Person hasn't shown up yet, it's time to make your room look like someone mysterious and fascinating lives in it (which is true!). Got a lamp? Got more than one lamp? Throw a red or pink sheer scarf over the tops of them, like they do in *Almost Famous*. A sheer T-shirt or tank top will work as well. When you flip the lamps on, the room will be bathed in a rosy, cozy glow. (Don't forget to take the scarves off after your visitor leaves—this is a potential fire hazard!)

Attack the top of your dresser, grouping and clustering items together until it looks like you planned for them to be with one another: makeup/scented items lined up in a row, photos in a cluster, and all figurines/toy models grouped together like a mini-shrine to teenagehood.

Finally, add carefully edited "mess" back into the room for realism. For example, hang a pendant necklace off the edge of your dresser, held in place by a trophy or figurine. "Accidentally" drape your favorite concert T-shirt on the closet doorknob.

Do a last lightning check. Did you: (1) put all garbage bags full of clothes or trash out of eyesight? (2) Hide your journal? (3) Erase any blinking computer chats that say something like "OMG!!! I JUST LOVE HIM/HER SO MUCH I CAN'T BELIEVE HE/SHE'S COMING OVER"?

Excellent. Your room looks like it belongs to a casually neat person, a person who never has to worry about someone coming over unexpectedly, because everything is always this way! Now put on your favorite album, starting it smack in the middle, because you've been listening to it this whole time, alone in your awesome room. ♦

MOD EYE MAKEUP IN LIKE FIVE MINUTES

You can tell people it took an hour if you want to.
Writing by Hannah.
Illustration by Cynthia.

I've always been most inspired by the 1960s, especially when it comes to makeup. Cosmetics in the '60s were all about enhancing your favorite features and making a bold statement, and icons like Twiggy, Penelope Tree, Peggy Moffitt, and Edie Sedgwick came up with looks that were all about more, more, more.

For this month's Transformation theme, I wanted to give you guys some ideas for transforming your eyes. A mod eye-shadow situation is guaranteed to make your peepers stand out and get people asking how much time it took to get them that way (you can lie and say it took an hour, but it actually takes only a few minutes).

WHAT YOU'LL NEED:

♦ A matte white eye shadow, like Wet 'n' Wild's Color Icon Eyeshadow Single in Sugar ($2, drugstores).
♦ A matte white eyeliner, like New York Color's Classic Brow/Liner Pencil in White ($1, drugstores).
♦ A matte medium-toned brown eye shadow, like NYX Cosmetics' Nude Matte Shadow in Underneath It All ($5, nyxcosmetics.com).
♦ A matte dark gray or black eye shadow, like NYC Cosmetics' Nude Matte Shadow in Stripped ($5, drugstores).
♦ A small, stiff-bristled eye-shadow brush like Sephora Collection's Classic All Over Shadow Small Brush #23 ($11, sephora.com).
♦ Gel eyeliner and a fine-tipped brush. I used Maybelline's Eye Studio Lasting

Drama Gel Eyeliner in Blackest Black, which includes a brush ($7, Wal-Mart).

HOW TO DO IT:

1. Cover your entire eyelid, from the brow bone to the lash line, with the white eye shadow. You can use your finger to apply it, if you want. I use my fingers all the time! I'm not fancy.

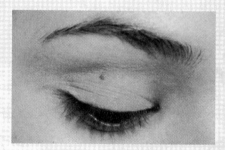

2. Use the white eyeliner pencil to color in your waterline (the inner rim of your lower lash line). This will make your eyes look much bigger and more awake.

263

3. Use the tiny shadow brush to apply the mid-tone brown shade in an arc, just above your natural crease. This creates an exaggerated, heavy-lidded look that a lot of mod models were known for. Extend it from near your tear duct upward and out toward the edges of your eyes, slightly above the outer corner.

4. Use the shadow brush to apply the dark gray or black shade to *really* exaggerate the "crease" line you drew in step three. Focus the color in the center, and blend it out to either side.

5. Dip your tiny liner brush into the liner. You can also use a felt-tipped liquid liner for this, but I think cream liner is a lot easier to apply. Apply the liner to your upper lash line, starting a few millimeters away from the inner corner, and extending slightly out at the outer edges of your eye. Build the coverage up until you have a reasonably thick line.

Try doing this at a desk or table where you can sit down, with a tabletop mirror. Rest your elbow on the table for balance and precision. It will make the eye-lining process a whole lot easier.

6. Make a line of thick dots with your liner, a few millimeters apart, along your lower lash line. Slowly draw them out so that they make slightly triangular shapes. Make them as long or as short as you like, but I think somewhere in the middle looks best.

7. Finish up with two coats of your favorite mascara and a nude-toned lipstick, like Revlon's Super Lustrous Matte Lipstick in Nude Attitude (about $8, drugstores).

If you're feeling more adventurous or having a really gloomy day, add color! Switch out the brown and gray shadow for shades of blue or green, or add accents of purple, pink, or yellow at the outer corners.

Boom, there you go. It's eye makeup that will look just as awesome with your cute floral minidress as it will with a sleek all-black outfit. Happy spring! ❀

OUTSIDER/INSIDER

You may ask yourself, "Well, how did I get here?"
Writing by Jenny. Illustrations by Minna.

I. In eighth grade, in the middle of reading lines from Shakespeare's *Comedy of Errors*—a play my English teacher insisted was "funny if you would just put in the effort"—the two girls who sat behind me, who weren't even the worst of the worst, took out a box of packing peanuts and dumped its entire contents on my head. When I came home with little bits of white fluff in my hair, my grandmother exclaimed, "You've gone white!" in Chinese and I mumbled, "It's freakin' Styrofoam!" in English and locked myself in my room, crying in that heinously dramatic way I had learned from watching my heroines on TV cry—the Lindsay Weirs and Angela Chases, who seemed to have pain rumbling from their every pore, and yet, unlike me, had friends who stood up for them, boys who tried hard to understand them, and a world that wasn't entirely hostile to every fiber of their being. I had packing-peanut pieces in my hair, a lifetime membership to the Itty Bitty Titty Committee, and the rest of my miserable life to dream about escaping a world that I swore could never ever understand me.

When middle school ended, I scrawled in my yearbook, "MEMO: Eighth grade was hell. I hope Glen Cove burns down to hell. I was THE outcast," and subsequently spent the summer feeling lonely and abandoned, like a fleck of paint flung out to a part of the world without buildings or walls, someplace where my small, negligible life did not belong. "My life will always be like this," I wrote in one of my many notebooks that summer. If no one was going to talk to me, then I would talk to myself. If there was no one who I wanted to listen to, then I was going to listen to myself. That summer, I filled up eight notebooks with poetry and song lyrics that you couldn't tie me up and drug me into looking at again.

In ninth grade, I mixed sugar with water in my mom's spray bottle and used the mixture to spike my hair. It would be another year before I watched *SLC Punk* and decided that I was a secret punker who was too good for the suburban hell I lived in. I was a misfit whose poetic sensibilities were just *too poetic* to ever be understood or accepted by the kids who traded last year's wide-legged JNCO skater pants for this year's Gap polos. I told myself that the kids who abandoned Green Day for Britney and would abandon Britney for whatever MTV told them to like the next year, who laughed at our 75-year-old math teacher when she fell off her stool in the middle of explaining proportional fractions and then laughed at me when I went to help her get up, who prided themselves on how little they ever thought about anything and publicly shamed me for how much I always thought about everything, would grow up to be the kind of people who talked about high school like those were the halcyon days, like life peaked back then and would never be as good—and, for them, it wouldn't.

Just to keep myself from sinking, I had to believe that these kids, whose meanness and cluelessness were validated and encouraged by the entire structure of high school, would one day lead miserable, dreamless lives while I filled mine with poetry and rock & roll and adventure and love. And one day, I would return to this town that once gave me so much grief for not wanting to wear what everyone else wore and not wanting to cheat on tests like everyone else cheated on tests and not caring about sports or cheerleading or bake-sale fundraisers or junior prom or senior prom or pep rallies or making fun of my teachers. I would roll through town and still be the weirdo I have always been, but instead of its being something grotesque, something to be attacked, it would be this dazzling, amazing thing. *Maybe I'm not too weird for this world*, I thought in ninth grade, hair sticky with sugar. *Maybe the world isn't weird enough for me.*

II. And it wasn't. It just wasn't. I wrote angsty poems about feeling hellaciously black in a world of sunny, cheerful yellows. I briefly dated a boy who was the lead singer of a screamo band called—I crap you not—NINTH DEGREE BURN. He drew Xs in permanent marker on his wrists and layered black rubber bracelets over them. For Valentine's Day he gave me a fake rose that he had dyed black, and I gave him two carnations like how you were supposed to do at funerals. All of my friends' screen names were like xNxOxOxOxIxWxOxNxT or xXwishyouweredeadXx. I started wearing clothes from my mom's closet, fun stuff like this white Heidi-of-the-mountains lace-up suspender skirt that had people yodeling at me in the hallways and asking if I was competing in the Ice Capades this winter.

I had a total of maybe four friends, none of whom I ever confided in or spent time with outside of school, but they were misfits too. One of them had been misfortunately nicknamed "the plumber" because someone had spied her crack in shop class; another wore her hair in a long, thick medieval braid right down to her rump and pretended that our little suburban town in decline was really the Welsh countryside, sprawling and giving. Another was a practicing Wiccan whose mother had pictures of naked, oiled rock stars in her house and once lent me a black cape to wear, just 'cause.

As high school went on, I became bolder, more contrarian. It seemed like I was one of four people in my school who read books outside of class. I argued with my English teachers whenever they insisted there was a "right" way to interpret a text. I disagreed openly with my teacher's Freudian reading of *The Metamorphosis* and tried to formulate my burgeoning thoughts on feminism and racism while the rest of the class was falling asleep or copying each other's homework for the next period's class. My English classes turned into one long dialectical conversation between me and my teacher about literature and privilege and criticism. I stomped around in platform combat boots and shredded sweaters and my mom's old clothes that I rescued from the Dumpster. On days when I just couldn't bear to step foot in my high school, days when I knew I couldn't take it, I would skip school and take the bus to Queens and then a subway to the East Village because I harbored some absurd delusion that if I stood outside Kim's Video in my combat boots and my shredded clothes and my sugared hair that made me the target of confused bees everywhere for long enough, I would eventually be swept up into a world of art and music and poetry. Deep down, as a 15-year-old misfit, I honestly thought that I would find my community just by standing around and doing nothing.

III. But I didn't, and I was learning that standing around and doing nothing would not get you any closer to finding your place in the world. I had to do something. If everyone said I was weird, I thought, then maybe I *was* weird, and maybe I liked it, because I had to like myself if I was going to keep on living, and I wanted to keep on living, and if I wanted to keep on living then I would have to like whatever it was about me that marked me as "different" from everyone else. So I embraced it. I did stuff with it. If I was a speck of paint in a world without walls, then I would build those walls myself. I convinced my parents to let me volunteer at a community center that put on punk-rock shows on the weekends and struck up a friendship with the director of the center, a 40-year-old former punker named Jim who gave me lists of movies to watch and introduced me to the Velvet Underground and Patti Smith and Television. When my dad brought home a crappy, old-school, dial-up modem that I wasn't allowed to use more than an hour a day because it made our phone lines busy, I spent that hour looking up profiles on AOL of people who liked Sylvia Plath poems and James Baldwin novels and lis-

tened to Jade Tree records, and put all of my energy into befriending them. I made friends with an anemic, sensitive, literary punker from Omaha, Nebraska. We sent each other care packages filled with Polaroids and mixtapes, collages that he had made for me and poems that I wrote for him. I was alone and I wasn't alone.

I spent my lunch period writing poems about escape and fantasy. I cut my hair short and dyed it burgundy. I applied to a summer program at Stanford University for high school students who wanted to spend three weeks intensively studying philosophy. I got in, and for the first time in a long time, I was happy. I felt like I belonged somewhere. I made more friends in three weeks than I had in five years. The first night, 10 of us sat around in a circle talking about faith and our relationship to God and debated about abortion and the death penalty. We stayed up every night until four or five in the morning just talking talking talking, frantic that there wouldn't be enough time to learn everything about each other, and there wasn't. "I'll never be the same again," I wrote in my notebook on the plane ride back to New York. And I wasn't. My suspicion that there was space for me in this world had been confirmed, however fleetingly, and I thought maybe if I could just get through high school and escape my miserable town then I would continue to find these spaces already inhabited by others who had made the same pilgrimage that I wanted so badly to make.

I approached my last year of high school with a level of misanthropy that I find embarrassing now. When I was voted "Most Individual," it felt like a backhanded compliment coming from my classmates, who championed conformity. I watched and taped religiously every single episode of *Freaks and Geeks* on my VCR, and I fell to the floor, overcome with vindication, when in the last episode the AV teacher drew an imaginary graph for Sam, Neil, and Bill, illustrating the rise and decline of the high school jocks and popular girls who would never know glory again after high school, whereas the freaks, geeks, and cretins would steadily rise. *I just have to wait*, I

thought. *I just have to wait until I graduate from high school, and then I'm gonna get the hell out of here.* I knew my people were out there, scattered like I was scattered, and somehow I was gonna traverse this fucking amazing universe and find each and every one of them and we would be one another's barrier to the horrific outside world that did not love us, did not appreciate us, and did not care that we spent the first 17 years of our lives so utterly alone.

IV. When I was 10, my legs grew too long too fast and my body was so bony that it hurt to lie down on the mats in gym class. My mom told me that growing happens only when you're asleep, so for weeks I tried to stay up and watch over my legs, hoping to stop them from growing, and for a while, I thought it was working.

"I'm not growing anymore," I said to my mom.

"Bullshit," she said in Chinese. "You're 10 years old, you can't stay this size forever." And I didn't; the growing happened despite my efforts.

The jabs and the jokes about my knobby knees and my next-to-nothing chest that were so much a part of the early years of my teenage life, that I thought I would carry in my heart forever like a wound that does not heal, disappeared one day. It took me some time to catch up with these changes, to switch my idea of myself as this awkward, gawky, hideously unwanted creature to someone who didn't need to move through the world so wounded all the freaking time. And no matter how much I tried to track these physical changes—to the point where I would sometimes spend entire afternoons sitting in front of a mirror, waiting to see something happen—it always came as a surprise. Like the time I walked past my university's post office and saw my reflection in the glass door and I felt so beautiful and happy that I wanted to cry, because the day had finally come when I had realized that I was no longer the person I was when I thought the pain I felt would be the pain I would always feel.

V. But how do you do it? How do you even get started? That was my question when

I was 13 and picking Styrofoam out of my hair. "How do you build a house from scratch?" I asked my father, who told me, "You just do. You pick up a brick and you just start."

"And how do traffic jams happen?" I asked him. "How does an entire highway get backed up for miles?"

"It just does," he said. "And it always starts with someone."

"But how does one person start a jam that affects like 10 thousand other people in their cars?"

"You just do it," my father told me, as if it were just that simple. As if all you had to do was just start doing anything at all, and eventually your little actions would become huge.

At some point, I just started. I read all the time and I wrote all the time and I listened to music I loved and I sought out people who I thought might know about music and books that I would love too. I rigorously researched colleges and universities to find ones that had strong creative-writing programs. I got into Stanford after spending months on my college applications, spilling my guts out into my personal essays; and at Stanford, I took every poetry and fiction class I could, joined every club that seemed even a little bit interesting, went to every reading I heard about or had time for in my schedule, met people who made art and played music, and started a writing group with my friends that still exists today, only now we are all published authors and journalists and novelists and poets. I applied for grants that allowed me to travel to Paris two summers in a row and spent six weeks obsessively researching the literary and artistic community in Paris, and when I got there I immediately went to Shakespeare & Company, the bookstore that Allen Ginsberg and William Burroughs and Anaïs Nin once frequented,

the bookstore that famously offered beds in exchange for poems, where I was determined to sleep amongst the books I had spent my whole life reading, and it turned out, all I had to do was show up with my big dreams balled up in my sweaty fists, and ask if I could spend the night. The answer was yes.

I spent my first summer in Paris tirelessly and relentlessly seeking out miscreants and weirdos, and came back the next summer to continue where I'd left off, hanging out with the crust punks from Germany, falling in love with a Swedish boy who had walked on a bed of hot coals, writing poetry on the Pont des Arts, and flirting outrageously with boys and girls who found my social awkwardness lovable instead of execrable.

I'm 28 now, old enough to know better—old enough to shed my old attachments to this idea of being the ultimate loser, the unknowable weirdo—but I'm still clinging. I can't let go of the scared, angry, alienated 17-year-old I was when I went off to college in California, where everyone was always "SO AWESOME" and so happy and so cheerful and so upbeat and I was always so "mysterious" (EW) and "artsy" (EW) and "quirky" (EW EW). I can't let go of that girl, even though at some point, I was so proud to be myself and so alienated by everyone else that I started to work really hard to find people who would never use the word *artsy*; and then I found them, and I started to date boys who didn't think I was "quirky," but just got who I was; and slowly, painfully, and ignorantly, I began to accept that things were changing. I couldn't cling to my old safety net of "everyone is against me!" because the happy, creative bubble I wanted for myself was happening, and in order to love it, in order to experience it, I had to acknowledge it.

So here I am, acknowledging it. Acknowledging that a few weeks ago, I went

on a poetry-and-puppets tour with the poet Zach Schomburg and the multimedia puppet troupe Manual Cinema. We spent a week driving down the East Coast in a Ford Econoline, listening to the songs I listened to when I thought I would always live on the edges of everyone else's world, except I wasn't on the edge anymore, I was right there in the center. I was still the cheerful, moody, puerile, poop-and-farts-obsessed wannabe poet I had always been, except I was in a van with other poets and musicians and actors and trapeze artists and puppeteers—the very people I had hoped to meet standing on the corner of St. Marks and Third Avenue—and every day we drove to a new city where we shared the things we made with people who had come to hear poetry, and there were nights when I stood there, trembling, with poems in my hands, wondering, *How did I get here?*

I got here because I *had* to get here. As soon as I stopped standing on corners, I began to find other misfits and explorers. So here I am, in it. Acknowledging it. Loving it. Wanting you to know that as much as it might look like nothing is happening right now, as much as you might think that it's possible for a person to be this lonely forever, in fact, slowly, bit by bit, the dust that has been gathering in your corner will clear, and one day, when you are returning to your lonely place for the hundredth or thousandth time, you will be surprised to find that the dust is gone and there in your corner of the world will be people like you who have been waiting for you this whole time as much as you have been waiting for them. ✦

BREAKUP BREAKDOWN

A guide to navigating the end of a friendship.
Writing by Amy Rose. Playlist by Rookie staff (lettered by Suzy).

Ending a romantic relationship is never easy. But it does have one thing going for it: there's a template for the end of love, and a generally agreed upon script. Someone breaks up with someone else, and it's understood that you two are no longer going to be spending time together, telling secrets, texting each other gross jokes, and all the other beautiful things that come with being connected to someone else that you like. Yes, that hurts, but it is of the Rookie staff's QUITE PROFESSIONAL opinion that there's another type of breakup that is even harder: the friend split.

Sometimes a relationship between you and a friend, a relationship that you took for granted would last for the rest of your lives, starts to change. It takes on a new shape, and that shape is not so pleasing. Maybe you're being inconsiderate of each other, fighting, or just growing apart—but you can tell something's off, and probably not going to be back on again anytime soon. How do you navigate the waning parts of a close friendship gracefully and with as few hurt feelings on all sides as possible? Hell, how do you even know when it's actually OVER? I mean, it's not like you can use the old "I hope we can still be friends" line with your *actual* soon-to-be-ex-friend.

As it happens, a good portion of us here at Rookie, like most other human people, have experienced lots of different kinds of friendship breakups throughout our lives and are happy to share our perspectives on them with you, because you've always got a friend in us, of course. Here's what we've learned so far:

1. CH-CH-CHANGES AIN'T SO STRANGE.

Change is natural, of course, and often for the best. But sometimes friends can feel left behind when you start doing newer things that don't necessarily include or interest them. Friends who are scared of the way you're changing might try to make you feel bad by saying things to you along the lines of "You've *changed*," like that is a monstrous thing that you are intentionally doing to be a dick to them, or that you're not as genuinely *you* anymore.

You know what, though? Life is about doing all kinds of different stuff, especially as a teenager. Who would want to stay the same forever? I mean, do these people not realize that they also, in fact, are not wearing the same corduroy overalls that they did in preschool, or are not still obsessed with the Wiggles? People grow up, man, and they continue to do so for basically as long as they are alive. Growing doesn't make you "inauthentic"—it means you're healthy. You should be encouraged, not criticized, especially by your close friends, while you're transforming and growing and exploring new things. Friends who are less than understanding about this are being kind of selfish, because they like you just the way you are and want you to stay that way. While I feel for them in this situation too, they are not being supportive of you, and that's not cool.

A big exception to this rule is if a friend is trying to express honest concern about new situations that involve things they're worried might be damaging to you, like drug use or crazy sex or that new cult you've joined. Even then, though, if you feel that what you are doing is safe and OK, you have every right to respectfully and calmly (even and *especially* if that's not how you were approached by this person) tell them that while you appreciate where they're coming from and that they care for you, you are going to continue to make your own decisions.

Of course, someone's criticizing you for changing is not always going to be some sort of mini-intervention about your choices with regard to substances or sexuality, which are the two most common things about which a concerned (or, you know, "concerned") party will be judgmental. Sometimes people are just trying to fence you in by being condescending about your new tastes or friends or whatever else have you. Tavi can relate: "In the fall, I was trying to keep a very special friendship afloat, even though I felt us changing into different people. Since the beginning of the falling-out she'd been doing a weird hostile thing, passive-aggressively insulting my newer tastes and interests, which I realized when I finally confronted her about it was way more about the fact that these tastes and interests were shared with new people in my life who I was hanging out with more than I was with her. To be fair, she also didn't make an effort to hang out with me, though that could've been because she assumed I wasn't interested. But she had new people in her life as well…and it wasn't about her personality, it was just that we had had time together to grow and learn and stuff and then we became different people and each had to feel comfortable following where that was taking us. Maybe we'll find each other again, or maybe we can just stay on good terms and be thankful for the strength of the friendship we had."

This experience is really common among the Rookie staffers, and I'm sure that many of you have been or are going through something similar too, because YOU ARE US AND WE ARE YOU AND SO ON. If you're trying to maintain the friendship, the most effective way to go about it is to address it openly, like Tavi did. Let your pal know that although you may care about different things now, you are still invested in your relationship, and then follow that conversation up by actually acting like it.

However, there are times when it's just not going to work out, which is totally OK too, even if it's really hard at first. Maybe you just *don't* have anything in common anymore, you know? Have a respectful conversation with your friend about this. If you're feeling it, he or she is too. Tell them that it's not anything they did, or you did, to spite the other party; it's just that things ain't the same. As Anaheed says, "It's GOOD to change and grow, and that means your friendships will also change, and sometimes change = the end of friendships." This doesn't mean that you won't treasure the time you spent together, nor does it void the friendship you DID have with this person and how great that was, when it was. It just means that not all friendships are meant to last forever, and now you can explore new relationships without feeling bad about moving gently away from one that just didn't work for you two anymore.

I also want to note that, obviously, you and your friend don't have to be the *exact same person* with the *exact same interests* in order to have an awesome relationship. My best friend from high school, who is still one of my favorite people ever, never really had much in common with me besides our huge love for each other and videos of cats being weird on the internet. But we're able to show each other lots of fun things that maybe we wouldn't have come across if we hung out exclusively with people who were cultural clones of ourselves. Having friends that are different from you is just as important as having ones that are similar, as long as they accept you wholly and vice versa.

2. "DON'T YOU KNOW THAT YOU'RE TOXIC?"

The fact of the matter is, not all friendships are going to end with your both amicably agreeing that you're growing in different directions. Sometime there'll be an issue of people actually being horrid to you, by lying, insulting you, spreading rumors, or otherwise being a complete booger.

A Rookie writer who was disrespected by a longtime best friend says the friendship started to get shaky when the following happened: "[She] didn't stand up for me when her boyfriend said something offensive about my identity. I was so deeply hurt because I realized, *WOW, she takes and doesn't give.* She'd cut me down publicly—she'd ask me what score I made on tests and not tell me hers, for example. I just realized that my values are different—I'm a ride-or-die kind of betch and she is all about looking out for number one." After a few years, our writer and her friend are cool again, but only because she put a stop to what was happening in their relationship at the time. A few others among us have been able to rekindle great friendships with ex-best-friends just because we refused to participate in the friendship when doing so wasn't healthy. Our writer did a tough thing, but it was the right one, and now she and her friend are able to hang again in a positive way.

Sometimes, though, you're going to want to be done with somebody for keeps. My most significant friend breakup happened when someone I considered my best friend for years, who worked with me, went to school with me, and was with me every day outside of those things, started to gradually reveal that she was using me for gross social-climbing purposes, among other things. Although that appeared to be the case with almost all of her other friends too, every last one of whom she'd trash-talk behind their backs, this person was so charming and awesome-seeming that I figured what we had was, you know, DIFFERENT. It was a classic case of my insisting to everyone who saw her mean side, "YOU JUST DON'T UNDERSTAND HER." Of course, it was me who didn't understand: an important and true life rule is that if someone is intensely negative about his or her other friends behind their backs, but is ultra-lovely and sweet to them to their faces, he or she is doing the exact same thing to you. This was the case with my ex-friend, who started flaking on all of our plans unless she needed something from me, at which point she'd send a barrage of super-affectionate texts/tweets/Facebook messages that would also oh-so-casually ask me to help her out with something, naturally. After this went on for about a month, I tried to see her in person and, when that failed, called her to explain that she was really hurting me, but she refused to address my feelings. It really sucks, because I loved her so much, as did all my other friends, but I didn't feel comfortable maintaining such a blatantly one-sided friendship.

If a person is doing things to you that a true friend wouldn't, tell them straight-up that their behavior is unfair. It's hard to do this without making the other person defensive, so try to express yourself as honestly as you can while still keeping their feelings in mind, even though they haven't exactly been extending you the same courtesy. Remember, too, that this person might have NO IDEA that they've been making you feel bad! So get together in person or give them a call, and put it out there. I highly recommend that you don't choose to address this online, where your tone can be misunderstood or you can say not-so-nice things to each other more easily. Instead, tell your friend *out loud* how much they mean to you, and then that you think they might not realize it, but they've been making you feel bad. If you give them the benefit of the doubt, your friend will be much more willing to speak with you without blowing up or closing themselves off. If they are genuinely apologetic and don't brush you off or try to shift the blame, accept that, and see how things go in the future. If they aren't open with you during this talk, or don't change the way they treat you afterwards, it's time to make a tough but essential decision: cut this wack person out of your life! You just deserve so much better.

3. GROUP THERAPY.

Some of the toughest friend breakups are the kinds that take place among more than two people. Maybe you're trying to slip out of your group of friends, or you don't like a member of your group with whom everyone else still wants to hang. Either of these situations can be totally insane-making, since you're not just dealing with your own feelings—you have to respect everyone involved, even if what you really want to do is just start freaking out and yelling GOD ENOUGH OF YOUR DUMB OPINIONS AND ALSO FACE GET AWAY FROM ME ALREADY at the person or people in question whenever you see them.

As a rule, that is never really a good idea, just so you know.

In the first situation, you might want to start exploring other friend groups for any number of reasons—you think your current pals exclude, alienate, or are rude to people outside the group; you find yourself no longer interested in the stuff you all do together or talk about; you start developing different opinions from the ones you all used to share; etc. and etc. and etc. These are all valid motivations to not want to hang as much or at all. Leaving a group is one of the only cases in a friend breakup where I think it's OK to start by doing a slow fade (usually, I think it's better to try and talk it out first, except in extreme situations)—just start gradually spending less time with your original group of friends. Sit with other people at lunch a few days a week, or go to different sleepovers on the weekends. If your old friends ask you about it, you can tell them that you feel like you haven't been socializing with other people enough lately. That's reason enough. Eventually, the old group will get used to doing things without you, and it probably won't be as hard on them as it was for you, because they all still have one another.

OK, but what if YOU don't want to leave your group, but you really want someone else to do so? Is there someone in the group with whom you'd feel comfortable discussing how you feel? Tread carefully, though: by "discussing," I mean "being honest about your reservations about this person while respecting that your confidante might not feel the same way," not "goading your friend into a smear campaign against this person that ends with you two instant-messaging her that she is ugly." I'm actually very serious about this—no matter how bad a breakup can be, no matter what this person has done or does to you in the process, DO NOT BULLY PEOPLE, not even a little. You will feel HORRIBLE about it later in life, if not immediately.

If your confidante agrees with you *of their own volition* that the person in question is bringing down your collective friendship, boom, you now have someone to support you in moving away from that person.

What happens when you find yourself on the other side of all of this—when you are the reluctantly broken-up-with person? Oh, man. I am so sorry if this is the case, because it can be so, so heartbreaking, whether or not your friends mean for it to be. What you need to realize, though, is that happens to EVERY SINGLE PERSON at one point or another, for real. Most friendships don't end because you are defective in some way, which is sometimes what people think after it happens to them (I know I did)— it's just what happens, eventually, to everyone at least once, especially in middle and high school. If someone doesn't want to be your friend anymore, it doesn't mean there's something wrong with you— it means you are a human being.

If you really examine your behavior—did you do anything resembling the stuff we mentioned above to your friend(s)?—and find that the answer is no, you're probably going to feel pretty confused and hurt for a little while. Luckily, there are ways to come out of these painful times gracefully while growing into an even better person than you already are in the process. It might be hard to believe right now, but these experiences will help you EVOLVE, like a beautiful and strong Pokémon who can only level up after a battle (God, I am such a poet sometimes). The result of most friendship breakups is this: you end up happier than you would be if you'd stuck with these relationships that no longer fit, no matter how difficult it can be at first.

In the meantime, you are going to be hurting a lot, and you might be tempted to cling to your ex-friends even though you know they're not invested in the relationship anymore. Don't do this, babe, really. (a) It doesn't work. (b) It's a misuse of your energy. (c) It distracts you from making new and better friends. (d) It's…well, embarrassing for you. Really.

How do I know? Well, oof: In eighth grade, my friends pushed me out of our group. They started ignoring me completely, as well as making fun of me online and spreading nasty rumors about me. It came out of nowhere. I was suddenly completely alone, and so I freaked. Instead of accepting the situation and trying to move on, which

would have started my ~healing process~ much sooner, I threw myself at the nonexistent mercies of the person I was once closest with in the group by writing her a three-page letter. In it, I apologized over and over (for what, I didn't and still don't know), and was just generally like, "WHATEVER I DID I CAN CHANGE I CAN BE WHOMEVER YOU WANT ME TO BE PLEASE DON'T DO THIS." Yikes, right? Years later, I'm still kind of cringing about it.

No matter how painful it is when someone ends a friendship with you, what's even worse is when you GROVEL like I did with that letter, which of course received no response at all. This kind of desperation doesn't have to take the form of a letter, and your friends don't have to have been as mean as mine were, to make a similar, too-clingy misstep. Maybe you keep trying to sit with your ex-friends in class, or calling them long after you've drifted apart, or writing on their Facebook walls even though you know it's no use. **Stop doing these things immediately**, because what IS useful is being a gracious and strong person who is able to realize that even though some people might not want to be friends with you, there are plenty of people out there who do, many of whom you already know.

I began coming to terms with the split by starting a conversation, funnily enough, with someone else my old friends hated. I fell in with her and her friends, who were, thank goodness, infinity times more fun and intelligent than the old group. They became my best friends throughout high school. That never would have happened if I had stuck to writing insecure letters to a person who thought it was awesome to joke about the fact that my family was poor.

Instead, KEEP IT MOVING and I promise you will be so much happier, so much sooner. If it's difficult to make new friends right away at school, get involved in organizations outside of it, which I found hugely helpful as well.

The internet is basically the devil in any friend breakup sitcheation. You might want to do a little Facebook stalking after the breakup at first, and that's understandable, but try to keep it to a minimum.

Don't be passive-aggressive. Tell someone honestly how you're feeling whenever possible, because manifesting your frustrations in ways like muttering "YOU WOULD" under your breath while your friend is telling you about their weekend doesn't actually accomplish anything besides making you look like a whispery weirdo.

There can be a certain awkward variable that I like to call the MOM FACTOR in some older friendships: maybe you are close with your ex-friend's parent, or your parents are also friends. Be as respectful and friendly as ever to your ex-friend's parent(s) if you still see them occasionally. If you ever have to field questions like "Now, what's going on between you girls??" just chirp, "I'm just so busy with school and stuff lately!" and then, like, bustle off. It's not rude—you totally have homework to do! You just explained that!

All told, no friendship breakup is going to be a perfectly clean split, even if you're really mature and awesome about it. Sometimes, you're just going to miss the person who isn't in your life anymore, and that part really stinks. Although, as we pointed out, these kinds of breakups are really different from the ~romantical~ ones in most ways, when it comes to getting over them, the process is the same. You need distractions from your hurt feelings, as well as a way to express yourself. Do you draw, or write, or make awesome collages out of tabloids in your spare time? Well, now is the time to do all those things, and more. You can cry, for sure, but also make time to put together all-new playlists (they can even be about the ex-friend, that's fair), put pictures of flowers on your Tumblr, or work on an actual garden! Most importantly, spend more time with or talk more to your other friends, or work on making all-new, non-terrible ones. They're out there for you. ◆

1. here comes the sun – the Beatles
2. Tunnel of Love – Wanda Jackson
3. hold tight – Dave dee, Dozy, Beaky, Mick + Tich
5. for today i'm a boy – Antony + the Johnsons
4. i'm coming Out – Diana Ross
6. Rollergirl – Anna Karina
7. Send me a Postcard – Shocking Blue
8. Walk on the wildside – Lou Reed
9. Sweet young thing ain't sweet no more – mudhoney
10. time of the season – the Zombies
11. Pretty Ballerina – the Left Banke
12. what am i going to Do – the Lovers
13. Shakin all Over – the guess who
14. Satan's theme – the Rondels
15. Gimmie Shelter – merry Clayton
16. after hours – the velvet underground
17. Landslide – fleetwood mac
18. Comment te dire adieu – françoise Hardy
19. All grown up – the Crystals
20. You're Sixteen (you're Beautiful and You're mine) – Johnny Burnette

here comes the sun

SECRET STYLE ICON: SHIRLEY KURATA

Talking tacos and the benefits of being a nerd with the smartest stylist around.
Interview by Leeann. Photos by Autumn de Wilde.

Stylist Shirley Kurata has described her look as "mod secretary," but with all due respect to the steno pool, this doesn't do her justice. Whether styling her own outfits or decorating her home in L.A., Shirley creates this giddy, Starburst-colored world full of winking mid-century references. She's whimsical without being precious, and referential in a way that feels totally fresh.

Shirley has dressed Miranda July, Zooey Deschanel, Cass McCombs, and Devendra Banhart, but I'm especially enamored of her editorial styling, which is smart, cinematic, and full of attention to detail. She has also been styling Rodarte's runway shows since their very first one in 2005. She shares an apartment with Kate and Laura Mulleavy during New York Fashion Week, where their horror-movie-and-taco night was once interrupted by a surprise visit from *Vogue*'s André Leon Talley (do you want to be their BFF yet?).

Shirley's own style is '60s mod (bright Crayola colors, A-line dresses, and opaque tights) meets '70s pottery teacher (slim-fitting turtlenecks, knee-length skirts, and little berets). She was awesome enough to answer some questions for us about her own inspirations. Read on for her words about developing your own style, her favorite Japanese horror movies, and the atheist Smiths fan who changed her life. Oh, and we get some deets on that star-studded taco night, too!

LEEANN I want to start by asking you: what were you like in high school?

SHIRLEY KURATA Well, I went to an all-girls Catholic high school in Pasadena, which I hated. I just never felt like I fit in there. It was a school for white, privileged, preppy girls. The turning point in my high school life was meeting my friend Sharon, who is dear to me to this day. Sharon was outspoken about her atheism and did plays about it in religion class (to the dismay of our teacher, a nun). She dyed her hair blue-black, loved Thoreau and Oscar Wilde, listened to the Smiths and the Style Council, and showed me that it was OK to be different. She was the one that took me to the great vintage stores in Orange County, which was near her mom's house, and that started my obsession with wearing vintage.

I actually liked wearing a uniform in high school. It's kind of nice to wake up and not think about what you have to wear, and there's something about school uniforms that's visually appealing. But I think it also gives you this drive to find your own identity. Being Japanese-American, I would go the Japanese bookstores in L.A. and get fashion magazines from there. I loved the styling in them because it was so not sexy—as opposed to what you saw in American fashion magazines. It was cutesy, androgynous, quirky. Because my upbringing at home and at school was so sheltered and contained, I naturally needed to break free from that world and be as different from everyone else as I could!

How did you get into styling? Was it something you always wanted to do, or did you have another career in mind?

I've wanted to be a fashion designer since I was 10. I had my mom teach me to sew, and I took sewing classes in high school, and then eventually studied fashion design in Paris at a school called Studio Bercot. Starting a fashion line was kind of a big

HELLO BEAUTIFUL

beast that I felt I didn't want to tackle, so I got into costuming and styling. I interned on a bunch of low-budget films and TV shows. It wasn't a meteoric rise by any means. But I think it gave me the constitution to stick to this line of work. Styling is not easy.

I love your runway work for Rodarte. Do have much autonomy in creating a vision for their collection, or is it more collaborative?

It's definitely collaborative. Kate and Laura [Mulleavy] are completely involved in the total vision of their collection and their runway shows. I'm not an ego-driven stylist that would push a designer to do something they didn't want to do.

Who are your favorite designers, and who would you love to work with?

Well, of course, Rodarte and Peter Jensen. From a historical standpoint, I love the work of Yves Saint Laurent, André Courrèges, Rudi Gernreich, Ossie Clark, and Cristóbal Balenciaga. I love Miu Miu and Prada and Marni, so I'd love to work with Miuccia and Consuelo.

Your personal style is so amazing, like Carnaby Street meets '70s pottery teacher! Can you tell me a bit about how it developed? What have your influences been beyond fashion?

L.A. has great thrift stores, vintage stores, and flea markets. Since I wasn't really finding new stuff that I liked in stores at the malls, I just tended to wear more vintage. Also, as a young student, it was more economical. And I loved the hunt to find a $10 Ossie Clark dress from Savers, or a Burberry coat from a Parisian flea market for two dollars. The mod thing kind of developed because I had mod friends and an obsession with the '60s. But I could never be the goth or rockabilly kid that dresses solely in one style. I really do like mixing it up. I wear a lot of modern stuff mixed with vintage from different eras—although mostly '60s, '70s, and some early

'80s. My second love after fashion is film, so movies definitely influence my personal style—French and Czech New Wave films, in particular. I also love subcultures—the metalheads, the skater kids. I love the way kids rebel in their otherwise normal suburban world.

Where do you look for inspiration?

Museums and galleries are definitely a source of inspiration. And I regularly pick up fashion magazines and books. I do read some blogs, but there are so many now that I kind of feel overwhelmed by them and am backing off a little.

What are your favorite horror films, and do you find they influence your work?

I still think the scariest horror film is *The Shining*. Whenever I dress identical twins, I feel like they HAVE to be dressed identically. And Shelley Duvall is one of my style icons. I tend to be drawn towards films with a surreal pagan world, like *Wicker Man* and *Valerie and Her Week of Wonders*. The innocent girl in the white dress is a horror film staple. I love Japanese horror films because there tends to be this perversity mixed with weirdness. My favorites are *Audition* and *House*.

I have to ask about this: I read that you always share an apartment with the Mulleavys during New York Fashion Week, and that one time André Leon Talley interrupted your taco night! Can you set that scene for me? I'm picturing him sweeping in wearing a giant fur hat and caftan and saying something really genius and bitchy about tacos.

OK, I'm glad I have a chance to fully tell the story, because it was condensed in an interview with me to just a quote saying "He's so tall," which made me sound dumb for stating the obvious. So it was after [the Rodarte] runway show [in 2010], and we hadn't slept a wink the night before, and we were famished and exhausted. We were staying at this place that we called Chateau Brioche. It was an apartment that

the Mulleavys rented that was decorated in this tacky '80s French style. We were all hanging out and had ordered Mexican food and were in the middle of eating our tacos and watching TV when Laura gets this phone call that André Leon Talley was going to stop by for a visit. So there was a slight panic because the place was a mess. But we agreed that he should see it for how it was, so we left the TV on and the food in front of us. In he walks with his assistant and the most enormous orchid arrangement as a gift. And yes, he was wearing a fur hat and a caftan. He walks in the room just as you would imagine—very grandiose and effusive. No bitchy comments whatsoever. Since the apartment was small, the only thing available for him to sit on was this little faux-French stool. So he's sitting there, all 6'6" of him, and I seriously felt like he could've been a character from *Star Wars* or some noble king from some far-off land. He seemed larger than life.

Finally, I know this is the cliché question, but is there any advice you'd like to give to teenage girls, something you wish someone had told you?

Yes, I've actually thought about this because I was a really gawky, self-conscious teenager. And because I went to an all-girls school, I was even more awkward around boys. I used to beat myself up for not being more cool. Now that I'm much older, and now that I've worked with the people that I have, I've found that some of the musicians or actors that I thought were so cool and so confident were surprisingly shy or socially awkward in person. Had I known that, I wouldn't have beaten myself up so much. The point is that we are all human, and we have our insecurities, and that's OK. What makes us cool, ultimately, are the sincere and interesting and unique things that we create and do and believe in. Some of the coolest people I know are self-professed geeks. So embrace your inner nerd! And your inner uniqueness! I hope that teenage girls find role models in women with intelligence and integrity and talent, and eventually become role models for future teenage girls! ◊

FULL DISCLOSURE

My coming-out story.

Writing by Arabelle. Illustrations by Minna. Playlist by Eleanor (lettered by Suzy).

I'm queer. I have always been queer. And so I get a lot of questions about queerness: how to tell if you're homo, if crushing on boys still qualifies you as queer, and what coming out was like. In this here article I'm gonna talk about that last thing.

The long and short of it is that I was very lucky. I never really had to "come out" to my friends and family, because they all suspected before I did that I was gay, and they were (mostly) OK with it. Even so, every time I come out to new people or to my mother for the hundredth (thousandth) time, I hold my breath a little because I still never know what's going to happen. It can be scary and it can be dangerous, and don't let anyone tell you otherwise.

According to one study, 26 percent of gay teens who come out to their parents are told they have to leave home. That's terrifying—we are meant to love our parents, but how can you love someone who can't accept who you are? When I finally told my parents, it was right after Tyler Clementi committed suicide. Tyler went to my school; he killed himself after his roommate secretly taped him kissing another boy and shared it with friends via Twitter. The people I had been living with at the time felt OK making jokes about Tyler when they knew I was queer. As a result, I was at my parents' house a lot, thinking about my queerness and how similar (and how different) I was from this boy who killed himself. I wanted to tell my parents why I felt so unhappy—it wasn't because I was queer, it was because it now felt *dangerous* to be queer. My sexual orientation loomed in my mind all of the time, and it felt like a physical weight on my shoulders. It was finally just too much. I had to say something to my parents. I needed them to tell me it was OK and that it didn't matter what the kids in my dorm were saying, because they loved me. I needed *someone* to say that to me. So during dinner, when we were watching a news report on Tyler's death, I blurted it out. And I just waited, nervous and scared and hopeful.

I knew my dad would be OK with it, which is why I am so lucky. I have the best dad—he is my best friend, he is my everything. My mother is another story. I knew that she wouldn't be OK with my orientation. I love her, and I know she loves me, but she has always been the most conservative person in our household. Still, it hurt when she said that my being queer was an illness and that she wouldn't want to go to my wedding if I had one. You can't really prepare to hear such a thing from someone you love. You just bear it. *This is my mother*, I thought, *the person who raised me and loved me and makes terrible meatloaf and drove me to swim practice every day after school. She loves me. How can she say this to me?*

I was afraid she'd kick me out of the house, but my dad would have none of it. If my mother didn't like it, *she* could leave, he said. This house was for me, he said, and everything they had done was for me. Whom I love was not up to them, he said. And he has stuck by me and supported me throughout. He asks me how my girlfriend is doing, he writes letters to newspapers on behalf of gay rights and sends me copies, he drives me to pride parades. He is the best man alive. I am unspeakably, wondrously lucky.

But the thing is, too, that I wasn't seeking my mom's approval. I still don't seek her approval. There comes a point when you realize that your parents make mistakes just as often as you do, and that they are people, too, and they can be wrong. When you come to terms with that, their approval becomes unnecessary. You don't ask them for their permission, just for their love. That's why I'm still on good terms with my mom despite the fact that she's grossed out by my queerness. When she asks me if I'm dating a cute boy, I just bluntly tell her that I'm more inclined to date a cute boi. It's a friendly but firm reminder. I still love her, and it's important to me that she knows exactly who I am. I know deep down that I am a healthy person, regardless of the gender of the person I love, and I am a good person because I am capable of loving, and my love is just as valid and beautiful as any hetero relationship.

The thing people don't really tell you about coming out is that it is a perpetual, never-ending event. You don't come out just once. You come out to your parents, you come out to your best friends, you come out to acquaintances, and you repeat this throughout your life with varying degrees of acceptance and success. It's not always a banner event. Sometimes it's just slipping "my girlfriend and I" into a conversation, or your partner's calling you when you're at work and a co-worker asking who it is, or the queer T-shirt you forgot you were wearing to class. You don't always plan it. But you shield your heart and hope for the best every time. You realize who your true friends are. You realize a lot.

Now, coming out to someone else is a little different than coming to terms with it yourself, which, in my opinion, is messier. I don't think I've met a lot of queers who knew point-blank from the very beginning that they were gay. We go through phases: I'm bi, I'm gay, I'm pansexual, I'm in a straight relationship but I'm curious, and so on and so forth. Not having a clue is fine, and it's normal. I identified as bi for a while in high school, but then I realized the only people I liked were girls, so I switched to gay, but then I realized I still crush on boys and **genderqueers** sometimes, so I went pansexual, but that still didn't feel right to me. Being un-straight is *hard*, because, before you can really come out as anything other than heterosexual, you need to figure out what the boundaries of each label actually *are*. And it's more complicated than it sounds. We all feel love and lust differently, and it's difficult to translate feelings into one word, especially when that word is supposed to encompass an entire identity. Most straight kids (and adults for that matter) never question their straightness and prefer to ask *us*, "How do you know you're gay?" Straightness is represented everywhere. It's the norm. It's in every rom-com. It's in every television show. It's in our laws. It's on the billboards. It's in the books. Gays stick out because we're different from what we're told to be, and that scares the crap out of some people. It makes them want to hurt us because it makes them question what the very definition of "normal" is.

Enough about that. I've told you my coming-out story, and now I want to talk about yours, especially if you haven't come out yet. I want you to know that it isn't your obligation to come out to other people if you don't want to. You don't owe anybody anything that might risk your safety or home or livelihood. If you do come out—and I hope that you do eventually, because it's fun on the other side of that closet door, and you can go to queer parties and make eyes with pretty ladies and not feel bad about it—know that you are so, so strong for being able to do so. It changes your life, ideally for the better, but you've got to be ready for it.

Once you've taken that step and admitted it to yourself and to the person or people you're coming out to, the rest is awesome. Or it should be. Find people who are out, too, and make them your support group. There is this thing called the internet (you may have heard of it?) that saves me every day that I feel down or unsure about myself. For instance, I like Tumblr, and fashion blogging led me to feminist fashion bloggers, who led me to queer feminist fashion bloggers. You can find friends and talk about things that you can't really talk to straight people about. (Queers talk about queer life ALL THE TIME. It's hilarious and awesome.) They will accept you for who you are. It might take a while, but that community is your home as much as your parents' house is/was, and it's something to cherish.

If coming out doesn't go well, there are other options, and you deserve love and support more than ever. Go to your nearest women's center or queer shelter, and keep in mind that you are not alone, you are worth more than what was given to you, and you will live through this.

We are family, and I love you for who you are. ◆

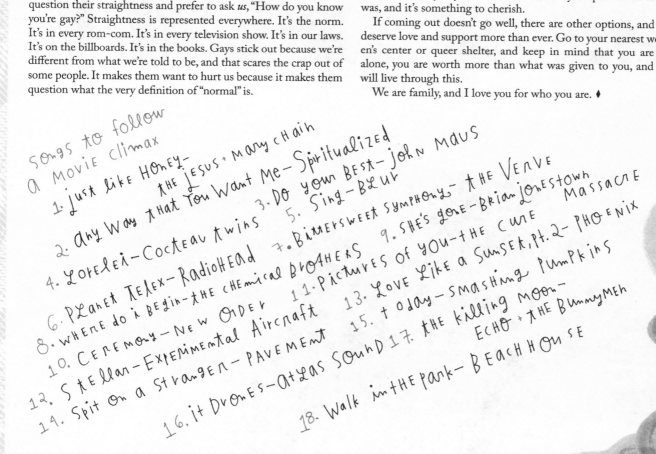

songs to follow
a movie climax
1. Just like Honey— the Jesus + Mary chain
2. Any Way that You Want Me— Spiritualized
3. DO your Best— John Maus
4. Lorelei— Cocteau twins   5. Sing— Blur
6. Planet Telex— RadioHead   7. Bittersweet symphony— the VERVE
8. where do i begin— the chemical Brothers   9. She's gone— Brian Jonestown Massacre
10. Ceremony— New Order   11. Pictures of You— the cure
12. Stellar— Experimental Aircraft   13. Love Like a Sunset, pt. 2— PHOENIX
14. Spit on a Stranger— PAVEMENT   15. today— Smashing Pumpkins
16. it Drones— Atlas Sound   17. the killing moon— ECHO + the Bunnymen
18. Walk in the park— BEACH HOUSE

ODESSEY

Blinding and blindingly wonderful photos by Petra.

AND ORACLE

By Petra. Thanks to Adrien, Amit, Erick, Jamie, and Kalale for modeling; Chloe Wise for styling, and Kealan at 69 Vintage.

What to do when the WORST happens.
Writing by Sady. Illustration by Minna.

The strange thing is, until the worst actually happens, it's impossible to predict the shape that it will take. Everyone argues with their friends sometimes; it's only when you get into that one, big, relationship-ending argument with your best friend that you realize losing her is an actual possibility. Rumors and mini-scandals are a part of high school life, like lockers and lunch periods—everybody's got one—but it's only when people start turning away when you say hello, when the flood of nasty emails hits your inbox or your Facebook wall, that you realize this rumor isn't a small one, that you've been targeted for a complete and vicious shunning. And everyone's parents have a particular arrangement and dynamic, and to be honest, I never really thought about the arrangement between mine, until my mother woke me up when I was 16 years old and told me that her "friend from out of town" whom I'd been asked to have dinner with the night before was going to be my new stepfather, and that her divorce from my current stepfather had been going on, quietly, politely, without my noticing, for months.

The worst happens to everyone, at some point. When I asked the other Rookies about it, I got so many stories: Failing a necessary course out of nowhere. Getting caught shoplifting. Living across the street from a crack house, with a roommate who steals your clothes, yells at you, and runs a borderline-illegal yoga studio out of your living room. Or having a roommate revenge-pee on your furniture. (A different roommate. WE THINK.) Or this: "All the girls in my sixth-grade class decided, as a group, that they hated me. Our teacher called a special meeting and ORDERED them each to name something they liked about me. A bunch of them were like, 'I can't think of anything; can you come back to me?' My stomach still hurts when I think about it."

Waiting for the worst to happen is impossible, and always embarrassing, like trying to find your glasses when you're already wearing them, or looking frantically for your keys when they're in your hand. When the worst finally hits, you always realize that it was there all along.

The good thing about this is that it's a waste of time, waiting for something terrible to happen, or trying to predict what that terrible something will be. The bad thing, of course, is that when something does happen, you'll know it, and it will not be within your power to stop it from happening.

So let's assume the worst has already happened to you, at least once. That something terrible and beyond your control has already come down the pike; that you're sitting here, reading this article, thinking that your life is ruined. Or even that you've ruined your own life. It's not my business to say whether what's happened to you is a big catastrophe, or a small one; whether you've had a falling out with a group of friends or lost a parent, it all feels huge while it's happening. My business here today is the recovery end of it. No matter how big this feels, one of these days, you're going to wake up in the morning, and you won't be in a catastrophe anymore; you'll be in your post-catastrophe life. It will have changed, but it won't have to be horrible.

Besides being impossible to predict, and always feeling inevitable, the worst things—big and small—share a few other distinct factors, some of which are very helpful when it comes time to get up and move on.

For one thing, you're about to find out who your friends are. When you're sad and alone, it helps to think about this: happy, popular people are constantly surrounded by a bunch of folks who don't actually like them very much. It's not that those people are cruel to them, or that those people are two-faced or deceitful. (Well. Some of them may be, but it's not really my business to decide.) It's just that happiness and popularity and power are attractive to people who want to be happy and popular and powerful themselves. The textbook-y term for this is "social capital": on the most basic level, people are more likely to be friendly if they believe you can help them get something, even if that "something" is just social status or more friends.

Which is all fine, but when you lose that social capital—when you've been made unpopular as the result of losing some friends or a social shunning, or when you're going through something so difficult that the only person you can really afford to take care of is yourself—you lose those superficial relationships. It's not your fault, and it's nothing to be ashamed of. My best friend, for example, is one of the most naturally popular people I've ever met. She's charming, and kind, and outgoing, and really fun, and people automatically and inevitably love being around her. She's always had about a thousand people who want to spend time with her. But last year, she had a serious illness—not something lethal, but something which definitely incurred a lot of grossness and vomiting and deliriously high fevers. (She's better now! Don't worry!) It lasted for a long time, and it made her extremely tired, and she was also going to school throughout, so she couldn't really pursue all her thousand different friendships in the way she wanted to. So some people dropped away. It wasn't her fault for being sick, she'd done nothing wrong; it was just a case of losing some social capital.

But you'll notice that I'm still referring to her as my "best friend." And so are lots of other people. The relationships that last through these hard times are the ones that aren't about getting something out of you. They're the people who can hang with you when you're having a panic attack, when you're crying your eyes out, when you're too tired to do anything but watch crap TV, when you're just no fun at all. They're the people who don't just like you—they love you. By the time this is over, you're going to know which friendships were conditional, and which ones to keep for the rest of your life. That's a tremendous gift.

These deeper friendships are essential to the second part of this equation: figuring out what goodness you still have. No matter how total a catastrophe may seem to be—losing ALL of your friends, having to move to an entirely new city, trying something and failing at it and being so humiliated that you can NEVER try again (you can, and should, try again)—there is always something good left over. If you don't have many friends right now, you might still have your art, your sport, whatever makes you feel like YOU (and, as it happens, a lot more time to practice). If your parents are getting divorced, you might still have your best friends. This stuff is essential to surviving a bad time.

When something awful happens, it's often hard to focus on the remaining good factors in a situation. Awful happenings are so intense and overwhelming that they often command the majority of our attention. But it's essential to look away from the catastrophe right now, to focus on the edges of the picture and away from the car wreck at its center, and see what's there. By doing so, you can come to a whole new appreciation of what you want and need. When something terrible changes your life, the actual shape of your life becomes clear: you suddenly realize, out of the million different little factors that comprise Being You, which ones were essential to feeling good. This sounds cheesy—like, you just realize what really matters, you know?—but it's not. Sometimes you only realize that something was essential to your happiness when it goes missing. Everybody hates their job, until they lose it, and then they're broke.

This process is great, because realizing what you need is *always* great. If you need new friends, well, you now know which kinds of friends you don't need, and you'll be on the lookout for people who are nothing like the jerks who just dumped you. If you're devastated because something you wrote is being made fun of, or you had a solo in the choir recital and flubbed it, suddenly you know how important it is to you to sing or to write well. And that kind of passion is what separates dilettantes from people who can devote their lives to a goal.

I used to be attracted exclusively to cool, smart, sarcastic, emotionally reserved, or troubled dudes that I had to chase—taking relationships seriously was so normal and boring and suburban, you know?—until I had my worst breakup ever, in which I lost my job, one of my two closest friends moved across the country, and this guy (whom I'd just moved in with) ditched me because I seemed depressed, and that was too much for him to deal with. It was *awful*. But after that, I knew that I did take relationships very seriously, and I wanted someone who wasn't afraid to take them seriously, too—someone who wasn't afraid to chase me, and to be emotionally expressive, even if that seemed uncool or sentimental.

And I got that. I got precisely that, in fact, from a friend who'd been around during the whole terrible breakup process, and we've been together for years, and I'm just absurdly happy. Like I say: when something terrible is happening and your life is changing, it pays to look for the good stuff in the picture.

Third, and finally, here's the best part about ruining your life: you find out who you are.

When things are going well, you can take yourself pretty much for granted. That's what happiness does: it lets you deal exclusively with the parts of yourself that you like and feel comfortable with. Happiness is like living in a big house, and only visiting a few big, sunny, well-cleaned rooms. That's great; I'm not anti-happiness. Who could be? But, in the house of anyone's mind or life, there are always rooms that haven't been cleaned yet. Rooms that no one visits, places where junk is piled up and mice infest the floorboards and make nests out of old newspapers, dark and dim and unwelcoming inner places that everyone would prefer just to ignore.

When the worst happens, you have to visit those dark rooms. Like a teen in a horror movie, you just have to go down into the basement and see what's hiding there. You get to know how you respond to stress, what grief feels like for you, and who you are when you're consumed with anger. You have to visit feelings and aspects of your personality you're not comfortable with; you have to (if you'll let me stretch this particular metaphor to its breaking point) start cleaning up your junk.

But what you find can surprise you in some good ways. Maybe you're resourceful in ways you'd never imagined. Maybe you have goals or needs or even good qualities that you've been ignoring; bad times have a way of showing those to you. Somewhere between my parents' divorce when I was 16—that stepfather actually disappeared when it was over; I saw him twice again in my life, for five minutes each time—and my relationship with a dude who disappeared in part because he couldn't be bothered to care for me when I was in need (and in part, let us be honest, because I am hell on toast when I'm upset; this is also an article about ruining your OWN life, after all), I found that I valued permanence and commitment and authenticity in relationships more than almost anything else in life. I've experienced a lot of unpleasant things, but what hurt me most was finding out that I had been wrong about how much people cared. But that's what made me a good friend, and a sincere person: someone who could stick around for others during their own hard times, someone who would stick up for people or reach out to them when they were being bullied, and who would listen to people when they were lonely or afraid or stuck in a bad spot. I wouldn't have known this about myself—and maybe I wouldn't even have those qualities in the first place—had I not been through my own world-ending catastrophes.

You'll never know what kind of a survivor you are until you have to survive something. Maybe you're strong. Maybe you're someone who can endure. Maybe you're just incredibly good at staging comebacks, at arranging things so that you can make the best of a bad situation, and come out on top. You'll never know, just like you'll never know what really matters to you, or who your best friends are, until you're called upon to live through a bad time.

When the worst happens, it's always unpredictable, and strangely inevitable. But it's only when the worst happens that you can discover the best in yourself. ◆

MAY 2012: POWER

Greetings and salutations, Rookies! This month's theme is Power. You know, like money. Or fame. Or…that Kanye West song? Dammit, today is May first and I don't even know. What is POWER? From whencehence does one's POWER cometh, eth?

Yesterday I was having a shitty day in what felt like a series of many shitty weeks. After the inevitable bathroom-stall sobfest/pity party, I spent my next class writing instead of taking notes. As I was venting, I ended up demanding to know why I was letting dumb things bother me and make me feel bad, and insisting on getting over it, and it slowly became a kind of personal manifesto, and then on the way to my next class I thought of that scene from *Girls* when Hannah is throwing her own pity party, how she could have listened to sad acoustic music, but chose Robyn instead. So I put "Dancing on My Own" on my iPod and felt like I was GLIDING through the halls and kind of smiled to myself on accident before I realized I looked mildly disturbed, and then I just kept smiling anyway. And I felt way better, and OK with myself, and with most things.

What's nice about the kind of power you create for yourself when you're able to change the way you feel about a situation instead of waiting for the situation to change for you is that you can't ever get nostalgic for that feeling, the feeling of having power over how you decide to deal with something. You can't ever miss it the way you miss the happiness that comes from nice memories of concerts or summer or vacations or times with friends or whatever, because it's really just you being you. Once you reach that mindset, you can always come back to it. And knowing that made me feel like the most powerful, in-control-of-my-life-so-eff-y'all person since Some Evil Dictator Person.

Different outlets work for different people, and I personally was happy that pure thinking and writing got me there. This month, we're gonna talk about inner-power-searchers of all kinds, but the ones from the '80s especially, when there were SO MANY GOOD ONES. Not just Madonna, but, like, I think John Hughes made coming to terms with your own weaknesses and really owning them and turning them into personal power a somewhat radical act. Then we have lots of '80s angst-dwellers like Morrissey, who always makes me feel like I can listen to depresso lyrics set to a somewhat upbeat tune and in that way kind of accept feelings of angst and anxiousness.

I really hope you like all of it. Plus, omg, SCHOOL IS ALMOST OVER, so we have all the more reason to bounce around to Culture Club as we write about prom.

LOVE,
TAVI

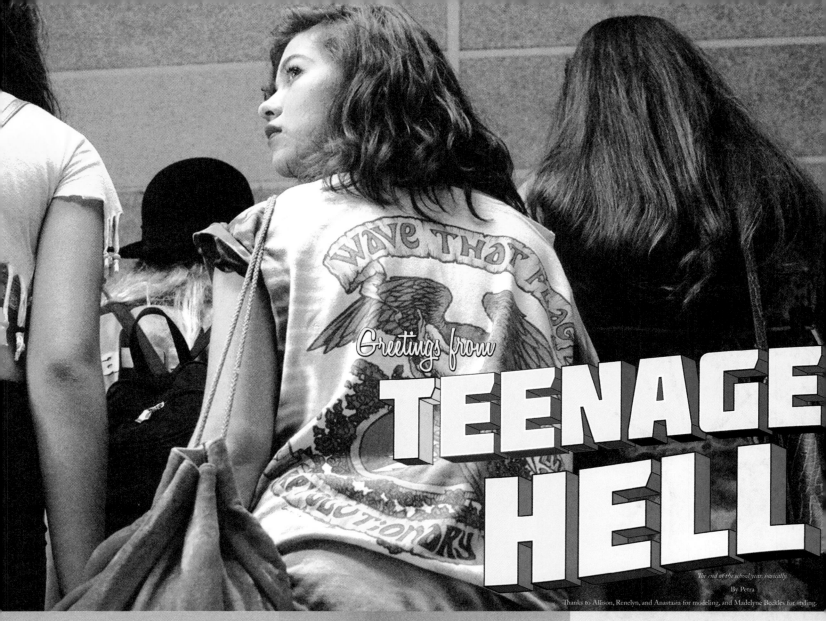

Greetings from

TEENAGE HELL

The end of the school year, basically.

By Petra

Thanks to Allison, Renelyn, and Anastasia for modeling, and Madelyne Beckles for styling.

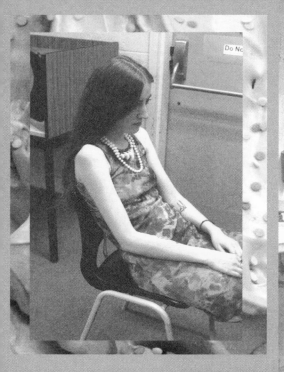

wish you

were here

Welcome to Paradise

Don't forget to SMILE

Disappear Here

Life Skills 101

Master these and there'll be no stopping you.
Writing by Krista. Playlist by Amy Rose.

When *Lara Croft: Tomb Raider* came out, I was blown away. Not only was it one of the first PG-13 movies I had ever seen (yes), but I quickly sensed that *here* was a cinematic *masterpiece*. It was everything I had ever wanted in a movie. It had Angelina Jolie playing a wealthy heiress in a very tight cat suit. She had endless amounts of time. She had expensive gadgets. She had a mission. I wanted to be her.

I went to see the movie four times in the theater (after the first time with friends, I went by myself to be alone with Lara), but you know what my favorite part was? It wasn't watching the high-kicking action shots. It wasn't even the close-ups of that gun strapped to Lara's bronzed thigh. No. My favorite part was when Lara lands unexpectedly on a raft floating down the river in Cambodia. Not only is she not surprised, but she casually greets the fisherman manning the raft and speaks to him for a minute *in perfect, fluent* Khmer.

I was so impressed. *Now* there is *someone who is prepared for life*, I thought. Lara Croft spoke the native language of Cambodia. Of course she did. She'd spent years learning it just in case it ever came in handy. And what do you know—she needed her random language skills when she least expected it.

That's how I wanted to be: prepared for anything, like Lara Croft. I wanted to be strong and confident in odd situations, to not lose my head when things got tough.

And things do get tough! Even when (unbelievably) you don't end up being a tomb raider with piles of money, there are some Life Skills that are really, seriously helpful to have under your belt. You never know when you're going to need them.

I can think of tons of Life Skills you'd be real happy to have at random times (starting a fire in the woods without matches, changing a car tire, figuring out if a mushroom is poisonous), but here are nine major Life Skills, in no particular order, that my friends and I agreed that we've randomly needed in our college-and-beyond lives so far:

1. HAGGLING

Haggling is what happens when you want to buy something, and you suspect (or know) the price stated isn't set in stone. Together, you and the merchant reach a bargain. In lots of countries, haggling is a normal way of doing business, and totally expected in places like outdoor markets and tourist-frequented shops, but in the U.S., it's sometimes harder to tell when the price listed is the actual price.

You can almost always haggle in situations where it's just you and a person selling something, whether it's a garage sale or a person offering a couch on Craigslist, but some surprising places where haggling is acceptable are: mall kiosks and antique or vintage stores. You can often get a *much* better deal if you're willing to just *try* haggling. Sometimes the merchant will let you. Sometimes not. But it never hurts to try.

But how to haggle? Well! Once you've found what you want, *don't let the seller see how interested you are.* This is the most important thing. No matter how amazing that gold sequined tube top from the '70s is, no

matter if your hands are actually shaking with excitement…*act bored*. A merchant would much rather make a sale today for a little less than it says on the price tag than let you walk off and not make the sale at all. But if he/she knows how much you want it, the price will be set in stone.

If there isn't a price tag at all, say, "So, this tube top…I don't see a price. How much is it?" Or, if there *is* a price tag, say in a bored tone, "This is a cute tube top. Oh, it's $60." When the merchant says, "It's $60," make a vague, noncommittal noise, like *"ahh"* and then go idly look at some other stuff. Then come back to the sequined tube top. Say, "I really like this tube top, but it's a bit more than I can spend today. I could give you ___ for it." Make ___ the amount you'd like to get this tube top for in a fair world. Don't make it absurdly low, like $20. I find that a figure around 75 percent works well. Say, in this case, $45.

The merchant will then either (a) say firmly, "No, I'm sorry, the price is set," or (b) realize she is dealing with a shrewd customer, and raise her eyebrows for a second before saying, "Mmm. No. I might be able to give it to you for $55." Then you meet her in the middle, and say, "How 'bout $50? I could maybe do $50." She'll probably agree, and you will have saved $10 and she will have made a sale on a gold sequined tube top from the '70s that she's had in her store for months. Haggling takes just a few seconds, and everybody wins!

2. INTRODUCING SOMEONE WELL

At some point, you'll have to do introductions that don't go like this: "Everybody, this is Kim. Kim, this is everybody." Sooner or later, you are going to need to introduce someone you want to impress to someone who is important to you, or introduce two people who you are certain would loooove each other, and the way you introduce them matters!

Introduce these two people with old-fashioned, 1950s-party-hostess style and grace. Include something personal, non-superficial, and interesting about each person when you do it, and act like they're the two most important and fascinating people in the world.

NEW ROMANCERS

1. ARE "FRIENDS" ELECTRIC? - TUBEWAY ARMY
2. GENIUS OF LOVE - TOM TOM CLUB
3. ENOLA GAY - ORCHESTRAL MANOEUVRES IN THE DARK
4. DON'T YOU WANT ME - THE HUMAN LEAGUE
5. PRINCE CHARMING - ADAM AND THE ANTS
6. (I'LL NEVER BE) MARIA MAGDALENA - SANDRA
7. WORDS - F. R. DAVID
8. EXTRAORDINARY - YUKIHIRO TAKAHASHI
9. ONE THING LEADS TO ANOTHER - THE FIXX
10. I'LL TUMBLE 4 YA - CULTURE CLUB
11. RIO - DURAN DURAN
12. GUILTY - CLASSIX NOUVEAUX
13. ONLY YOU - YAZOO
14. TRUE - SPANDAU BALLET

No: "Jenny, this is Matt. He loves blondes with big boobs. Matt, this is Jenny. She has blonde hair…and you can see the rest hahahha."

Yes: "Jenny, this is Matt. Matt has a black belt in karate, but he won't show you any moves unless you really beg him. And Matt, this is Jenny; she's one of the funniest people I know—we were actually just talking about what happened to her at the calculus finals on Friday. OK so Jenny, *what* happened?"

BOOM! They have two possible conversation topics, they're both fascinating… and you quietly excuse yourself, you Grand Puppet Master of Matchmaking.

3. REALLY APOLOGIZING

We all screw up, and when we do, the way we apologize is important. Now, no one has to accept your apology—that's their right. But! No matter how sorry you are, you can make things a hundred times worse by using one single word: IF. Watch!

You didn't invite your less-popular-but-very-good friend to your house for a sleepover on purpose, because more-popular girls are coming and they think she's weird. You tried to hide it, because you know not inviting your friend is an assy thing to do, but she found out and now she's pissed and not speaking to you.

Bad apology: "I'm sorry **if** you feel left out, or like I didn't want you there or something."

Look at you! You're not sorry! Look at that *if*! You're basically blaming her for feeling the way that *you* made her feel. "I'm sorry if you…" is a shit apology. You're sorry? BE SORRY. Don't blame the other person or use sneaky words like *if* to shift things around to sound like you're not really to blame. Apologies involving the *if* word tend to turn into major fights, because one person believes they are trying to make amends, and the other person doesn't hear any actual sorry-ness.

Good apology (always happens in person, btw): "I'm sorry I didn't invite you to my house. That was a shitty thing to do. I won't do that to you again. I understand if you're still mad at me."

Look at all those *I* words. *You* did the bad thing, *you* take the blame. Nice!

4. SWIMMING

Well, duh. I only bring up knowing how to swim because one of my friends quietly admitted to me last year that she didn't want to come to the lake because she couldn't swim. I was completely shocked—what did she *mean* she couldn't swim? She was 24 years old! But my friend told me that she never had swimming lessons and never lived near water, so she had never learned. Which happens to lots of people, it turns out.

But—*but*—what if she got pushed in a pool? What if she fell off a boat? What if she lost her balance on a boardwalk? Water is everywhere! I grabbed her hand. "I will teach you," I said fiercely. We spent about a week in the shallow end of the pool at her gym, and she learned to swim. No one drowns on *my* watch.

5. THROWING A PUNCH

Sad but true: someday, you might need to hit someone. There have definitely been times in my life (hi, college) that I needed to get a boy off me, like right then, and I wish I would have known how to throw a good punch to make him see things my way. Now, I'm not saying go pick some fights, or punch someone for insulting your mother, but knowing how to throw a punch that means business is a good skill to have under your survival belt. I mean, make no mistake: please try not to fight. Get away; run from fighting if you can. We're not talking fighting for the sake of fighting. We're talking a good punch to stop some fighting, or to get yourself the hell away from someone who is physically all up in your business.

When throwing a punch:

⚬ Use the hand you write with.

♦ Make a fist *with your thumb outside, not tucked inside*. If it's tucked inside your fist, when you punch someone, you might break your thumb. The thumb goes across your fingers, not on the side.

♦ Don't be like in the movies—don't aim for the face. Face punches don't usually stop people, and you can miss when they duck their head or break your hand on

their jaw. If you want to get away quickly, or end a fight, aim for the chest, or the ribs. If you really want to do some damage, e.g., you're being attacked, aim for the throat, which will make it hard for your attacker to breathe for a hot minute.

♦ When you punch, you want to aim and hit with your first two knuckles. Not the flats of your fingers, and not your ring or pinky knuckles, which can break more easily. You can use your weight, if you're on your feet, to add wallop, and spring into a punch with your feet and torso.

♦ When the person is momentarily distracted by either pain, or being winded, or the fact that you, a girl, hit them—run away. Which leads us to…

6. RUNNING A MILE

Running for one mile isn't so bad. And it isn't the exact distance that's important—what's important is being able to run for several minutes without having to stop and pant for breath. So, practice until you can do this. Run! Catch that bus that's pulling away from the corner! Catch the lady who left her wallet on the counter two minutes ago! Catch your cat after she slips out the front door! Get away from a big scary dude who's harassing you! Run, dammit, run!

7. TIPPING PROPERLY

Tipping is easy. Tipping makes service people love you. (Did you know that waitresses, bartenders, and most coffee-shop workers make minimum wage? They live off their tips.) Tipping ensures you'll get great service next time, and is good-ass karma. People remember good tippers. Plus it's effing classy.

So: whom do you tip? You tip people who are doing something personal for you. (That being said, you don't need to tip your gynecologist. Wokka wokka wokka.) The people you tip are: Waitresses. Baristas. Hairstylists. Manicurists, taxi drivers, valet drivers, hotel concierges, and anyone who touches your luggage, ever, whether it's a shuttle driver or the guy at the airport who loads your bags outside so you don't have to wait in line.

How much do you tip? Waitresses: 15–20 percent of the total bill. An easy way to do it is this: If the bill is $30.05, take 10 percent, which is $3 (move the decimal point one number to the left), and double that. Ta-da! The (generous and unexpected-from-a-young-person) tip is $6. If you can't afford to tip the standard going rate, you shouldn't go out. Or you should go somewhere you don't have to tip. Period.

Coffee-shop baristas: $1 per espresso drink. These people remember who tips and who doesn't, I promise you.

If someone has done something extraordinarily nice, like let you sit at your table for super long after you're done eating without giving you attitude, or picked you *and your wet dog* up in their taxi, or broken a sweat in any way, give them more than 20 percent: 25 percent is good.

Everyone else gets 10-15 percent. Wheeee doesn't everyone just *love* to help you?

8. MAKING ONE DELICIOUS, ADULT MEAL

I can't cook. I really can't. Not only that: I am not interested in ever learning to cook, and I don't care what anyone says about it. However! When I really need to impress someone, e.g., I HAVE A DATE WHO IS COMING OVER FOR DINNER AND SHE DOESN'T KNOW ME WELL ENOUGH TO THINK MY NONCOOKING IS ADORABLE, I make my patented Roasted Chicken Impressive Meal.

Here you go!

1. Buy a whole rotisserie chicken in the deli section at the grocery store. Also buy broccoli and three large Idaho potatoes.

2. Go home. Take the roasted chicken out of the plastic container it comes in, throw the container away (hide evidence), and put the chicken on an oven-safe plate. Set the oven to 250 degrees, and pop the chicken in. (We're just keeping it warm, crisping it a li'l, and also making it look like we *made* the chicken.)

3. Wash the potatoes and cut them into large chunks. Put the chunks into a pot of boiling water. Wait about 20 minutes, or

until the potatoes are soft, and then drain them. Mash up the pieces with a big spoon or whip them in the pot with an eggbeater (way more fun), and add a little bit of milk, some salt, and some butter, until the potatoes taste like mashed potatoes. Keep tasting and adding things until it tastes right.

4. Wash the broccoli and cut it into bite-size pieces. Put the broccoli into a pot of boiling water, and put a lid on it. Let the broccoli sit in the boiling water until it's bright green and you can easily bite through a piece.

5. Take the chicken out of the oven, put it on the table as your Impressive Chicken Centerpiece, and dish up the broccoli and mashed potatoes on two plates.

6. Act casual, like you do this all the time, and it's really nothing. SOON YOUR DATE WILL BE HOPELESSLY IN LOVE WITH YOU.

(If you and/or your date is a vegetarian, buy a package of pasta, a jar of pasta sauce, an onion, and some fresh garlic. Boil two servings of pasta, according to the instructions on the package. While the pasta is cooking, heat up a big glug of olive oil in a small to medium pot, then add half a diced onion and a thinly sliced clove of garlic to it. If you have red pepper flakes in the house, add a shake or two of those. If you have access to red wine, add a splash of that, too. [The alcohol in the wine will evaporate in the cooking, and adding all this stuff will make it seem like you made the whole entire sauce.] The heat should be on the low end of medium. When the onions become kinda see-through, add a cup or two of store-bought sauce to the pot. At this point your pasta will probably be done—take it off the heat and drain it. When you see steam coming off the sauce, add the warm pasta to it, and give everything a minute or two to become friends. Turn off the heat and add grated parmesan cheese, or skip that step if you or she/he is a vegan. Serve this with the broccoli described above.)

And finally…

9. SCALING A FENCE

Sometimes, you just have to. Let's not dwell on why.

First, tuck in any jewelry. Tie your hair back so it doesn't get in your eyes. Fence-climbing is all about toeholds. If it's a chain-link fence, you're in luck. Just stick your toes into the holes and clamber up like a monkey. If it's a high chain-link fence, don't look at the ground—just focus on your hands and footholds. When you get to the top, gently ease your legs over (make sure your pants don't get caught!), hook your toes in on the other side and climb down. If, however, it's a chain-link fence with extra strips or coils of wire up at the top, abandon all plans to climb the fence. That's razor wire, possibly *electric* razor wire, and razor wire doesn't play around.

If the fence is brick or stone, again: look for toeholds, the little ledges or edges that stick out slightly so you can put your foot on 'em. These are some of the easiest fences to climb, because the tops tend to be flat and inviting. When you get to the top, though, you usually have to jump.

If the fence is tall, metal, and has pointy spikes at the top, like a city park fence, well, that fence is just begging to be climbed, isn't it? Except you usually can't. Metal fences look easy and then are deceptively difficult to scale without getting hurt. Believe me, I've tested this again and again. (I like sunset picnics in old, grand cemeteries.) Don't climb this fence. Walk around the perimeter until you find another way in. (There is *always* another way in.)

If the fence is wooden, get a friend to give you a boost to the top, or climb onto something nearby to get closer to the top. And hey: watch for dogs, OK? ♦

HAIRSTYLES OF THE MUSICIANS OF THE 1980S: A TAXONOMY

Unlocking the mysteries of the weirdest hairdos in the musical pantheon.

By Eleanor and Marie

BOY GEORGE

HAIRSTYLE MAY OR MAY NOT RESEMBLE:
JACK SPARROW TEACHING YOUR ART CLASS

NECESSARY TOOLS:
NINJA-LIKE BRAIDING SKILLS, SCRAPS OF FABRIC IN EVERY COLOUR, SILK SCARF, BOWLER HAT, AND A TOUCH OF HOPE-LESS ROMANTICISM.

HAIR GEL RATING:

GRACE JONES

HAIRSTYLE MAY OR MAY NOT RESEMBLE:
FUTURISTIC MILITARY CAPTAIN

NECESSARY TOOLS:
GRAVITY-DEFYING HAIR, SHINY HOODS, FEARLESS FASHION SENSE, GENERAL BADASSERY.

HAIR GEL RATING:

MADONNA

HAIRSTYLE MAY OR MAY NOT RESEMBLE:
PROM-QUEEN ROADKILL

NECESSARY TOOLS:
GIANT BOW, HAIR BLEACH, UNAPOLOGETIC DARK ROOTS, CURLING IRON, REBELLIOUS ATTITUDE.

HAIR GEL RATING:

MORRISSEY

HAIRSTYLE MAY OR MAY NOT RESEMBLE:
A POMPADOUR FILLED WITH TEARS

NECESSARY TOOLS:
AN UNFATHOMABLE AMOUNT OF HAIR GEL, A BROKEN HEART, AND THE WIT OF OSCAR WILDE.

HAIR GEL RATING:

ROBERT SMITH

HAIRSTYLE MAY OR MAY NOT RESEMBLE:
ONE OF THOSE GIANT FAKE HALLOWEEN SPIDERS SITTING ON A BIRD'S NEST.

NECESSARY TOOLS:
YOUR FAMILY'S COSTCO CARD (FOR STOCKING UP ON CASES OF HAIR SPRAY), A GHOST TO SCARE YOU EVERY MORNING WHILE YOU'RE DOING YOUR HAIR, A POCKET CALENDAR TO COUNT DOWN TO FRIDAY.

HAIR GEL RATING:

STRAWBERRY SWITCHBLADE

HAIRSTYLE MAY OR MAY NOT RESEMBLE:
CYNDI LAUPER GETTING READY TO GO TO A GOTH CLUB

NECESSARY TOOLS:
POLKADOT RIBBONS, MILLIONS OF BOBBY PINS, FAKE FLOWERS, OR JUST A BANANA PEEL TO SLIP ON AND FALL INTO MICHAELS' BARGAIN BIN.

HAIR GEL RATING:

SIOUXSIE SIOUX

HAIRSTYLE MAY OR MAY NOT RESEMBLE:
A PORCUPINE STRUCK BY LIGHTNING

NECESSARY TOOLS:
CRIMPING IRON, TEASING COMB, HAIR DYE AS BLACK AS YOUR SOUL, AN ELECTRICAL STORM.

HAIR GEL RATING:

Prom Night: The Prologue.

Sometimes the pre-party is the best part.

By Lauren P. and Laia

Photos by Lauren Poor; styling by Laia; hair by Liana Le at Marie Robinson Salon; makeup by Arabelle. All clothes are vintage. Thanks to Marie, Amy Rose, Lily, Rie, Paula, and Arabelle for modeling; to Riza and Laura at Screaming Mimi's and Evan at Frock for the clothes; and to Emma S. for letting us use her beautiful house!

Breaking In A Broken Heart

How to draw power from a truly crappy experience.
Writing by Liz Armstrong. Playlist by Hazel.

Bummer truth time: being heartbroken is honestly one of the worst things that can happen in life. If you know right from the start I'm being truthful, then maybe all of this forthcoming talk about turning a really crappy experience into something empowering will seem less like lilting fairy-speak and more like a reality. Without spending a bunch of time telling you about the relationship endings where I was destroyed and cried nonstop and didn't think anything good could possibly come of them, I'm going to take a shortcut and promise you: everything in here really works.

Let's start off by talking about what your heart does for you. Besides pumping all your blood so your cells get oxygen and nutrients and you don't die on the spot, your heart is also, metaphorically, the capacitor of all your emotions, the place where the internal YOU resides. It is the home of your fortitude, resilience, bravery, self-respect, and softness. It's where you give and receive—and being good at both of those things is important, because real love of all kinds involves exchange.

So when your heart is broken, your aorta may be just fine, but all the experiential things associated with this crucial organ turn into a hot mess. That may seem obvious, though when you consider that our brains process the pain from heartache the same as they do the pain from physical injury, feeling romantically busted is kind of serious.

To be able to love freely, bounce back during tough times, and fearlessly explore the joy in all things...well, I guess there are some people who just get all that right away. The rest of us need an ass-whipping to understand how to do it. And that's how heartache can become an empowering experience.

We all know or have heard of at least one person (not naming names) who got their heart broken and became a little hard and jaded, and they possibly got a really weird tattoo that may or may not involve a zombie hand holding a rose, busting out of a grave bearing a banner with the phrase "R.I.P. Love" to commemorate the experience, and after enough time has passed, you just feel a little sorry for them for having to carry their scars so publicly for so long. That isn't you! So start by saying thank-you to your banged-up heart for teaching you how to be a hero (and avoid bad permanent art).

Now let's get started. Here's what got me to the other side, and might get you there too:

REALIZE THAT THOUGHTS DRIVE YOUR BEHAVIOR.

Whatever you believe you are fundamentally, that is the truth. This isn't where you go, "I fundamentally believe that I am Drew Barrymore," because that is crazy talk. This is where you go, "I'm awesome, and I might be hurting right now but it's OK, because I'm going to be better in the long run," or "I'm a sad loser who doesn't deserve a damn thing because it's all gonna get taken away anyway." Whichever one—or some variation—you choose, you will act it out somehow or another, and you will be treated accordingly. It's entirely your choice!

DEVELOP COMPASSION.

Now you know what it feels like to feel like garbage. So you can recognize that feeling in others, and empathize. It strangely becomes a healing experience for both people when this happens. You get over your heartbreak even more, and so do they.

DISCOVER THAT YOU ARE LOVED.

Go ahead and try to reject this because it sounds corny and you don't like feelings. I'm sorry, it's just the objective truth of the matter. When you understand that you are loved, that there are, really, people who love you, that you DESERVE their love, and that you really do have huge, undying support in this world, from your friends and/or family and/or pets and/or God if you believe in that, the love that you lost begins to feel smaller in comparison. Some ways you can do this:

♦ Say thank you. When you express gratitude for things you have in life, that appreciation will become happiness. Genuine happiness that comes from you and isn't bestowed by outside forces (like certain people who once used to make fuzzy caterpillars dance in your stomach and now are total a-holes who ruined your heart) leads to bigger and better things, things that actually matter. What these things are will look different for everyone: Better grades? More confidence? Finding a little bit of peace with your mom? Whatever they are, they'll put you in a more positive frame of mind for generating whatever it is that feels good to you personally. Even if you have to force yourself to keep a journal of three things you're thankful for every day, and one day it's "I'm thankful for veggie chili," at least you've got veggie chili on your side.

♦ Ask your friends for help. Your real friends are going to listen to you, and then shut you up when it's time to stop talking about it. They will call you at night and listen to you cry, and then remind you of all the good things you have going on in your life. They will help you stay strong and ignore your ex's late-night texts. They will pay you amazing compliments that almost feel too good to be true, though deep inside you know they're right—they see who you actually are.

♦ Hang out with animals. Animals rule. They love your affection and want to return it.

LEARN HOW TO BE ALONE.

You're no longer half of a pair, and you're still at least somewhat functional. Yes, you need your friends (and now's the time to depend on them to help you out when you're sad, which we talked about above)—you're not an isolated hermit whom no one loves. As much as you can, get into that space of You Power, because enjoying solitude is an important life skill.

When you're alone, the things that are exciting to you as an individual will become beacons of inspiration, if you let them. Whatever you deem your "work"—and it can be anything: personal collage projects, tracking down awesome comics (hint: Ron Regé Jr.), acing your history paper, beating the top score on that video game, concocting the perfect Pandora station (Top Girls + Diva Dompé + Enya + Grimes + Tomita + Sun Araw), focusing on emotional growth, powering through your Netflix documentary queue, getting your Tumblr in shape with some homemade custom CSS, or exploring some aspiration that doesn't have a shape but is right now just a "feeling" inside you—starts to have focus, detail. These are the things that come to the forefront when you can be happy by yourself. You can burn all your anger and sadness as fuel, and this "work" becomes a rocket that transports you to your personal goals.

Plus, not everything is better if you share it with another person. All those fries are *yours*. And you get to explore whatever you want on your own time, go into your dream world, sit in the bookstore and scheme up random correlations between subjects, dress up for the special occasion of bonding with your favorite pinball game…it's like being five again, only you know how to cross the street by

yourself and not get hit by a car. These small things are glitter treats for your independent spirit, and you're the only one who can provide them. In other words, you learn that you are your own source of validation, and that *you* decide when you're cool, which is always.

Developing your independence means you know how to protect and take care of yourself, you'll be able to lead when the situation arises, you dress better because you don't care what anyone thinks, you're able to make decisions for yourself without consulting seven and a half people first, you learn how to share without being weird about it, and generally you just get radder. Seriously, you know those people who are nice to everyone yet mysteriously don't seem to need company every minute of the day? How do they do that? Maybe they got their heart broken once.

DEVELOP YOUR WILL.

You're not really supposed to have all this self-control in life right now. It's not your job to be calm and rational and know how to cope with everything and have the perspective that it all "happens for a reason" (it drives me insane when people shrug and say that—why would you hand over your power of choice to some outside force, a.k.a. "the universe"?). However, it is important to have the experiences that give you the chance to cultivate self-discipline, because knowing how and when to bite down and power through really comes in handy in life. Mentally getting a grip and refocusing—even just distracting yourself, if that's the best you can do sometimes—takes hard work. You don't have to take the high road all the time, but it's good for you to be able to quit checking your ex's Twitter or Facebook, because it hurts to keep looking. Plus, you can't pass your driving test if you're crying over your ex.

FIND WHAT YOU'RE REALLY MADE OF.

It's always good to have a starting point from which to measure everything that comes after. Do you wallow? Want to smash stuff? Say horrible things to your ex that you really wish you could take back? Good news! You've gotten a chance to identify parts of yourself that show up only when you're in mega pain, and now you know what lives inside you. When else do you get to do that? The fantastic thing is, once you see who you really are, you can make a better decision about who you want to be. Also, you get to see where you're solid and dazzling, and can still be nice to someone who might not deserve it. Maybe you realize you're worth something better than what you previously had. Maybe, actually, you're stronger than you ever thought you were. Nice work. A++. I knew you had it in you. ♦

Liz Armstrong lives in Los Angeles, writes for a living, believes no amount of glitter is too much, and currently aspires to better pinball chops.

HANGING OUT WITH
~~DETENTION SLIP~~

NAME: ALLISON REYNOLDS

1. CLOSE TO ME - THE CURE
2. THERE'S A WORLD OUTSIDE - THE PSYCHEDELIC FURS
3. LOVE WILL TEAR US APART - JOY DIVISION
4. SHOW OF STRENGTH - ECHO AND THE BUNNYMEN
5. CASCADE - SIOUXSIE AND THE BANSHEES
6. BEING COLD - STRAWBERRY SWITCHBLADE
7. LEAVE ME ALONE - ALTERED IMAGES
8. SET-UP - AU PAIRS
9. PALE SHELTER - TEARS FOR FEARS

WE WILL NOT BE BLINDED

Springtime in the city.
By Lauren P.

Thanks to Claire Marie Christerson for styling help; and to Claire, Sepeed Emambakhsh, Mars Hobrecker, Angela Munoz, and Mike Bailey-Gates for modeling.

HOW TO MAKE A ZINE

Zine-making isn't about rules or knowledge; it's about freedom and POWER.
Writing by Emma D. Playlist by Leeann.

YOU'LL NEED:

♦ *A cutting knife (like an X-ACTO)*
♦ *A ruler*
♦ *An A3 sheet of paper (you can use another size, but an A3 will make a postcard-size zine—ideal for snail mail).*

YOU WILL NOT NEED:
♦ *Glue*
♦ *Tape*
♦ *A stapler*
None of that junk is necessary!

HOW TO MAKE YOUR ZINE:

1. Fold the paper in half so that the two longer edges line up.

2. Fold it again the other way, so that the two shorter edges line up.

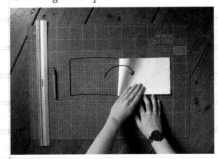

Zines are self-published, small-circulation, often nonprofit books, papers, or websites. They usually deal with topics too controversial or niche for mainstream media, presented in an unpolished layout and unusual design. Everyone, from a major NGO to a teenager like you, can be an author (and also an editor, art director, and publisher) of a zine, and that's part of what makes them so awesome.

Since the invention of the photocopy machine, zine-making has been one of the most popular forms of independent publishing, especially in underground communities. But it's hard to generalize about zines, the same way it's hard to generalize about *culture*. Not just hard—impossible. Because like all art and media, zines can be anything and everything. And they are.

If you type "zine making" into Amazon, you'll get 10 pages of results. But to be honest, I've never read a book about zine-making, and I don't think you have to, either. For me, zine-making isn't about rules or knowledge; it's about freedom and (guess what?) POWER.

Zines are super powerful! They can communicate rebellious words and strong ideas. People who feel a burning need to share their energy with the world make zines, so it's no coincidence that zine culture is often associated with some of the most energetic movements: punk, feminist, queer, etc. Some publications that sprang from those subcultures, like the punk fanzine *Chainsaw*, enjoyed cult status; others, like *Bitch*, got so popular that they turned into regular magazines that you can find in bookstores.

But zines are not looking for a broad audience. They're not supposed to appeal to everyone. That's the point: they're exclusive. And "exclusive" can mean anything from "anyone interested in *Doctor Who*" to "only you and your girl gang" to even "only you."

Nowadays (boy I sound old all of a sudden) you can make a digital zine/mag and reach people on the other end of the planet in a blink, but what's nicer than a little handmade book you can hold in your non-virtual hands? Or the unique feeling of being one among a tiny group of special people in possession of a carefully made publication?

There are tons of ways to make a zine, of course. But the one I'm going to show you is one of the cheapest, quickest, and easiest—perfect for spreading your message widely! You will need only three items (that you certainly own) to make it, plus a one-sided printer to make copies.

3. Fold it one last time, in the same direction as you did in step two, so that it's the size of a standard postcard.

4. Unfold the paper. In the picture below I've mapped out where on the paper the different pages of your zine will live, as long as you've folded the paper the way I've laid out here. (It's OK if you folded it some other way, but this map of pages won't be the same for you.)

5. Cut a slit in the paper, lengthwise between the two outer folds (the pictures below do a better job of describing this than words ever could).

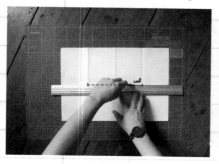

6. Fold the paper along that same line, bringing the two longer edges of the paper together.

7. Grab the two sides of the paper and push them together to form a cross, like so:

8. Take the top and bottom legs (arms?) of that cross and fold them over so they sandwich the arm (leg?) on the right.

9. See that last double page that's sticking out on the left? Fold it over the top of the other pages (you'll move it clockwise, as shown below).

10. Flatten the zine by creasing the edges with your finger. It's almost ready!

11. Now you can start working on the art and the rest of the content. This is one of my zines, inspired by old punk/feminist zines that were made from newspaper cutouts (it'll look really cool when I Xerox it in black and white!):

12. As you probably noticed, all the pages are double, giving them a blank inside layer—that's because we only used one side of the original sheet of paper. You can add secret notes in the "hidden pages" that are different for every copy of your zine.

That's it! You're now an independent publisher. Congratulations! For more inspiration, I suggest you check out publishers such as PO-GOBOOKS, Café Royal, BOLO, and Nieves, all of whom are doing a great job navigating zine lovers through the sea of boring stuff flooding the internet, and plucking out only the very best for your enjoyment. ♦

IT HAPPENS ALL THE TIME

A private conversation about street harassment, made public.
By the staff of Rookie

Here's an unexciting secret: the Rookie staff has a hidden Facebook group wherein we discuss themes and ideas and assignments. We also go there to chat and gossip and joke around and blow off steam. Sometimes things get serious, as they did last month, when Jamia told us about a gross incident of street harassment that had happened to her that day. As everyone began to chime in with support and tales of similar things that had happened to them, we all got so sad, and so MAD. It dawned on us that you can take any random group of girls and women, and EVERY SINGLE ONE of them will have multiple stories of terrible things that were said to them and done to them on the street by strangers, as a matter of course. Just the normal state of affairs when you are out in public, being female. Like, we're not special. This happens to everybody.

We're publishing that conversation here today. If you're not a girl, you might be surprised to learn what all your female friends go through. It might help you understand why we don't think it's cute or cool or flattering to be hollered at, commented on, ogled, or groped as we just try to get from one place to another. This wasn't a conversation we had for the public—this was just what came out when we talked about this stuff in private. Any girl you know can tell you her own horror stories, if you're willing to listen.

Warning: strong language throughout, by necessity.

APRIL 16, 2012

JAMIA OMG nasty street-harassment moment in my lyfe… I was sitting in Grand Central's food court today eating soup. My nose was stuck in a book, so I didn't notice what was going on around me. When I was done eating, I turned around and saw this old man sitting two seats away from me. He looked over at me and was masturbating in his pants and talking to himself. UGH. I got up right away and tried to find a cop, to no avail. I am still pissed off about it.

JAMIE This sucks and is gross. I am adding my own story to this. One time I was in T.J. Maxx shopping for bathing suits. I was not trying them on, just browsing the aisle, and I looked over to the novelty-lotions gifty-crap section, and there was a man staring at me and jerking off with the lotion from the tester. I was 15.

ANAHEED GOD. I am so sorry, both of you. I always wish I had the balls to YELL at those people, but I get too grossed out and freaked out.

AMY ROSE Oh my god, Jamia, I am so sorry. I've had strangers touching me a LOT in the past week (seriously, what the fuck is going on here?) and I flip out enough over that. I hate street harassment so much, and I have so much love and empathy for you.

JAMIE I think it has something to do with spring. All the creeps come out of hibernation. I've been getting "Hey…smile!" a lot

COMMENTS

EMILYJN
Ugh I was on holiday in New York when I was 13 (!) and a man in his 60s came up to me in Times Square and asked to have sex with me. Ugh still makes me go red.

ALIENOR
Not too long ago, I was in the subway on my way to school. It was very crowded and everyone was pushed against each other, but that happens all the time, and people keep to themselves so that it's not too gross. At one stop, people got out and people got in. And this guy got behind me, and started "pushing himself" against me. I started breathing heavy to calm down, telling myself he would stop but HE DIDN'T. He kept pushing more and more, and I started crying so much, so I grabbed this girl standing next to me and told her, and she helped me get out at the next stop. I was crying until I got to school. Getting on the subway is now very scary to me.

ARGIGLE
This really is sad. I know I've had plenty of experiences and tried to explain to my guy friends that it is scary having to wonder if you're going to get raped or attacked or something when walking down the street, or in a store, or at a party.

IDONTEVENKNOW
One time my friend and I were going to a sleepover and she was holding a huge blanket and this guy stuck his head out of a car window and said "Can I get under there with you?" She's 13 and I'm 14 and it's just fucking scary.

LUCY23
Ughghghgh This all makes me so mad! I was standing at a train station once and was texting and out of nowhere this older man came up and put his arm around my waist and said some VERY gross stuff. Luckily, someone saw and got him to leave, because I was too shocked to even move!

more, too, from weird paternalistic men on the street.

JAMIA I usually say, "Show some respect," but I was so shocked today. Another time this guy came up to me in Washington Square Park and yelled, "I want to eat your pussy" and made this hand motion at me… it was so gross that I burst into tears and yelled at him. GROSS GROSS gremlins.

ANAHEED When guys used to yell that at me I used to say, "Oh wow, really, that would be amazing, I have been waiting all night for some gross turd to offer to eat my pussy." (They don't yell that at me anymore, 'cause I'm old.)

JAMIE My plan is to yell, "Would you say that to your mother?" and see what happens.

AMY ROSE I always fuh-REAK. Even at catcallers. My method has advanced recently: now when people holler at me from cars or on the street, I go into full pretending-to-be-a-horrible-tortured-monster mode and growl and act like a lunatic.

JENNY Dang, you girls are way better at fending off street harassment than I am.

When I lived in France, I had it so bad that I literally had to look down at the ground whenever I went outside, because if I even accidentally looked up for a second, some dude or a gang of dudes would go apeshit. Oftentimes I had to factor in extra time when I would walk to the train station or go outside to do errands, because guys in cars would block the crosswalk or intersection so they could harass me. Probably once a day some guy would jump out from seemingly nowhere and do some "kung fu" move that would have been hilarious if it wasn't in service of harassing the fuck out of me, and I didn't go a single day without 10 to 15 dudes following me and whispering every single Asian-language word they knew while trying to grab me and pull me into their disgusting arms.

HANNAH I was on the Greyhound once and noticed a guy a few seats behind me moving his hand around in his pants area and staring at me intently. I freaked and moved closer to the driver, and when I looked back he had moved closer! I texted my dad to make sure he was at my station right away to pick me up and kept my hand inside my pocket on my Swiss Army knife. Also, this one time a guy

stopped his car and asked me if I wanted a ride and I said, "Only if you've got a toilet in the back, 'cause I've gotta pee." He drove away.

EMMA D. Once I fell asleep on the public beach (full of people) and woke up an hour later because I could tell that something was GOING ON. As it's rather difficult to figure out what's going on when you're wearing a swimsuit and OMG WHERE ARE MY GLASSES, it took me about two minutes to locate an old, naked man jerking off in the bushes one meter away from me. I ran away, and promised myself I'd yell at someone like him next time. So the next time it happened I yelled at the guy making nasty comments on the street and was all woohoo female power, but he ANSWERED BACK in a vulgar but somehow CLEVER way and it left me speechless. 1:0 FOR THIS ASSHOLE. I STILL CAN'T GET OVER IT.

NAOMI I was *13* when I first got asked if I wanted a "lift." I had no fucking idea what to do. Actually, I think I was *11* when I was in the park with my friend and this guy asked us to keep watch while he pissed in a bush. We thought he was probably a flasher, so we just ran like hell.

UNEFILLECOMMETOI
Three weeks ago I went swimming with some friends—there were like 15 of us, guys and girls. We were the only ones in the little lake until a group of guys swimming in their underwear arrived. It wasn't until we were getting out of the water to leave that I noticed that the guys were TAKING PICTURES OF US and VIDEOTAPING us! They filmed us while we changed too. Now I wish I had taken their fucking camera and thrown it into the lake.

HAN_SOLO
When I was TEN, a boy in school deemed it acceptable to stick his hand up my skirt when I was standing on a chair putting up a wall display. What the fuck.

FARAWAYFAERIE
I feel so insecure when people shout at me from their trucks, it makes me want to crawl into a hole, but then I get angry that they have that *power* over me, but it happens EVERY TIME AND I JUST WANT TO BE INVISIBLE.

TEA
When I was 11, I had just had a growth spurt, so I was finally starting to look less like a little soft-faced kid and more like a teenager. I was on the subway and a man in his mid- or late 40s looked at me, patted his lap (he was sitting down), and made kissy faces at me. I just turned away and tried to ignore it. I felt violated and didn't really know how to express it.

Once, also on the subway, it was really crowded and a man moved up closer to me, from behind, and

I felt his erection pressing against me. I said "Oh my fucking GOD, what is your DEAL?" and turned to him sharply. He just moved on. I told a woman next to me what happened, and she looked at me like I was the crude one.

I've been followed by men from class and work, they would say things like "I really like the way you wear your clothes and how your body moves in them" or "Can I come home with you?" I would always say, "Get lost, asshole." No smile, no anger. Just

TAVI I am so sorry and grossed out for everybody here. On Sunday I was having the worst day and was on the phone with my sister while I was walking home, and these guys outside the library whistled and I WISHED I'd been like ANJSJSIDNSA AMY ROSE GREMLIN or at least like NO-BODY ASKED YOU but instead I just gave them a dirty look and was like "ugh" to my sister. Then you have the guilt trip you put yourself through for not saying anything even though it is totally alarming.

JAMIA One of the creepiest street-harassment experiences happened to me in France too—what is it about France? This gang of dudes circled me and one of them picked me up and pretended he was going to carry me off somewhere. I was kicking and screaming, "Va te faire foutre!" ["Fuck off!"] over and over, and my friend Sandy came over and yanked me out of this asshole's arms.

ELEANOR One time when I was having lunch in a café, this man sat near me. I could see his hand moving around under this giant blanket. Then the other week me, my sister, and a friend were walking to a party and a guy asked to borrow a lighter from my friend. She passed it to him

and he held her hand, then he was following us down the street, and then a massive dude came out of an alley and joined him, and then ANOTHER joined him until these three guys were like storming along behind us down this empty street at midnight. We were literally running at this point, and they were saying such disgusting, terrifying stuff, and thank god we got into the house before they got to us. I hate London because every time I visit I get disgusting comments thrown at me and weird guys shouting at me from car windows. I hate that I have to live in fear while on public transit and have to make sure I get off the train just before the doors close so that people don't follow me…

HAZEL One time at Target there was this man who was yelling at me and saying VULGAR things. I told my mom, and when we left the store the parking lot was dark, but we saw him. My mom drove around him very quickly in tight circles, like almost hitting him and basically stalking him in our car while screaming at him insanely, and I swear to god he was actually scared.

JENNY I love your mom, Hazel.

STEPHANIE I have now had THREE experiences of riding the train in Chicago and seeing a man sitting nearby, leering at me and masturbating. Once it happened when I was on my way to a job interview. Seriously, how fucking unsettling was that? I've always been too freaked out to yell or press the train call button, except for once when I happened to be on the phone with my husband and said to him really loudly, "I'M SORRY, I HAVE TO MOVE BECAUSE THE MAN ACROSS FROM ME IS MASTURBATING." This caused a very suburban-looking dad and son to take notice, and the dude fled the train at the next stop.

TAVI Stephanie! The fucking El! That happened to me once. UGH. I was just reading my diary from March 2011 and it was around the time when I got contacts and started wearing more-flattering clothes, and all of the entries are like, "Can I do this all without these creeps assuming it's for them?" Yeesh. That was when the thing on the El happened, and it was my first time on the train alone, too, which was so off-putting! The next time I took the train was on the way to SlutWalk, so I was like SYMBOLS FOR PERSONAL GROWTH BLAH BLAH. Can we all have a communal hug?

matter of fact. I have more in my life to think about.

I'm so sorry young girls and women, both cis- and transgendered, have to experience this constant harrassment. I want to hug you all, my sisters.

KELSEY RUE

Just this Saturday, my best friend Inga and I were walking down the street in Sacramento and this guy is singing and talking to his friends and grins at us. He says, "This is where you

two start snapping and singing, 'If you think I'm sexy, love me,'" and we shook our heads and kept walking. He yelled after us, "Ooh you little bitches!" She's 14 and I'm 13.

VICTORYBELLE

On one occasion I was walking to the Tube after having a meal with some friends and a man walked past me and said something I didn't really make out in this really pervy way. I was a little intimidated but just carried

on and walked a little faster. At the next junction in the road, I looked behind me only to discover this guy had started following me. When he saw I'd noticed him he sped up and started saying what he'd said before and getting louder and louder as he got closer, he was yelling "big legs" at me (??!!). I ran to an island in the middle of the road as soon as the opportunity came up and he got stuck on the other side of the road staring at me and yelling louder and louder. I got home and cried my eyes out.

And once a group of us were having a picnic in Brighton on a super sunny day. We'd just finished eating and my friend was lying back on the grass with her knees bent up. A pair of repulsive men took this as an invitation to shove their hands up her skirt. We were all just so shocked we had no idea what to do, and they just stood there smirking at us. I then yelled at them and dialed the police on my cellphone, and the men ran off. The thing that saddens me is that I didn't know wheth-

STEPHANIE Communal hugs for sure. And seriously, the fact that these guys think that women dress up so we can play a role in their personal porn is so annoying. I hate that it makes me self-conscious.

HANNAH I dressed very "masculine" once I hit puberty because I was the first one in my class to "develop," and boys thought they had a right to snap my bra or touch my thighs, so I figured if I covered myself in baggy clothes and made myself look boyish no one would see my female-ness and I would feel tougher. I only really started to celebrate my femininity around 16 or so, and even then I chopped off all my hair as an act of anger toward harassing dudes.

TAVI I always thought it was interesting that Mary-Kate and Ashley dress so baggily now when there were entire websites counting down the days till they'd turn 18 and be "legal."

HANNAH The thing is, even when I am not dressed "attractive," I still get car honks and hoots. I can be bundled up in a parka and rain boots, with my hair pulled back and essentially looking like a genderless blob, and still, pervs will act out.

NAOMI Exactly! I was beeped at on one rainy day—this was last week—and I was like, "I am in jeans and a raincoat and my hair is in a greasy ponytail and I have no makeup on and my face is probably screwed up trying to see through the rain," but no, people still think it's funny to make a girl jump out of her skin.

HANNAH But it definitely heightens on those days when you dress up and feel good about yourself, and then some jerk makes you feel like garbage and it's just like THIS ISN'T FOR YOU, A-HOLE. THIS IS FOR **ME** I AM A QUEEN GODDESS AND YOU ARE A LOWLY WORM.

TAVI I was complaining about this in class with some other LADIEZ and this douche dude said, "Don't you think you're being a little CONCEITED?" God, this isn't about being like, "IT'S SO HARD TO BE POPULAR!"

HANNAH If a homophobic dude were hit on by men constantly, he'd never shut up about it, meanwhile at least once a week from puberty onward I've been made to feel like someone's personal entertainment when I'm doing something as banal as walking to the bus in the middle of the afternoon.

ANAHEED It is crazy how hard it is for most dudes to understand this. How they're like, "I would love it if people told me how hot I was all the time." How they tell you, "You should be flattered." I feel like boys need to be educated about this from a young age! On what it means to be leered at and touched way before you're even equipped to understand what's going on, and how that makes you feel shame and guilt and finally anger for the rest of your life.

NAOMI We need some kind of an intervention for men to make them see, LOOK, THIS HAPPENS EVERY DAY. I don't know about you gals, but I think about it EVERY time I go out. I think most men can't really comprehend it, because they don't have to deal with it every day of their lives. I mean, I think I got my first wolf whistle when I was 12? NOW TELL ME WE DON'T NEED FEMINISM.

ANAHEED We should just publish this whole conversation.

JENNY Hell yeah, publish it. ◆

...er what happened was serious enough to tell the police about. I'm so glad I did, though, because they took us really seriously. Street harassment is a serious crime.

DANA SUSAN

One time a man literally grabbed my vulva as I walked past him in a bar. I was livid and disgusted, but I didn't do anything because it happened so fast. Guys get away with murder in bars. I always try to scream, "NO. You cannot do that. You cannot TOUCH

someone without their consent. I DON'T KNOW YOU." It always amazes me that they always put up a fight, but I will keep repeating myself till they walk away.

RUBY B.

I'm 14 and things like this have happened to me a few times. I remember that I was out somewhere with my mom (in public) and this random guy started staring at me and masturbating. It was SO CREEPY and I didn't know what to do, so I just ignored him. A few

weeks ago, my friend and I were just walking around and this guy pulled up in his truck, rolled down his window, and said in this creepy voice, "Hello, ladies." We just RAN. I hate how this isn't even recognized as an issue most of the time.

MRS. FLOYD

The first time I got hollered at I was 13. I was riding my bike wearing shorts. I stopped at a light, and some creep pulls up next to me and says, "Is it legal for a girl your age to have legs that sexy?"

and then proceeded to drive off whilst chuckling. Makes me nauseous. I was so scared I would see him again I took a different route home the next day.

SAGE

Once, when I was nine or 10 years old, I was waiting for my dad in our car with my baby sister. Suddenly, a truck pulled up in the "no parking" zone and just sat there for a while. I was like, "What the heck is this guy doing?" and took a closer look. The

driver was masturbating. Did I mention I was nine or 10? Who does that? I was disgusted and felt guilty and I couldn't stop crying. Worst day ever. Scarred for life.

POLLYANA
I live in NYC, which is notorious for its train creepers. Once when I was on a very crowded subway I sat down next to this guy. I was reading a book and from my peripheral vision I could see him put his hand in his pants IN FRONT OF ME and begin to tap me on the shoulder. I willed every muscle in my body to not turn around and ninja-assassinate him. Thankfully there were only like four stops till my station. The saddest thing about it is that that's not the worst thing I have experienced in terms of street harassment.

RAYFASHIONFREAK
I can totally relate to this (isn't that sad that we girls have all been objectified like this in this day and age!). Exactly a year ago today (funnily enough) my friends and I went on a school trip to Morocco. We were at a water park, and a man pushed us into the river. Each time he pushed one of us out he felt us up and started whispering vulgar things to us. I was 14, of course I felt really awkward and creeped out. We spoke to our teacher, but even she said there was nothing we could do about it (that was the thing that enraged me most!).

ANNEBELLE
Gosh, reading all of these comments have made me sad to live in a world where misogyny is commonplace. I have had this happen to me since I was 11 or 12, I get

it lots in my school uniform, but the beach is pretty bad too. When I was 12 I was too scared to do anything, but when I was 13 or 14 I'd just scream FUCK OFF I AM 13 BITCHES, that'd make them stop. I swear a guy followed me home from the gym one time too, it's pretty creepy, I just hate it.

EMKLUMPEN
When I was seven years old, my friend and I were walking to my house from the park, which was a block away, and this old guy rides up beside us on his bike and says, "I'll pay you 10 cents to see me naked." We ran to my house and told my parent right away. They called the cops, but I don't think anything was done about it because we had different accounts of what this guy looked like. Another time I was waiting for a train and, again, an old guy starts speaking to me in a language I didn't understand, made sexual hand gestures, then tried to take my hand out of my pocket. I smacked his hand away, but I was on the verge of tears the whole way home. Then there is the usual honking, calling from moving cars, guys making kissy noises, guys asking gross questions.

CARNEECE
My college doesn't have enough parking spaces for every girl who lives on campus, and although there are PLENTY of commuter spaces that go unused, we get fined if we park in them at night. Just a few months ago a female student was held at gunpoint by three men, kidnapped in her own vehicle, and barely escaped from being gang-raped. Where did this

occur? Literally feet away from her dorm, in the street where she was forced to park. I've spoken to security numerous times about it, and they tell me that I just have to park in the street and buy a taser. It disappoints me that so few people want to stand up for girls or consider street harassment and danger a legitimate issue.

STACEY
I always try to avoid eye contact with any guy, anywhere, for fear of them doing anything to me. I hate when you're walking and you can see and feel creeps staring at you. It's disgusting. I don't go out too much, but on a Saturday two weeks ago, I was out shopping with my family, and I was shouted at, honked at, and whistled at, in the time span of an hour when walking from the parking lot into the stores. It made me feel horrible.

CARO NATION
I was 12 when a man accosted me from his car, hollering, "Hey sexy!" while his friends made vulgar noises. I flipped him off, screamed, "Up yours!" and nearly kicked his tailpipe clean off. A feminist perspective is imperative when you're growing up. But I do not recommend damaging the perpetrator's car. They will try to run over you.

LOROBIRD
When my friends and I were like 11 we were in the playground and a guy on a bike stopped on the other side of the fence, took out his junk and waved it around in front of us for a while. It was gross and fascinating. We ran to

tell our (woman) teacher, who was with other (women) teachers, and they all LAUGHED and told us to run along. This is what rape culture looks like.

LORI
Two days ago I walked into this restaurant/bar place to inquire about summer work, and this group of like 40-year-old men wolf-whistled. I'm 15! Then as I was walking out one of the guys said something like "Give us a smile." I was so insulted, angry, and creeped out. It made me feel so bad, even though I didn't do anything wrong! Ugh!

BECCA-JADE
God, sexual harassment is the worst! How would guys feel if we stared at their crotch, tried to touch them inappropriately or make rude comments? Will they only then understand how vulnerable and self-conscious we feel when stuff like this happens? WE DON'T FEEL FLATTERED OR INCLINED TO SLEEP WITH YOU!

DEARBH
I don't think it's an issue of being "pretty" or "hot"; misogynistic assholes just get a kick out of intimidating people. It's happened to me a lot recently so I've perfected my bitchface and just flip them the bird. It's harder though when (usually) older men start leering at or talking to you on the street and it may look really innocent from an outsider's perspective—but it's not. I hate when I get leered at or I feel men's gazes on me when I walk down the street. It's like, "I didn't give you permission to look at me, so, STOP!!!"

FIRKY

When I was 14 I'd walk to Country Style (local coffee and doughnut place) after school with my friends. There was a super creepy man that would come every day at the same time we were there, sit down and stare at me. When I got up and left, he got up and left. This happened for about a week. I didn't tell my parents because I wasn't quite sure if it was just a huge coincidence that everywhere I went, he went…it wasn't! One day I walked outside, saw him get up and wait for me to make the next move. I walked to the video store next door, he walked in too. I looked up, shaking. He was staring at me across aisles of videos. I called my mom from the store's phone, and she freaked at him. To this day we regret not calling the police.

LONGSTOCKINGS

The other day I chose to shout back at a guy who yelled out of his car to suck his dick, but when I did, the girl I was with looked embarrassed and a couple across the road gave me a filthy look, as if I was somehow the one in the wrong. As if by not ignoring it I'd gone against some kind of chaste-girl law.

LEANNA

When I was 14 I was walking to school with my best friend. A man came up behind us, grabbed my friend, and tried to pull her panties down under her skirt while saying, "Oh baby, I want your pussy." He was a well-dressed man in his 30s, and it was in broad daylight on the same block

as our school. I was frozen for a second, but then I started hitting him with my lunch bag and screaming at him and calling him a fucker. He ran away. I'm still so infuriated that I couldn't save my friend from feeling hurt and ashamed, though. I told school officials and the police. There were even witnesses. But to my knowledge he was never caught.

SKATAPUS

I was on public transport a few months ago and went upstairs to sit and read. Some older guy came over and started talking to me, and while it felt sketchy, some kind of stupid politeness kicked in and I didn't just leave. I sat there and talked to him, told him my age, answered his questions until he said, "Girl, you're beautiful, you should be a model," at which point I made an excuse about it being too hot out and fled downstairs. Absolutely ruined my day; I was furious with myself for telling him information and for not just leaving straight away. I guess because he wasn't saying anything particularly creepy for the most part, I felt like I couldn't just get up and leave, which is terrible!

MOLLYWOBBLES

Last week I was walking from college to band practice and a guy pulled up beside me and rolled down his window. I stopped because I thought he was asking for directions, but instead he leered at me and said, "Can I lick your pussy?" I just stared at him in complete shock and then said, "No… really no." He laughed and drove off. I hate the fact that I was left

disgusted and on the verge of tears after this episode, and still thinking about it a week later, yet he drove off laughing and probably forgot about it as soon as he got home. It isn't fair.

YOURENOTFUNNY

When I was 12 I was walking home from the store and a grown man FOLLOWED ME DOWN THE FUCKING ALLEY and asked me for my number. When I didn't answer (I thought I was gonna piss myself), he laughed at me and drove away.

DEARBH

Actually the more I think about it and the more stories that are here on this thread, the angrier I am getting. Like what the actual fuck makes guys think they can get away with this or that this is accepted behaviour?!! Do they actually wake up in the morning like, "Oh, time for some public masturbation!" or what? To everyone commenting here and everyone who has felt demeaned or embarrassed or harassed in public, I'm sorry, and I hope that someday we can walk down a street anywhere in the world and not feel intimidated.

STARSINYOURHEART

Two weeks after I turned 15, I was walking by myself and some random 40-year-old followed me home. I kept telling myself to stop being paranoid and that he wasn't following me, but he ended up pushing me down an alleyway up against a wall, kissing me and forcing his hand up my skirt. I felt so ashamed and awful and dirty, like a whore for so

long, always showering and stuff. Now I've just turned 18 and I look back and it makes me so mad someone did that to essentially a little kid!

SORCHA M

Since I started developing at like 12 or something, I've had to cope with disgusting comments, being groped and followed. Until fairly recently, I didn't even know it counted as harassment, because whenever I tried to complain about it, a boy would pop up and be like, "You should be flattered people find you attractive!" What, like I'm meant to be HAPPY a middle-aged man gets turned on by a 14-year-old girl in her school uniform? I'm still mad at myself for never retaliating, but I live in London and I often feel like it's never that safe to say something back.

CHANTEMOI

The thing is, when this kind of shitty thing happens to us, we freak out. It's only after the freaking out/panicking fades that we get angry. We are almost paralyzed and our protective instinct (which I strongly believe is stronger than with men) kicks in and we opt to get away from the danger. This is, of course, the wise thing to do. But when you think that those jerks will do the same thing to a million other girls, you know you should have done something to teach them a memorable lesson. I felt guilty many times for having done nothing. But we should be more forgiving of ourselves. The one story I have of a brave woman is that of my friend's mother. In Paris, my

friend, her mother, and I were on a very crowded subway train—as in can't move or breathe, body stuck to body, urgh disgusting. The man standing behind my friend's mother took the opportunity to place his hand on her butt. At the next station, as soon as the door opened, she grabbed that guy's hand, held it up so everyone could see, and yelled, "This hand was grabbing my ass. Whom does it belong to?" I swear everybody looked, and the guy turned red and ran off.

SALTWATER

When I was 15 years old, some ass-hole took an upskirt photo of me. I was just waiting outside a shop in a busy city center, and didn't fully realize what had happened until a very distressed woman who happened to spot him told me. I was angry and upset but also a little guilty. I'd been wearing knee-high socks and a pleated miniskirt, and I felt like I couldn't complain about that sort of attention when I was dressed in a way that could be interpreted as this "sexy schoolgirl" trope. I think this guilt is such a good example of how rape culture influences the way women perceive themselves.

KATIEDYD

When I was 15 I was taking a commuter train by myself from Hartford to NYC. A guy in his late 20s sat down next to me. He started moving his leg closer to mine, and then closer again when I moved away. I was really uncomfortable, and then he got up to leave and I was like YAY until he GRABBED MY BOOB. On a train full of people WHO SAID NOTHING TO STOP HIM, HE GRABBED MY BOOB AND SMILED IN HIS GROSS WAY. And then he left and I really wish I would have kicked him in the balls or something because that was not OK in the slightest. And no one around me told him to fuck off. I was scared and surprised and I couldn't think until I got off the train at my stop. What a dick.

MADDZWX

Once a man outside a movie theater offered me $50 to suck his dick before I was old enough to have gotten my first period. Gross.

CEE

One thing makes me the most angry is when a guy acts like you are obligated to talk to him or that there is something wrong with you when you ignore him. Some perv masturbating is gross and scary, and some aggressive guy shouting stuff and following—totally scary. But at least with those guys, they are upfront about what screwed-up freaks they are. What makes me sooo mad are the guys that say something sort of innocent sounding like "You are the most beautiful girl in the world" or "Smile girl, you're gorgeous" or whatever. You are just out walking—that doesn't mean you are obligated to talk to them. If you smile and respond, they think they can flirt with you so it's better to ignore. But when you ignore, they yell at you and call you a snob or a bitch or ask you if you are gay or ask why you are in a hurry, and suddenly they get MEAN. That's the Big Bad Wolf sort of creep. Acting all nice and then they turn around and show their teeth.

PEANUTBUTTER

The biggest problem with street harassment is that it is so insidious. It's hard to pin down, and often the victim may not even realize that what happened was unacceptable. It wasn't even until I had read through most of this article that I began to realize that it had happened to me, too. Numerous times, in many different ways, starting as early as when I was 10 or 11. What bothers me most, though, is the fact that my knee-jerk reaction to these memories was to make excuses for the perpetrators. He was drunk, he was just a teenager, he was clearly mentally incapacitated. Part of it is me not wanting to admit that a normal, rational adult would do these things, but it's also the fact that we are geared to think "Oh, it's not a big deal. I'm weak if I let it get to me, and annoying if I speak out about it."

TINABALLERINA

All the way through junior high I experienced sexual harassment by my classmates. They didn't see me as attractive, but still they were creepy, touching, and just disgusting. One guy wrote on my Facebook wall that I should suck his dick, and there were just so many comments. The school actually reported this to the police, but when he was expelled for three days, the whole school hated me. People started following me around, saying I had ruined his life for something that I should have accepted, etc. After this, I deleted a lot of people on Facebook, and changed classes for the last six months. I was approached by all his friends (literally the whole school) every day when he was expelled, saying how stupid and wrong I was. I walked around with a lump in my throat every day, and even suffered from post-traumatic stress disorder afterwards. I'm still angry, and get frightened when I see people from my old class at the bus stop. Now I go to a different school, where guys have a lot more respect for women. :)

ELIZA

This is what I hate about people!!! When jerks do creepy things, nobody does anything, but everybody silently supports us. But as soon as WE retaliate, they become the victim!!! Like, seriously?! This one guy and his friend blocked me on Facebook and were commenting about what a slut I am on a photo of mine that they had taken in class. There were about 60 comments discussing stuff about me that were truly demeaning! And nobody stood up for me except two guys. The first guy did it only because he wanted to get in my pants. And the second guy gave me his password and I printed the photo along with the comments, submitted it to the principal and got their ass suspended for three sweet weeks. And then suddenly the entire class was calling me dangerous and saying that people should not even talk to me and beware. But you know what, Tina babe, we gotta stand up for ourselves and do what we gotta do. We owe it to us and to our self-esteem. As for the rest of the world, they can just go and fuck themselves.

MOXX

Just this past Friday, I went to the Yankees game with my fam-

ily. On the subway on the way there, there was a guy staring at me. My mom said, "You shouldn't wear that top if you're using public transportation." I felt so gross! It made me never want to wear that shirt again. And it wasn't even that low-cut or anything. I told her how gross I felt about that and she just did the "Oh well, it happens, it's not a big deal, boys will be boys" thing.

SUNSHINESHOEGAZE

Once I was in a park with my best friend, and this really ugly old guy was staring at us and yelling some stuff that wasn't nice to hear. We went to the park police—all of whom were male—and were told, "Well, you can only blame yourself for wearing such a short skirt. Besides, he did not do anything to you."

NOTREALLYCHRISTIAN

Not the worst but the most disturbing street harassment I've had was when I was in Italy, and while walking home from a friend's house at night (yes I know, I shouldn't have been by myself, but it was a five-minute walk) I was catcalled by POLICE-MEN IN THEIR POLICE CAR. How was I ever supposed to feel safe?!? My Italian friends don't understand why anyone would ever be offended ("but it's so flattering!") but I never felt flattered by the guys who followed me home at night, or randomly hit on me when I was in the supermarket.

CAROLITA

I get a lot of this, maybe because I'm old and should be grateful? It's what happened to me practi-

cally every day in my old neighborhood in New York. I stopped wearing dresses while I lived alone in that neighborhood, just because I felt too vulnerable. I noticed that none of the other women in my neighborhood wore dresses, either. How sad is it when a woman doesn't want to look pretty because she thinks it'll just get her harassed every time she goes out?

ROMANE

I wish I could be a boy and oblivious about it all. I wish I didn't feel so afraid that I can't even wear dresses anymore.

LELELIKEUKULELE

I hate that this is the way it is, that whenever I go downtown by myself I am constantly scanning the streets for any threatening-looking guys, and whenever someone so much as touches my arm I just about jump out of my skin. We shouldn't have to be afraid like that.

LOLR

I signed up just so that I could tell this story. Today I stopped in a parking lot to make a phone call like a good, law-abiding person. I parked, turned down my music, and took off my sunglasses, when a man came up and knocked on my window. I pretended to ignore him for a while but he kept knocking, so I rolled down the window a tiny bit just to hear him, and found myself the recipient of a stream of insults that went something like this: "YOU FUCKIN' 15-YEAR-OLD-LOOKIN' ASS WHAT ARE YOU DOIN' HERE YOU CAN'T DRIVE FUCK YOU YOU

FAGGOTS SHOULDN'T LIVE LOOK AT YOUR FAGGOT-ASS GLASSES WHO TOLD YOU YOU WERE AL-LOWED TO DO THAT FUCK YOU AND YOUR PUSSY ASS ONLY ROLL DOWN THE WINDOW A CRACK WHAT YOU SCARED OF FAGGOT." I was shocked and scared, but I wasn't going to let him know that, so I rolled up the window, turned my music back up, put the car into drive and hit the gas, spun around and laid on my horn for about 20 seconds while giving this guy the finger, and drove off. I still feel disgusted with myself though. I don't know what I did to deserve it; all I did was park my car.

PAT

When a guy comes up and says something to me, I LAUGH. I laugh as hard as I can. Because they are just trying to intimidate me. I laugh to show them that I think they're stupid, and I'm not afraid of them, and they will NOT win. And you know what? By the time I'm on my second burst of laughter, most of them have walked away, embarrassed or nervous. And then I forget about it. Because I didn't feel intimidated, and they didn't win. Try it. Laugh your freaking head off.

EXTRAFLAMEY

Having large breasts I am sadly accustomed to this. I've had the catcalls, the jeering, the jerking off, and the staring. If I can meet their eye I try and stare them down with the meanest glare I can muster. Most of them have backed right down. I really hate how this isn't made a bigger issue and is just chalked up to "men will be men."

KEAVY

I was harassed a lot in middle school for having short hair— I lived in a southern state, so I got a lot of homophobic nonsense tossed at me. I was prepared to deal with that kind of harassment, and had reported it to several teachers, and had moderately good results. Then, when I was in the seventh grade, a kid who I was uncomfortable around anyway (mostly because I had seen and heard him harassing other girls, but been too afraid to say anything) talked to me at a rehearsal for a show. He said things like "You cut your hair short, are you a dyke?" "Do you got blonde pussy hair?" "You shave your pussy hair?" It quickly went from harassment to assault when he stuck his hands up my skirt and pushed me up against a wall using his pelvis against my face. I never told my parents or any teachers about it because I felt like it was my fault, like I had been stupid for going into the hallway with him. He assaulted two other girls that year, and nobody did a damn thing about it. Nobody told any teachers or administrators; we all felt like it was our fault.

That was almost 10 years ago and I still wake up in the middle of the night thinking about it, still regret not reporting it, still fear being left alone with any male person who I have even a shadow of a doubt about. If the system actually dealt with this shit as HARASSMENT instead of "boys will be boys" bullshit, maybe every woman could live without fear of harassment/assault.

TORIRO

These stories are all horrible to read, but men don't limit themselves to calling attention to the desirability of a woman's body. I've been pretty overweight for most of my life and have been steadily chipping away at it for the past year. It was a huge accomplishment to hit the 85-pound-loss mark and to finally be considered "overweight" and not "obese" by my BMI. Riding high on the confidence of my accomplishment, I went for a run outside in my workout clothes (loose capris, two sports bras to keep the goods from jostling, and a T-shirt). Some guy yelled from his truck as he drove past me, "Keep running to the McDonald's, fatty!" It completely destroyed my self-esteem, and now I refuse to work out outside of my apartment complex's shitty gym, because I don't want other people to see me. Why do men feel they have the right to comment on women's bodies to their faces?

SCHALY

I've had two instances of public sexual assault, and been stalked and followed home more times than I can count. That's aside from the constant lewd comments and public displays of "self love" men give to themselves while watching me. It got so bad for me during my teenage years that it was one of a few factors that caused me to develop strong social anxiety and agoraphobia. Nowadays I don't leave my house because I'm afraid of strangers approaching me.

KATE B

I went to SlutWalk this past September, and I was NOT prepared for the immense number of creeps who were taking pictures of my tits. In retrospect, I'm not surprised, but I went into it all excited to have duct-taped my nipples and be all risqué and support the cause, and I was so freaked out by it that I cried. These guys were on the sides of the road but they also got in on the march, and when all the feminists were hugging each other afterwards they were there too, saying things like "Move your arms down to your sides, honey." All I wanted was a safe space.

KILLERTEETH

Why do (some) guys think it's OK to catcall and do all that other gross stuff to us ladies? Is it cultural?

KRISBA

Guys really don't understand. Even if we ladies took a day and decided to catcall vulgar things at men, they still wouldn't understand—because it'd be only a day, and we have to put up with it all of our lives.

BECKYR003

I wish every man on earth would read this article. I think a lot of them just don't realize how often this happens to women (except when they're the perpetrators, of course). Every woman I know (including myself) has at least one street-harassment story. The other night a creep followed me home shouting that I "couldn't dress that way and not be any fun." It was horrifying. Everyone should check out Hollaback!, an organization that aims to end street harassment.

JOHANN7

I'm willing to bet that most of the men who are not also part of the problem don't realize that this happens, or that it happens with the frequency it does, or possibly don't understand precisely how terrible it makes most women feel. I knew sexual harassment was an issue, but not really the extent or the myriad ways in which women are subjected to it on a daily basis. I think the avalanche of stories in posts and discussion threads like this is a good way to help men understand how much of a problem it is. It's not fair to expect (mostly) women to take the initiative to fix a problem with (mostly) men's behavior, and I'm so sorry you have to put up with this, but please keep speaking up about it online and in person. There's still a long way to go.

REIDMCC

I am a straight man. I find the type of harassment described in the posted conversation disgusting. What I'm surprised by is that, despite wholeheartedly rejecting this sort of behavior, in a sense I really don't comprehend. When I read articles like this which describe such extreme frequency of harassment, I find myself automatically thinking "Really? It happens that often?" It's not that I believe that any of these reports aren't true—it's just that the idea of the frequency that baffles me. The idea that I'm part of a group that is so often horrible is not something I like to believe. How can it be this bad? How can so many men do these things?

JUST SAMMTHING

I never would have expected to be "one of those clueless guys," but obviously I am. Most of my closest friends are girls; we tell everything and anything to each other. Maybe because I'm straight, harassment is the one topic they won't talk about with me, or maybe they have never experienced something like all the things described here before. I feel sorry for all of you to go through all of this and wish this would all stop.

NAOMI

Sadly, I think it becomes something we are used to. Unless it really affects you on a specific day, and I think you are more likely to share it with people who also have firsthand experience, like Jamia did to start the conversation above. Maybe we should tell guys more, but I think unfortunately the reaction isn't always as understanding as yours.

EMANON

Another boy here. This is so painful to read, and I wish I could avenge every single one of you. A message to all boys out there: never be a creep and never for-give them.

TANIA

I had an experience on the bus about a month ago that was violating and horrible and disgusting, but the worst part was how angry and on edge I felt about the whole thing in the weeks that followed. It was the most emotionally draining experience of my life. It temporarily turned me into this on-edge and pessimistic person, and THAT made me MORE angry, because I never thought of myself as somebody who could be semi-permanently scarred by one disgusting guy. I'm still coming to

terms with the whole thing, but all sexual harassment is about power, so I'm determined not to let it take hold of me anymore. It doesn't. Despite that guy's efforts, I live a happy life and feel more empowered and determined to speak out about this kind of BS than I did before. So next time instead of just getting off the bus as fast as possible I think I'll try out the ol' public shaming. It's good that this is being talked about. I don't really know what to do to change how things are, but this seems like a good step.

RANGERBAGEL

There's a street guy who hangs out on Shattuck Ave. in Berkeley who harasses and catcalls women. It's obvious he's doing it strictly for the pleasure of making women uncomfortable. Finally one day as I walked by he leered at my chest and said, "That's a nice shirt on you."

I lost it: "I'M NOT FLATTERED! LEAVE ME ALONE!"

"I WAS PAYING YOU A COMPLIMENT! SAY THANK YOU!"

"DON'T TELL ME WHAT TO DO. IN FACT, DON'T SAY ANYTHING TO ME EVER AGAIN!"

I pass by him at least three days a week. He hasn't said a word.

Ladies, I encourage you to scream at all harassers. It singles them out and scares them, which is what they wanted to do to you.

CLAIRE

A super creative thing that random guys like to scream at me is "Nice tits," because I rock my 32A's and they're being ironic, get it?! The last time it happened, I took a note from Tina Fey and yelled "Suck my dick!" while riding my bike down the street. Success.

MJADE97

There is an amazing class I took this year that opened my eyes called Impact: Self Defense for Women. We learn ways to defend ourselves, be it verbally towards people we know, or waking up with someone on top of you, trying to rape you. It makes me so much more comfortable and confident. It is the most empowering class in the world and I would recommend for everyone to take it.

YELL

I got a guy sent to jail for jerking off on the subway. True story. This is what you do. Stand up, point, and yell at the top of your lungs and don't stop until a cop comes. Follow the guy and keep yelling if you have to, and he will be arrested. People will get the cop for you. Nobody knows what to do, but if you yell, and tell people to get a cop, they very surely will. Don't let them get away with it. Don't run away from it. Stand up and yell, "This guy has his dick out! Hey, everybody, this guy right here has his dick out!" Keep yelling. IT WORKS. Also, juries love it. These harassers WANT you to be ashamed and run away. Don't give them what they want. They bank on women and girls being shame-able. Send them to jail.

JENNAF

Here are my own pointers, as someone who went through this, figured out some strategies, and then aged out of it (as Anaheed says, once you get old enough it usually stops):

♦ Cultivate a thousand-yard stare.
♦ Be ready to be loud and obnoxious in return—I found that once

I steeled myself for that, the harassment tended to happen less. I think the fact that I was ready to strike back was apparent.

♦ Go ahead and be loud and obnoxious if it happens (especially if it's in a public place).
♦ Whip out your cell phone and record anything that's happening.
♦ Speak out! I have made it a bit of a mission to get men to understand how damaging this sort of thing can be. It's so insidious and cumulative that sometimes it's not as obvious as we think it is. (That is, a catcall sort of thing by itself isn't necessarily that big of a deal—it's when it keeps happening day after day, week after week, month after month, that it really takes a toll.) It helps a lot when the nice guys help censure the jerks.

♦ And if you yourself see something happen to another girl, say something. I've got a menacing stare and look tougher than I am, and when I've seen something that looks like it might be a harassment situation I usually go over and say, "Everything OK here?" while glaring at the harasser. It's been pretty effective. I think a lot of people want to stay out of it, but that helps create an environment in which the jerks feel like they can get away with anything—and they often do.

MISSMADNESS

The worst EVER was I was working in a bookstore and this creep kept looming over me while I was restocking (in the children's fiction section, no less!). I tried to ignore him but looked up and he had his dick out and HE WAS MASTURBATING OVER

MY HEAD. I got up and casually found my manager (I didn't run because I wanted him to get caught) and we called the police. He left before they got there. Fucking AWFUL.

BUT, a few notes:

1. For you girls wondering if you should call the police, the answer is ALWAYS YES. Sexual harassment is scary, dangerous, and ILLEGAL, and the cops will come. Even if the creep is gone, you can still give a description, and that way when he harasses someone else, the cops have a record of him doing it more than once.

2. For you girls in school who say boys are grabbing you or making lewd comments, tell your teacher, your guidance counselor, tell SOMEONE. I'm in the education department, and when we find out about sexual harassment we are LEGALLY required to report it. This means the fuckface who keeps grabbing your ass can have a CRIMINAL record as a result. Also, we will try to make sure you're not on his bus/in classes with him, etc.

BHAUS

One time my friend and I were walking home in the wee hours of the morning having just left a zombie fest. We were in our best zombie punk clothes with really realistic makeup. These two guys walking towards us were like "Hey ladies" and seemed ready to harass us, but just then we stepped into the light. They saw our faces, said, "Oh shit!" and recoiled in horror. Heh heh. So what I'm saying is we should all wear zombie makeup all the time to teach those perverts a lesson. ♦

I KNOW WHERE MY FRIENDS ARE NOW

By Petra

Styling by Petra and Celia. Thanks to Celia, Georgia, Maya, Carmen, and Fraser for modeling.

Dear Diary

Excerpts from a weekly series on Rookie by four (real! live!) teenage girls.

September 7

NAOMI

My name is Naomi and I live in a little town on the outskirts of Birmingham, England. This has its good and bad connotations. One of the bad ones is that it's hard to find good magazines—I have to order *Lula* online. Another one is that I don't have what outsiders think of as a "British" accent.* No, I have a light Brummie accent. Not very noticeable to my ears, but it usually produces a response if I'm anywhere else in the country. I'll give you a little Wikipedia fact: "A study was conducted in 2008 where people were asked to grade the intelligence of a person based on their accent and the Brummie accent was ranked as the least intelligent accent. It even scored lower than being silent, an example of the stereotype attached to the Brummie accent." Oh, the joys of stereotypes.

Well, about where I live. We are right slap-bang in the middle of Britain, so unfortunately, we are furthest away from the sea. My town is so small that word gets around if on a given day the thorn-bush branches are sticking too far over the vicarage fence to the footpath behind. I live in that vicarage. Yes, my dad is a vicar—otherwise known as priest/minister. I'm not sure why, but it seems that people have a lot more interest in you when the vicar introduces you as his daughter.

It isn't a quaint English village. We still have a white-van man** honking at anybody in a skirt, which in my opinion means you are situated in an area with a dense enough population for there to be an urgent need for window cleaners, plumbers, and conservatory fitters. I remember being wolf-whistled in the summer by a window cleaner and then his coming to my house, so I had to hide under the bed. These are the lengths I go to to avoid being embarrassed.

To be honest I have pretty extreme anxiety, such that I don't really venture out very far from my house. Luckily, the internet has given me a connection to some things outside that restricted area. My first foray into the World Wide Web was Tumblr. I discov-

ered it about three years ago, when I was 14, and I am so thankful for all the music, books, film, art, politics, and feminism I have been exposed to there and have been able to soak up like a sponge. Plus the internet has given me this, my first "published" piece of writing, which feels like a big opportunity for a little insignificant person like me.

* *There is really no such thing as a "British accent"—little geography lesson, the UK consists of England, Wales, Scotland, and Northern Ireland, each with dozens of their own accents.*

** *Another Wikipedia definition: "'White van man' is a usually pejorative stereotype used in the United Kingdom to describe drivers of light commercial vehicles such as the Ford Transit. Such vehicles are commonly painted white in order to facilitate easy sign-writing on the panelled sides. The stereotype represents the drivers of such vehicles as having poor driving skills and/or an aggressive and inconsiderate manner. The stereotypical 'white van man' is often self-employed or the owner of a small business such as builder, carpenter, or plumber."*

September 7

DYLAN

I think the greatest expression of my self is a thought I had once while riding the bus through downtown L.A. one night. I was trying to decide which part of the day was my favorite. I love the night, I thought, when all the debauchery and fun of the world happens. But late afternoon feels so whole and comforting. And being out before 8:00 AM is always incredibly huge- and open-feeling. But also, the space between night and the next morning is like this magical purgatory when you feel like you're the only one alive, but fully alive. I couldn't decide which part of the day I loved best, and I realized that this must mean I just love all 24 hours, and that by this principle I just seriously love life.

It was a great realization.

September 7
KATHERINE

When the sixth grade started, I was still a sensible-underwear kind of girl. My Hanes accompanied me to after-school activities like chess club and book club, and I thoroughly enjoyed the security that only thick elastic bands and huge swaths of cotton can provide.

One afternoon that school year, my panties drawer was rocked.

I was lying on the floor of my bedroom, working on a school project, when my grandmother walked in. She said that she had a surprise for me, that it would be "our little secret." I was thrilled. A gift that had to be kept secret must be good. From behind her back my grandmother produced a tiny drawstring bag. I opened it slowly and pulled out what I thought was a piece of white tissue paper. "Do you like it?" she asked. I didn't answer because I had no idea what the hell it was. On closer inspection it revealed itself to be a tiny lace undergarment. A thong. My first piece of lingerie.

I wasn't shocked that my grandmother had randomly bought me a thong. If you talked to her for five minutes or even merely caught a whiff of her perfume—a scent named Poison—you wouldn't be surprised either. What really got me were her parting words: "Have fun." *Have fun?* What was that supposed to mean? Suspecting that the having of this fun could somehow lead to trouble with my parents, I stashed my new acquisition away in my underwear drawer for a year.

In my mind, this thong became something of a "new girl" in the drawer. One can only imagine how my other underthings reacted to her presence. Perhaps they were jealous of her floral lace pattern; maybe all of the high-rises dreamed of being just like her. Or maybe the other panties saw her as some kind of celebrity. A rock star. No matter how this thong got along with my other clothes, it would be about a year before I would work up enough nerve to "have fun."

Finally, one Friday in seventh grade, shortly after getting my braces removed, I woke up and put on the thong. I felt great. I felt sexy. I had a wedgie that I feared would have to be surgically removed. I went to first period with high expectations of fun-having and classmate-shocking. I went through all of my classes hoping for at least one "Something about you has changed, but I just can't put my finger on it," or maybe even a "Wow, Katherine, no panty lines today." But nothing happened. Nothing had changed. I realized that I was expecting to be treated differently based on the fact that I was wearing what I considered to be daring underwear. What had once felt cool and defiant now felt kind of silly. The thong went back into the drawer, along with my expectations.

September 14
KATHERINE

I caught myself starting to pray the other day and quickly stopped, surprised at my thoughts. I hadn't prayed in at least a year. Why did I do this? Why was I offering a prayer that I know no one will hear?

I used to pray all the time. I went to Sunday school every weekend, and I believed in God, most of the time. As a teenager I even attended several youth retreats organized by my church. They were usually held at campsites with funny names and always were near a lake. On these trips, I would sit around campfires with other Christian teens and confess my sins and beliefs to my peers. I'd even cry.

Eventually I started resenting Sunday school. There was this youth pastor there who really rubbed me the wrong way. One time on a mission trip I was standing by myself and he came up to me and said, "HEY LOOK! THE QUIET AWKWARD KID." I tried to be civil, but really I was thinking: *Thanks. I really love it when people point out my greatest insecurities in front of large groups of kids I want to think I'm at least somewhat cool.*

As I became more frustrated with the pastor and the whole youth group, I started to fight with my mother on Sunday mornings. I would beg to be able to stay home, and she would either win the fight and drag me along to church or lose and leave the house alone and upset. I started paying more attention in science class, and reading more on my own, and thinking about the fact that God's existence could not be proven. It started to bother me. The Sunday after I got my driver's license I drove to church, walked in the door, told my Sunday school teacher that I was really sorry but I just didn't believe anymore, and walked out.

So, now I'm in my senior year at a small Christian school in Nashville, and I'm required to take a class titled "Christian Dynamics." Being neither Christian nor dynamic, I'm not really sure how to go about this class. I disagree with most of what the teacher says, but I don't want to fight him all the time. But I also don't want to stay silent in our class discussions. There's this really sweet girl named Krista who sits behind me. One time in class she was talking about a girl who she met at camp one summer. She told us how the girl was an atheist and that every time she tried to tell this girl about God, the girl would just tune her out. She ended with the statement "I know where she's coming from, but at the same time, I just don't want her to go to Hell."

I don't buy into Christianity anymore. I can't. But the religion surrounds me every day. It's a part of the Bible Belt culture I live in, and it was a huge part of my youth. A majority of my friends believe in God, and my parents are attending church and Wednesday-night Bible studies more frequently. Most of my teachers start class with a prayer.

So I guess it's not really so weird that when I was super stressed about homework this week, I reflexively started to pray. The prayer was kind of like when you eat a burrito and burp up the flavor a few hours later. It was an aftertaste of who I used to be.

October 6
NAOMI

A lot of people are excited by the prospect that almost anything can happen. This thought makes me reach for the nearest blanket and climb under it.

I think almost my whole life I have been varying degrees of frightened, terrified, frustrated, and paralyzed by life itself. I spend a lot of the time dreaming the day away on things that will probably never happen, and some things that have a possibility of happening, but at the slightest notion that they will, I get the sudden urge to run as fast as possible in the opposite direction. Because I'm sure the reality is very different from the picture in my head. And obviously in my head I must be a completely different person, someone who doesn't get scared.

It's hard to differentiate between anxiety that is perfectly normal for a human being, anxiety that is a personality trait, and anxiety as a reflection of whatever situation I am in. Am I socially anxious naturally or because I have been more isolated ever since I started taking classes online instead of going to regular school? How much do I have to fight it and how much do I accept it? Can it ever really fundamentally change?

There are things I have adopted over the past few years to deal with other difficult things. It is a vicious circle. It's embarrassing and I don't want to be specific because, to be perfectly honest, I am ashamed. Because of my fears and anxieties, my life is very restricted. I can't go to school or parties or on independent excursions or take driving lessons, etc. Most of the time I just dream about having a fulfilled life, full of "normal" things. Sometimes I am very happy with what I've got. This week, I just wish I could expand my sphere, for my limits to be nonexistent. It makes me incredibly sad that in a world full of potentially beautiful experiences, my instinct is to hide and stick to my imagination.

November 9
DYLAN
I would not be surprised if every moment of this past week in my life came to theaters near you, because everything felt scripted and kind of stupidly romantic. Let me know if you want to buy the rights to my life to write the cutest screenplay ever, ALL ABOUT ME.

Last Thursday I met up with Sara, one of my best friends. We went to a rock show together, and guess who showed up? The long-haired boy I have a crush on. He and I made plans to see each other the next day, and then I ran to Sara's car to hide and giggle because I'm never going to grow up and aaaaah, Crush Boy!!

The next day I looked at the clock every other minute until I was finally out of class and free to meet up with him. It didn't matter, because when I got home around 8:30, he couldn't meet up until a few hours later because of band practice (OH MY GOD BAND PRACTICE). We eventually met at the extremely shady drive-in around the corner from me. I got a milkshake and we walked back to my house together.

At my place, I turned on my Christmas lights, worked on my milkshake, and watched him flip through my vinyl, talking about his favorite tracks on each record. Normally I can somewhat fluently engage in such conversations, especially when they're my own damn records. But I have such a dumb crush and I mostly just nodded and went "uhuh!" because I'm a baby who can't speak English when confronted with a Crushing Subject in Bedroom. We finally settled on top of my bed and talked about stuff we have in common, like how we are both the same age, and how unusual it is for us to

be hanging with people our own age. It took a few awkward silences for the inevitable to happen, but then we finally kissed.

He spent the night. I skipped my noon class. Every little thing he said or did during our time together was just, like, who does this in real life? Who is smart enough to be this cute? In the morning we traded off sharing favorite rarities on YouTube and random '60s garage tracks that I ripped off compilations, like a 21st century version of a high school crush mixtape. We didn't get out of bed until 4:00 PM. Neither of us wanted to let go, so we didn't.

November 16
NAOMI
If you live in the UK, I highly recommend you watch the TV series *Rev* (Thursdays, 9:00 PM, BBC2). Usually, on any drama or comedy, priests are comedic characters—blundering, out-of-touch white-haired men. But *Rev* gets it right. It shows vicars as they are. They smoke and drink and have doubts and swear and have to figure out how to balance their home life and their church life. They have irritating parishioners to please, and homeless people ringing the vicarage doorbell. I should know. My father is a vicar.

Most of the time, the fact that my dad is a priest is just another normal part of my life, like anyone's dad having a job. But there are certain ways in which it is really different.

For instance, we don't own our house. The church owns it. I used to worry that visiting friends would think we were rich because of its size—especially the size of our garden. Because the truth is that vicars do not get paid very well, especially for how much work they actually do. But at least we have a free house to live in!

Dad knows *everyone*, and everyone feels like they know Dad. Whenever I'm with him when people approach, I feel bypassed and a little awkward, standing there with nothing to say while apparently whatever these strangers are saying to Dad is of the utmost importance. It can be frustrating to watch these interactions, because these people don't *really* know him. They don't live with him day in and day out. So many people pull his attention and energy in so many different directions with so many different demands. They don't realize how hard it is for him to please them all. The church can occasionally attract strange people—I suppose it's good that it accepts everyone for what they are. Sometimes, though, it seems like accepting everyone is impossible, and I step back and wonder at how Dad can be such a good, wise, humble man.

It's not surprising that everyone wants a piece of my dad. Another name for priest is *preacher*, but my father never really preaches, you know? He isn't patronizing. He doesn't use his authority to control people. He is invariably kind and considerate. He never turns anyone away. For some people, he is their only hope. He manages to balance all these people that invest so much in him, and he earns their trust. He is very good at his job.

The freedom that my parents give me is something I try not to take for granted. I've been able to shape my ideas and spiritual identity on my own terms. I've never been forced into anything. We are a liberal family primarily—pro-choice, in favour of gay and female priests, not denying the fact of evolution. I am not forced to go to church on Sunday. We rarely say grace before meals.

I'm a teenager, so I haven't had time to figure everything out just yet, while my mind is already full to bursting. My relationship with spirituality is fluid, changing and developing from one day to the next. I like my relationship with God the way it is—personal, almost private. My father respects that and lets me be. I am pretty sure God's all right with it, too.

There are people at our church who understand the pressure that my father is under, and thank goodness for them. Church might not be full of saints or people who would agree with my interpretation of the Bible, but there are a lot of fundamentally good people who mean well and have a lot of love. But my dad still trumps the lot of them.

December 14
NAOMI
Being ill gave me the ability to check out of life for a while, which I felt I needed to do. But now I am trying to check back in. I am starting simple, doing things that most people take for granted, like going to the dentist and getting my hair cut.

When all of the bad stuff hit me, it was my fundamental instinct to not be involved with life, because I thought that would be easier. I took a year off from everything—I stopped going to school completely, and stopped going out almost at all. I thought hibernating like this would help me figure things out, but it didn't really get me anywhere. In fact I feel like I dug myself in a little too deep. Sometimes I think it would have been easier in the long run if I had stayed in school, stayed the course, taken my A-level exams, and carried on into the next year. But I didn't. Right then I couldn't cope with it. I felt like I was at the edge of a precipice… and I took a step back.

Some good news this week is I am able to sit my exams in June at school as an "outside student." I'd be lying if I didn't admit that it is a terrifying thought. All my memories of those paint-peeling classrooms and carpeted halls come to the surface…it will be odd to return to a place that I thought I had left behind. My feelings are so jumbled up over the whole silly concept of what is essentially a building (and what it contains).

I've been studying so hard over the past couple of weeks, and I've been so tired at the end of every day. I have become unused to that feeling. I know all of this is progress, but it's nerve-racking. The other week I had a mini-breakdown (hiding in bed and sobbing) and decided I wouldn't do my exams after all. But little breakdowns are actually a good sign for me—they're how I get out all my heightened emotions so I can move on. They're a sign that I'm taking something seriously.

That feeling, of being serious about something, reminded me a little bit of the self I was when I was still going to school—tinged with hope along with the anxiety. I get nostalgic about that old me occasionally, but who doesn't? All the time you are changing, and that means leaving good things behind as well as bad.

Something else happened recently. You know when you see a family member or friend and immediately your instinct is to say "I love you" out loud? The other day I looked in the mirror and had that instinct. I haven't had it again since, but still, I paused, looked myself in the eyes and said it. And I meant it.

January 4
DYLAN
Sometimes I hate myself for feeling a certain way. Like: *God, I'm so frustrated that I'm still mad at so-and-so for flaking out on plans.* Or: *I hate myself for hating the way I look today.* Clearly, that pattern doesn't get me anywhere; it just gives me another negative emotion to deal with on top of the original one. So 2012 is all about getting over that, and not apologizing to anyone about the way I feel! Because otherwise I will die alone in a beige land of numbness because I was too embarrassed to acknowledge what it's like to be a sentient being. But, there's a problem. Right now I think I do owe the world, and specific people contained therein, an apology for my feelings, or lack thereof.

My mom's dad died last week, a few days after Christmas. He was 94, and is the perfect example of the live-every-day-like-it's-your-last ethos. He was just *loud*. Always belting Sinatra songs, making old-man hurrumphs when he wanted attention, and punctuating every other moment with proclamations of gratitude about how awesome his life was. When he would visit us every Thanksgiving in Seattle, I'd take him to my all-girls Catholic school for a tour, and he would hit on the nuns and the underage students alike. He kissed a lot of my friends' hands. Everywhere he went, he made a show of himself and a friend of any stranger. He was a social fixture in Kansas City, where he lived most of his life and raised my mom and her sisters. We all called him Papa, and he was a pretty dope grandfather, who is now gone.

Papa was put in hospice care right before Christmas; we knew it was coming. My mom and I talked to (well, at) him on the phone an hour before he died. His death happened the day before my second annual After Christmas Blues Party, an idea I stole directly from him. He used to have these big open houses every year after Christmas (which now my mom says were her idea—all right, Mom), which of course were torture for my cousins and me when we were younger—they were essentially conventions for local adults seeking to pinch our cheeks. But now that I'm older, wiser, and obviously more awesome, I thought it was a great idea to appropriate, and given my mom's somewhat recent approval about my general party habits, why not have it at her classy little townhouse in the middle of the city? The party was quite a success, with 50 buddies stopping by to flick cigarette butts into my yard and accidentally drink my mom's champagne from the fridge. It also felt like a perfect way for me to honor Papa's memory. I'm not into the whole all-black-wearing mourning tradition; I'd rather celebrate life. And considering that Papa died in basically the ideal way—after a long, happy life, in his sleep, surrounded by loved ones—it didn't seem appropriate to be all morose about it.

But: I feel like I'm being less than honest. Like I'm rationalizing my insensitivity and disguising it as a well-considered joie de vivre and a superior take on death and mourning. I think my outlook of

"Oh, he was really old, he had a great life, IT'S ALL OK" might be a strategy I've adopted to keep from feeling sad. And now I feel guilty for not being sad.

My mom, for the first few days after Papa's death, would have little random bursts of crying. I'm pretty terrible at comforting people (getting better with my peers, but comforting people older than me feels really awkward…why?), so I'd just nod my head and be like, "Yeah, Mom…it's sad." Then she asked me if I ever even felt like crying. Shit! I should be crying!

What's really going on is that I'm distracted. I'm unbreakably obsessed about returning to California after winter break. How selfish do I sound right now? I can't help it, and I'm sorry about it. I left my sense of life back at college, and it's all I can think about. Not to mention that my Crush Boy is going to be back in town upon my return, and thoughts of seeing him have taken up a lot of brain space. God, am I really so selfish that thoughts of a cute long-haired boy override my sadness over the *death of my grandfather*?

I know I'll be sad at the funeral, when I'm immersed in the moment of it. But for now I can't stop wanting to be back in MY own apartment, doing MY own things. My feelings distribution is jacked. I wish I could feel the feelings that this moment in my life is calling for. But all I can think about is my apartment, my friends that I miss, the feeling I get when I wake up and have the entire day open to me and no one else. And I'm so, so sorry.

February 8
NAOMI
I've been thinking and trying to figure out how to express what has happened to me this week; it feels like it has contained more than seven days' worth of experiences. It's been a little overwhelming. Let me start here: as you might have gathered, if you've been reading my diary these past five months, I've been dealing, for a long time, with a lot of fears and restrictions. It's been hard for me to venture very far from my house. New experiences tend to frighten me. I get anxious easily; I fall into depressions with ease.

Well, Friday I actually went to two places that I hadn't been to for over a year! They were just two stores, and I know that to most people that sounds like no big deal at ALL, but for someone like me, it was really hard. I have agoraphobia, even though I've been reluctant to say so out loud, at least here on Rookie, because I get embarrassed about it. Staying close to home was, for a long time, a coping method to deal with my anxiety. I've been breaking myself of that habit slowly over the past year, with walks around my neighborhood and to the library and to my best friend's house, and volunteering in the church office, answering the phones and things.

I have a lot more to say about this and will someday, but I feel like I want to wait until it's more definitely behind me, when my feeling so trapped is a distant memory. Plus, like I said, I'm still a little embarrassed and ashamed about it. I'm also *scared*. Scared of life! But I think fear is a sign that something's changing, and that's good.

February 15
NAOMI
For so long I've been living with this thing. This thing that was casually described as "Naomi finds it hard to go out." I don't know why this was the case. I don't know why it kept getting worse, or why it started to get better. Or how this thing has hindered me, and in some ways helped me.

It was hard for me to do things that I was not comfortable with. That's the definition of comfort, isn't it? Things that are not hard to do. Thinking about going to school, or even just riding in a car, started to give me panic attacks. Then I started being anxious about the panic attacks themselves—a vicious cycle that could only be avoided by not considering leaving home in the first place. So I stopped considering it.

Last year was the unhappiest period of my life—it's when I really saw clearly all of my limitations, how deep the hole was that I had dug myself into. But I was so tired. Too tired and lacking in motivation to do anything to change my situation. I gave up before I really did anything at all.

The less you do anything, the harder it gets to do. Ultimately, it was easier to stop fighting my urge to stay home all the time. But then, one day, that began to change. I regrouped, and decided that instead of trying to *act* differently, I would first focus on *feeling* better. I worked on alleviating my depression before I worked on leaving the house. Then when I did leave, I didn't try to go far. I took small walks right near the vicarage, then I started going to the nearby library, and those things felt good, and safe, and I stuck with those for a long time before venturing farther.

In some ways agoraphobia is just another destructive habit, like smoking, or cutting, or procrastinating. You know you are not helping yourself by staying home again, but you do it anyway. You know that you are making everything harder for yourself, but that doesn't matter, because right now you are choosing instant gratification, where the anxiety decreases and you think that makes it the right decision. And that is what is important. You are blinded to most other things.

I don't think I am blinded anymore. I think I actually want to go places. I don't want to miss out any longer. I don't want to hate myself every time I realize I can't go somewhere. I don't want to let down the people I love anymore. I think there is only so long you can live with something like that. It's a continuing thing, though, with no clear beginning or end.

March 7
KATHERINE
In an ideal world, farting would be the most OK thing ever. It would not have to be 100 percent socially acceptable, as I believe that teenage-boy farts are gross and sloppy (double standard, I know), but I do think that if someone lets one slip at school or work, everyone should give that person a pass. For a second I sounded altruistic, didn't I? However, I assure you that my motives are super selfish. If farts were no big deal, I would have someone to call when I needed advice and something to do each Saturday night.

When I was in second grade, I changed schools. In the first week at my new school, I farted in class. Loudly. Embarrassingly. Painfully so. There was no smell, but I can assure you, the sound alone bought me a ticket to a solo lunch table seat for the next few years. I would eventually find friends in chess club and book club and the girls who collected weird rocks on the playground instead of playing house or four square, but I would identify as an outsider throughout my middle school years. I started out at that school as the girl who farted and, as a result, became the girl without many friends. One fart robbed me of the opportunity to meet new people and find a group.

I began seventh grade at my current school with no self-confidence. I avoided talking to people. I dressed poorly. I barely spoke in class, and was hostile to those I perceived as too popular or too pretty. Because I acted this way in junior high, I had few friends as I started high school. And now, even though I talk to many of my peers, I believe that my social history and loner mindset have led me to alienate myself.

You know when you accidentally overhear someone talk about their weekend plans and they end up inviting you? I always turn them down. And when prom or a school dance comes up, I struggle to decide whether to go, and with whom. I don't want to be too imposing. I tell myself that I have no friends. And I know that it's my fault for not accepting what I suspect is a pity invite, or just going ahead and asking to be in a group for a dance. I could even call someone up and ask said person to hang out. BUT I DON'T BECAUSE I'M A TOTAL IDIOT AND BECAUSE OF THAT DAMNED FART.

FARTS AND SUBSEQUENT FART-SHAMING RUIN LIVES. Either super-genius scientists need to eliminate this phenomenon altogether (even though farting is really fun and cathartic), or people need to get over the idea that farts are gross. IF I ever decide to have kids, I will teach them not to judge anyone based on one fart, nor to let one of their own farts become an enemy.

But it can't just stop there. EVERYONE should know that farts are just a bodily function that mean YOUR COLON IS FUNCTIONING. When I stop being the laziest person ever, I'm going to start an anti-fart-shaming activist group that will change the way our culture looks at the act forever.

Tell your friends. Tell your family. Farting is OK. FARTACUS HAS SPOKEN.

March 14
DYLAN
My life in gentrification nation has been a formative experience. From moving into a house with my mom in a historically black, quickly transitioning neighborhood in Seattle back in high school, to now living with my friends in a notoriously sketchy section of Oakland, I've experienced two areas of two different cities that are in the midst of socioeconomic transition. It's obvious that I'm a part of it because I'm new here, and white, and I come from a middle-class family, and I think things like *I'm so happy my neighbors put the petunia planters here. I hope it will discourage the discarding of hypodermic needles!*

There's a lot of social complexity in neighborhoods undergoing gentrification, which are often characterized by fascinating but awkward phases of tension between the lifelong residents and the people (such as me) who move in and, over time, drive rental costs up and the old residents out, altering the area's demographic.

This is a BIG can of worms to open, but it's a huge part of my adolescent experience, and speaks to how comfortable I feel in places that Girls Like Me (blondish, occasionally dressed like a kindergarten teacher) historically might not. But I worry I may have become too comfortable walking by myself late at night, too accustomed to daily life in somewhat questionable neighborhoods. Not that there was much I could do to change the situation I'm about to describe, but I guess that it was a wake-up call not to take my safety for granted.

At least a couple of times a week, I take the bus back from campus at night, then walk eight blocks through downtown Oakland to my apartment. I walk swiftly, with my pepper spray–equipped key ring in hand and my cell phone in my pocket, taking only busy, well-lit streets. Last week, on Monday, I was only three blocks from home when a man stormed up to me, got in my face, and called me a "white bitch." I tried to slip past him, responding, "Yep, you're right." Street harassment is common in every major city. Not reacting has worked for me in situations like this thus far.

But as I tried to keep moving, the guy chest-bumped me and repeated his insult. As I fiddled with the switch on my pocket spray, I yelled, "Get OUT of my FACE!" I was almost done getting the safety switch off the thing when he did it again, pushing me backwards. Gathering all of my strength, I looked into his bloodshot eyes and told him to "get the FUCK off of me." But I wasn't quick enough, because he socked me in my left eye. It made me dizzy, though I remember hearing the group of people he was with collectively gasp in protest as he pushed me to the ground, where I fell on my right arm underneath the brightest street lamp on the block. I was in adrenalized-survival mode, struggling aggressively. I was feeling a mix of shock and the most extreme level of anger I have ever felt in my life. But what could I do? I protected my head to the best of my ability, but that left my back and neck exposed. He kicked me in the face and the back of the neck four or five times before one of his companions pulled him off of me. They got into a car and sped around the corner, but he walked away on foot. I regained my vision and fuzzily focused in on my Mace, aimlessly spraying it in the air like it was Febreze. I screamed vengeful thoughts at him as he walked away, making sure he knew that there's a special place in hell for people who randomly beat up girls. I vaguely remember threatening to make his eyes bleed.

I looked around the block and saw one dazed face, and I realized that my only witness appeared to be totally cracked out. No one was at the window of the drive-through across the street, nor the gas station on the next corner, so I called my roommate Leah and had her open the door for me as I stormed home, still on the phone with her, still screaming revenge at the attacker.

All of my neighbors in our complex came upstairs to help me clean up the cuts along my earlobe, scalp, knee, and elbows as I cried in a few bursts. They checked to see if the bleeding on my scalp would need stitches, and if I had a concussion. Fortunately, I didn't have to go to the hospital. They called the police. When they hadn't shown up after three hours of waiting, I gave up and tried to go to sleep. It was 3:00 AM. The next day I skipped my first class, but woke up early anyway to call my mom. My neighbors made me kumquat biscuits and visited periodically.

I was dizzy for much of the next week, and it was hard to write or hold a thought for a few days. Having people in my classes ask me about my developing black eye was helpful at first, because talking about it made me less anxious. Otherwise I would get too in-my-own-head, and forget to put the incident in perspective: my body was OK, save for the scratch on my cornea. I sort of pride myself on being the kind of person who can take things in stride. I told myself, *Let's be real. This stuff happens to people. It is a thing that happened to you that will not change your life.* But, as I continued to take public transportation alone at night, I'd get uncontrollably anxious. My favorite activity—drinking with friends—made me more depressed than happy.

Now I'm feeling OK again, and I'm waiting for my second chiropractic appointment and a meeting with a school counselor next week. I've mostly received comforting responses from the people in my life, but a couple of them suggested that I leave the area. Oh sure, I'll go pay twice as much to live in San Francisco, which I love half as much. Some kids I know who live deeper in the hood viewed it as a rite of passage. Other people, such as my dad, told me to do something differently next time, or just avoid walking at night, because that is *so possible.* (Yeah, I should've pulled out the pepper spray sooner, and next time I go from peacefully walking home to bleeding on the ground in under 10 seconds, I'll try to remember that!)

Those responses have driven me nuts. It's true, if I lived in a place that wasn't experiencing growing pains, this wouldn't be an everyday risk. It's also true that my presence in Oakland is part of the mechanism of change. Gentrification is personal and political, and it's associated with plenty of polarizing effects, both positive and negative. There's only one thing I know for sure: there is no pure and perfect truth for the questions that arise regarding urban neighborhoods in transition. My incident does not define my experience of living here. The area between right and wrong, that's where you can find me, loving my home and trying my best to live my magical life.

March 28
RUBY B.

Sometimes there are less-than-ordinary moments in life in which, on paper, nothing MAJOR happens, and yet we can never forget them. Rare, singular moments that we share with our loved ones. These are the moments that make us think, *Man, my life would be an awesome sitcom.*

Last week was spring break at my school, so my little sister, Celia, and I headed to my grandparents' house. My aunt and uncle and their two babies came along. With the addition of two lazy excuses for obese dogs and one cat that people tend to fight over, it

was an interesting few days. One of those Special Moments happened over dinner at an Italian place in North Carolina.

Ryan is my mother's brother. He's a chef, with hair almost down to his shoulders. My grandmother, Nonny, says he's lost weight since we last saw him. He finds everyone amazing and likes to make fun of his parents.

Liz is Ryan's wife. She rolls her eyes. A lot. I like Liz.

Jack is the baby that's just old enough to toddle around and say some words. He is delightful but attached to me like glue. I woke up every morning to "WUBY! WUBY!" and little sausage hands grabbing my foot. Lilah is Jack's newborn sister.

Nonny is an imposing woman with a loud Rhode Island accent and feathered hair. She says *cah* instead of *car.* She wears purplish eyeliner, brown mascara, and perfume, and she complains a lot. She likes things to be neat and fancy. She owns khaki nail polish. Babies love her, and she *really* loves for babies to love her. She likes them to learn her name before other words.

Papa is Nonny's husband. He gets angry about wars that happened over 40 years ago and Communism, as well as DVD stores. His favorite movie is *Little Miss Sunshine,* and he won't listen to anyone who says it should not be shown to small children. Someone at Panera Bread once got his order wrong and he never went to another Panera again. He runs marathons and tells us how sometimes he pees blood after he runs. He has an indifferent relationship with the cat.

Celia likes to tattle, talk about my mother's texting habits, and gossip. She watches courtroom shows with the two slobby/evil/lazy/boring dogs. She is convinced that Jack likes her more than he likes me, despite his crying whenever someone pries him from my grasp. She shows off her flexibility whenever possible by falling into a split in unexpected situations.

While deciding where to go for dinner, Nonny and Papa said anywhere would be fine, but then rejected every option presented except for the Italian restaurant, so that's where we went.

When we arrived at the restaurant, Jack screamed at the top of his lungs. He then laughed when he saw everyone's alarmed faces, and then screamed some more. Lilah began to cry, and Celia started whining about something or other. Nonny tried to yell to me as Jack tried to bolt out the door, and I called after him. We were placed in a little corner next to the kitchen, under some stairs.

The meal began with my sister and me being picky vegetarians and everyone else growing annoyed, followed by Jack's dumping Celia's water all over him and me. "COLD! COLD!" he shrieked, and Celia stuffed a napkin into his wet onesie. Nonny made a comment about how someone needed to go over and control him, while doing nothing (she likes to sit), and Liz gave Ryan a knowing look (and rolled her eyes). The exasperated waiter scowled as he mopped the water up with a towel, telling us it was no problem at all.

Then, bread and olive oil arrived on our table. Jack grabbed for them, got hold of a plate instead, and threw it on the floor. I handed him a piece of bread, and he threw that, too. When I wouldn't give him any more, he started squealing, so I turned away. "WUBY! WUBY!"

"Look how smart he is," said Liz. "Where are your eyes?" Jack pointed to his eyes. "Where is your nose?" Jack pointed to his nose. "Where are your boobies?" Jack pounded on his chest like an ape. Everyone laughed. "Jack, do you have a wiener? Where's Jack's wiener?" My family loves to talk about nether regions in public.

Dinner finally arrived. We had ordered the "family-style special," which meant that we got four big salads, pastas, and desserts to share. Celia's chair slipped backwards and hit the wall, Jack shrieked, my sister cried. Nonny snapped at Celia for making noise as Jack laughed and held up the empty bottle of olive oil, whose contents he had just poured all over the floor. Papa got angry that no one had prevented the spill. Celia got angry and cried over Nonny's insensitivity, and Ryan backed her up while Nonny pleaded that she didn't even know what was going on.

"What dessert should we order?" asked Liz.

"Anything but the tiramisu. I hate tiramisu," said Nonny.

"We'll have the tiramisu, please," Ryan told the waiter. Papa laughed.

Getting up, I slipped on the spilled olive oil and brought down a plate with me. Jack threw his own plate down too, and Liz removed Lilah from the scene.

All in all, it was a pretty good day, and even though nothing really exciting or funny happened, it made me realize that I'm part of *one of those families*. I feel really lucky to be part of something that's not dysfunctional enough to be really sad, but not proper enough to be functional.

That moment at the dinner table was a long one. It lasted over an hour, in fact. So maybe it didn't count as a moment, but whatever.

April 11
RUBY B.

Last Wednesday morning, as usual, I went to my favorite bathroom. It's right between the entrance of the school and the hall that leads to the main classrooms, so I can make sure I didn't line just one eye or put my shirt on backwards before I walk into class.

Then, in an open stall across the bathroom, I saw my name. "Ruby?" it said. I had no idea what it meant, but it pissed me off, so I started trying to get it off, but it was in permanent marker. Grr.

Later that day I pulled my friend into the bathroom to show her the "Ruby?" and ask if she knew what it meant. There was one thing I had missed before: it said "BURN WALL" above it in red. Three people had made their "burns" already since I got to school: *TOTAL FREAK. Emo. Secret slut. Weird.* I wasn't the only name there, but mine had the most (and meanest) comments.

I tried to make myself believe that all of the comments were probably from one mean girl who was having a bad day (and carried three different pens). But they probably weren't. Maybe that's what people think of me. I'm weird, a freak, an emo…and a "secret slut," whatever that means. "Aw, that's so mean!" said my friend, and she took a picture of the wall with her cell phone. I told her I didn't care and that was the end of it.

Until Friday.

Our school is Quaker. A couple days a week we all have Quaker meetings in the Meeting House, where we basically just sit in si-

lence for 40 minutes. If someone has something important to say during that time, they stand up and say it. Then the silence continues. Most kids consider this a boring time. I love it, even though I'm not Quaker. It lets me think. Not necessarily about God, but about everything in my life. It's a nice break from the world.

The next meeting we had was very quiet. Nobody shuffled around or coughed or got up to go to the bathroom. Everyone was waiting for something. Everyone was just waiting.

I felt the pressure build, pushing down on me, forcing me further into my bench. I had spoken in a meeting only once, and it was a generic comment about how wonderful my education is during Thanksgiving, and a bunch of other people had gone before and after me. I didn't want to say anything. I didn't want anyone to notice me.

The eerie silence continued until I couldn't wait anymore. I stood up. Every head turned, much more noisily than I would have liked. I just stood there for a second, and then I cleared my throat. All eyes were on me.

"I noticed something on the bathroom wall this week." I heard a few muffled *oh*s. They weren't the eye-rolling kind, though. I continued my speech.

I don't know exactly what I said. I don't know if I got really into it and started yelling or moving around, and I don't know if I started to cry or laugh or if I did nothing. I hope I didn't swear, but I can't be sure. The whole thing was a three-minute blur, and it felt amazing. Everyone was listening to me! The girls who pushed passt me in the halls listened, the boys who made fun of my clothes listened, my friends who I didn't really connect with before listened, and the other people who were on the burn wall just *listened* as I talked.

I said my closing line, and then paused to breathe and take in what had just happened. I looked around, and sat. For a moment, everything was quiet.

Then, out of nowhere, like something falling onto concrete, I heard applause. In a Quaker meeting. I had made people clap where they weren't allowed to! I didn't know what to think, because I hadn't thought.

It was what I needed. I let myself be vulnerable, and nothing bad happened. A feeling came over me that I can only describe as *healing*.

May 16
RUBY B.

It was a perfect day outside on Friday at my mom's funeral. It was about 70 degrees out, with a gentle breeze and not a cloud in the sky.

My grandmother had taken me shopping at the mall for a black dress, because the only one I owned was a party dress. We got the first one I tried on. It was simple black lace, shaped like a big T-shirt. I'd put a plain black cardigan over it. I will never wear it again, probably, so I didn't care that it wasn't really my style.

When we got to the funeral home, we were ushered into a small "family room." My grandmother was using my mom's old cell phone case on her own iPhone, and my dad politely asked her to take it off. He said he didn't mind her having it, but it was hurting him to see it. She quickly put it away and we were all silent for a long time. In the room were my mother's parents; her brother, his wife, and their baby; my father; and my brother and sister.

People came in and hugged us or shook our hands in a line. There were about 300 people. A bunch were from my school. Some of the kids who came weren't even my friends, and some were usually just plain snotty to me. A teacher later informed me that they were just there for the drama.

I was smothered by school faculty, distant cousins, family friends, my mom's college friends whom I had never met, and people I had never even heard of but who knew me. It was just weird. A bunch of people skipped over my little brother in the hug/handshake/ "sorry for your loss" line. This made me angry. I let it go, and I think he did too. We were soon all herded into the main room, with long wooden benches that went back for miles and miles. We came in last and sat in the front row.

My dad gave his speech. It was really beautiful and she would have liked it. I know he got a lot of compliments for it, and rightfully so. It was funny, too, which she would have liked even more. He talked about how they had met and what she meant to him. A few people cried. I didn't because I don't think I could have if I tried. I just couldn't cry anymore after doing so much of it for the past week or so.

We moved out of the funeral home after a prayer (just one, because she was agnostic) and a few more speeches. Everyone drove to the cemetery. I tapped the casket twice with two fingers, like I always do to the door when I'm getting on a plane. I don't know why I did. I think it was a goodbye.

It's a Jewish tradition for everyone to bury the casket in turns, starting with the immediate family, and to put the first shovel of dirt in upside-down because it's more difficult and demonstrates reluctance. My dad put in one upside-down shovel and two regular ones. I did one of each. Then everyone else came.

It was a beautiful day, but she would have been freezing. She was always cold.

May 30
RUBY B.
My mom once told me to write a heavy diary one week, a lighter one the next, then one heavy one, and so on. She said that way people would know I could write but wouldn't feel stressed reading my stuff. I wanted to do this, but I'm finding it really difficult to think about anything light right now.

I feel like I should never take anything for granted again. I feel angry because I feel I *should* have been able to take her life for granted. Everyone should be *granted* their parents, and other important things. If I feel that it should just be a given that everyone needs fresh water, of course I will take it for granted, and be even more disturbed when I find not everyone can. Is this optimism? Is it anything?

If that is optimism, I can no longer be optimistic. My world is half empty. God, that sounds stupid. She would say it sounds

cheesy, cliché. I don't really feel bad for myself, I just feel extremely shitty, and I think that's reasonable, which makes me feel selfish. I'm supposed to think that I deserve this. But nobody deserves to have a parent die when they're 14, and I'm somebody. Or am I supposed to have horribly low self-esteem? Am I supposed to be nobody?

I dyed my hair dark brown. I like it (my sister says it looks weird, and surprisingly my dad says it looks nice). My mom will never see it. That feels so weird, and I feel like it should be sacrilegious to change anything now. Pretend it's all the same, don't rearrange the furniture, don't put up a new picture in the living room, or we're doing it behind her back.

I have always been extremely logical. Maybe not in my actions, but in my head. The only exception is with ghosts—such a scary idea for me. It seems to kind of make sense but not *really*, like psychics. In sixth grade I was deathly afraid (ha) of ghosts for some reason; I couldn't look in mirrors or down hallways. I was afraid to open my eyes at night; there were times when I was afraid of closing my eyes in case I'd see one inside my head (those were the worst). I was also afraid of dangling my feet off of beds because that's supposed to summon them or something. Now I sleep with my feet off the bed, I stare into mirrors at night, I walk down hallways when I'm alone, and I never see anything.

Is it going to be like this forever? I know I won't ever wrap my head around why this had to happen. But will I always wonder? ◈

JUST Wondering

You've got questions, we've got (totally subjective) answers.

Do you really think that sex sells, and why? —María, Barranquilla, Colombia

Dear María,

You know what? I do think sex sells. I think romance sells and I think "love" sells too. But who's buying?

Everyone wants to believe they can buy a fantasy, and certain advertisers would like us to believe we can buy it from them, but we can't, because it's a big fat capitalist lie! Don't believe it, María!

In the end, corporations make a lot of money while the rest of us are stuck with a bunch of unrealistic ideals. Sex is not Sookie and Bill in the middle of a misty forest under the full moon sucking each other's blood. It's not that nervous chick and the hot dude from *Twilight* either. It's not (usually) silk sheets and fine wine, and it normally doesn't happen on the beach (rolling around in the sand is not ideal for sex).

That being said, I love *True Blood* and watch it weekly. I love all kinds of rom-coms and sexy things. I like fantasy. It's fun. But it's just that. I have to make sure I remember that it's not real life.

I started smoking cigarettes because I thought it looked cool (sex). I wanted the popular jock to fall in love with me, the weirdo, in high school, because that's what happened in *Pretty in Pink* (romance). Now I just smoke cigarettes and can't quit and spend $13 on a pack and might die from them. When I made eye contact with the popular jock in high school he laughed in my face. The good news is that even though "sex sells," the real-life, non-fantastical version of it is better. Yes, it makes us nervous and awkward, wear the wrong things, sweat too much. That's the real feeling of something that no one can buy or sell.

Real romance doesn't take place under silk sheets while you're listening to R. Kelly or whatever. Real romance is when maybe you accidentally spill your water all over the sheets and feel stupid. It happens when you trip over your words, or a crack in the sidewalk, and you blush and feel embarrassed and vulnerable and the guy or girl you like still likes you anyway. Actually, it makes them want to kiss you more. Then you feel crazy rushing feelings in the pit of your stomach that you don't know how to explain. That feeling is actually butterflies having sex with other butterflies; it's a scientific fact. So let me ask you this: do you think that's something you can buy? I hope that answers your question.

xx Lesley

♦ ◊ ♦

How do you kiss? What are tongues supposed to do? —Anonymous

The lean-in should be at an angle, but it doesn't matter which way you tilt your head. (Eventually you'll alternate—try switching directions when it's time to take a breath.) Coming in straight on, at least at first, makes it too easy to bonk noses or clash teeth. These run-ins are bound to happen anyway, but just giggle and keep going. That part doesn't usually make the movies, but in real life it might lighten the mood. Just kiss your partner on the cheek, smile and start again.

Once the lips actually touch, it's like dancing, but not like dancing for a normal person—dancing like you were born knowing how to dance and were already super good at it. Fit your lips together like Tetris blocks, every which way, puckering your lips and releasing until you find a rhythm. If one way doesn't work, just adjust. No one is going to take kissing privileges away from you, and since they've already agreed to kiss you, your special friend is bound to be understanding. You get unlimited tries!

Tongues! Ew. (But also, wow!) Don't lead with your tongue, because you're not trying to lick their face. But once your lips are waltzing together, you can gradually open your mouth wider to indicate it might be time for your tongues to touch. If you've made it this far: CONGRATULATIONS, you're making out. Now, with your tongue, you can cross the threshold of your own chompers. Feel free to go slow at first to keep your spit in control—there's plenty of time and no one likes a slobberer. BUT! The only thing worse than a Too-Much-Tonguer is a Total-Tongue-Hider. Making out with no tongue is like eating a Blow Pop but never getting to the gum: it's still a lollipop, so it's pretty good, but you probably want the soft inside part, too. Maybe you're like a Sour Apple (tons of tongue flavor) but your partner is more of a Cherry (less out-there, just the basics). The only way to know is to try. Flavors can mix! Present them with yours and if they greet you back, keep sharing. You can graze or wrestle, even gently bite or pull your tongue back altogether. Part of the reason people can kiss for so long is that you can switch styles, speeds, directions, and it's still good.

Better than the Blow Pop gum, the flavor doesn't fade in two minutes. And never mind what they say on TV—it doesn't get stuck in your braces either.

Love, Joe

◆ ◇ ◆

None of my "friends" know who I am. Personality, I mean. They see me as whoever they want me to be. I feel empty because of it. What do I do? —Anonymous

Oy, this! I hate this. It's pretty common for people to be so caught up in their own lives that they cannot, for the life of them, bother to notice others. It sucks and is awful. But let us not discuss how much it sucks! Instead, let's discuss what I am hearing, in your question: you are very keyed in to what your friends think of you. Maybe too keyed in. If they don't see who you are, you start to feel "empty," as if you don't exist. And this, to me, indicates that you are giving too much power to your friends.

Everybody wants to be liked. One of the easiest and most convenient ways to do that is just to reflect your environment; you're into music with the musicians, you talk about dating with the friends who do the date-talk, you're a sci-fi nerd with the sci-fi nerds. Etcetera, etcetera. I was all about this, at a certain point in my life. And there was a pretty obvious reason for that: I did not like myself. I had absorbed the message that, whoever I was, I wasn't worth people's time or care, and that the only way to "fool" anyone into thinking otherwise was to imitate other, better people. The sad part? All the people around me had gotten the same message. Especially the girls. So we had an entire world built around trying to reflect one another, and seeing ourselves only as reflected in one another, and...have you ever seen a mirror reflecting a mirror? It's not that interesting. It's just a whole lot of shiny, empty space.

This is a really crappy way to live. It results in shallow, empty relationships. It results in having dozens of friends, and feeling lonely every time you hang out. Fortunately, the solution is simple (if not exactly easy): you figure out who you are, and you share it fearlessly.

Do you have a journal? Get a journal. Write in it, until you figure out which topics fascinate you. Then, start conversations about them, and see who takes up the challenge. Make a list of all the weird interests you have—English folk music! Woodworking! Screen-printing your own T-shirts! Whatever!—and then figure out why you like those things, and how you can get really knowledgeable or skilled when it comes to at least one of them. Then, tell everyone about how much fun you are having, with your woodworking and such. Your friend-sorting process begins here. Some people are going to be all, "Ugh, you build cabinets?" These are not the friends you need. Toss 'em. Some people are going to be all, "Whoa! I don't know anyone else who can build such awesome cabinets! Good for you!" These are real friends. Keep them. And then, unbelievably but inevitably, someone is going to share with you the fact that they are building their very own spice rack, and you are going to have someone who shares this "weird," previously lonely portion of your life. In fact, you are going to draw all sorts of new people to you. People who do not NEED to project a convenient personality onto you, because they are really into the personality that you have RIGHT NOW. Which has been your goal all along.

Don't get me wrong: you're always going to relate to most people with only a portion of your full self. Only very rare and very good friends can handle absolute, unfiltered honesty. But as you get more comfortable and honest in your relationships, you're going to create an environment in which comfort and honesty are acceptable. And at that point, your friends are going to start relating to you in a new way. And you are probably going to find out something shocking: you weren't seeing the "real them," either. And they're happier to know you, now that it's OK to be themselves. —Sady

◆ ◇ ◆

How do I get over a guy that treats me like shit, and has been treating me badly for the past oh say year and a half? —Anonymous

This is a great question, even though at first glance it appears not to be. Anyone will tell you, "Duh! If he treats you like shit, dump his ass and move on!" But for girls like you and me, it's not that easy. And if there's two of us, well, there's gotta be a ton more. You're not alone, you're not crazy, and you're not someone who deserves to be treated like shit.

The bad news is that it doesn't matter how often we hear this. It doesn't matter that we ask ourselves (and others), "If he's treating me like shit, why can I still not get over him?" We're not flawed people, or rather, not more flawed than anyone else. We just happen to have a higher threshold for pain. And maybe a lower amount of self-esteem?

I dated a guy who treated me like shit for a while, and I got over him by going out with someone else, who then treated me like more shit. I got over that guy by going out with, yes, another guy, who also treated me like shit. But there was a catch. He wasn't treating me extra-shittily, he was treating me like he treated anyone else. And the more I wanted things to be different between us, the more I realized that I was kinda treating him like shit too. I wanted him to be a different person! Of course he felt insecure. Of course he was "treating me like shit." I was making it perfectly clear that I didn't love him for who he was. I feel sad even just writing that down, but also relieved that I don't have to do it anymore.

It took me a long time to figure that out.

It didn't happen by someone telling me it would. I had to get to a place where the pain of letting go was less than the pain of being with him. I saw my pain on a scale. I knew, *OK, I hate being with this person, but I'd hate being without him more.*

And then one day, the scale shifted its weight. And yes, it does just happen one day. Just like that. Everyone has their own "bottom." My bottom was verrrrry low. I hope yours doesn't get as low as mine did.

My apologies for the long-winded answer. If you want the short answer, it's this: there is no way we can predict when we get over someone. I've tried every single trick. Nothing works.

It's like being in the Hunger Games. It sucks, then it sucks more, more pain, killer bees, invisible force fields of fire, fighting your way through it...and then it's over. The good news about this stuff is that you won't die, whereas in the Hunger Games, you just might.

Hope I didn't give anything away there.

xx Lesley

♦ ◊ ♦

Why is being skinny so important to so many girls? Why is it portrayed as such an amazing thing in the media? —Ava, Minnesota

Hi, Ava! There are several answers to the "skinny" question. And all of them are, in my opinion, pretty ominous.

The first answer is this: if people can get you to worry about how skinny you are, they have already taken away a substantial chunk of your time and energy. Seriously. Look at how many "solutions" there are to the problem of girls not being "skinny enough." Are you doing yoga? Are you running? Are you swimming? Have you gone vegetarian yet? Have you gone vegan yet? Have you tried eating only meat? Are you using diet pills? Are you drinking diet shakes? Are you wearing slimming clothing? Have you tried fasting? Have you tried surgery? Have you tried spinning around counterclockwise while saying "I want to be skinny" backwards 300 times? You're not trying hard enough! Try harder! Be more skinny!

Oh my god, it is TOO MUCH WORK. Exercise is nice, and you should definitely do that, and healthy food is really super, too. But I also like to, you know, read books, and go to movies, and learn things. And all of that is stuff I would not have time to do if I worried full time about being skinny. But this relates to another unpleasant fact, which is: if people can get you to worry about being skinny, they can get you to buy things. They can get you to buy books about how to be skinny, and magazines about how to be skinny, and clothes, and exercise equipment, and gym memberships, and all the rest of it. "You should be skinnier" is the core premise of an entire industry. Not a small industry. So if you are really focused on being skinny, you are helping to fund someone's summer house in Florida, and he is going to go run over a manatee with a Jet Ski or whatever, and do you know how grateful he is to you, for buying his Jet Ski with your subscription to his brand-new diet plan that will finally get you skinny? Not a lot! That dude runs over manatees! He's a jerk!

Which relates to part three: if you worry about being skinny all the time, and buy all the things, you are never actually going to achieve magical "skinny enough" status. If you take this to an unhealthy level, you can get really physically sick and die. So you can be both "not skinny enough" and "too skinny," literally. But no matter how much weight you lose, you are always going to turn on the TV or open a magazine and hear the message "Be more skinny!" Even if you work on being thin like it's your full-time job, no one ever shows up at your house with a trophy, like, "Congratulations! You did it! You can stop worrying and feel good about how you look, because you are now skinny!" So it never ends. You keep buying things, and you keep worrying and wasting energy you could be using to becoming a Supreme Court justice, and it lasts for the rest of your life, except that after a certain point people also start selling you fancy moisturizers because it turns out you are now "aging."

I think "skinny" is portrayed as an amazing thing in the media, and something girls should aspire to, in part because it is very rare. The people who are best at "skinny" are people who have a genetic predisposition to it, and who are also models or actors who literally work on their appearance as if it is their job. Which it is. (And even they get Photoshopped to death. Nobody's a winner here.) That means a ton of the women we see as "sexy" or "fashionable" are living a lifestyle that we will never live, and have genetic gifts that most of us don't have. And we see them, and we see that everybody knows who they are, and that people are constantly sending all this love their way, and they're rich and go to fancy parties and hang out with our favorite movie stars and have cool jobs, and we think, *Wow. How much more people would love us, how much happier we would be, if we were skinny!* It's not about being "attractive." It's about the idea that looking a certain way guarantees happiness and security. It doesn't. But this idea—that all of the richest, happiest, most loved people are very skinny—puts us in a position where we become poorer, less happy, and less likely to love ourselves. And guess who benefits from that? Two teams: the one that wants girls not to reach their fullest potential, and the one that makes money off of girls' buying things. Girls think it's important to be skinny because rich adults profit from girls' thinking it's important to be skinny. And that is how it is. That is not, however, how it has to be. Save a manatee; eat a burrito. Is my lesson for you today. —Sady

♦ ◊ ♦

I want to be a strong, independent feminist, but in the face of a square jaw or an Adam's apple I turn into a simpering sycophant. How can I stop being obsessed with guys and just be happy being me? —Kshemani, Toronto

Oh lord, I understand! I consider myself a very strong, independent woman of the world, and yet a dreamy pair of eyes can leave me in a state of recklessness. I think daydreaming is perfectly fine and healthy—I spent many a day in my 20s reading Anaïs Nin and lusting for my own Henry Miller to come and sweep me away—however, I cannot stress enough how important it is to keep your feet planted on the ground whilst daydreaming (this is an art I have yet to master...but I try). When you get carried away with boy-craziness, ask yourself if the boy you're attracted to at the moment is really so great, or if you're

transferring your personal hopes and desires onto someone who's not worth them. And when you're feeling obsessive, try to distract yourself with the things you love in life (aside from boys): projects, hobbies, friends, etc. Speaking of friends, sometimes talking to them about your crush and getting it off your chest can help you relax. And if you feel really obsessive about a guy, I think it's a bad sign; move on. My best advice, which I should also follow, is to remind yourself of reality and to remain the badass that you are. If you feel like you have to play down your independence for a guy (or, for that matter, a girl), walk—no, RUN for the hills! —Karen Elson

♦ ◊ ♦

Why are girls and guys obsessed with losing their virginity? All I hear about from my friends is "the V-card" or "popping the cherry." Why can't people just keep it to themselves? I honestly don't understand why being a "virgin" is such a big deal. —Olivia

Oh, the eternal "V-card" question. Honestly, you are lucky that the kids you know are not as corny as the ones I grew up with; in our school, kids kept little plastic leis around, and when someone lost her virginity, she'd wear the lei to school to signify that she had—wait for it—"gotten lei'd." Arrrrrrrgh.

I think the "V-card" question is easy for people to obsess over because it is supposed to signify two really important things. One, that you're sexual: Look! You even got one whole other human being to want to have sex with you! And two, that you're "an adult." You can "have sex," which is for adults, therefore you are one.

One tiny problem: neither of these things is true.

First let's examine the idea that "losing your virginity," whatever that means, makes you "sexual." Really coming to terms with your sexuality isn't one definitive experience; it's a long, personal process of learning about what you want, and what feels good to you. I once attended an all-day conference about virginity at Harvard. And even people who were smart enough to speak at Harvard didn't actually, definitively know what "losing your virginity" meant. Every new sexual experience, even masturbation, could be considered a kind of "virginity loss." Not to scar you for life with my over-shares, but I learned how to have an orgasm by myself at 14, made out with another person for the first time at 18, had penis-in-vagina intercourse for the first time later that year, and didn't figure out how to have an orgasm with another person until I was 20. I "became sexual" in a different way during each of those experiences; I found out something new about myself and my sexuality every time. As I do every time I try something new, sexually, whether I do it by myself or with another person.

And then there's the idea that "having sex" makes you an adult. Which is even more ridiculous. There are plenty of people who've never had sex, who are adults. There are plenty of people who are asexual, and either try sex and figure out that it's not for them, or refrain from sex altogether; they live productive adult lives, paying rent and making friends and doing their jobs, and some of them also have romantic relationships. And, crucially, there are TONS of people who've had sex, and are very sexual, and who still aren't grownups—and I don't only mean the other teenagers at your school. I mean the 26-year-olds you date later on (if you're unlucky) who are late to pick you up because they got really caught up in playing Xbox Live or reorganizing their iTunes. "Becoming an adult" is one more thing that we want to think happens all at once, and which actually takes your entire life: I "lost my virginity" when I was 18, but I didn't figure out how to do my own taxes until this year, and I can tell you that one of those experiences (guess which one) felt a lot more mature and responsible than the other. Although, given how awful my first partner and I were at sex, the two experiences were equally stressful.

But when you talk about it like this, it becomes clear that Losing Your Virginity—however you define that—isn't that big a deal. It doesn't "make" you anything. It doesn't change anything essential about who you are, and it doesn't even necessarily change anything important about your sexuality. It just means that you've learned a new skill, which is having sex with other people. And sex is great! I really like sex! It can help you to form close, loving relationships, or help you to feel connected to your partner; it can relieve stress, and take your mind off a bad day; it's a nice way to celebrate a good day; it can just be something that feels really nice, when you're in the mood. But sex can also be really boring, or sad-making, or uncomfortable, or even harmful—especially if you're not emotionally in the right space to have it, or if your partner doesn't pay attention to what you need, or if you don't know enough about safe sex to make sure that you don't get sick or pregnant. And I'm just talking about less-than-good consensual experiences, there. Some of my earlier sexual experiences—being touched or groped—were not consensual at all. I don't personally consider those to be part of "losing my virginity," because they weren't about sex; they were about force, and I didn't have a choice as to whether or not I wanted to participate. Choosing to be sexual with someone else for the first time is, in fact, pretty special. But having someone else force sex on you…well, I certainly don't think that should define how anyone views your sexuality, let alone how you define your own.

In fact, I hate the idea that people are defined by sex, period. By how they have sex, or who they have sex with, or what kinds of relationships they have sex in, or whether they have sex at all. There's a whole lot of being human that has nothing to do with sex. Defining people by their sexual lives is just a way of defining people as less than human.

People would really, really like virginity to be a big deal. That way, they can call you "dirty" or "slutty" for losing it, or, conversely, a "loser" or a "prude" for not losing it. Often, people think losing or keeping their virginity "proves" something about them, and that other people have the power to decide what that is. Which is just a recipe for feeling crappy about yourself, for no real reason. It makes no sense whatsoever. Which is where I give you, Olivia, the good news: You are about 80 percent less likely to feel crappy about yourself, or buy in to this BS. Simply because you sent in this question. —Sady

I've found myself falling out with my old friends, and I've realized it's for the best. Now I need some new ones. There are some girls I'd really like to be friends with, but I'm so shy. Any good friend-making tips? —Cleo

OK, so first: are you sure about renovating your entire friend list? You don't have any keepers in the bunch? I just ask because sometimes it's tempting to wipe the slate clean and meet new people, even when the old ones are still worthwhile. But maybe your friends are suddenly getting into hard drugs or kicking puppies. I don't know.

So what do these new girls like to do? Is it stuff that you like to do? Maybe they like to go to coffee shops and hang out, or maybe they like to go to concerts? If you guys are interested in the same things, and you're pretty sure you could be friends, it should be easy to find some common ground.

A good way to start making friends without coming off as overeager is just to smile— in the general direction of the girls you want to be friends with. I know, DUH, but I'm not kidding. If you want to let them know that you're approachable, your default expression should not be bitchface. Look like the friendly person that I'm sure you are.

Next, separate one from the herd. Which girl in the group do you have the most contact with? Does one of them happen to be in a lot of your classes? Who seems the nicest or the most at ease with everyone? She is probably your target: she's good at making friends, and is probably open to talking to new people.

It's OK to be shy. You can work up to talking. Start by saying hi in the hallway to the girl in the group you see most. Does she, um, know who you are? If she doesn't, and she looks surprised, just say, "I'm Cleo, we have [FILL IN CLASS OR ACTIVITY] together." One of these days, work in a "How was your weekend?" And then LISTEN to the answer, so that you get a sense of what you two might have in common. She might ask you what you did in return. If not, you can always offer it: "I went and saw/did this AH-MAY-ZING band/play/sports thing/whatever. Do you like poetry/ hip-hop/theater/modern dance/horror movies?" People who love to do a particular thing also looooove to find someone else who feels the same way. BOOM! Something in common.

Eventually, you'll probably have to be brave. Tight-knit friends often stick together, figuring they already have their dynamic sorted out. But that's only before they get to know you. Keep up the friendliness. Talk to your favorite prospective friend when you see her in class, or when you pass her. Maybe in a few weeks, tell her you're going to go hiking/to the beach/to walk your neighbor's Great Dane/to a cute cafe on Saturday, and does she want to come? If she does, great! If she doesn't, or is busy, it's fine—you just put the idea in her head that you like to do things, and maybe she will ask you out the next time she does something.

Remember: new friends don't happen overnight. It takes a while to build up a core group of good friends. Keep doing the cool shit that makes you happy, keep being friendly, and people will be drawn to you, I promise. —Krista

♦ ◊ ♦

I've recently started seeing this guy who already has a girlfriend. I like him a lot, and as far as I can tell, he feels the same way. He says that they're only staying together because they made a "promise" to finish out the school year before he goes to college. From what I gather, he expects me to keep sneaking around with him until June. I want to be with him, but I also respect myself more than this. I don't know if I should give him an ultimatum—me or her—and call it off if he can't make a decision, or if I should just continue until it works itself out? —Anonymous

Let's get a couple of things out of the way: complicated situations do not magically smooth themselves out. Also, when you deliver an ultimatum, you're placing the power in the hands of one person, and it's not you.

But you know that already, so let's suppose we give this guy the benefit of the doubt and accept the premise that he didn't plan any of this and is in over his head. Feelings are messy and overwhelming and sometimes spring up out of nowhere to muck everything up. But he's sort of beside the point. The point here is you.

Feelings swimming around in your head and your guts and your quivering knees can make it hard to see straight, but it's essential for you to recognize that remaining in a situation that (rightfully) makes you uncomfortable will take a toll on your self-respect. And the relationship you have with your self-respect is a lot more profound than what you might have with this guy.

When faced with confusing situations, we often feel tempted to impose an ultimatum —me or her or else—or we waffle, thinking, *This is better than nothing.* Let me lobby for option C: you decide what you want and/or are willing to put up with and communicate it clearly to him. Find your boundaries and enforce them. You could say: "I really like you. I think you like me. I understand that the situation with your girlfriend is complicated, and I respect that. However, until you've resolved things with her, I'm not comfortable kissing you/holding hands/sleeping together/buying you ice cream/hanging out/whatever."

Maybe you guys keep getting to know each other as friends. Or maybe he's lying about everything and two-timing both of you. The only way you will know any of this is to clearly articulate what you need and ask him to respond in kind. If his response is insufficient, move on. This way, no matter what the outcome, your self-respect will remain intact, and that's worth so much more than any guy. And if he's worthwhile, it'll make him respect you more, too. —Emily C.

♦ ◊ ♦

Tavi, as a blogger, editor-in-chief of this fine magazine, high school student, social being, and pursuer of many other hobbies—how do you manage your time? I struggle to manage going to school, working, doing schoolwork, and pursuing creative stuff such as writing and making collages. You even find time to reply to comments on Rookie, although I am sure you are just sitting upon your leather throne, eating pomegranates and shouting replies to your minions who type for you and fetch you exotic fruit. Much like Ellen DeGeneres does. All my lovin', Ally.

Hi, Ally! Hold on, let me adjust my sitting position, carefully so my leather seat doesn't make it sound like I'm farting. AH, THERE WE ARE. Now, to your question. Since you've asked about my own experience—my day has five parts: sleep, school, Rookie and related commitments, homework, and either hanging out with friends or doing something on my own, which can mean either being super creative and productive, or watching TV, which I consider important because sometimes you need to shut your brain off. It was by no means easy to finally find the right balance, mostly because to keep everything in its time slot, I had to cut out all the little things that would make some parts of my day take longer than they need to, keeping me from having time for all of them. Things like procrastinating, listening to music while studying (which made it go slower), trying to videochat with a friend while working on Rookie, etc. It's hard to stop procrastinating, but once the stress gets to a certain level, you realize the value in just GETTING SHIT DONE. Then you can never go on Tumblr again without thinking about how nice it would be to just finish your paper and then have time to watch a movie later, and then you just shrug and get back to discussing Aristotle or whatever.

Another ~tip~ is to focus on one thing at a time. I don't know if you do this, but for a while I had a habit of getting distracted from homework to start making another page of my notebook into a comic or letter or something. I would justify this by telling myself that my doodles were different and important and LIFE homework. Which is a little true, but I still have to be in high school for 2 1/4 more years, and it's easier to just do the work and be done with it and then be able to put time into one thing I'm really proud of later instead of tons of little doodles.

Look for holes in your own different time slots that you could use to work on other things. It's way different from getting distracted and procrastinating, because sometimes a time slot might involve waiting. Like, I don't know what you do for work, but you can bring a book to read if you often find yourself waiting around, and then there's some "me time" that you've gotten in. The important thing to remember to keep this from ALSO getting stressful is that you don't have to be DOING SOMETHING ALL THE TIME. Like, I use my study hall to work on homework, but during my lunch period I just want to relax and enjoy my Gushers with my friends. I guess I could use it to finish all of my homework for the day, but by sixth period my brain is too mushy and needs a break.

Oh, that's another thing: figure out when you work best. I, for example, cannot do homework immediately after school. I need to recharge and get started later at night. So my Rookie time or hanging-out/me-time usually comes right after school. It would be wasting time to try and do geometry when my brain is in no state to get it all done as quickly as I could at another time.

I'm going to tell you what my school counselor, a wonderful lady who understands the thinking behind both my academic and creative pursuits, told me: something's gotta give. It would be impossible to both do everything you want to do and do it well. So, you have to prioritize a bit, and maybe the priorities shift from time to time so that one section of your life doesn't collapse.

For example, I have at times decided that I just can't do exceptionally well in a certain school subject for a while because it's become really important that I have time to write in my diary every night while something in real life is going on. Or, I can oversee Rookie in the way I normally do but not be as involved in the comments section as I'd like to be because I have lots of tests and projects due one week. Or, not be social or work on any personal creative projects for a couple weeks so I can go to bed early instead and get as much sleep as possible, because I realize I've been tired all the time lately.

Overarching to-do lists and planners are daunting to me and just looking at them stresses me out. I can't tell you how many times I've been like, TODAY IS THE DAY I START GETTING SHIT DONE, FOR I JUST BOUGHT A BEAUTIFUL CALENDAR FROM BORDERS. That's too intimidating for me. Instead, I make mini to-do lists when I sit down to work on a different time slot, for the satisfaction of crossing things off and so I don't get off task on doodling or Facebook or whatever. Different things work for different people, but I recommend trying either the full-on planner or the little to-do lists, and seeing what helps you.

So...I hope this helps? (1) Get rid of tiny slower-downers and procrastinating. (2) Focus on one thing at a time. (3) Look for empty chunks of time when you can slot something in, even if that thing is "sit down somewhere and breathe." (4) Know when your brain and energy are able to work on each task in your day. (5) Understand that you may need to compromise and reprioritize. (6) Write it all down if it helps.

Now, bring me my pomegranates! —Tavi

◆◇◆

I've been having sex with this guy for about a year and a half. I'm 17 and he's 43, married with children and a pregnant wife. I don't want him to leave his marriage, and I know we will never be a couple. I wanted to ask for help from someone who wouldn't look at him as a pedophile or me as an idiot, because sometimes I really do feel that I'm in love with him. But I want to have a real relationship, and this is changing the way I relate to guys my age. I know that I should leave the relationship, but I can't seem to do it. Because when we're together, I really am happy, but I want a normal relationship with a guy who only wants me. I don't know what to do. Please help. —Anonymous

First of all, I sure don't think you're an idiot. I was in a similar situation when I was 15—the guy wasn't 43, he was 24, but he was also married with a child and a pregnant wife. He was the first person I had sex with. It was exciting, and the sex was great, and I wasn't having the best time at school or at home, so having this sophisticated (so he seemed at the time) older "boyfriend" really helped me feel like I had something good in my life, something that other people in my high school, the people who made fun of me for being shy and dressing weird, didn't have. I loved it when he'd pick me up from school in his car, before anyone in my class had a driver's license. That was fun, you know? And I'm about to say something possibly controversial: I don't regret that relationship for a minute. I don't want anyone to feel like they're damaged because something like this happened to them, and just because I was 15 doesn't mean I didn't on some level understand what I was doing. I don't feel like I was dumb to get into it, and I don't feel traumatized or damaged by it now. I needed it at the time, and even though I now understand that he was kind of a loser (more on that in a minute), he was never mean to me. He was nicer and smarter than most of the boys in my class, and he made me feel special. For a little while.

That feeling ended when I was talking to a cool, loud-talking girl from another high school and I mentioned his name and she said, "Have you had sex with him yet? It's like a rite of passage." I mean, I was naïve enough to believe that I was the only person he was seeing outside of his marriage. I was also naïve enough to believe him when he told me that his wife was a bitch, that they never had sex anymore (then how'd she get pregnant?), that his parents made him marry her when she was pregnant with their first kid, etc. I bought all of this BS from him even though I was a smart person. Why? Because I was 15 (which doesn't mean I wasn't savvy; it just means I didn't have a ton of experience) and I wanted him to love me. When I realized that what was, like, rainbows & kittens LOVE for me was just a piece on the side for him, I cried for like two days and never slept with him again.

Now that I'm 41, basically the age of your guy, I see this all really differently. I feel for the wife of the guy I was with. I understand now why she was bitchy to me—she probably knew her husband had a thing for teenage girls, and saw that I was always hanging around, and put two and two together. Poor woman, right? Can you imagine that feeling? I hope for her sake that they're not together anymore.

I also see, from this side of the age gap, that your dude, sorry to say it, is an asshole. Listen to what he's doing: he is lying to the person that he married, who is about to give birth to their baby, and carrying on a relationship with a teenager. If any of my my-age friends were doing this...well, honestly, they wouldn't be. I wouldn't be friends with a person who did this! A man my age who was cheating on his wife with a high school student would seem like a person with a problem. He would seem gross and sad. I really wouldn't want to hang out with him.

I asked one of my 43-year-old guy friends, Chris, if he would ever consider dating a teenager on the side, and what he would think of a peer in that situation. Chris is married and has three kids. He is really cute and funny and smart and decent—the kind of person you will be friends with when you're our age. Here's what he said: "Middle-aged dads with wives and kids who sleep with teenagers are, by definition, skeevy liars with power issues and deep unresolved sex stuff. As much as he may pretend it's all normal and lovey-dovey, he knows how slimy and awful and embarrassing he's being."

I agree with Chris! The man you're involved with knows full well that what he's doing isn't fair to his wife, their kids, OR YOU, but he keeps on doing it. That is because he sucks! Even though he's nice to you! (I also feel obligated to inform you, even though you probably have already googled this, that depending on where you live, this guy might be breaking the law.) It's OK! My guy sucked, too! I still don't regret it. But: I carried on with him for only six months. If I had kept up the relationship for a year and a half, I might feel differently. Six months I feel I can chalk up to "Oh, that was an interesting and helpful, though not ideal, experience." A year and a half starts to get into "Why did I waste so much time on this person?" I don't want you to live to regret this relationship, so here is my advice.

You say that you want to have a real relationship, and that you know that your relationship with this man is what's holding you back, and you KNOW you should leave. So you already know what I'm gonna tell you. Leave. Now. Go have a normal, fun relationship with someone closer to your age, someone who doesn't already have a significant other. Know that you'll feel sad for a while and cry and cry and want to call/text/email the married dude. But RESIST. I know it's hard, but a lot of things that are worth it in life are hard. Be brave. You already know that you've outgrown this grown man. Zoom past him. Go to your next thing. When you're 30 you'll see him the way Chris and I do, I promise. But for now, find someone who can be your actual boyfriend, and don't look back. <3 Anaheed

♦ ◊ ♦

I know high school years are supposed to be hell, but is it ~normal~ to feel unable to connect with anyone, and utterly lonely? —Anonymous

Honestly? No. I don't think it's normal. This doesn't mean there's anything wrong with you, or the people around you, it just means that you are in the middle of many incompatible circumstances. Knowing this can be a burden, because the truth can hurt, 'cause who wants to admit that they're lonely? But it's really a blessing, because it means you can give yourself the power to fix it, which would never happen if you didn't know or acknowledge that there was something to fix. You can try to take advantage of this terrible feeling.

One good thing about loneliness is that it helps you access the emotions you need to fully experience some of the world's greatest art, movies, writing, music, and such. That great, awful feeling where you feel so in love with a song at the same time that your chest physically hurts from how much things seem to suck. Such feelings broaden our life experience and make the happy, un-lonely feelings stronger. "BUT I DON'T WANT LIFE EXPERIENCE! LIFE SUCKS!"—you, maybe, or at least me a lot of the time. Unfortunately, life is all we have, so DEAL WITH IT, or at least TRY to make the suckiness of it less sucky. For these times, I recommend "At Seventeen" by Janis Ian, *No One Belongs Here More Than You* by Miranda July, *Ghost World*, and lots of Woody Allen (just try to avoid learning about his personal life for a while). And, after you've developed these obsessions, you might want to create some of your own art, too, and let me just say that it is extremely satisfying to be able to make some kind of sense out of shitty feelings, be it through drawing, collaging, photography, writing, etc.

The problem with this specific brand of sadness—loneliness—is that it's so dependent on the people around you, and you can't change them, and you can't change yourself to relate to them when it doesn't feel right. So, now that you've gotten to know yourself more by *exploring* your *obsessions* (TWO ROOKIE THEMES IN ONE SENTENCE, GO ME), and you've developed your taste, you can use all that to relate to others. Keep an eye out for events that pertain to your interests: authors speaking at local bookstores, concerts, sports events. Do you live by a city? Does it have a record store of any kind? A *ROCKY HORROR PICTURE SHOW* SHADOW SHOW? Other people will be doing the same thing you are, looking for people to enjoy the author/concert/festival/game with, and so you are bound to find someone else who will understand your reasons for being there.

Now, maybe you're lonely not because you don't have friends but because you actually have quite a few friends but don't relate to any of them. It is a terrible feeling to spend all night with a group of people and go home and realize that you kind of hated yourself and everyone around you for the past three hours. If you feel this way, they probably feel it too, and so no one will think you freaky for kind of fading away from the group. You might deal with the paranoid suspicion that people are judging you because lately you've been spending more time at home making things than hanging out, but you don't really want anything from them anyway, and you're not hurting them, so it's not worth your or their caring about. (Also, don't feel discouraged if you don't make things that you like right away. Nobody does. And even just watching movies and developing your tastes and figuring out what you like is an effective use of time, in my opinion.) Or, maybe you feel lonely because you don't have a romantic partner, and you're sick of the optimism it takes to be like, "Hey, I can relate to Janis Ian! Take THAT, people who are happier than me and make out with each other!" I am honestly lost on this one, but I do think this is the most NORMAL kind of loneliness here, so at least it's not like everyone is having some giant orgy and you're not invited. Just please promise me that you will remember that YOU are not the problem. It's just that people are complicated, and it is rare for two of them to find each other and say and do all the right things that make it work out. But there's nothing wrong with you that is keeping you from getting a lover of some kind, even though it's easy to think, like, *If only I could be more X, less Y, just the right kind of Z*. It is also easy to feel this way if you have the notion that your loneliness might have nothing to do with the people around you, and is just something you feel all the time, regardless of your circumstances.

When you are met with the burden of understanding things and why they make you sad, to a point where it's hard to relate to others and you eventually become lonely, you may hate yourself a little bit, and want to make yourself more boring, pretty, passive, submissive, easier to get along with, uncontroversial in any way. But by that point, you know too much about the world and what you do and don't like about it, you know that you feel rather attached to your opinions, your tastes, your ideas, the things that might make you un-boring or un-pretty, and you don't want to compromise them, because they make up who you are, after all. The comfort in knowing that you are being your full self, or, if you don't know who that is, just doing what feels right in the moment, will triumph over the comfort of knowing that some hypothetical other person is into a boring, pretty, one-dimensional version of you that doesn't exist. Or at least the discomfort of smiling and nodding when you have so much you'd rather say will be so awful that you'll prefer the discomfort of confusing people. It does not feel this way in the moment, but I believe it is incredibly important in the long run, in the health of YOU, and that's who you gotta take care of.

NOW. What happens when you don't want to take care of yourself, when you're so MAD at yourself for being LONELY, when the person you feel alienated from is you? When everything you love has turned against you, your favorite song just reminds you of YOU, and you feel like that person is someone who just sucks?

First of all, know that you don't suck as much as you think you do, ever, especially if you are a teenager, especially if you are a female teenager. Because we are SCIENTIFICALLY PROGRAMMED to hate ourselves more than we should right now. Because puberty sucks. (It will be over soon, or at least relatively soon, considering how long life typically is.) (Also, therapy. It's a good idea to investigate therapy if your feelings of loneliness and disconnectedness persist no matter what else you've tried.)

It's all about striking a balance between being Liz Lemon and being Stevie Nicks. You are not perfect, because you are a human being, and in moments where you dwell on this and start to hate yourself, you need to keep a Liz-like sense of humor about your flaws. But you also need to give yourself some credit, know that you are awesome and sometimes other people just don't get it. Know that your flaws are interesting, your loneliness is interesting, that you, you are a force of NATURE, a BEAUTIFUL, COMPLICATED human. And you think about these flaws and you feel these feelings because your world has color and depth to it, which can make the things that hurt, hurt more, but can also make the things that feel good, feel more good.

And so few people understand, because this kind of persistent, all-encompassing loneliness, as we have established, is not "normal," but your bonds with the other few people who do understand will be the most special of all, once you find them, which you will. You and your wild heart, you're like Stevie Nicks. Stevie Nicks wants the sadness and the emotion, she wants to scare people by expressing them and presenting people with the part of themselves they're afraid of. You're not afraid—you're aware. And if you're tackling your loneliness with the right combination of acceptance and optimism, you're DOING something about it. You're trying to make something BEAUTIFUL out of it. You are Stevie fucking Nicks.

"I think if you are really into words and poetry and situations of life, there is always a little kiss of sadness on everything you do… It's just the kind of person who I am. I always look carefully beneath the outward appearance of things. I want to know what's really going on in somebody's heart."

A-fucking-men, Stevie fucking Nicks. Now, listen to "Rhiannon," watch some *30 Rock*, and take a nap.

Love, Tavi ♦

People Reviews

Literally just reviews of random people we have interacted with or observed.

COLBY THE DISNEYLAND GUIDE

There is nothing so faith-renewing as an adult who believes in the magic of Disney. When I went to Disneyland we had the BEST tour guide. His name was Colby and he moved to California to be an actor but started working at Disneyland because he figured he should "make [him]self useful." A utilitarian, I see! His sincerity perfectly matched his plaid vest and red pants, and his nose was even upturned a little bit like Mickey Mouse's. Whenever we couldn't decide what to do next and asked him what he would recommend, his eyes would widen as if we'd just asked him to steal us the princess costumes so we could run around in them and clobber children, disguised as representatives of the Walt Disney Corporation. He would take a step back, hold up his hands, and say, "I am just here to make y'all happy." But Colby's best moment was when we recalled a fellow we'd met earlier named Paul, and he said, to no one in particular, "Oh yeah, Paul. Paul the rubber ball." Then, after a quiet chuckle, "I just came up with that out of nowhere." COLBY 4EVER. —Tavi
★★★★★

COFFEE SHOP DOUGHNUT GIRL

Near my apartment there is a coffee shop that is famous (at least to me) for their delicious doughnuts—which are advertised as being AS BIG AS YOUR FACE—so every Sunday before work I stop in and grab one. Recently, right after I was done ordering, a girl walked in and asked for a coffee and a glazed doughnut—the last glazed doughnut, that is—and as she was paying the unspeakable happened: the doughnut fell off the counter and while in midair it fell out of the little bag it was in and then SMACK right onto the floor. We all looked on horrified as she quickly picked it up, and a sense of panic started to fill the room. The baristas tried to offer her another doughnut, but alas, it was the LAST one! What happened next was the best thing I have ever witnessed in my life. She asked. "Well, is your floor clean?" to which the baristas replied, "We clean it every morning," and she said, "Don't judge me," and I said, "I am only judging you BETTER now because you are going to eat it." We all had a good laugh about it and cheered her on for her A+ attitude. She went outside and sat on the bench and ate her doughnut and drank her coffee and I give her five stars for knowing that a good doughnut is a terrible thing to waste. —Laia
★★★★★

PEOPLE PROTESTING AT THE LOCAL LIBRARY

I saw four people rather meekly protesting the closure of my tiny local library. I give their handmade signs one star because they were not very colorful, creative, or eye-catching. They didn't have a good slogan to chant, but I give them four stars for trying. Involved was the rather crazy lady who also works in the charity shop and calls everybody "Curly-locks" no matter what their hair-

style and randomly bursts out singing. I give her five stars for her enthusiasm and for the confusion she caused passers-by deciding whether they liked her or were scared of her and for entertaining me and making me smile despite myself. —Naomi

★ / ★★★★ / ★★★★★

HI, OR NOT

My older sister, Laura, is one of my best friends in the world. This review isn't about her, though; it's based on the same joke that we've been telling each other for 15 years, the centerpiece of which is one unforgettable human being. It all stems from a supermarket trip that took place when I was five and she was six. Our mom would send us together to run errands for her in the store, and on one of these jaunts to the canned foods aisle or wherever, we met the girl who would leave us irrevocably changed. We turned a corner and almost ran directly into the cart that she was sitting in, buckled up top in the baby seat. We were super bewildered in that moment, (a) because we had nearly knocked over a toddler, and (b) because of what, exactly, that toddler happened to look like. She had blonde hair that PUFFED in perfect spheres of fuzz in three directions, I think maintained with bulky scrunchies: one on each side of her head, and one perched directly on top. The rest of her face reminded me of a woman from the comic strip *The Far Side*, despite the fact that those characters all look well over 40. On its own, the wacky appearance of this little girl probably wouldn't have made a permanent impression, but it was burned indelibly into our memories when she spoke. She glared at us with the craziest consternation you could ever expect to see on a small child— it was SERIOUSLY bitchy—and, in a voice that was half-bored, half-accusatory, sassed, "Hi, or NOT?" To clarify, the underlying message of

this was "Are you going to say hi to me, or are you going to KEEP IT MOVING already?" We were able to squeak out a tiny "…hi" before simultaneously having to turn tail and laugh our goddamned crazy heads off about this wonderful weirdo. Hi or NOT, to me, starts with five stars for her punchy personality and overall look, as well as the lasting power of the impression she made on us, but maybe loses one for being mean 2 me!! —Amy Rose

★★★★

MY DENTIST

I went to the dentist after one of my teeth started hurting like crazy. After she had taken a look at my mouth, she decided to write me up a prescription for antibiotics. She looked me up and down and said, "I can see that you're really skinny, so you probably don't eat a lot. You have to take this medicine with food— real food, not like water or a salad or anything, so mentally prepare yourself." For being a totally judgmental asshole, I give this dentist ONE STAR (only not zero because she did cure my mouth pain). SCREW YOU!!! —Laia

★

THIS ONE KID IN LINE AT SIX FLAGS TWO SUMMERS AGO

In the summer of 2010, two friends and I rented a car and drove to New Jersey to pass the day at Six Flags Great Adventure. The whole day was spent observing HUMAN BEINGS and what weird creatures they are—especially the child variety, who just do crazy shit in public with zero embarrassment and no apparent awareness that they might be observed. Which they were, with a vengeance, by us. The best example of this has become a legend in our lives. I was in line for a ride with my friend Julie. The line was long and wind-y, so that you'd be standing right next to people way farther down the line for like half an hour waiting for this damn ride. Two of these other people were a pair of boys, probably about nine years old. One was big and one was small. They were unremarkable. UNTIL! The big one suddenly, out of nowhere, grabbed the small one around the waist and violently humped his butt for five seconds, calmly stating, while doing so, "Nuts. Nuts. Nuts." Then he loosened his grip and they both acted like nothing had happened. When in reality EVERYTHING HAS HAPPENED. I give this kid five stars for showing me that you just can never tell what is going to happen anywhere at any given time. —Anaheed

★★★★★

LAUGHING THUMB LADY

All best people-review stories come from Six Flags. Once I was there in the bathroom stall getting ready to relieve myself (a thing which I still don't totally understand as meaning "to pee" but whatever), and said to my friends who were waiting for me, "Crap, guys, I'm wearing a one-piece!" I guess I was annoyed because it's annoying when you have to pee and you have to basically take off your whole swimsuit? LIFE IS HARD. Anyway, right after I say this, I hear through the stall wall next to me a horrendous laugh, which I can only describe by asking you to imagine a giant thumb melting while trying to slurp spaghetti while chuckling at a thing a co-worker said earlier that day at Being a Thumb Work. The laugher left her stall before I got the chance to get out—another thing I imagine she enjoyed about my misery is that she would have time to make a getaway after LAUGHING AT IT—but my friends say she was most definitely a grown-up and also didn't wash her hands. She gets four stars, because I would totally laugh at someone for being such a whiny annoyance too, but I wouldn't flee the scene and I would definitely wash my hands first. —Tavi
★★★★

DANCING DUDE AT A SHOW

I went to see my friend's band play last Friday night, and the room, at first, was kind of quiet, because people were still shuffling around and doing that head-nod thing they do when they're trying to rev the rest of their body up enough to actually move it to the dance floor. Eventually a bunch of people pushed toward the band and began dancing around and yelling or whatever, but one dude, who was probably 25–30 years older than everyone else, just shut everyone else down as soon as he hit the floor, jumping and kicking and spinning and smiling and FEELING IT CAPITAL F CAPITAL I in a punk-rock display that was miles above everyone else's dumb little "your band is cool" shimmy. I suddenly recognized him as the sweet, mild-mannered guy who runs a store in town. Whenever I've seen him at his job, he's been in "have a nice day" mode, but on this night, he was in his own rock-out universe and I LOVED him, because he was the epitome of someone just going to a show to kick that shit out and have some fun. Also? He was wearing a shirt that said "Old Guys Rock." You know when you recognize the secret side of someone, and you realize that they've been around far longer than you have, and have more stories and more nights out and more dance moves and they don't intend to slow it down anytime soon? That is an awesome thing to see. "Look at that dude," one of my friends said, pointing in the dancer's direction. "That dude kind of rules." Yup. —Pixie
★★★★★

TAN MAN

I knew it was officially summer when I was biking around the lake last week and saw TAN MAN. He is tanned to an extreme degree like the New Jersey mom who was recently accused of taking her five-year-old daughter to a tanning booth. However, I am fairly certain that TAN MAN does most of his tanning the natural way, by biking around the city barely clothed. He wears neon-pink swimming trunks and has long tousled bleach-blonde hair, surely engineered to accentuate his tan. I give TAN MAN five stars for enjoying the short summers we have in Minnesota to the fullest, but remove one for putting himself at such a high risk for skin cancer! —Kelly
★★★★

MY BRA FITTER

This is a shout-out to the woman who conducted my first bra fitting in years. I don't think we even exchanged names. With her swiftness and knowledge, she was like some kind of bra magician. Because let me tell you, I had been wearing the wrong bras. Something that could have been embarrassing and uncomfortable was worth it for the wonderful knowledge she gifted to me that day. Like, I may be a 30FF, but that is still in the medium section of bras! She reassured me with her expertise. She was awash with bra and boob knowledge, and that puts her high up in society in my eyes. Thank you, kind bra-fitter lady! I am forever indebted to you. Or at least until my next bra fitting. —Naomi
★★★★★

BLACK SABBATH COVER BANDS

Melissa Auf der Maur, the former bassist for Hole and Smashing Pumpkins, had a Black Sabbath cover band in the early naughts. I thought that was a cool time to have a BS cover band. It was called HAND OF DOOM. But the BEST Black Sabbath cover band name I have ever heard—and possibly best cover band name I've ever heard—lives here in Whitehorse, Yukon (where I currently reside), and that cover band name is: A Bunch of BS. I give this a 4 out of 5 stars. A solid B for BULL. —Sonja

★★★★

OLD MAN ON THE CHAMPS-ÉLYSÉES

Last week, I went to Paris for the first time, and it was beautiful and old and overwhelming in many ways, one of which was the incompetent feeling of exploring such an incredible city with only the smallest workable French vocabulary. Many people didn't seem to like this, despite the amount of times I would sputter "JE SUIS DESOLÉE" after butchering yet another phrase. I was visiting the Champs-Élysées on the third or fourth day of my trip, and I had let people's dirty looks get to me a little. While I should have held my head up high and continued to at least TRY to speak French, albeit in my weird, slurring pan-European accent that sounds like it belongs to the offspring of Pepé le Pew and Super Mario, I minced around silently instead, responding to people with mute shakes of the head and so on, because that totally isn't a weirder way to communicate at all. I walked into one small shop that sold scarves and other accessories, the proprietor of which was a man who looked to be 80-plus years old. He sagged into an armchair near the door, but it was clear from the way the other employees deferred to him that he had the run of the place. As I walked in and very quietly looked around, he asked in French where I was from. "Je vis à New York City," I carefully responded, hoping that he wouldn't roll his eyes when he heard my poorly pronounced answer. Instead, he smiled and made polite conversation for another minute or so. I left after browsing a little, my French-confidence slightly elevated. Since I had to wait for friends to come out of a nearby shop, I stalled on the block for a few moments. All of a sudden, I saw the man slowly approaching me with a white paper bag in his hands. When he reached me, he handed it over and said in English, "I wanted you to go home with a souvenir," then walked away as I called out, "Thanks," dumbfounded. I opened the bag and found a gorgeous black, white, and gold scarf with locks, chains and keys all over it, which I proceeded to wear wrapped around my head like some babe protecting her hair in a convertible for the rest of the week. Five stars for this guy for renewing my desire to improve my French unabashedly, as well as for giving me a lovely scarf and an lovelier better memory. —Amy Rose

★★★★★

MY FRIEND'S LITTLE SISTER

Lauren is the little sister of my friend Megan. She's 10 years old and enjoys insulting me, making song parodies with her friends, insulting me, and coning. She has fiery hair and she wears cute Boden-style outfits that she picks out herself. The other day I was with Megan at the mall, and Lauren was with us. At Dairy Queen, she ordered a cone, and sweetly asked the cashier if he believed in unicorns. When he said no, she angrily shoved the cone onto her head like a unicorn's horn. "Well, ya should!" she yelled, and strutted away, ice cream dripping onto her face. I truly do like Lauren for her spunk, but I will have to deduct one star for her calling me a shiny-nosed moron (or some variation) on a regular basis. —Ruby B.

★★★★

LONDON MESSIAH

A couple of months ago I was sitting at the front on the top of a double-decker bus in London. The bus had momentarily stopped at the Liverpool Street station. I watched the rather bored- and sullen-looking faces of suited businessmen droop along the sidewalk. It was a cold English winter, and everything was looking predictably gray and fed up. Before I knew it, I saw a flash of color whiz out around a corner. There he was: a man, wearing only a pair of orange Hawaiian shorts, with a beard and long waving hair, both down to his waist. Barefoot, he skateboarded down the street, his long locks dancing through the air wildly as he slalomed around passersby, high-fiving every dreary Londoner as he passed. His happiness was contagious, and I watched through the bus window as everyone he touched instantly grew an enormous grin. A man in a gray suit spun around and laughed as he made contact with this man, who, I'm almost sure, was a reincarnation of Jesus. And I give that man five stars…not just from me, but from the whole of London. —Eleanor

★★★★★

MY FRIEND CHARLIE'S MOM (MUM)

Important background information: I have both a British friend on my improv team named Charlie whom I love because he's crazy easy to just hang out with, and a dark apartment in a com-

plex called "Carolina" that I hate because it doesn't have Wifi or gas, so I can't internet or cook. Charlie has both an awesome and hilarious personality and an awesome and hilarious giant family. His awesome and hilarious giant family has a GORGEOUS home and welcoming personalities. Thus, I am at their house, like, ALL the time. In a span of two recent weeks, I managed to spend nine days at their house. And when I say "days," I don't mean we hung out for an hour or two each time. I mean eight hours a day, comprising two meals and at least one movie or television marathon. Two of those days happened in a row, because I ended up drinking wine and chatting too late to drive home, so his family fixed me a bed. Occasionally Charlie had to leave to go do some standup, and I just sort of hung out at the house, cleaning up after dinner or jumping on the trampoline with his brother or whatever. This seems like a glowing review of Charlie, or maybe an abstract "person" review of the house as a living thing (I AM in college, I could do it), but I now come to the focus of my review: Charlie's mom. Or should I say MUM?! I shouldn't, I'm not British (USA! USA! USA!). Although I am extremely mild-mannered and have decent hygiene, I was still a guest in her home. She did not have to be happy about my being there. But she was so nice, you guys! SO NICE! Even better, she was really, sincerely OK with my basically living in her house. We chatted! We joked! She alerted me when I had some rice in my hair and gently asked Charlie and me to quiet down when we were talking too loudly in the kitchen. It's really cool and—I'll say it—beautiful when someone can just accept another human being into their home seamlessly. It shows a certain compassion and level-headedness to not let yourself be flustered or upset by a whole new PERSON in whatever order you've worked to establish. And for that, Charlie's mom, I give you ALL THE STARS IN THE WORLD. But for the sake of space, let's make it five. —Shelby

★★★★★

P.S SUPER IMPORTANT BONUS STAR because when I woke up, in their home, for the 25TH HOUR STRAIGHT Charlie's mom greeted me with: "Good morning. Did Charlie make you tea? If you saw someone creeping around your bed this morning, it was the termite man—as in, the man to exterminate termites, not some sort of half-man, half-termite. I forgot he was coming today! Charlie better have made you tea." —Shelby ◆

347

ORDINARY PEOPLE

Classmates created by one of our favorite artists when she was 13.

By Leanne Shapton

Summary of Persons

(1) Name: Morgan Abwaithe
Age: 17
Personality Type: Pleasant but practical joker
Boy/Girl Friends: None
Pet Peeve: Club Monaco sweatshirts/socks/pants
Nickname: "Ya Twit!"

(2) Name: Susanne Brougham
Age: 17
Personality Type: Soft-spoken, secretive, happy
Boy/Girl Friends: David Chauncey, Nancy Gordon
Pet Peeve: McDonald's salads
Nickname: "Sue"

(3) Name: David Chauncey
Age: 17 3/4
Personality Type: Sporty, moody, nice but sometimes sarcastic
Boy/Girl Friends: Susanne Brougham, Alex Narter
Pet Peeve: The color "mustard"
Nickname: "Jock"

(4) Name: Jéanette Delemonde
Age: 17
Personality Type: Friendly, cheerful, somewhat quiet
Boy/Girl Friends: Benjamin Hart, Gayle Jennings
Pet Peeve: Her nose
Nickname: "Fifi"

(5) Name: Kier Fredrickson
Age: 17 1/2
Personality Type: Smart-alecky, funny, bright
Boy/Girl Friends: Benjamin Hart, Jessica Snow
Pet Peeve: Shrimp
Nickname: None

(6) Name: Nancy Gordon
Age: 18
Personality Type: Peppy, leader, trendy, cheerful
Boy/Girl Friends: Susanne Brougham, Alex Narter
Pet Peeve: Hippos
Nickname: "Curly"

(7) Name: Benjamin Hart
Age: 18 3/4
Personality Type: Preppy, brainy, nice, sarcastic
Boy/Girl Friends: Jéanette Delemonde, Kier Fredrickson
Pet Peeve: Converse All-Stars
Nickname: "Sir Prep"

(8) Name: Gayle Jennings
Age: 16
Personality Type: Happy, energetic, sporty
Boy/Girl Friends: Jéanette Delemonde, Nick Preston
Pet Peeve: People who refuse to dance
Nickname: "Little Girl"

(9) Name: Leonard Melton
Age: 17
Personality Type: Quiet, sporty, creative
Boy/Girl Friends: Wendy Truffner, Peter Roland
Pet Peeve: Rainbows
Nickname: "Lenny"

(10) Name: Harriet Nedrow
Age: 18
Personality Type: none
Boy/Girl Friends: none
Pet Peeve: Ritz crackers
Nickname: "Watzername"

(11) Name: Alex Narter
Age: 17
Personality Type: Active, artistic, hockey-goer
Boy/Girl Friends: David Chauncey, Nancy Gordon
Pet Peeve: Blood
Nickname: None

(12) Name: Darlene Partridge
Age: 17
Personality Type: Shy, quiet, picky, sometimes whiney
Boy/Girl Friends: Paul Tucker
Pet Peeve: Stickers
Nickname: None

(13) Name: Nick Preston
Age: 18
Personality Type: Strong, snobby, criticizing
Boy/Girl Friends: Gayle Jennings
Pet Peeve: Gino's
Nickname: "Snob"

(14) This is dumb. ♦

THE DJ SAVED MY LIFE

Suzy X. // 2012

I WAS ALWAYS GROUNDED AS A TEEN. USUALLY FOR MY GRADES. OR MY SARCASM.

I OFTEN SPENT SATURDAY NIGHTS TUNED INTO FORBIDDEN PLANET, AN INDIE RADIO SHOW IN FLORIDA. FOR YEARS I CALLED IN WITH SONG REQUESTS. WHEN I WAS 17, THE HOST FINALLY RECOGNIZED MY VOICE.

HEY, I KNOW THAT VOICE—YOU HAVE REALLY, REALLY GOOD TASTE!

FROM THEN ON, I CALLED HIM EVERY SATURDAY. WE'D TALK ABOUT EVERYTHING—FROM MUSIC, TO DATING ADVICE. MAYBE WE GOT TOO CLOSE.

BUT HE DROVE ME TO DO BETTER.

HE DID LEAVE ME SOMETHING:

HIS SHOW WAS COMING TO AN END. THE STATION WAS BOUGHT OUT. I MISSED HIS LAST SHOW WHILE I WAS GRADUATING. ALTHOUGH,

HIS WHOLE MUSIC LIBRARY.

"YOU MAY BE A PUNK, BUT YOU'RE NOT STUPID. YOU'LL BE JUST FINE."

THE BEST OF
ROOKIE
IN PRINT!

COLLECT ALL THREE BOOKS
FEATURING:

★LORDE★KELIS★

★SKY FERREIRA★

★EMMA WATSON★

★CLARESSA SHIELDS★

★SHAILENE WOODLEY★

★AMANDLA STENBERG★

★NEIL DEGRASSE TYSON★

★ZOOEY DESCHANEL★

★DAVID SEDARIS★

★MINDY KALING★

★LENA DUNHAM★

★MORRISSEY★

★GRIMES★

AND MORE!

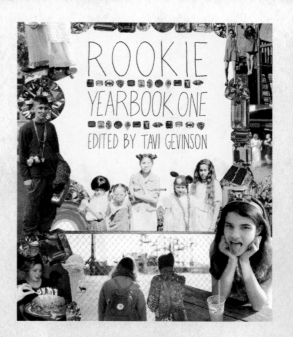

ROOKIE
YEARBOOK ONE
EDITED BY TAVI GEVINSON

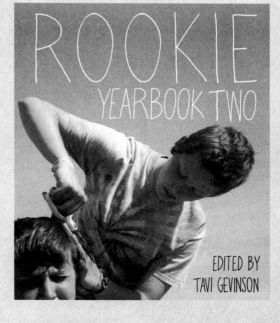

ROOKIE
YEARBOOK TWO

EDITED BY
TAVI GEVINSON

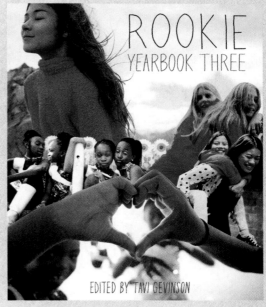

ROOKIE
YEARBOOK THREE

EDITED BY TAVI GEVINSON

STAY GOLD

ROOKIE!
I LOVED OUR TALKS!
YOU DEFINITELY MADE
THIS YEAR WAY MORE
BEARABLE. LET'S HANG
OUT OVER THE SUMMER.
YOUR FRIEND,
~Jess~
LOVE JD

LOVE
Kate & Laura
RODARTE

Dear Rookie,
This year I loved
trading secrets w/ you, copying
★ your style (LOL!)
and learning beside you.
Thanks for being you!
Have fun at camp and
don't forget me once
you grow boobs - hehe
♥
love,
Lena D.

I love
corrupting
young minds—
John Waters

MILWAUKIE LEDDING LIBRARY
10660 SE 21ST AVENUE
MILWAUKIE OR 97222

56375199